THE
PROMISED CITY

THE
PROMISED CITY

New York's Jews

1870-1914

By

MOSES RISCHIN

HARVARD UNIVERSITY PRESS
Cambridge, Massachusetts
London, England

Library of Congress Catalog Card Number: 62–11402

ISBN 0–674–71501–2 (paper)

Printed in the United States of America

To OSCAR HANDLIN

Preface to the Paperback Edition

It is over a quarter of a century since I mapped out the research for *The Promised City* published in 1962 by the Harvard University Press. At first my aim was to identify those currents of human and institutional vitality central to the American urban experience that converged on the Lower East Side in the era of the great Jewish migration just as New York emerged as the nation's and the world's most dynamic metropolis. It soon became evident, however, that I was engaged in portraying the most rapid and the most revolutionary transformation in the millennial history of the Jewish people, a paradigm of modernization so universal in its unfolding and so vivid and dramatic in its New York setting that it answered the need of an ideal model exceeding all expectations.

In retrospect, it is apparent that *The Promised City* was published on the threshold of an era of unprecedented historical scholarship, creativity, and specialization. Within less than a decade, a host of new historical specialties would emerge with a methodological and technical sophistication that seemed to revolutionize the historian's craft. Almost overnight, so it seemed, a dimly charted urban history had become the new urban history; social history, the new social history; political history, the new political history; economic history, quanto-history; immigration history, ethnic history, and so on. The history of childhood, of the family, of women, of social mobility, of popular culture, of education, of labor, of race relations, and a host of others acquired an autonomy and an esprit that ingeniously and imaginatively expanded and advanced our understanding of whole sectors of the historical landscape. But in the process, subspecialization and quantification, untethered to a larger sense of the human experience, often threatened to rob the past of historical context, tone, proportion, and ultimately credibility. When present concerns and an obsession with methodological hardware overwhelm all sense of past times the result is fiasco. The medium becomes the message.

Fortunately, when *The Promised City* was conceived and written there was as yet little temptation to methodological adventure. In the 1950s the embers of New York's classic Lower East Side still smouldered on East Broadway although "the first authentic study by an outsider of the inner life of an American immigrant community," *The Spirit of the Ghetto* by Hutchins Hapgood, published half a century earlier, had been virtually forgotten. Newspaper offices, bookstores, theaters, synagogues, settlement houses, schools, storefronts, and tenements, however blighted and mouldy, sustained more than the illusion of direct continuity with a vital earlier time. Aged proprietors, tenants, clients, and heirs gave living evidence of a strenuous epoch that protruded wistfully into the present. But already by the mid-1960s it was no longer so. When I interviewed Lower East Side survivors in preparation for writing a biography of Abraham Cahan, which will be a collateral work to *The Promised City,* I suddenly knew myself to be a latter-day Rip Van Winkle. By then it was all too plain that time had nearly run out. The last remnants of what once had been the densest and most pulsating concentration of humanity in history would soon be no more. By 1976 the landmark ten-story edifice of the octogenarian *Jewish Daily Forward* had become an empty shell; its illuminated flashing sign for over half a century visible for miles around was no more to be seen. On a recent visit to New York I found the *Forward* offices relocated in the tastefully remodeled former brownstone mansion of Harper & Brothers—publishers, ironically, of the *Forward* editor's classic novel of the failure of success, *The Rise of David Levinsky.* Even as a symbol of a rich and complex Jewish immigrant universe, the Lower East Side seemed on the verge of extinction.

The final passing of the historic Lower East Side is of course but a minor symptom of a major realignment on the American urban and ethnic scene. Like the nation's other great aging industrial cities, New York, the hub of megalopolis, the nation's cultural center, and the world's capital city, has reached the limits of its growth and its proverbial generosity. The decentralization of population and economy, new job patterns and life-styles, the seductive pull of the sun-warmed cheaper-energy regions, suburban, ex-urban, and minicity alternatives, almost effortless interregional mobility, and the growing centralization of federal functions in Washington have divested the nation's New York-centered dominant manufacturing belt of its traditional hegemony. In the late 1950s New York still was, as it had been for a century, the country's most diversely industrialized metropolitan region. But in the two decades after 1950, a static population that abruptly declined in the early 1970s, the stagnation of the whole New York metropolitan region, and the city's tragic fiscal insolvency seemed a grim testimonial to the end of an era of longtime competitive advantage that had been especially pronounced in the years of the great Jewish migration.

Indeed, New York's general population decline was paralleled by an even more precipitous fall in the Jewish population of the city. Ever since the second decade of the twentieth century, New York boasted the largest concentration of Jews in history, mounting to two million in the 1930s and 1940s and consistently comprising well over one-quarter of the city's inhabitants. By the mid-seventies, Jews have become less numerous than at any time in the preceding six decades, accounting for but fifteen to sixteen percent of the city's population. And for the first time, the number of Jews in the New York metropolitan region also decreased.

If the promise of New York—and the other magnetic high density great central cities that reached maturity in the first half of the twentieth century—has become problematic, the need for cosmopolitan, urbane, internationally individualistic and self-conscious centers of civilization is likely to become more acute than ever even as the poor and the abandoned further tax the survival capacities of the great cities to which they have fled from the hopelessness of the countryside, particularly of the South, Puerto Rico, and Mexico. The postmodern and post-industrial era continues to be at least as fraught with cultural shock and personal and social dislocation as the era of the great

Jewish migration. The fading away of neighborhoods; the demolition of buildings, institutions, and other landmarks; the imminent dissolution of the rural countryside; the withering of the urban immigrant heartlands of America; and the severing of the fragile threads of ethnic, group, and family continuities have threatened to diminish indiscriminately all our identities and loyalties without making adequate provision for comparable new ones. The revolution in American consciousness, law, and social etiquette with respect to the issues of race, religion, and ethnicity and many others that emerged in great part during the vast social and cultural upheavals of the 1960s and 1970s has yet to be assimilated and transformed into a broad national consensus supportive of imaginative change appropriate to a nation virtually become a belt of supercities. A new national urban and posturban historic and social consciousness must energize and link all Americans into a national network of public trust. The finiteness of the urban, no less than the natural, habitat in an overwhelmingly urban nation that still rebels against urbanity leaves no sane alternative.

Let us hope that New York's usable past drawn from an age not unlike our own may offer example, insight, vision, and faith for a truly cosmopolitan America extending to all its inhabitants. Great cities like New York, without equal in the world in opportunities for culture, education, alternative life-styles, recreation, and sheer atmosphere continue to provide the critical massed varieties and stir of peoples essential for national renewal and rehumanization. New York's first great encounter with the problems of the city has become that city's and the nation's problem writ large. Its travail has been its glory, an earnest to a tradition of a promised urbane land.

Moses Rischin

January 1977

Preface

THE Greeks of the ancient world looked upon a city of ten thousand as an ideal community for the practice of democracy. The citizens of New York, the national metropolis after 1870, had lost all sense of community and were skeptical about democracy. The Jews of Eastern Europe, on their way to New York, had never heard of the Greek ideal but they had been displaced from real communities, from the *shtetls*, or small towns, of their birth, and they longed for the communal spirit.

This is a book about the search for community in New York between 1870 and 1914. It is the story of the encounter between New York and the great Jewish migration. It is a twofold study. First, it explores the profound changes in every aspect of the lives of Jews torn from the villages of Eastern Europe, cast into the great metropolis, and in search of links to bind them to the life of New York. In the process, these small-town Jews were shaped into new people. Gradually, at times swiftly, and at considerable cost, they were to be transformed. Physically, economically, and spiritually, they were on the way to becoming modern Americans. By the early years of the twentieth century their quest for community made them builders of a city that itself was striding toward new urban dimensions. But this is more than an epic of a group resettlement; it is the story of New York's first great meeting with the social problems of the modern city as told through the experience of East European Jews. Urban problems were not new. But in these years reformers came to accept the city as the hope of democracy and the solution of its problems, a test of the validity of the American way of life. Sweated industries, great poverty, unemployment, economic exploitation, packed and unsanitary housing, and corrupt politics became the foci for civic reform. For the first time, social and cultural institutions appeared to bridge the gap between immigrant and American, to educate and to inspire, to make immigrants into Americans and to allow them to be themselves. In facing the social problems of the city together, East European immigrants and reformers met on common ground and attempted to bring a sense of community to a metropolis that is still engaged in that quest.

Part One portrays New York between 1870 and 1914 as it was reaching new heights in every phase of its development, but paying the price of indifference to communal responsibilities. By contrast the Jews in Eastern Europe were possessed of a communal tradition that was being shattered by multiple revolutions in their lives and they yearned to belong. Part Two is concerned with the terms of settlement of East European Jews in New York, where they became the victims of the metropolis as well as its builders. Their bondage to factory, shop, and slum, and their apprenticeship to the established German Jews in American urban living initiated them into the life of the city but failed to provide for their full dignity as human beings. Part Three explores the development of a new group consciousness on the part of East European Jews under the pressures of the modern city. In the process, Judaism became secularized, unleashing new social energies that encouraged East European Jews to confront a chaotic world with forthrightness and optimism. Part Four examines the major social problems of the city, especially the labor question, that brought East European Jews, the most conspicuous victims of New York's social abuses, and reformers into contact with one another. It depicts the advance of reform into every phase of the city's life and the emergence of East European Jews as new people after the turn of the century. Finally, the story is not complete without an examination of the effect of group prejudice upon the integration of Jewish immigrants into the city.

The theme of this book, the search for community in New York between 1870 and 1914, is both general and special. Other American cities, with somewhat different problems and peoples, faced the same challenges in these years. To the degree that the New York experience is both representative and seminal, it will, I hope, cast light on the total American urban scene.

ACKNOWLEDGMENTS

It is the scholar's besetting fear that he may not show a due humility, indeed, a conscious awareness of his many debts. Since this book draws upon a whole education, my obligations know no end. I hope that I shall be forgiven by the many for citing only the few.

My foremost debt is to Oscar Handlin. His quiet fostering of the intellectual and personal integrity and independence of his students can be appreciated fully only by those who have had the good fortune to come under the direct influence of his keen and wide-ranging scholarship. Professor Handlin fortified me in my determination to do this book, read the manuscript at successive stages of its writing, and encouraged me whenever the spirit flagged.

The following friends and teachers read the complete manuscript, raising provocative questions and making thoughtful criticisms: Professor Solomon F. Bloom of Brooklyn College, Professor Paul H. Buck of Harvard University, Professor Jacob M. Price of the University of Michigan, and Professor Richard L. Schoenwald of Massachusetts Institute of Technology. Mr. William V. Shannon read the early chapters in a first draft and I profited from his comments. Mr. Benjamin Barondess, Dr. Thomas N. Brown, Professor Louis Filler of Antioch College, Dr. Isaac Levitats, Mr. Ephraim London, and Professor Max Weinreich of The City College cordially answered my queries on specific points. The late Paul Abelson graciously allowed me to study a wealth of fugitive materials that he had amassed in a lifetime's association with civic and labor affairs and that are now the property of the School of Industrial and Labor Relations, Cornell University. Mrs. Jean Barondess and the late Miss Nina Hillquit generously permitted me to examine the scrapbooks kept by their fathers. Mr. Solon DeLeon invited me to see photostats of official documents relating to his father and the late Dr. Herman Frank kindly made available to me rare issues of the *Freie Arbeiter Shtimme* of which he was the editor. The following persons granted me interviews and shared with me their reminiscences of the era of the great Jewish migration: the late Louis Boudin, the late Abraham Cahan, the late August Claessens, Mr. Israel Gottlieb, Dr. Mordecai Kaplan, Dr. Horace M. Kallen, the late Algernon Lee, Mr. Max Maisel, the late Max Meyer, Mr. Abraham Mitchell, Dr. David De Sola Pool, Mr. Joseph Schlossberg, Miss Rose Schneiderman, Dr. Alexander Seldin, Dr. Abraham Wolbarst, and the late Max Zaritsky.

For access to the records of the past, I am indebted to the following: Miss Florence C. Thorne of the American Federation of Labor; Professor Jacob R. Marcus of the American Jewish Archives; Mr. Harry Alderman of the Blaustein Library; Rabbi Isidore S. Meyer of the American Jewish Historical Society; Professor Henry J. Browne of the Catholic University of America and now of Cathedral College; Mr. M. Halsey Thomas of Columbiana and now Princeton; Professor Gerson Cohen of the Jewish Theological Seminary of America; Mr. A. K. Baragwanath of the Museum of the City of New York; Miss Grace Mayer of the Museum of Modern Art; Dr. Abraham Berger, the late Joshua Bloch, Mr. Robert Hill, and the late Edward B. Morrison of the New York Public Library; and Mr. Max Meyer of the University Settlement. The staffs of the libraries at Columbia, Harvard, and Cornell universities, the Library of Congress, Madison House, the National Archives, the Library of the School of Industrial and Labor Relations, the Tamiment Institute, and the Union Theological Seminary were always cooperative. I should like especially to thank Miss Dena Abramovitch of the YIVO Institute of Jewish Research for good-humoredly aiding a novice to find his way in the early Yiddish newspapers and periodicals. I owe a debt to Mrs. Freda Limberg, the most cheerful of typists, who worked from illegible drafts studded with transliterations that would have intimidated less loyal practitioners.

My mother, Mrs. Rachel Rischin, and my sister, Mrs. Frances Abrams, gave the moral support these many years without which this book might not have been written. My father, who taught by example, would have understood why this book had to be written, for he was the most worthy of antagonists in the good fight between the generations out of which history is made. It is my great regret that he can not share in the fulfillment. My last word of appreciation I reserve for Ruth, my beloved partner in life and literature.

Moses Rischin

August 19, 1961
Cambridge, Massachusetts

CONTENTS

LIST OF ILLUSTRATIONS

Part One

NEW WORLD AND OLD

∾ I ∾

City Unlimited

> The courage, the heaven-scaling audacity of it all and the lightness withal, as if there was nothing that was not easy, and the great pulses and bounds of progress, so many in directions all simultaneous that the coordination is indefinitely future, give a kind of drumming background of life never felt before. I'm sure that once *in* that movement, and at home, all other places would seem insipid.
>
> William James to Henry James (1907)

In the half century after the Civil War, New York's growth from a seaport "city of masts and spires" to the skyline symbol of the Western Hemisphere dazzled Americans and foreigners alike. Still a distant outport of Europe in 1870, New York by 1914 had emerged a metropolis, binding the civilization of two worlds. During this period the most ethnically diverse of the nation's cities continued to add to the variety of its inhabitants. More so than ever before, New York became the gateway, toll station, and hostelry through which immigrants passed in their abandonment of the Old World for a better life in the New. The city's leading citizens prided themselves on their enthusiasm for "taking it for granted that all men are not of one pattern, and that we are to live by allowing others to have their liberty as we have ours." The acceptance of differences, reiterated the Reverend Samuel Osgood in 1866 before the New York Historical Society, was the essence of New York:

The national diversities are not hostile, and we are seeking out their best, instead of their worst, qualities. Italian art and French accomplishment, we can appreciate without forgetting that we are

Americans. We are . . . learning to appeal to the sterling sense and indomitable love of liberty of the countrymen of Luther and Gutenberg. The Irish among us . . . we are studying anew, and discerning their great service to industry and their great capacity for organization . . . and are bound to acknowledge that in purity, their wives and daughters may be an example to any class in America or Europe.

Jews too were the city pride:

Old Israel is with us too in force, and some thirty synagogues . . . manifest the power of the oldest organized religion, and the example of a people that cares wholly for its own sick and poor; willing to meet Christians as friends and citizens, and learn our religion from its own gospel of love, than from its old conclaves of persecution.

Nor were only Europeans welcome:

We often see other types of the Oriental mind in our streets and houses, and it will be well for us when Asia is here represented by able specimens of her mystical piety, and we learn of her something of the secret of her repose in God, and give her in return something of our art of bringing the will of God to bear upon the stubborn earth.[1]

THE ECONOMY

Manhattan Island acted as a magnet more powerful than ever before, incessantly drawing the able and the aspiring into its vortex. New York's "life is so intense and so varied and full of manifold possibilities, that it has a special and peculiar fascination for ambitious and high-spirited men of every kind," exulted Daniel Van Pelt. Yankees from country stores in Connecticut, small towns in Massachusetts, and even from the American Athens, Boston itself, continued to migrate southward to test their business mettle on the metropolitan battlefield. From 1845 to 1875, except for an eight-month lapse, sons of the rockbound soil had presided over the New York Chamber of Commerce. In 1890, James W. Gerard noted that "New England thrift and pertinacity have made the New Englanders . . . comparatively at the head of our commercial life." Thereafter, the Chamber's growing membership became more varied, but the Yankee stamp persisted.[2]

The Dutch founding fathers could not have imagined a mart of New York's dimensions, nor have foreseen that few traces of New Amsterdam were to remind their successors of the city's trading post beginnings. Yet, if the scale of New York's growth eluded the Dutch grasp, far-sighted burghers might have anticipated the city's commercial pre-eminence. With the best harbor in the Western Hemisphere, New York was without rival as a site for the transfer of South Atlantic and Gulf Coast products to ocean-going vessels. The opening of the locks of the Erie Canal in 1825 had assured the city's place as the nation's commercial terminus. The laying of track for railways that were to crisscross the continent elaborated New York's solid advantages.

At no time before or since did the city pre-empt so large a portion of the nation's trade as it did in the final decades of the nineteenth century. In 1874 nearly 61 per cent of all American exports passed through the New York port; in 1884 almost 70 per cent of the nation's imports flowed through its gates, more than twice the total for all American ports combined. By 1910 the rise of Gulf Coast and Pacific ports reduced New York's share to about 47 per cent of the country's imports and exports, but the absolute combined value of the city's foreign trade had doubled. New York received three fourths of the coffee and sugar, nearly half the tea, and more than three fourths of the cotton, silk, and wool manufactures entering the United States. About 90 per cent of the India rubber, tin, and diamonds and precious stones, as well as nearly 64 per cent of the wines and almost 60 per cent of the hides and skins, were routed through New York.[3]

Allied to New York's function as the nation's entrepôt was its role as the country's credit and banking center. Between 1888 and 1908 New York's banking resources grew nearly 250 per cent, dwarfing the 26 per cent increase for the country as a whole. With J. P. Morgan as symbol and underwriter of national prosperity, the city became the security market of the nation and the home of the four largest life insurance companies in the country. Climbing capitalization and titanic mergers drew the country's industrial leaders to Wall Street, and adopted and native New Yorkers came to own or control much of American industry. Of the 185 largest industrial combinations in the nation at the turn of the century, 69, directing 2416 plants, had their main offices in New York.

The management of New York's commerce and finance empire and the direction of the nation's industry were closed to all but a few immigrants. But other spheres of the economy were not. An unparalleled growth in retail trade and interstate commerce in the 1880's solidified the city's role as the nation's leading jobber and distributor. Variety, five-and-ten-cent, and department stores multiplied, augmenting the dry-goods and specialty shops, bazaars, and emporia that catered to the city's visitors. In the higher realms of commerce, jobbery, and brokerage, old native and foreign-connected firms prevailed, but in the retail market opportunities beckoned to even the humblest from among the foreign-born.[4]

New York's economic growth was not restricted to national industrial control and business administration. In the single decade of the 1880's, local industry shot up to a new prominence. The city's plants doubled in number and in capitalization while their labor force increased by 49 per cent and the value of their products jumped by 50 per cent. In the first decade of the twentieth century the dry statistics of the census reminded Americans that "New York City is not only the leading city and commercial center of the United States, but also the industrial metropolis." In 1914, New York City produced almost 10 per cent of manufactures in the nation and was exceeded only by Pennsylvania and New York State itself. New York offered manufacturers grand retail fairs and wholesale markets, an international exchange for goods and ideas, ample credit facilities, and above all, a ceaseless flow of low-priced immigrant labor. But the industries which prospered were those that were able to accept the terms of the island: costly land, expensive construction, high taxes, and exorbitant transportation and transshipment charges. As a result, the city became primarily a center of light manufactures, the refining and processing of heavy and bulky raw materials finding their sites closer to the sources of supply.

At the close of the century New York was as distinct in its industry as it was in its commerce. While shipbuilding—once a major industry—languished and other heavy industry persisted largely as an auxiliary to commerce, finishing and processing industries and a network of specialized skills reinforced the city's role as the country's greatest market of men and materials. The most populous of the nation's cities was the perfect site for the manufacture and distribution of an infinite variety of consumer goods. The buying fever spurred manufacturer and merchant alike to experiment with the different and the novel. Aspiring jobbers, wholesalers, converters, commission and manufacturers' agents, and buyers descended upon the city, while first Castle Garden, and later Ellis Island, daily fed ready hands into the labor hopper.

Such special conditions promoted an industrial design unique to the state and to the nation. The city's twenty-five leading industries, with products valued at over $20,000,000 each, and most of the 261 smaller branches of manufacture enumerated by the federal census in 1914 were but slightly represented upstate. The trend toward giant plants accentuated the smallness of the city's factories. A profusion of entrepreneurs scrambled through all branches of manufacture in the city, so that in 1914, excluding home industry and shops where manufacturing was incidental to merchandising, almost 68 per cent of the state's factories were located in the city, a 14 per cent jump in fifteen years. In 1914 women's clothing was the leading state industry. In the preceding decade its workshops had doubled, its work force increased by half, and the value of its product had risen to more than 98 per cent of the total state product. The advances in the apparel trades only elaborated the city's special bent for small-scale manufacture. After 1900 as before, the corporate form of business was most poorly developed in the agricultural Southeast, the country's least advanced region, and in New York, its most sophisticated metropolis.[5]

Much of the city's commerce and industry was widely dispersed, but tradition and convenience combined to center like businesses in one district. In this way, misunderstanding and friction was minimized and the business pulse quickened. South Street was as much the symbol of grand commerce as Wall Street was of high finance. Strung along Maiden Lane and John Street, jewelry shops sparkled with goldsmiths' and silversmiths' wares. From Broadway to West Broadway, between Canal and Worth streets, the wholesale dry goods houses were to be found. The retail dry goods emporia lined 14th Street, 23rd Street, Broadway, and Sixth Avenue. The wholesale grocers clustered below Canal Street, mainly off Chambers Street where West Broadway and Hudson Street led into College Place. The "Swamp," the longtime leather district with its sharp odors, bordered the impressive approaches to the Brooklyn Bridge, while William Street accommodated the wholesale drug houses. Nearby sprawled the Fulton Fish Market and Newspaper Row, topped by the golden-domed World Building opposite City Hall. The apparel trades, the city's liveliest domain of manufactures, were to migrate northward and westward colony by colony through much of the city's central business district.

The geographic partitioning of the economy was paralleled by an ethnic pattern of labor that led immigrants and native Americans alike to cleave to their own. The size and strangeness of the city, the barriers of language, the peculiarities of special skills, and the desire to aid one's own, gave most trades a distinct ethnic cast. So universal was this situation that excellent mechanics were unable to find employment without the aid of a friend or relative. Total strangers, when sufficiently numerous, carved out colonies of their own, each with occupational patterns molded by past training and tradition yet often reconstructed by new expectations and conditions. German immigrants accounted for the greatest range of skills. In industries such as piano manufacturing, for example, a German community persisted for many decades. In less highly skilled trades, technological change, the coming of new immigrant groups, and new vocations altered the ethnic makeup of the industry. Irish receded before Italians as laborers and longshoremen, and Germans and Negroes gave way before Italians as barbers. But the most rapid turnover came in the apparel trades, where Irish and German tailors were engulfed in the 1880's by East European Jews, who in turn began to be replaced by Italians and Lithuanians at the turn of the century. New opportunities in commerce, government, and the professions linked the Germans and the Irish more closely with older Americans, but the new status of the Schmidts and the Fitzpatricks did not divest them of their distinctiveness.[6]

THE HUMAN GEOGRAPHY

The newly arrived were not at a loss to find their place in New York. Ever since the middle of the nineteenth century the foreign-born and their children had outnumbered older stock Americans; by 1900 they constituted over 76 per cent of the city's population. At that time those of recent German origin led all other nationalities and, like the Irish, exceeded native whites of native parentage. By 1910 New Yorkers of German and Irish parentage, though still more numerous than the others, were being overtaken by immigrants from Russia, Italy, and Austria-Hungary: for the first time the foreign-born from Italy and Russia exceeded the foreign-born from Germany and Ireland. In the same year, Scandinavians, British, Dutch, Belgians, French, Swiss, Greeks, Finns, and Syrians also were numerous in a city where representatives of virtually all mankind were to be counted.

Some immigrants were dispersed throughout the city, but most collected in districts where they set the tone, driving earlier residents to more congenial and less congested quarters. New York's immigrant enclaves, in a port of continual immigrant renewal, remained the half-way house between Europe and the great American continent extending westward three thousand miles. The Irish wards in the lower city, and neighboring *Kleindeutschland* with its beer gardens and *Apfelwein Stuben* (where only cider and mineral waters were served) retained an air of permanence that disguised the ever-changing composition of their inhabitants. "Klein Wien" on lower Second Avenue and an earlier Little Hungary off East Houston

Street retained their distinctiveness after the Lower East Side became largely East European and Jewish in the 1890's. Bohemians settled between 60th and 70th streets on the East Side, alongside newer colonies of Germans and Hungarians. In the 1890's, the Italians of Mulberry Street founded a second Little Italy in East Harlem, and Central Harlem began to fill up with Jewish immigrants. Smaller and less conspicuous groups, such as the English about Gansevoort Street in Greenwich Village and a French community south and east of Washington Square, clung to well-defined quarters.

The growth in the diversity of New York's population was matched by the growth in its numbers. Between 1870 and 1915, the city's inhabitants increased from 1.5 to 5 million. Older New Yorkers, pressed by the newer waves of immigrants, dispersed to the farthest corners of its five boroughs. In 1870 nearly two thirds of the inhabitants of Greater New York resided in Manhattan; slightly over two fifths lived there by 1915. Manhattan's population more than doubled in these years, but the population of Brooklyn, the Bronx, and Queens multiplied fourfold, sixteenfold, and ninefold, respectively. Even the population of remote, thinly settled Richmond nearly tripled.[7]

New York's rate of growth in the nineteenth century exceeded that of all the world's great cities which antedated 1800, and defied the comprehension and control of its inhabitants. All improvements came late. So pressing were the demands, so inadequate were the legal and political forms, so unruly the physical growth, and so unprecedented the necessary expenditures, that the city became a veritable wilderness in which near anarchy reigned.

Yet some of New York's problems were on the way to solution. The Croton system, begun before the Civil War, continued to grow, providing a sanitary water flow that contributed to the city's relative freedom from epidemic diseases in the last two decades of the century. Public education had acquired a respectable place, though the religious issue was intermittently rekindled. Police and fire protection also became recognized parts of the official civic structure. These were spheres amenable to control by tried agencies; other areas were less easy to regulate.[8]

Ever since the influx of the 1830's and 1840's housing in tenements had been the lot of the city's immigrants. As older residents retreated before the flood of newcomers, living quarters in lower Manhattan became progressively more unkempt and dangerous. In 1901 a state law with strong enforcement provisions set up tolerable standards for future building. But the city's housing was only gradually affected. So voracious had been the speculative appetite for land that virtually all the greenery and open lots in the lower city had been covered with factories, stores, and dwellings. Between 1860 and 1907, the assessed value of the land and buildings on Manhattan rose from $1,700,000,000 to $6,700,000,000. Even the unventuresome profited from rising values. "They have not toiled, neither have they spun; yet while they have slumbered in idle comfort, their inherited acres have changed to city lots, and city lots, no matter how situated, represent dollars and produce income." [9] As a result of the tenacious efforts of Andrew H. Green the city was able to rescue and develop the Central Park tract at the geographic center of the island. But few patches of grass or shrubbery obtruded in lower Manhattan where the city's inhabitants were massed.

Only prodigious feats in engineering and construction enabled the city to service New Yorkers. Progression from a predominantly commercial port to a metropolis taxed the narrow island to the limit. Its truncated width made all efforts to modernize the city a costly burden. Street improvements, water and gas pipes, telegraph and telephone lines, and all means of transport were crammed upon less than one dozen thoroughfares that traversed Manhattan north and south.

In the early nineteenth century New York's magnificent harbor had interlocked a water transportation town and the designers of the city's "pettyfogging parallelograms" assumed that north-south travel would follow the waterways, even though the many ferries that crossed the East River, the Hudson, and Upper New York Bay never proved popular with commuters. The city's growth and developments in ground transportation, however, quickly made the gridiron street pattern of 1811 obsolete. Omnibuses, horse-drawn cars, steam railroads, and cable cars supplemented and succeeded one another in an effort to solve New York's transit problems.

Every extension in transportation facilities hastened the consolidation of the city. By the 1870's, the villages of Bloomingdale, Yorkville, and Harlem had been absorbed into the city in the course of its northward march, and the East Side as far north as 86th Street had become settled. The remarkable growth of the East Bronx, in Westchester, was hastened by the steam railroad, followed by the elevated. In 1874 the Bronx townships of Kingsbridge, West Farms, and Morrisania were annexed to the city; in 1895 the city added the remaining Bronx townships. In 1898 New York completed the metropolis by attaching Brooklyn—the nation's third city a few years earlier—and the boroughs of Queens and Richmond. As impressive as the growth of the city, was the growth of continguous areas. By 1915, 1,929,183 nonresidents lived within the thirty-mile commuting radius. New York and its suburbs, with a population in 1870 of 1,900,000, contained in 1915 nearly 7,000,000 inhabitants.

The city's outward expansion was paralleled by the upward surge of the downtown business district as the flurry of early skyscrapers rising from Manhattan schist intensified the traffic snarl. "Sitting like a feudal castle surrounded by a moat spanned by a single bridge, Manhattan forces those living to the east and to the west literally to fight their way over the barriers," recorded James Creelman. In 1908, the Public Service Commission reported that surface, elevated, and subway companies carried over 3.5 million passengers daily, nearly two thirds more than the total passenger traffic carried by all the steam railroads in the United States. Twenty per cent of this travel took place in a single "rush" hour. Despite the multiplication of tunnels and bridges and the extension of subways, the waterbound isolation of the core borough posed a transportation dilemma that would never cease to test the patience of New Yorkers.[10]

THE POLITICS

The business community was no longer an effective force in the political life of the city. The majestic dimensions of commerce, finance, and industry, and the cumulative intricacies of the law, pre-empted the energies of men of wealth and talent, leaving them little time for the cares of municipal government. Men of leisure from the old families, "enthusiasts in yachting, horse-racing and fashionable functions," according to Matthew P. Breen, were even less likely candidates for the responsibilities of municipal statemanship. Even had they been so inclined, social separation from the ever-growing city of strangers limited contact and sympathy. "With its middle classes in large part self-exiled, its laboring population being brutalized in tenements, and its citizens of the highest class indifferent to the commonweal," New York was bereft of political leadership, concluded Frank Moss. The affairs of government fell to those for whom politics was a livelihood and a way of life. Men who were the social companions of the people of the tenements were to become the city's rulers.[11]

The Irish quickly assumed leadership of the immigrant electorate. Their natural gregariousness, outstanding position in the Catholic Church, and familiarity with English facilitated their rise in politics. And Irish solidarity contrasted with the lack of organization and indifference of the other immigrants and Yankees. Proving themselves "as vivacious and excitable as the French," they injected a Celtic flavor at all levels of the city's public life. St. Patrick's Day parades and Fourth of July bonfires rivaled Election Day festivities in the American as well as in the Irish calendar. The Democratic Party became the party of the Irish Catholics (and to a lesser extent of other Catholic immigrants) for the Irish regarded the Republicans as aristocratic, anti-Catholic, and antiforeigner, and their unquenchable sense of persecution buttressed their political loyalties.

Politics was big business in this era. In 1898 with the consolidation of Greater New York, the city's annual budget exceeded $90,000,000; tens of millions accrued from assessments for street improvements, bond sales, fees, fines, interest, rents, and other sources. Political power, accompanied by the jobbing of contracts and the dispensing of privileges and favors, suggested pecuniary opportunities. At a lower level, political patronage turned professional politicians into labor entrepreneurs and personnel managers. Tens of thousands of jobs in the police, fire, and other municipal departments were channeled through leading stalwarts and their ward associates. The political boss and his lieutenants also doled out employment to unskilled laborers on the private construction projects invested with a public interest; often even skilled mechanics were obligated to politicians. The building of hospitals and schools, the laying of streets, the digging of sewers, the provision of transportation facilities, and the furnishing of conduits for gas, electric, and telephone service, all required a continual supply of labor. The minor amenities and social services performed by the worthies of the political club and corner saloon—the picnics, parties, dinner baskets, and sacks of coal—welded constituencies whose ballots were dependable.[12]

Seasoned New Yorkers accepted the division of labor between the politics of business and the business of politics, between Yankees and Irish, as a matter of course. Only flagrant violations of these allocated functions aroused more than fleeting indignation. The colossal peculations of the Tweed Ring were of such magnitude, however, that even New York's chastened citizens were shocked. The County Court House, designed in 1868 to cost $250,000, had by 1871 cost somewhere between $8,000,000 and $13,000,000 (including $7500 for thermometers), and was still unfinished. The Committee of Seventy, consisting of the city's most distinguished citizens of various political allegiances, undertook to investigate the mayor, high city officials, and the judiciary. But despite their revelations, popular excitement soon cooled. Fraud, conservatively estimated at $75,000,000, brought imprisonment to the "Boss" alone. Businessmen, especially those connected with the new public service corporations, and politicians were far too dependent on one another to countenance more than a temporary rift. By 1876, "Honest John" Kelly, Tweed's heir in Tammany, succeeded in electing his candidate, William H. Wickham of the Committee of Seventy, to the mayoralty. Despite factional conflict among Democrats and the election of such troublesome independents as William R. Grace, the city's first Irish Catholic and foreign-born mayor since colonial times, and Abram S. Hewitt, who defied the custom of the city fathers by refusing to review the St. Patrick's Day parade and fly the Irish flag at City Hall, the Wigwam remained in control of the city. Indeed, in 1894, when the Democratic Party carried only five Congressional districts north of the Mason-Dixon line, such was the strength of Tammany that three of these five were in New York City.[13]

The 1890's witnessed the beginnings of slow change in the political life of the island city as it became a metropolis that had no place for the old-time boss. The heirs of Richard Croker, whose triumph capped this decade, were outwardly a more respectable lot. Tammany's inner circles no longer welcomed the rough-hewn "fire laddie" and the retired bare-knuckled boxer. Disclosures of corruption precipitated fusion and reform parties led by the "aristocracy of social position," the "aristocracy of religious morality," and the "intellectual aristocrats" (as they were characterized by the newspaperman D. G. Thompson) who attempted to divorce municipal issues from national affairs. The campaign of the Reverend Charles Parkhurst, the Lexow investigation, the revival of the Committee of Seventy, and the election in 1894 of the independent Republican William L. Strong constituted the first major challenge to the pact between Tammany and Boss Platt's Republican organization for the division of patronage in the city and state. "This city cannot be redeemed" unless able men accept office, Strong informed the New York Chamber of Commerce. With Col. George E. Waring, Jr. as head of the Street Cleaning Department and Theodore Roosevelt as Police Commissioner, the Strong administration bequeathed a tradition of civil service and efficiency to the nation's largest urban bureaucracy. But with the election of Tammany's Van Wyck in 1897 for a four-year term, the city reverted to a tolerance for the social customs of its inhabitants, the frailties of its officials, and the needs of

its businessmen, as a more resplendent Wigwam than ever
supervised the city's destinies. Yet in the succeeding decade under a revised charter, opportunities opened for municipal statesmanship.[14]

In the 1870's old Knickerbocker society had retired into relative seclusion. New York hummed with the exertions of rapid
change but the heirs of the old merchants and landowners no
longer participated in the workaday life. Old business directories, where "the trades and occupations of the founders of
our modern aristocracy are set out in cold type," were rarely
consulted as reference works. The older families, aloof from the
tumult of trade, manufacture, and government, abandoned the
market place, factory, and legislative chamber to energetic outsiders, native and foreign. Increased fortunes stimulated a taste
for libraries, art galleries, and museums, and charitable institutions attracted attention in especially grim times for the unemployed. But few old New Yorkers ventured into public pursuits, social, cultural, or political, until the opening of the new
century.[15]

In the late nineteenth century many of the older families,
and others not so old, melted into a new society, rendered con-
spicuously public in the *Social Register*. Almost daily, the Four
Hundred glittered in newspaper headlines, as Mrs. William
Astor, squired by the elder August Belmont with his thick German accent, led the elite in antics before the city's millions.
"Being a millionaire had become a distinct calling or profession," acknowledged Ward McAllister, society's self-appointed
social secretary and guide. Fifth Avenue became a fairyland of
European architectural styles suited to the most eclectic tastes.
Yet by the century's turn, newly arrived magnates from the
West had submerged the Four Hundred, and the new society
lost all semblance of coherence. "New York society consists of
a whirlpool of tentative novices with a sediment of permanent
members," noted Ralph Pulitzer. These sojourners, detached
from their moorings and the multitudes around them, made
the city the seat of unexampled pomp and indulgence; in the

summer Newport fed their appetite for frivolity. Where the older families had been restrained by a lighter purse and a cultivated reticence, their wealthier successors outdistanced European royalty in their extravagances. The Bradley-Martin ball earned nation-wide notoriety. Arising one morning in 1897, Mrs. Bradley-Martin, informed of the depression, volunteered to underwrite a ball to stimulate trade and promptly spilled $360,000 into the market place. Equally prodigal but without the philanthropic pretensions were James Hazen Hyde's ball at Sherry's, Harry Lehr's "dog dinner," and Randolph Guggenheimer's sponsorship of "New York's most costly dinner" ($250 per plate).[16]

The cultural life of the city long had reflected a cosmopolitan inquisitiveness superimposed upon easygoing Knickerbocker ways. Its more prosperous citizens looked seaward to Europe as the true home of the higher attainments. Business travel and pleasure trips abroad cultivated liberal tastes, which were reinforced by European emissaries of learning and the arts who made New York their headquarters and first port of call. Cultural delights, like all aspects of a progressive world, seemed to be only slightly less inspired than the business faculty itself. To Carl Schurz Gotham gleamed as the "recognized center of civilization in America . . . People from all parts of the continent congregate here to find of the enjoyments of civilized life, the best to be had on this side of the Atlantic."[17]

After 1870 as before, the higher dramatic, musical, and artistic tastes continued to reflect a medley of European influences; but the growing wealth of the period encouraged lavish appointments. The Academy of Music, patronized by the older families, gave way in 1883 before the more magnificent Metropolitan Opera House, built by the newer society; there Leopold Damrosch supplanted customary French and Italian opera with German musical dramas. In 1879, the Metropolitan Museum of Art, a consolidation of private art galleries, began to function as a semipublic institution, the first of its kind in the city. Libraries were slow to gain public support and, except for the Astor and the uniquely unpretentious Cooper Union Library, retained an air of genteel privacy. Yet by the century's

close the city stood on the threshold of the democratization of
its higher cultural life.

As cosmopolitan as the higher culture were the circuses, the
dime museums, the minstrel shows, the theaters and music
halls, and the beer saloons. Newspapers and magazines were no
less responsive to the metropolitan milieu. Immigrants and
Americans mingled in front page article and comic supplement and jostled shoulders upon the stage. In the early twentieth century, New York provided the pioneers in the motion
picture arts with curious and hospitable audiences. As a cultural way-station between Europe and America the city was
without rival. New York's welcome to the strange and the novel,
the "absence of the granite of crystallized tradition" in its make-
up, provided a milieu where the cultural implications of an
urban democracy were becoming visible. In New York's unmatched ethnic diversity, one of the city's historians detected
its true vocation.

The late considerable increase in variety and numbers of those
who claim citizenship in the metropolis has . . . induced a corresponding animation in her intellectual progress. At no time has the
curious mosaic of nationalities that make up our community given
such abundant evidence as now of growth in culture and in a capacity for transmission through influence and example to the country at
large of what it has acquired.[18]

∽ 2 ∽

The East European Captivity

It was as if all the Jews of Russia were to be violently
crowded in and piled on top of each other, like grasshop-
pers in a ditch; here they were to be miserably crushed
together until the fruitless struggle for life should have
done its work.   *The Russian Jews* (1894)

THE major East European migration that was to enter into the
epic of New York's growth did not come until after 1870, but
its roots were laid much earlier. Bold and restless Jewish lads
from Prussian Poland, like Haym Salomon, abandoned their
birthplaces in the latter half of the eighteenth century and
sought new moorings in America. Others followed in the early
years of the republic, encouraged by a dip into Campe's *Discovery of America.* Translated from the German into Hebrew
in 1823 and then into the vernacular in 1824, this was the first
book, neither fable nor moral tract, to stir the imagination of a
Yiddish-reading people. Tsarist conscription laws, effective in
Russia in 1827 and in Poland in 1845, which bonded Jewish
boys to twenty-five years of military service—measures tanta-
mount to actual if not formal de-Judaization—impelled many
youngsters to steal across the Prussian border and eventually to
wander overseas. Polish revolutions, recurrent after 1830, also
contributed a sprinkling of political exiles. But the dearth of
travel facilities and information, the distance and hazards of the
journey, and the fear that Judaism would be lost in the outside
world deferred mass migration.[1]

After 1870 a decisive change occurred. With the decline of
emigration from Central Europe, the German trans-Atlantic

shipping companies hastened to broadcast America's allure to the poorer classes farther east. Most of the earliest Russian Jewish immigrants came from the provinces of Kovno and Suvalki adjoining the German border. Ship captains did not have to press their bid too hard. The cholera epidemic of 1868, the Polish famine of 1869, and the 1871 Odessa pogrom generated a mild emigration fever. In the 1870's, 40,000 East European Jews migrated to the United States, compared to a trickle of 7500 in the century's first seven decades. Thereafter the flow, steady and strong, generated its own momentum. In the 1880's over 200,000 crossed the ocean to the United States; in the 1890's another 300,000 followed. From 1900 to the outbreak of World War I, the pioneers were joined by 1,500,000 of their kin, as young men sent steamship tickets to their wives, children, and fellow townsmen; with the tide of families on the move, the number of immigrant women rose appreciably. During the Russo-Japanese War of 1904–1905 thousands of army reservists earmarked for slaughter in Siberian wastes stole across the frontier into Germany and struck out for America.[2]

A folk exodus of two million, one third of Eastern Europe's Jews, might have been expected to alleviate the distress of the impoverished remainder. But it produced the reverse effect. The immigration of such vast numbers thinned the ranks of consumers and intensified the crisis for stay-at-home artisans, cutting further into their meager living. Only steady remittances from overseas kinsmen propped the limp economy. Economic paralysis and political reaction in Russia, political and economic repression in Rumania, and the hopeless Galician poverty converged to effect a mass migration of unparalleled impulsion and volume. This migration, made up of Jews seeking a homeland, was to help shape New York into a unique metropolis.[3]

THE JEWISH PALE

In the thirteenth century Boleslav the Pious, King of Poland, in an effort to encourage commercial growth in an economy characterized by great landholdings and an impoverished peasantry, invited European Jews to settle in his kingdom. As in-

**EASTERN EUROPE IN THE
ERA OF THE GREAT MIGRATION**

〰〰 Boundary of the Pale of Settlement

tended, these settlers found places as money-lenders, tax col-
lectors, innkeepers, whiskey distillers, grain merchants, factors,
stewards, artisans, and general middlemen. Except for brief
intervals of religious fanaticism, Jews went unmolested, being
recognized as intermediaries indispensable to the economy. For
four centuries, their numbers were swelled by refugee out-
pourings from the strife-torn west. Within fifty years of the end
of the benevolent reign of Stephen Batory (1575–1586), the
climax of a "golden age," the Polish kingdom entered upon a
fast decline. Successive invasions by Cossacks, Swedes, and Russians, accompanied by civil war, laid waste a nation that once
extended from the Oder to the Donets, from the Baltic to the
edges of the Black Sea. The high civilization attained by Poland's Jews in the middle of the seventeenth century sank pre-
cipitously at its close. Decay followed in the eighteenth century.

Poland's dismemberment in the eighteenth century reflected
the new political reality. A minority of Poland's Jews fell under
the rule of Austria and Prussia, but the majority were swept
under the hegemony of Russia. The tsarist autocracy, impelled
by fear and superstition, confined the annexed Jews to an area
which became known as the Pale of Settlement. Congress Poland, Lithuania, Byelorussia, and the Ukraine (excluding Kiev)
constituted this great ghetto which endured until 1915, two
years before the downfall of the Romanoffs.[4]

Throughout the nineteenth century, tsarist despotism severely tested Jewish middle-class patterns. In locality after locality Russian officials schemed to eject the Jewish lessee, innkeeper, and middleman. More often than not, edicts expelling
Jews from the villages were rescinded, but not before wreak-
ing havoc upon thousands of families. Less cruel and more far-
reaching were the tsarist plans to divert Jews from commerce
and trade into agriculture; these proved unrealistic and went
unsustained. Eager Jews, cherishing visions of the redemptive
fig tree and vine, were induced to apply antiquated methods to
land situated amid desolate steppes, remote from main roads
and rivers. Freshly fashioned Jewish peasants lacking marketing facilities, and proper tutelage, faced malnutrition, ruin, and
death. Those who survived were without the promised seed

corn, cattle, implements, or dwellings, while the land remained unallotted and unsurveyed. A like fate befell tsarist designs for ushering in large-scale factory industry. Lacking incentive and experience, neither Jews nor Russians were prepared for such ventures.[5]

The middle of the nineteenth century saw the enfeeblement of traditional Jewish middle-class roles. The emancipation of the serfs in 1863 dealt the medieval division into economic spheres, a blow that devitalized the functions of moneylender, factor, petty merchant, and steward. The provincial nobility, compelled to take an interest in their own affairs, sought means to reduce costs and services, while the emancipated serfs, forced to become self-reliant, began to market their surpluses through the great merchants. The swift growth of cities, the spread of banking and credit facilities, and the extension and multiplication of railway lines, further upset the precarious position of Jews. Few had the training, capital, or privileges needed to scale their businesses into substantial commercial, industrial, or banking enterprises. Forced into an unequal race with government-subsidized ventures and mushrooming foreign concerns, their economic lot steadily deteriorated. A handful of Jews astutely slid into the changed order and even rose to become grandees in St. Petersburg, Moscow, and Kiev. But their achievements were as remote from the sordid experiences of the Jews of the Pale as were the splendors of the tsarist court itself.[6]

In the face of change the tsarist government remained obdurate. Absolutist decrees thwarted all possible escape from an economic morass meliorated only by official corruption and inefficiency, custom and habit sanctified by religion, and the degraded lot of the surrounding peasantry. Liberal policies of the 1860's enabled privileged Jews to elude the ever-tightening vise of the Pale, but did not relieve the plight of the Jews as a whole. Merchants owning a costly business license, professional persons, midwives, university graduates, students, master artisans, and discharged soldiers who had served before 1874 were permitted to live throughout Russia. However, the terms for settling in the Russian interior were so onerous that at the close of the century only one twentieth of Russia's Jews lived outside the Pale.

The promise of the 1860's proved short-lived. Restrictions punctuated the 1870's. In the 1880's tyranny was codified in the May Laws, which prohibited Jews from owning or renting land outside towns and cities and discouraged them from living in the villages. Quotas limited the entrance of Jews into the gymnasia and the universities. In 1891 thousands of privileged Jews were expelled without warning from Moscow, St. Petersburg, and Kiev. Thousands more were deprived of their livelihoods as innkeepers and restaurateurs in 1897 when the liquor traffic became a government monopoly. Finally, coercion culminated in violence. The "spontaneous" outbreaks of 1881, the massacre at Kishinev in 1903, the pogroms that followed, and the revolution of 1905 obliterated hope. The accompanying economic crisis reduced Russia's Jews to penury.

Despite the barriers and restrictions Jews were continuously on the move within the Pale, for the pressure of numbers was relentless, creating a crisis of Malthusian proportions. Where there had been one million Jews in 1800, there were four million in 1880. Economic suffocation was imminent. From Byelorussia and Lithuania, with their populous cities, scrubby land, and puny industry, Jews streamed southward to the bountiful Ukraine and westward to a rapidly industrializing Poland. In the latter half of the nineteenth century, Jews forced from the villages thronged into the towns and cities. Urban centers rose overnight. Lodz, the Russian Manchester, a village with 11 Jews in 1793, had 98,677 Jews in 1897 and 166,628 in 1910; the older city of Warsaw, with 3532 Jewish inhabitants in 1781, numbered 219,141 in 1891. This movement from village to town to city, the migration from one section of the Pale to another, and the exodus overseas were all part of the mass flight from poverty.[7]

Until the 1880's Jews clung to their traditional middle-class occupations. Their refusal to bend put village lessees who administered inns, mills, taverns, and estates in a desperate pinch. Landlords might dispossess them at will; the pathetic scene of a Jewish innkeeper cast upon the road with his wife, children, and household belongings in any season of the year was common. Their only resort was to drift into the towns, bloating the numbers that already struggled to exist. Once there, Jews were restricted in their residence, were unqualified for government employment, and, with few exceptions, were barred from the professions. While economic and technical change imposed new ways upon industry and commerce, they were driven into the traditional handicrafts and into petty trade.

Declassed Jews, subsisting on the slimmest of margins, constantly changed occupation. A popular street song gave melancholy expression to the dejected state of commerce and the desperate improvisations of its practitioners.

> Brothers ten were we, o,
> Flax did we ply, so
> One departed this life and nine remained.
>
> Nine brothers abided, o,
> Freight did we handle, so
> Another passed away and eight remained · . . .
>
> One alone do I tarry, o,
> In candles do I traffic, so,
> Daily do I perish, o woe,
> For want of a morsel to relish, o.

With jobs so scarce, earnings so scant, "it [was] hard to draw the line between the 'schnorrer' (mendicant) and the 'luftmensch' (a man without any regular source of income), who has not yet resigned himself to beggary, and yet cannot tell in the morning whence he is to draw his sustenance at noon. These include artisans, sweatshop workers, agents and go-betweens, a city proletariat of the very worst kind," reported an observer of ghetto prosperity.[8]

Meager earnings, a low technical level, and middle-class gentility had traditionally restricted the crafts to the more humble. And throughout the Pale virtually all artisans were Jews, for the Russian peasant aspired neither to commerce nor to the handicrafts. Cobblers, tailors, blacksmiths, tanners, hatmakers, carpenters, tinsmiths, harnessmakers, butchers, bakers, watchmakers, jewelers, and furriers were invariably Jewish. These craftsmen both manufactured and marketed their goods, supplying town, village, and countryside. The modest demands of their patrons and the backward Russian economy kept their products inferior to those of Western Europe. But many Jewish artisans were superb craftsmen, and the gentry relied on them almost exclusively for a variety of services. Prior to the 1880's the living standards of artisans had been rising steadily, but the subsequent overcrowding of the crafts reversed this trend.

Factory production also made inroads into the economy of the Pale, notably in Poland, threatening the position of the craftsmen. There German capital, organization, and technology assumed a dominant role, and Jewish artisans were forced to compete with the domestic and foreign factory product as well as with their fellow craftsmen. They frequented villages, hamlets, estates, fairs, markets, and religious festivals, in search of customers for their goods and services. The drain on the time and energy of the roving craftsmen invariably led the more enterprising to become merchant capitalists in the domestic system. Scarcity of capital, inadequate borrowing facilities, competition from the factory product, government restrictions, a scattered labor force, and the individualistic Jew's aversion to factory labor contributed to the rapid growth of this kind of manufacture throughout the Pale. The first Russian census of 1897 testified that the proportion of gainfully employed Jews in manufacturing exceeded those engaged in commerce; in Lithuania and Byelorussia the ratio stood at nearly two to one.[9]

At the turn of the century hundreds of towns, dense with workshops and sweatshops, entered into the production of a variety of ready-made goods. The textile industry led the way, with Lodz brooking no rivals in cotton manufacture and Bialystok excelling in woolens. Czestochowa produced toys, Smargon and Kreslavki tanned and refined leather, Mezeritch converted hog's bristles into brushes, Grodno made cigars and cigarettes, Odessa, Warsaw, Vilna, and lesser commercial and governmental centers attracted their share of activity in a score or more trades. The chemical industry in its many branches—ink, shoe-blacking, dyes, soap, candles, turpentine, and tar—absorbed the newly unleashed energies of many towns. Even the sacred trades were harnessed to the new capitalism. Five hundred artisans of Dubrovna, engaged in the weaving of prayer shawls, depended on three or four middlemen who bought the entire product and marketed it throughout the Pale.[10]

Rapid urbanization boomed construction and multiplied opportunities in the building trades. Mechanics who had plied their crafts in the townlets and on the estates of a progressively insolvent Russian squirearchy flocked to the bursting cities. Despite the restrictions of the Christian guilds, Jewish carpenters, locksmiths, tinsmiths, plumbers, and masons multiplied. As they were excluded from government work, few were bricklayers or streetpavers. But Jews were permitted to work on high buildings "because they were more competent to do the work"; virtually every church spire in the Pale had been tiled by Jewish workmen.[11]

The industrial transformation affected the role of Jewish women as well. Jewesses customarily had acted as helpmates to their men in the management of the family business; frequently they assumed a major share of the responsibilities so that their husbands might devote themselves to religious study. Lower-class girls made *shaitels* (traditional wigs for married Jewesses) or, more commonly, were hired out as domestic servants. But in the 1870's the Singer sewing machine began to revolutionize the Jewish home; by 1900 even the daughters of respectable householders had turned their energies and talents to it. Aided by his wife, daughters, and the sewing machine, the marginal Jewish tradesman struggled to sustain himself. In the larger towns and cities women worked as tailoresses, seamstresses, sockmakers, modistes, and flowermakers, trades that they later were to practice in New York City. In the 1890's young women took the final step and left home to work in cigar, cigarette, and match factories.[12]

In the three decades preceding the First World War, factory production made remarkable strides. Despite restrictions, Jewish entrepreneurs were active throughout the Pale, particularly in Poland where their legal rights were less circumscribed than they were elsewhere. Jews were especially prominent in the production of textiles, lumber, tobacco, hides, soap, bricks, tiles, and mineral waters; they managed creameries and to a lesser extent were active as beer brewers and distillers. Owing to insufficient capital, Jewish-owned factories remained small, and largely employed hand machinery. Although individual production was trifling under these circumstances, total production of the Jewish factories was considerable.[13]

The proportion of Jewish factory workers was initially small. But in the final decade of the nineteenth century Jews constituted over 21 per cent of the factory hands in the Pale and nearly 28 per cent in Poland. Heaviest was the concentration in the textile mills of Bialystok and the tobacco factories of Grodno. Lodz, Russia's greatest textile center, attracted Jews from the blighted towns, but they reluctantly entered the factories; weavers from the nearby townlets preferred the squalid home labor to the more sanitary discipline of the factory. The traditional independence of the artisan and trader, the difficulty in adjusting religious observances to the factory routine, the inability to compete physically with migrating peasants in heavy labor, and the open hostility of non-Jewish factory owners, deterred Jews from entering the factories. Jewish entrepreneurs who used mechanical power in their workshops were reluctant to shut down two days a week to accommodate Jewish employees. They chose instead to hire non-Jews, who more easily adjusted themselves to the routine. Jews consequently were to be found largely in factories operated with hand machinery, where their absence on the Sabbath did not curb the manufacturing processes; where there was a small capital investment, both the Jewish and the Christian Sabbath could be honored.[14]

Unskilled day labor traditionally had counted few Jews in its ranks. The low status of "black labor," the inferior muscular development of the underfed city-bred Jew, and above all the unlimited reservoir of peasant labor, particularly in the Northwest, discouraged Jews from entering such occupations. Yet so unsettled had conditions become, despite a rising manufacturing economy, that in the 1890's 2 per cent of all Jews eked out livelihoods as agricultural laborers, cabmen, diggers, stonebreakers, ragpickers, teamsters, porters, and water carriers. In the towns and townlets of Lithuania and Byelorussia Jews monopolized one ancient vocation: the census of 1897 counted 5878 Jewish water carriers. In Poland and the Northwest the building of railroads curtailed wagon and coach traffic, largely conducted by Jews; the construction of electric trolley lines similarly unseated Jewish cabmen, who, hovering about the city squares, became *gassmenschen,* ever ready to undertake the most arduous assignments.

At Kasimilch, at Grodno, and at Vilna, it is almost solely Jews who lash tree trunks into rafts. On the banks of the Dnieper, are seen the Jewish porters who unload wood from the ships—some of these between sixty and sixty-five years of age—pass days of from twelve to fourteen hours in water to their waists, unloading boats . . . At Vilna, the *vachevniki,*—whose work consists in separating the trunks of trees that form the rafts and piling them up—work on horseback, and their dangerous trade demands much daring and skill; there are 480 of them, all Jews.

As early as the 1880's, the leading Black Sea port of Odessa had from 8000 to 9000 Jewish day laborers with over 1700 employed on the docks. In Southern Russia where their more powerful country-bred physiques made them equal to their tasks, 10 per cent of all gainfully employed Jews worked at day labor.[15]

The most dwindling of occupations, agriculture, attracted few Jews. Artificial colonization by the tsarist government on barren distant soils in unfamiliar climates, and administrative caprice that at once encouraged and prohibited settlement, left but 190,000 Jews on the soil in the 1890's, the hardy remnants of earlier experiments. But agriculture as a supplementary source of income was commonplace. In the villages almost every Jewish family owned a cow or goat, often the sole dependable source of income, as well as some fowl. Jews cultivated their own gardens; they raised the "Jewish fruits"—beets, carrots, cabbage, onions, cucumbers, garlic, and horseradish; and, despite restrictions, many rented orchards on a seasonal basis from neighboring peasants and gentry.[16]

The crisis in the lives of Jews was accentuated rather than disguised by the hum and bustle of trader, artisan, factory worker, and day laborer. Bulging cities and withered towns rivaled one another in their raw poverty. Two- and three-room huts, stuffed to bursting with "lean, cadaverous caricatures of humanity," housed from seven to thirty people. Only the city of Berditchev outdistanced Vilna, the "Jerusalem of Lithuania," in the melancholy state of its Jewish inhabitants. Even the violently anti-Semitic *Vilna Journal* made no attempt to conceal the distress of the city's Jews.

One Jew who was a bootmaker, kept himself alive during many weeks on new potatoes, until at last he became dangerously ill; another a weaver, fell down dead whilst engaged at his loom; he had died of starvation . . . They live in miserable hovels, dirty and badly ventilated. Filth is everywhere—inside and outside. In the same dwelling may be found four, five, or even six families, each of them having a number of children of tender age. To add to the misery, neither beds, nor chairs, nor tables are to be seen in the wretched hovels, but everyone has to lie on the damp and infected ground. Meat is an unknown luxury, even on the Sabbath. Today bread and water, tomorrow water and bread, and so on day after day.

In the 1890's booming Lodz presented an equally dismal picture. "The Jews are crowded together in the Balout quarter where the atmosphere is almost unbreatheable. In one single room . . . three persons [were] eating, working, and sleeping. They had no beds and slept on the floor, summer and winter alike. The unfortunate wretches have bad health and their misery is indescribable." [17]

The decaying townlets with their one- and two-room brick and timber cabins wallowed in "the extreme of squalid dilapidation."

The sanitary condition is, if possible, worse than in the very poorest of the Russian country towns. Household refuse of every kind is simply thrown into the streets. The liquid portion slowly percolates downwards, while the solid debris stamped into the sand, forms a crust in dry weather, and a swamp that is simply indescribable after a few hours of rain.

Parsimony and wits were joined to sustain life on buckwheat and potatoes.

Several Jewesses were selling herring which were sliced into small pieces . . . One of these merchants . . . is a widow with five children to support. She buys every morning four or six herrings, and cuts each one into six or eight pieces, each of which sells at a kopek . . . If she succeeds in selling a half a dozen herrings in this manner, she can manage to exist with her family.

Nineteen per cent of the Jewish families in Russia and over 22 per cent in Lithuania buckled under the strain of poverty and applied for communal assistance to meet the exigencies of the Passover in the 1890's. These percentages would have been far greater had not pride and expectation of migrating to America restrained many more potential applicants.[18]

GALICIA AND BUKOVINA

Elsewhere in Eastern Europe the position of Jews differed only in degree from that of their more numerous coreligionists in Russia. True, Jewish political and civil disabilities had almost disappeared in Austria-Hungary by the late nineteenth century. But the material plight of Jews in the easternmost provinces of Galicia and Bukovina was equal to if not worse than that of the Jews of Lithuania and Byelorussia. Galicia's gross poverty, retarded industry, sparse and undeveloped natural resources, and poor transportation facilities rendered all economic activity backward. The rise in Galicia's population, from 150,000 in 1772 to 575,000 in 1869, choked an economy that annually saw five to six thousand Jews starve to death. Only the hoped-for intervention of the Almighty, "Gott hilft schon," shielded them from despair.[19]

Galician Jews were concentrated in retail trade, brokerage, the sale of beverages, and the handicrafts, and many worked on the land. But change affected all economic sectors adversely. The growth of peasant cooperatives made Jewish traders superfluous. Governmental monopolization of the tobacco, beverage, salt, and railway industries drove Jewish restaurateurs, tobacconists, retailers, and innkeepers to suicidal rivalries. The completion of a railway network in the 1880's and 1890's deprived Jewish teamsters and draymen of their sources of livelihood.

Jewish artisans, less numerous than in Russia, in the 1890's were largely self-employed master craftsmen. Yet by 1900, despite the delayed emergence even of the domestic system, the number of Jewish factory employees had grown considerably. They were engaged in tool-making, weaving, printing, and the wood and machine industries, where they worked in tiny establishments. The stagnation of the Galician economy, as industrial change crept forward, however, aggravated the frustration of the masses.[20] But many Galician Jews were to rise from an apathy decades deep to seek a new homeland in America—their destination, New York.

RUMANIA

Like tsarist Russia, Rumania burdened its Jews with severe political disabilities. Even Jews who had lived there for generations were treated as aliens. They were not admitted to schools, were barred from public employment, could not buy land, and were banned from the villages.

Yet, however handicapped, Jews were well-integrated into the Rumanian economy. They were dispersed throughout trade and commerce, small and big industry, and were to be found even in agriculture. They were conspicuous in the exchange and marketing of grain, cattle, and timber, and also excelled in retail trade. To a greater extent even than in Russia, Jews predominated in the handicrafts, particularly as tinners, glaziers, housepainters, coopers, watchmakers, bookbinders, tailors, and modistes. In many Moldavian towns practically all gainfully employed Jews were artisans. Even in Bucharest, tinkers, tailors, painters, braidmakers, silversmiths, coppersmiths, woodturners, cabinetmakers, bookbinders, lampmakers, hatters, and brushmakers were preponderantly Jews. With the penetration of western technology, Jews attained a new level of pre-eminence in the textile, clothing, glass, wood, and furniture industries.

Rumanian Jews, partaking of the general material well-being, were less pressed than Jews in Russia and Galicia. But when Rumania modernized, earlier barriers for Jews, especially those affecting education, became acutely disabling. All hope for improvement or a reversal of policy shriveled with the crowning of political reaction at the turn of the century. After 1899 Jewish migration from Rumania was to be proportionately heavier even than that from tsarist Russia.[21]

In a little more than three decades, over one third of the Jews of Eastern Europe left their homes. Over 90 per cent of them came to the United States, the majority settling in New York City. These immigrants packed their few household belongings, pots and pans, samovar, pillows, and bedding, much of which would be lost or pilfered on the way, and forsook their native towns and villages to embark on the greatest journey of their lives. They parted with loved ones, seemingly forever, and made their way by foot, coach, and train, to the bewildering port cities of Western Europe. There they sailed direct from Hamburg or Bremen at a cost of thirty-four dollars, some for a saving of nine dollars traveling by way of Liverpool. Crammed into steerage for as long as three weeks, Jewish immigrants were confined to herring, black bread, and tea by their loyalty to dietary laws, until the water journey's end. It was "a kind of hell that cleanses a man of his sins before coming to Columbus' land," insisted a popular immigrant guidebook that attempted to minimize the torments of the ocean voyage.[22] Whatever the spiritually therapeutic values of that epic crossing, few immigrants would ever forget its terrors.

✎ 3 ✎

Torah, Haskala, and Protest

High above aspires my being
Up into my land of dreams
Where source of thoughts fresh and mighty,
Reason flows in clearest streams.
"Ahin, Ahin" (1890)

THE Jews of Eastern Europe gloried in their separateness with
no need to apologize and less to explain. Rendered conspicuous
by their dress, language, and customs and confined in their occupations and habitats, they knew they were Jews, anchored in
religious traditions by their needs, their convictions, their communal life, and the state of the surrounding peasantry.

Adversity fashioned an inner existence that flamed up in
direct proportion to the bleakness of an outer world that was
shaped by the rumors and realities of forced conversions and
persecutions. Everyday life was transcended and embellished
by a rich heritage of learning, liturgy, custom, and special observance. Renewed torments, made more vigorous the conviction of Israel's superiority, however erring it might be. For was
not the Almighty but testing the faithfulness of his chosen from
among all the nations? If these trials seemed excessive, it was
only that the sinfulness and waywardness of the children of
Israel merited retribution. What was the history of Jewry if
not a glowing testament to the triumph of the spirit over the
flesh, the weak over the strong, the humble over the proud, the
few over the many, the Eternal People over their remittent
destroyers? It had been so in the days of Matthias the son of

Johannan, in the days of Mordecai and Esther. Each such triumph was but added proof of the imminence of the Messiah ben David, who would redeem his people and bring them to final salvation in Zion when Israel's sufferings had become unendurable.[1]

Religious practice and observance, lightened by a sense of religious uniqueness, constituted the Jewish life. Divine thanksgiving hallowed each daily task, so that the spiritual intertwined with the mundane. The *shulchan aruch,* Karo's manual of religious ordinances and its many abridgements, governed the minute aspects of everyday life as well as the cycles of fasts, holy days, festivals, and inevitable bereavements. The Giver of the Law in all his prescience and wisdom supervised work and rest, dress and deportment, reading and writing, food and drink, cleanliness and health. So fused were all phases of life that Jews accepted as divinely ordained the *shtraiml* (cap edged with fur), the *shaitel* (wig for married women), the *kaftan* (long gabardine cloak) and the *peyes* (ear-locks). To deviate even in detail was heresy and invited ostracism.

Religious learning, the only kind of learning comprehensible to Jews, disciplined all. Its core, the compendia of the Law (the Torah), consisted of the Babylonian Talmud and the Midrashim (homilectical commentaries on the Scriptures), and at the last, the Pentateuch. The mastery of this civil and religious code was the acme of educational endeavor. Hidden meanings and contemporary applications perennially were unearthed as each passage and codicil elicited renewed commentary and debate. Talmudic scholarship, an unrelenting taskmaster and an end in itself, earned the highest social esteem.

Although relatively few Jews became rabbis, official interpreters of the Law, or semireligious functionaries, many spent their early years and leisure hours in later life wrestling with the Law in yeshiva (Talmudic seminary) and synagogue. Only in the final decades of the nineteenth century did religious learning falter in the face of the increasing attractions of modern knowledge, an unprecedented increase in semiliteracy, and economic decline.[2]

The pious Jew believed that in many and marvellous ways—

as Father, God of our Fathers, King and Redeemer—did the creator of the world reveal himself to his Chosen of all nations. The justice and righteousness of the Holy One was beyond the cavil of a doubt. At times, the God of Abraham, Isaac, and Jacob might be berated, for the burdens placed on his Chosen Israel often seemed inordinate. Jews might question details in the works of the King of the Universe and meticulously examine authorities. But in prayer services thrice daily they implicitly affirmed the magnificence of God's work, the Messianic coming, the mission of the children of Israel, and the promise of a future life. Jews were reminded of the transience of all worldly achievements, the vanity of vanities in a universe whose perversity made life and fortune ever uncertain, for even the most privileged among them might be stripped arbitrarily of human rights and earthly goods.

But ever certain, ever regular, the repose "of the Sabbath bride" separated the sacred from the profane, and banished the humiliations of the weekdays. Passover, above all the other holidays and festivals that re-enacted the annals of a people, bore witness to the deliverance of Israel from beneath the yoke of the pharaohs. This holiday, celebrated with symbolic precision, testified to the trust that gave dignity to the poorest Jew. A nineteenth-century satirist of the Pale ironically expressed the faith that calamity never was final.

Certainly it is bad! But Jews become accustomed to everything. Well, God will help anyway. Things will be a bit pinched; we shall eat a little less, somewhat less of this, a trifle less of that. No matter! The townlet is leveled by fire!—O, that is terrible, terrible indeed. What a terrible misery! But what is to be done! God is a father and the children of Israel are the merciful sons of the merciful. Messages are written, messengers are sent out. One hopes, one waits— and what comes of it! Not a thing! Messengers are also human, flesh and blood with wives and children. The poor wretches need a great deal upon which to subsist. Along comes a cold wet autumn, strongly intimating that they can no longer remain outdoors; so they bundle together, as is, in makeshift lodgings. Cramped a bit? Never mind, as long as they are all cramped together. Along comes an unexpected disease and death strikes one of their number down. A fast day is declared—and they fast! Want waxes ever more bitter, penury ever greater. Well, whosoever can, hastens away. God's world is large, somewhere in Volhynia a plump corner waits.[3]

Beyond the daily devotionals, religion bound its ethical prescriptions into the social fabric, making charity an obligation. Voluntary societies, or *hevras,* flourishing in every hamlet and *shtetl* (town), competed in raising free loans for the needy and dowries for orphaned girls. These *hevras* aided the sick, boarded the transient, and educated the children of the poor. Honor and social prestige were the reward for such good works, to say nothing of benefits to be derived in the world beyond. Although the merchant of means was set off from the artisan, the townsman from the villager, and above all, the learned from the unlearned, neither erudition nor wealth conferred caste privileges. The blessings of affluence, though hardly undervalued in worldly terms, had a social and religious purpose, that of *tsedaka,* charity conceived as justice. *Tsedaka* was to be acquitted with infinite tact, personal generosity, and humane feeling for the less fortunate of Israel's children. This social responsibility, which prosperous Jews were to bear with humility and self-effacement, served as the standard of the world's respect. If practice deviated from precept, if wealth at times showed itself neither generous nor kind and learning neither wise nor virtuous, still these ideals established the moral tone. Even the most delinquent and least literate of Jews was measured and measured himself by the ideals of Torah.[4]

But the homogeneity of circumstance, the binding overtones of religious life, the intellectual vitality, and mutual dependence in an unfriendly world also strained relations among Jews. Wealth and learning, copartners in authority as well as in social esteem, tended to slight the poor and the unlearned. Within the confines of the synagogue—house of prayer, house of study, meeting hall, and general social center—were mirrored all the irritants and vanities of Jewish life. Particularly in the larger towns, the mandate to participate personally in liturgical readings and ceremonials sanctioned a measure of social discrimination against the poor, who were unable to compete in the petty monetary bidding for these honors.

Where possible, artisans asserted their independence. Poverty did not detract from their religious ardor nor dull their sense of equality. In the larger towns and in some of the villages, *hevras* of artisans avidly supported humble houses of prayer and study. Within the measure of their scant earnings, tailors, cobblers, and carpenters petitioned and exhorted the Holy One in their own synagogues. There they delighted in the highly prized readings of the Sacred Scroll on the Sabbath, on the special days, and in the honorific ceremonials that were fully accessible to them. They were not relegated to the rear, but earned full religious privileges and could even occupy the coveted benches near the east wall that looked toward Jerusalem.[5]

Only during the reign of Tsar Nicholas I (1825–1855), when the well-to-do shifted the burden of twenty-five years of military service—with the prospect of death, or its equivalent, conversion—onto the shoulders of the twelve-year-old sons of the poor, were social relations lastingly embittered. At times the poor became suspicious of disproportionate taxation and sumptuary regulations that were enforced by the oligarchical *Kahals* (Jewish community councils). But their ire could be allayed. Much was tolerable on this earth, since this world was only an anteroom to the Hereafter and all Israel had a portion in the world to come.[6]

Whatever the strains between the well-to-do and the poor, all Jews shared in the pervasive personal and familial ties of the small towns. They were sustained by their sense of community, by a belief in a common destiny, and by a feeling of moral superiority to the surrounding world of lords and peasants. They at least were spared the chasm that divided the former serf from the nobleman and the brutality and indifference accompanying such relations. But this self-contained Jewish world was bound to crumble before ideas and forces that were to gnaw away its base.[7]

THE NEW LEARNING

The early 1800's saw the invasion of modern western influences. The proponents of Haskala, or Jewish enlightenment, in Warsaw and other cosmopolitan centers called for the modernization of customs and thought so as to place Jews on an equal plane with non-Jews. Such steps were to be the basis on which they could appeal for political emancipation. But the Haskala soon became more than a Jewish reform movement. In Russia, Nicholas I turned the Jewish enlightenment into an instrument of governmental policy, establishing schools to wean Jewish youngsters away from their folk loyalties and practices (without offering them the rights of citizenship that would enable them to enter into professional careers). Jewish leaders were quick to see the tragic implications of the tsarist policy and opposed enlightenment under any auspices.

As long as we are not granted civic rights, education will only be a misfortune for us. In his present state the Jew does not disdain the humiliating livelihood of a broker or usurer, and finds comfort in his religion. But when the Jew will receive a modern education, he will become sensitive to his legal disabilities, and then dissatisfied with his bitter lot, he will be prompted to desert his faith. An honest Jewish father will never agree to train his child for conversion.[8]

Against this wall of resistance, the Tsar's educational program was still-born. In 1841 only 15 of 2866 students enrolled at higher institutions of learning and 48 of 80,017 pupils in primary and secondary schools were Jews.

Yet, the broadening affect of the commercial occupations, coupled with widespread intellectual hunger, casually but continually brought privileged Jews and interlopers into touch with western influences. The masses of Jews were not disturbed by manifestos in the enlightened Russian and Hebrew periodicals, which urged them to reassess their whole way of life, for these were limited to a social and intellectual elite. But in the popular vernacular tales of Mendel Moicher Sforim the brute facts of the decaying old order were revealed to all with a starkness that mocked paper programs.

To your health, Gloops, you great Jewish city, you consummate ghetto! Where one meets thousands of creatures with faces boney and white as death, where one meets very many paupers, gaunt and deformed, sick luckless people because there is no good order and they are led, lost, hidden and a few wander about like blind sheep! To your health, you luckless city! Where there are many *hevras*, many collection boxes, many sextons, many genteel, many do-gooders, and many poor Jews . . . To the health of that section of the city where the poor sit in tiny low hovels, in holes, in cellars up to their necks in mud. To the health of that barren part of the city . . . where people fare worse perhaps than in hell! Observe the miserable conditions of the pauper, the way he sits, the way he sleeps, what he eats, the way his wife lies pregnant, the way his chil-dren roll about, the way they are clothed, and the way they are raised.[9]

The Haskala, penetrating the larger cities as a matter of course, proved most disturbing in Lithuania and Byelorussia where Talmudic study had sunk its deepest roots and where the cultivation of the mind had attained its highest development. Renowned yeshivas that huddled in obscure towns attracted in-quisitive youngsters from every sector of Russian Jewry. Vilna, a meeting place for Jew and German, Russian, Pole, and Lithu-anian, became the headquarters for the dissemination of en-lightenment and diffusion of "gentile" learning. At the turn of the century this "Jerusalem of Lithuania" broadcast the many modern ideologies that pulsed through Jewish life to the re-motest backwaters and farthest outposts of the Yiddish-speaking world.[10]

The cities quickened the pace of skepticism and intensified the malaise of a learned but careerless youth. Young men who had pored over the Law turned to Haskala literature and gentile knowledge. The sensitive at first were shocked, then in-toxicated, by the imminence of worlds only dimly compre-hended. (Later they would pay the price of acute tensions for their draughts of new learning.) Many Jewish youth, like the fictional Shloimele, were to bring minds tinged with historical romance to their visions of a new cosmos.

It is only a few years since Shloimele has begun to study the Torah. In every respect he is still a child. Yet, Lord God of the Universe, what has he not experienced, where has he not been in this time? Verily, he has roamed as far and as wide as an ancient who has out-lived the years of Methuselah! He has been in Mesopotamia, in Canaan, in Egypt, in Persia and Medea, in Susa its capital, and in multiple other lands as far as India and Cathay; also the wilderness and the desert has he frequented, and there he has hearkened to many marvelous things . . . of a sort which to all other people are an incomprehensible mystery; but among Jews it is a common everyday event. Only with Jewish children does it transpire that they sit day and night rooted to one spot, not knowing what is happening roundabouts, what they need learn to do in order to live among people . . . All thoughts are in another world, in other epochs; they are oblivious to the world right under their noses and devote themselves wholly to that which transpired long ago, for which eyes and the other crude human senses are not so much needed as an acute imaginative faculty—a stark naked soul—devoid of body, devoid of life itself!

He is wandering in Egypt, in the lands of Sihon, of Og, king of Bashan, and Nebuchadnezzar, emperor of Babylonia; his mind is agitated by the Red Sea, the Salt Sea, the river Euphrates and the Jordan; for him people exist whom one must address in the sacred tongue and even in Aramaic.

Shloimele has only been born here; he is not exactly a native but resides somewhere over there . . . His times are beforetimes, his world is another, of long ago; here he is a stranger, there—an antique resident! He comes home but only to sojourn, like a guest at a railway station, sups, rests overnight,—and tramps over yonder, again indeed over yonder!

And as this life is a dream, what wonder is it that he is aroused by the likes of which has never been and never will be.

In such a mood of expectancy unsettled youth, caught between a decrepit past and a forbidding future, became eager disciples of a new cosmology of hopes and assurances. They awaited seers who would replace Jewish practices with a new faith and who would reveal the scientific causes and teleological logic underlying so tremendous a cataclysm.[11]

> High above aspires my being
> Up into my land of dreams
> Where source of thoughts fresh and mighty,
> Reason flows in purest streams.
>
> Fair and radiant, outscaling life,
> Joy of freedom everywhere,
> Proud spirits through its currents glide
> Aloft in truth's eternal sphere.

There dawns forever waken
Youth released from time
Heroes, questing virtue's action,
Blest by love and peace sublime.

Where deep and holy is all feeling
And even pain brings purest joy
Boundless, the will, man's good achieving,
With a heart content and unalloyed.[12]

As the new learning spread in these years, the number of young Jews at the universities grew from 3 per cent of the student body in 1865, to 9 per cent in 1881. Eager to train for the professions and to acquire the higher values of Russian and Western culture, Jews had found a means of entry into the non-Jewish world of promise.[13]

REVOLUTION

But the new era of liberalism, in which Jews readily were admitted to the gymnasia, had come to a close. In 1886 Russian institutions of higher learning barred all but a few, so that opportunities suddenly vanished for many Jews who had abandoned traditional studies to prepare for professional careers. Once having broken with the past, they could not be put down. Many persisted in independent study, stirred by an ardor that was to flame into revolutionary fervor. Tutored by their fellows, they consumed every scrap of modern knowledge within reach. Others went abroad to study. In the final decades of the nineteenth and early years of the twentieth centuries large colonies of Russian Jews were to be found at the major continental universities, particularly in those of Germany and Switzerland. Intellectually emancipated, these students emerged as the leaders of the revolutionary movements that were to agitate Russian Jewish youth in the two decades before the First World War.[14]

The passion of the intellectually Russified Jew turned to radicalism, but it did so slowly. In the 1870's a few Jews played a minor role in the Narodnaya Volya (People's Will), a Russian revolutionary group. But tsarist policy in the 1880's drove Jewish students to turn to the dilemma of their own people. As a large Jewish working class emerged in the cities, Marxian Socialism achieved a more widespread appeal. Jewish workmen were to be inspired by a vision of a new era when all men would be united with a solidarity that through the ages had bound Jews together. Jewish students prepared workmen for their prophetic role by tutoring them in the mysteries of gentile learning—Russian grammar, astronomy, and geography, with the socialist creed thrown in as a special fillip. But this program attracted only a handful of aspiring workmen and their new accomplishments tended to detach them from rather than to unite them with their laboring fellows. In the early 1890's Social Democrats, caught up in a wave of strikes, recognized that unless they appealed to more basic needs they would have few followers. "The masses of folk are not drawn into the struggle on the strength of theories," they concluded, and they turned to economic agitation. "The struggle that will be aroused by such an agitation, will accustom the workers to defend their own rights, lift up their courage, create in them a faith in their powers, a consciousness that unity is needed and ultimately the more crucial questions will be presented to them." Soon a popular movement was under way chanting Winchevsky's hymn of liberation, "The Free Spirit," imported from the immigrant colonies overseas. "In the streets, the spirit of freedom calls to all folk of humanity's oppressed peoples." The revelations of a newly dawning age were to commence with a campaign for the twelve-hour day.[15]

Enlightened reformers, who once had carried the socialist gospel to students, now directed their message to the working classes. These leaders, few of whom spoke Yiddish, became committed to Jewish consciousness and sensibilities, and their socialist rhetoric became colored with the imagery of the Yiddish vernacular. In this new climate the Bund was organized in 1897 in an obscure alley in Vilna, spiritual and intellectual center of the Jews of Russia and internment city for suspected revolutionaries. There five intellectuals and eight artisans, representing the cities of Vilna, Bialystok, Minsk, Kovno, Vitebsk, and Warsaw, launched the General League of Jewish Workers in Russia, Poland, and Lithuania (Der algemayner idisher arbeter bund in rusland, polen, un litauen), the first attempt to organize Jews for secular independent political activity. For the first time in European history, Jews applied the admonition of an ancient sage to this worldly social action. "If I am not for myself, who will be for me; but if I am only for myself, what am I; and if not now, when?" [16]

The Bund's program embodied all the restless social forces that had been gathering momentum in tsarist Russia for over a generation. A resentment against the suppression of elementary civil rights, the longing of Russian subjects for civic and political freedom, the aspirations of factory workers for higher wages, and a widespread yearning for social justice, were joined in the Bund's credo. Its comprehensive mission, its humane spirit, and its role as an ally of all who worked for constitutional guarantees made the Bund more than a labor movement and gained for it universal support. [17]

As early as the 1870's Jewish workmen, driven by desperation had resorted to sabotage and violence in strikes that were without form or program. In 1888, however, Social Democrats founded strike funds and strike treasuries in a variety of trades, beginning with the stocking knitters of Vilna. As relations between masters and journeymen lost their intimacy, the guilds fell apart and workmen formed their own benevolent societies, which Social Democrats helped to transform into unions. In 1893, in Vilna, Minsk, Warsaw, Homel, and Smargon, Social Democrats led strikes of cobblers, carpenters, tailors, brushmakers, quilters, locksmiths, and glovemakers, who had been laboring fourteen to eighteen hours a day for a weekly wage of two to three rubles. In 1895 strike victories by tobacco workers in a large Vilna factory and thousands of weavers in the textile city of Bialystok set the stage for a great labor upheaval. In the same year, the first national trade union in Russia was organized, the Universal Union of Bristle Workers in Russian Poland—a trade which was monopolized by Jews. After 1897 the Bund extended and coordinated strike activity throughout the Pale beneath "the bright beautiful sun of socialism." Between

1897 and 1900 the Bund led 312 strikes that brought improved working conditions and higher wages.[18]

But under Russian despotism the Bund program invited martyrdom. The Russian government, alarmed by strikes and boycotts, attempted to destroy the Bund by sponsoring its own trade unions under Zubatov, head of the Okhrana, the Russian secret police. The Okhrana's *agents provocateur* also infiltrated the Bund. In 1898, immediately following the organization of the Russian Social Democratic Workers' Party in Minsk, the secret police arrested seventy of its members. The government's sudden enforcement of ancient factory laws further curtailed the revolutionary activities. But meetings in the seclusion of forests and back streets, that often led to armed encounters with the police, did not diminish in frequency. Illegality and secrecy cloaked the Bund in romance and mystery and tantalized a rebellious youth.

Leaflets that anathematized tsarist tyranny and that proclaimed "the coming bloody struggle with despotism" to "all the suffering and enslaved, all the exhausted and exploited" were secretly printed and widely circulated despite the peril of imprisonment, banishment to Siberia, and execution. In 1902 Hirsh Leckert attempted to assassinate Governor Von Wahl of Vilna in retaliation for whipping May Day demonstrators; his subsequent hanging aroused anguish among all classes of Jews. Copiously elegized, the martyred young cobbler became an almost sacred symbol of the struggle for freedom; the Jewish proletariat, whose revolutionary inclinations hitherto had been doubted, now became clothed with divine sanctification.[19]

"The quiet sleepy Pale, [once] . . . described as a stagnating pool of economic degeneration, became the hotbed of revolutionary work." Between 1901 and 1903, of 7791 persons imprisoned in Russia for political reasons, 2269 were Jews. From March 1903 to November 1904, 54 per cent of those sentenced for political transgressions were Jews; over 64 per cent of the women who received such sentences were Jewesses. In 1904, of an estimated 30,000 organized Jewish workers, 4476 were imprisoned or exiled to Siberia.[20]

The pogroms incited by tsarist minister Plehve at Kishinev,

the Revolution of 1905, the ruthless counterrevolution, and the subsequent rash of pogroms throughout western Russia drove young Jews to deeds of valor that contrasted with the submissiveness of their elders during the most vicious persecutions. In "the struggle for the light and warmth of the Socialist sun" in anticipation of "the sacred day," Jewish youth, with the Bund as their "redeeming angel," exhibited unprecedented daring and fearlessness. "Once again rivers of blood. Again great mountains of flesh on the bloodied altar of the bloodied idol of Russian despotism," shrieked a leaflet circulated in the wake of a pogrom. In many towns and cities the Bund coordinated self-defense units to combat the brigands of the government-sponsored Black Hundreds. "From the pusillanimous people that the Jews were some thirty years ago," Count Witte recorded in 1912, "there sprang men and women who threw bombs, committed political murders, and sacrificed their lives for the revolution." [21]

The massacres and brutalities that convulsed the Pale between 1903 and 1907 stoked the fires of Jewish nationalism. Jewish youth marshaled courage in an effort to salvage its self-respect and that of fellow Jews. In the face of unprecedented barbarism the Zionist impulse, which had remained dormant despite the existence for over a generation of the *Hibbath Zion* (Lovers of Zion) and other Zionist groups, acquired life. While the Bund demanded national cultural autonomy for Jews within the Russian empire, Zionists—general, Socialist, and labor—and Territorialists, heartened by sympathetic voices from abroad, drew up schemes and programs for the rescue of oppressed Jews that helped sustain morale in these terrible times. [22]

Quickened by the ascendancy of the Bund and other popular movements, Yiddish emerged as a democratizing force, with the success of the Yiddish press in America providing example and inspiration. The insistent challenge that "a working class that is content with the lot of an inferior nation will not rise up against the lot of an inferior class" was forthrightly met by a thousand pens. The central organg of the Bund, the *Arbeter Shtimme,* began to appear in 1896, and subsequently Bund journals were set up in Minsk, Vilna, Warsaw, and Bialystok. In the wake of the Revolution of 1905, Bund papers appeared openly and were not finally suppressed until 1907, long after the Russian Socialist press had been thoroughly smashed. The broad diffusion of a deeply moralized Yiddish fiction, able, through its artistry, to transmute the idiom of a folk language into a national literature bolstered popular morale. Yiddish literature, investing readers with a newly found dignity, inspired a heightened sense of Jewish identity and moral superiority at a time when overt evidence bore witness to the helplessness of Jews in the face of technological change and social and ideological chaos.[23]

Elsewhere in Eastern Europe, the forces of inner disintegration and outer catastrophe worked similarly if less dramatically. In Jassy, in Moldavian Rumania, exiled Russian revolutionaries organized a socialist educational society in 1895 and published the first Yiddish socialist weekly. Even in Galicia, where the rise of Zionist groups more generally reflected the stirrings of the modern spirit, one can discern traces of Bund and other socialist influences in the early twentieth century.[24]

Part Two

THE TERMS OF SETTLEMENT

~ 4 ~

Urban Economic Frontiers

These people are dazzled by the brilliancy of the city, and believe that there is room for everyone in the Metropolis, where they suppose they can quickly earn a competence and follow all the laws, minor as well as important, that they had been led through so many generations to believe to be as vital as life itself.

Report of the United Hebrew Charities (1893)

For East Europeans of the great Jewish migration New York was the promised city. There most of them were to find their first American employment and strike permanent roots. They had been preceded by a considerably smaller migration of Jews from Germany at mid-century which had engulfed the old Jewish families of the Knickerbocker mercantile community. A few of the German immigrants with connections on the continent became agents for the investment of German capital in American enterprise. Others became jobbers of Central European products and fashions, and wholesale trade invited their talents. Retailing, which had not counted a single Jewish firm in its front ranks, also attracted the thrifty and the industrious. German Jewish initiative and imagination led in the 1870's and 1880's to the growth of the modern department store out of the dry-goods bazaar, clothing store, and crockery shop. Altman's and Stern's came first, followed by the Strauses at Macy's, the brothers Ehrich, and the brothers Bloomingdale, creating a consumer's mecca that energized every aspect of the city's economy.[1]

In 1890 Max Cohen of the *American Hebrew* systematically surveyed the role of Jews in New York enterprise. That investigator, aided by R. G. Dun, the leading credit-rating agency, sketched the business progress of Jews over the preceding thirty years. The most spectacular advance came in the wake of the Civil War. Between 1860 and 1870 Jewish firms worthy of commercial rating rose from 374 to 1714, as a multitude of the newly prosperous with capital to invest flocked to New York. After 1870 declining profits, tighter margins, and greater difficulty in acquiring capital curtailed the entrance of newcomers into the front ranks. In 1890 Jewish firms with a Dun rating stood at 2058, an increase of only 20 per cent over 1870. While in 1870 only about 10 per cent of the firms were capitalized at over $100,000, in 1890, 496 firms, nearly 25 per cent, reported a minimum capital of $125,000.

"Dry and fancy goods," which included the manufacture and sale of women's wear and materials, and household linens ranked as the top Jewish industry in 1890 as it had in 1870, with 125 firms capitalized at over $125,000 each. As clothiers turned to the manufacture of ready-to-wear clothing, men's wearing apparel and "gent's furnishings" rose to second place. Jews, in addition to being distributors of house furnishings, glass and paints, furniture, upholstery, and bedding, became prominent in the refection trades, including tobacco and smokers' articles, wines and liquor, and the meat business. But for long Jews were so rare among wholesale grocers that Park and Tilford even furnished Passover supplies. They were well represented in the sale and manufacture of jewelry, precious stones, optical goods, and in the hide and leather trade; more unusual was Samuel Adler's Marble and Granite Works, noted for turning out products "in the most artistic manner." Among the leading investment bankers were Kuhn Loeb & Company, Speyer, the Wormsers, and the Seligmans. But more typical were the small private bankers, whose transactions lubricated the credit mechanism of the city. Although Jews had been associated with the Stock Exchange ever since it was organized around a buttonwood tree, they did not become numerous in Wall Street until 1900. Booming land values also opened successful careers in real estate for many.[2]

In scarcely a single generation, many German immigrants

and their American sons had achieved a moderate prosperity. But before the turn of the century few Jews were to be counted among the city's multimillionaires; the exception, Henry Hart, a member of an older New York Jewish family and chief owner of the Third Avenue Elevated, was ranked thirty-second, far below such grand proprietors of wealth as John D. Rockefeller, the Astors, the Vanderbilts, and the many lesser magnates who chose to make their homes in the nation's greatest city. In 1892, of the 1103 New Yorkers in the *New York Tribune* list of 4047 American millionaires, approximately 60 were Jews.[3]

The leading German Jewish merchants of New York, at the center of American foreign and domestic trade at the close of the nineteenth century, exuded optimism and proudly asserted the business virtues.

The causes of the remarkable progress made by the Jews in commerce are the simple homely virtues sung in rhythmic prose by Franklin and Smiles; patient toil; zealous application; intelligence infused into labor; frugal thrift and temperance in all things. They have had the self-denial to confine their wants to necessities until the means were provided for comforts; and to limit their desires to these until luxuries could be afforded. Realizing that the same social conditions which enabled others to amass wealth even with the most penurious beginnings to look back upon, held similar possibilities for themselves, they did not waste their energies in fruitless fretting at the conditions and fruitless efforts to change them, but devoted themselves to energetic endeavors to utilize them at their best.[4]

These middle-class Central European Jews contrasted sharply with their coreligionists from Eastern Europe. The East Europeans landing in New York between 1870 and 1914 arrived with energies spent, nerves frayed, and purses emptied. Only a handful of them benefited from overseas ties, for they came from regions which had little direct trade with the United States. Wiadro of Kiev opened a tobacco factory in New York in 1892. The following year the Fain brothers brought their own textile machinery from Latvia and established the Fain Knitting Mills in Brooklyn. In 1903, A. Lubarsky came as an agent of the Wissotsky Tea Company, makers of "the only true Russian tea," packed in Moscow by "the world's greatest tea company." And several Jews employed their Russian connections in the fur trade. But these were the exceptions. The Russian government, although anxious to advance trade, forbade Jews to do so.[5]

The East European Jews entered New York's social economy and attempted to make their place as had other immigrant groups before them. The new immigrants were not eager to leave for other parts of the country and efforts to disperse them met with limited success. Interior communities failed to cooperate and often returned newcomers to the city. So wretched were conditions in 1888 that 200 immigrants were shipped back to Europe in cattle steamers. Even the United Hebrew Charities, the Baron de Hirsch Fund, and the Jewish Agricultural and Industrial Aid Society showed unimpressive results. The more effective Industrial Removal Office, founded in 1901 specifically for the purpose of distributing immigrants, helped over 60,000 East European Jews to find a place outside of New York City in the following decade. Between 1906 and 1912 the Galveston Committee attempted to divert immigration away from the eastern seaboard to the trans-Mississippi South and West directly through the gulf ports. Zigismund Pestkof, newly of Dallas, wrote:

I may say that the south is a place where every emigrant will find the best chances, for his future; also Texas even it is a young state, but will raise some day, and will be the largest business state in the union. No matter who it is, a "balabos" [householder] or a tradesman, a young one or an old, a Socialist or a Zionist—for them is the best place only here in the south than in the ever crowded New York. This is my practice.

But only a small fraction of the Jewish immigrants were so aided and this new Texan, who signed himself, "yours for the freedom," proved exceptional. The absence of a wider Jewish fellowship, the abrupt break with the past, and the limited educational opportunities in the rural areas and small towns discouraged immigrants from leaving New York. New York was their lot, and their presence offered a challenge that long would affect the city's economic design.[6]

BUSINESS AND THE TRADES

The peddler's pack still provided the most direct introduction to American ways, the most promising school for the study of the country's speech, tastes and economic needs, and the broadest field for the play of the aspiring tradesman's imagination. Potential peddlers were warned of the decrease in opportunities, but few failed to put this caution to the test of personal experience. The lure of commercial success, starting from the humble peddler's role, was magnetic. In the late 1880's, along the East Side from the Battery to Harlem, merchants in shoestrings, neckties, and sausages could be seen vending their wares. "Suspenders, collah buttons, 'lastic, matches, hankeches—please, lady, buy," went a familiar refrain. Compared with the alternative of seasonal sweatshop labor, peddling proved exhilarating. The rebuffs of housewives, the torments of young rowdies, and the harassment of the police intimidated the less venturesome and the more sensitive. But the number of peddlers at any one time barely suggested the multitudes who passed through this apprenticeship.[7]

As the immigrant Jewish population swelled, the Lower East Side became the center of the pushcart trade. "Whole blocks of the East Side Jewry [were turned] into a bazaar with high-piled carts lining the curb," as few commodities failed to find a seller or buyer. "Bandannas and tin cups at two cents, peaches at a cent a quart, damaged eggs for a song, hats for a quarter, and spectacles warranted to suit the eye . . . for thirty-five cents." On Thursday night Hester Street, the chief market center, resounded to the cries of bawling wives making their purchases for the Sabbath. "Big carp, litle carp, middle-sized carp, but everywhere carp." Here only the limitations of space contained the crowds engaged in commerce, as the pinched economies of hundreds of transplanted *shtetls* competed amid plenty. "Every conceivable thing is for sale, chiefly candles, dried fruit, and oilcloth; and the yolk or the white of an egg, or a chicken leg or wing, or an ounce of tea, coffee or butter is not an uncommon purchase." Peddlers, able to sell in small quantities—from a penny's worth up—accommodated a bargain-eager clientele with limited storage space for perishable foods. Avid competition among sellers, crippling to the peddlers, reduced living costs for many an immigrant family from two to three dollars weekly.

The pushcart traffic, regularly increased by a host of seasonally unemployed garment workers, counted 25,000 peregrinating tradesmen in 1900. Predominantly Jews, augmented by Greeks and Italians who dominated the fruit and vegetable trade, they spilled over into Little Italy and on Saturdays intruded upon the Irish West Side to form the Paddy's Market. Many an energetic pushcart peddler earned 15 to 20 dollars weekly and was able to advance to more settled types of commerce, leaving the itinerant trade to newcomers and to the less successful.

The Lower East Side developed a fervent commercial life, infused with a vitality that made it something more than a mass of tenements. "Hurry and push, . . . the optimistic, whole-souled, almost religious passion for business," permeated the community. In 1899, within the Eighth Assembly District (coinciding essentially with the tenth ward) 2897 individuals were engaged in 182 different vocations and businesses. A total of 631 food mongers catered to the needs of the inhabitants of this area. Most numerous were the 140 groceries which often sold fruits, vegetables, bread, and rolls as well as the usual provisions. Second in number were the 131 butcher shops which proclaimed their wares in Hebrew characters. The other food vendors included: 36 bakeries, 9 bread stands, 14 butter and egg stores, 24 candy stands, 62 candy stores, 1 cheese store, 20 cigar stores, 3 cigarette shops, 7 combination two-cent coffee shops, 10 delicatessens, 9 fish stores, 7 fruit stores, 21 fruit stands, 3 grocery stands, 7 herring stands, 2 meat markets, 16 milk stores, 2 matzo (unleavened bread) stores, 10 sausage stores, 20 soda water stands, 5 tea shops, 14 tobacco shops, 11 vegetable stores, 13 wine shops, 15 grape wine shops, and 10 confectioners.[8]

Religious laws concerning the preparation and handling of foods had a decided effect on choice of occupation. Especially strict requirements for meats drew many immigrants into the meat and poultry business where earlier Jewish immigrants already were prominent. Markens estimated that in 1888 approximately half of the city's 4000 meat retailers and 300 wholesalers were Jews. From among them had emerged Schwartzchild and Sulzberger, subsequently the Wilson Company, and other leading meatpackers. By the turn of the century 80 per cent of the wholesale, and 50 per cent of the retail, meat trade was reputedly handled by Jewish dealers. In a period when other Eastern cities had come to depend upon Midwestern abattoirs, the mounting demand for kosher meat kept New York an important slaughtering center.[9]

Bakery products also required ritual supervision. The 70 Jewish bakeries catering to the Lower East Side at the turn of the century soon grew to nearly 500 in the city. Those on the Lower East Side were bunched on Hester and Rivington streets, where peddlers sold much of the product, calling: "Buy Jews, buy wives, buy girls and buy young gents, buy fresh cakes, buy little white loaves and eat them in good health." Family enterprises competed for the Sabbath trade, employee and employer laboring underground side by side continuously from early Thursday morning until Friday at noon. Investigators of factory conditions reported:

> The bakers worked in deep and dark subcellars, without ventilation or hygienic conditions. The walls and ceilings were moist and moldy. The shops were infested with rats and reeked with dirt. The air was pestilential. The bake ovens were primitive. No machinery was used. The work was all done by hand.

In 1910 Goodman and Son with 114 employees, Gottfried and Steckler with 102, and Nathan Messing with 60, were the leaders. Five factories employing 20 to 34 people, among them Horowitz & Margareten and Rauch and Strumpf, specialized in the preparation of matzos.[10]

The flourishing soda water business was directly attributable to the nonalcoholic drinking habits of Jewish immigrants. In immigrant Jewish neighborhoods where saloons languished, the imputed health-giving propensities of "the workers' champagne" proved irresistible. Two Jewish soda water firms in 1880 grew to well over one hundred by 1907, and comprised 90 per cent of such establishments in the city, almost all on the Lower East Side. With a rise in the price of sugar, seltzer came to replace soda as the staple beverage of Yiddish New York. If saloons ministered largely to a transient trade, coffee houses, cake parlors, lunchrooms, and restaurants thrived on Jewish custom.[11]

While bakers, meat merchants, and sellers of soda water were building characteristically Jewish industries, many immigrants sought less perilous opportunities for independence than those afforded in commerce. Skilled craftsmen were singularly blessed: "An artisan will sooner or later obtain work and will not be forced to work for someone else," counseled a popular immigrant guide book. But before 1900 artisans made up only a small fraction of the immigrants. In 1892 newcomers of less than a year's residence, placed by the United Hebrew Charities in 132 different branches of industry, were largely unskilled. These placements, the UHC employment bureau reported, were made "in addition to the lines that custom has made more prevalent among our immigrants, of which unfortunately report seems to assign as their sole means of making livelihoods, cigar-makers, tailors, drummers, clerks and salesmen." Skilled workmen were directed to places where their specialties could be employed but many qualified artisans were squeezed out by the factory system. The mechanization of the shoe industry, for example, prevented cobblers and bootmakers from exercising their crafts. Others, such as blacksmiths, found it difficult to resume the village routine amid the roar of a strange city. Many immigrants, without industrial experience, were intimidated by machines. One of the rules governing labor-employer relations in the needle trades reflects the workmen's awe of the sewing machine: owners, rather than workmen, were to maintain, clean, and oil the machines. Numerous artisans abandoned their craft as soon as an opportunity showed itself. As little as one third of 225 heads of families, according to one study, retained their original vocations. Most accommodated their skills to the labor market, turning to those industries where they might adhere to their religious habits and where the stranger could not mock.[12]

The arrival, after the turn of the century, of many skilled and semiskilled Jewish workmen from a growingly industrialized homeland transformed the Jewish economic structure. An estimated 66 per cent of the gainfully employed Jewish immigrants between 1899 and 1914 possessed industrial skills—a far greater proportion than that of any other immigrant group. Jews ranked first in 26 out of 47 trades tabulated by the Immigration Commission, comprising an absolute majority in 8. They constituted 80 per cent of the hat and cap makers, 75 per cent of the furriers, 68 per cent of the tailors and bookbinders, 60 per cent of the watchmakers and milliners, and 55 per cent of the cigarmakers and tinsmiths. They totaled 30 to 50 per cent of the immigrants classified as tanners, turners, undergarment makers, jewelers, painters, glaziers, dressmakers, photographers, saddle-makers, locksmiths, butchers, and metal workers in other than iron and steel. They ranked first among immigrant printers, bakers, carpenters, cigar-packers, blacksmiths, and building trades workmen.[13]

In the late 1880's, Harry Fischel, a pioneer East European tenement builder, encouraged Jews to enter the building trades by keeping the Sabbath and affording his employees half-pay on that day. Otherwise, religious observances, language barriers, differences in work standards, and the paucity of Jewish contractors discouraged newcomers from entering this field. Yet, as early as 1885 a society of Russian house painters had formed, and by 1890 nearly 900 Jewish painters and carpenters lived on the Lower East Side.

Jews flocked to this industry when the building boom hit the late nineties and first decade of the twentieth century, when migration from the Lower East Side filled the newly built sections of Harlem, Washington Heights, Brownsville, Williamsburg, and the Bronx. As mortgage credit kept pace with the housing needs of a mounting populace, immigrants were able to enter the construction industry with but a small fraction of the price for lot and buildings. Barred by the unions from well-paid new construction, immigrant iron workers, housesmiths, tinsmiths, masons, plumbers, plasterers, electricians, carpenters,

and painters concentrated upon alterations and the remodeling
of old tenements.[14]

Auxiliary to the building trades were the swiftly developing
metal trades. Formerly, brass work had been limited to trained
craftsmen, "workmen of artistic tact . . . as well as mechanical
skill." But the rising demand for brass supplies and the available cheap labor encouraged mass production. In 1890 Jewish
"locksmiths and jobbing tinkers and plumbers with their keys
and their tools strung on a wire heap that rests on one shoulder"
numbered over 400 on the Lower East Side. Frederick Haber-
man's Central Stamping Company, employing over 2000 men in
the manufacture of tin house-furnishings, included many Jewish immigrants. Jewish tinsmiths and locksmiths crowded into
metal shops producing wash boilers, barrels, pipes, and kitchen-
ware. Ironwork shops where structural steel, doors, gates, steps,
and fire escapes were turned out also offered jobs to the newer
immigrants. Others found employment in installing ironwork
and cornices, in roofing, and the laying-in of skylights in new
and renovated buildings. Small shops founded by former workmen readily hired green *lansman* (fellow townsmen) at a five-
or six-dollar weekly wage. At the turn of the century when a
vogue for Russian brassware created a demand for workmen in
copper, 100 skilled coppersmiths in a dozen Allen Street basement shops modeled and forged candle sticks, ash trays, kettles,
and samovars. Toiling for a ten-dollar weekly wage, the city's
newest artisans slaked the thirst for "imported Russian" uten-
sils.[15]

Workmen in fine metals, jewelry, and the printing trades were
to find a ready market for their skills. In 1890 specialists in
hand-made ornamental metalware numbered 287 on the East
Side. Collectively described as "goldsmiths" in the Baron de
Hirsch study, they probably included all those engaged in the
jewelry trades. A decade later, 2000 Jews comprised 40 per cent
of the industry's labor force. Printers encountered little difficulty in gaining employment once the immigrant community
attained sufficient size. In 1890 over 145 Jewish printers lived on
the Lower East Side, offering to many immigrants opportunities
in the collateral bookbinder trade as well. The expanding field

of Yiddish journalism and job printing soon became saturated. but openings in general printing mounted in one of the city's top industries.[16]

THE GREAT JEWISH METIER

Most immigrants, unequipped to earn a livelihood in trade or skilled industry, arrived in a period when the manufacture of such consumer goods as clothing, cigars, and household wares was becoming less skilled. As mechanization routinized production, dexterity, speed, patience, and regular habits became the prime work requisites. So endowed, undersized and underfed immigrants could compete without handicap. And for the shrewd and aggressive the closeness of workshop to sales counter opened doors into the world of business.

Jewish immigrants, separated by religious prescriptions, customs, and language from the surrounding city, found a place in the clothing industry where the initial shock of contact with a bewildering world was tempered by a familiar milieu. Work, however arduous, did not forbid the performance of religious duties, the honoring of the Sabbath, and the celebration of religious festivals. Laboring in small units, immigrants could preserve the integrity of their families.

The homes of the Hebrew quarters are its workshop also . . . You are made fully aware of it before you have travelled the length of a single block in any of these East Side streets, by the whir of a thousand sewing-machines, worked at high pressure from earliest dawn till mind and muscle give out together. Every member of the family, from the youngest to the oldest, bears a hand, shut in the qualmy rooms, where meals are cooked and clothing washed and dried besides, the livelong day. It is not unusual to find a dozen persons—men, women, and children—at work in a single small room.

However wretched the externals, here a measure of self-respect was attainable, while hearts beat and minds stirred with hopes and thoughts of a brighter future.

The manufacture of men's clothing had been one of New York's major industries long before East European Jews appeared. Between 1828 and 1858 the apparel trade showed proportionately greater gains than any other branch of manufacture, as Elias Howe's sewing machine transformed the garment-making process. In 1858, with an estimated 130 clothing establishments of "character and standing," the city's $27 million garment industry employed 32,000 workers; Hanford and Brother, reputedly the nation's largest clothing firm, alone employed over 2000 workers. Although the ready-made clothing trade was geared to supply the simple needs of the southern states, the West Indies, and South America, pioneer manufacturers, such as George Opdyke, the city's Civil War mayor, produced better garments to meet growing middle-class demands. The needs of the Union armies during the Civil War revolutionized the ready-made clothing trade. For the first time uniform standards and measurements were adopted and a growing labor pool made possible efficient factory production.[17]

In the 1880's the apparel trades led the general advance of industry in the city as technical improvements in cutting sent factory production soaring. So irresistible had the combination of cheap immigrant labor and the newest machinery become that an inspirational pamphlet entitled, *Genius Rewarded: or the Story of the Sewing Machine,* saluted new arrivals as they landed in New York, "the great mart of Sewing Machines for this country." By 1881 the *Sewing Machine News* featured advertisements for 22 different sewing machines, while the Singer Company alone sold an average of 1700 per day, 700 more than the entire industry had sold in 1867. Symbolic of this growth was the 47-story Singer Building, rising in 1908 to twice the height of its nearest rival.

The machine process did not attain maturity until after 1900. But the sword knife and the slotted table had replaced shears in the cutting room by 1880. The electrically operated knife followed and advances in electric motor construction led to the perfection of the small portable rotary and reciprocating electric knives. Finally, after the turn of the century, the adoption of the steam pressing iron in place of the gas- or coal-heated irons and the electrification of the sewing machine completed the mechanization of the factory.

The census figures for 1890 list only the factory product,

while those for 1880 include both factory and custom-made work, but these incomplete statistics attest to the clothing industry's remarkable growth in that decade in New York. The number of men's clothing factories rose during this decade from 736 to 1554 and the aggregate capital employed jumped from $22,396,895 to $48,591,055; in 1880, 47,647 workmen were engaged in custom and factory-made work as compared to 37,811 employed in factory-made work alone in 1890. The value of ready-made clothing in 1890 exceeded that of the combined product ten years earlier. Between 1880 and 1890, the manufacture of women's cloaks became important for the first time. The number of cloak establishments rose from 236 to 740, capital from $4,805,665 to $20,809,872, the number of employees from 12,366 to 24,712, and the value of the manufactured goods from $18,930,555 to $42,315,352. Paralleling these spurts in the clothing industry, during the same decade the number of fur goods establishments grew from 60 to 232, the capital invested from $1,950,875 to $8,032,134, the workmen employed from 2,440 to 4,337, and the value of manufactured goods from $4,474,018 to $10,665,997. Throughout the apparel trades the number of workmen per plant fell, as did the ratio between capitalization and product value, reflecting the rise of the contractor. As these increases occurred in the face of a considerable fall in prices, the upswing in manufactures was even greater than the figures would suggest. In the 1890's, despite depressed conditions, the rising tariff wall stimulated production as the value of ready-made clothing imported from Germany fell from 12,000,000 marks in 1891 to 2,000,000 marks in 1894.[18]

For fashion-sensitive industries, New York City was an unsurpassable location. Despite a wage scale higher than that of any other clothing center in the world, New York's many assets outweighed the unfavorable wage differential. No other city provided a labor fund so abundant, compact, youthful, and varied. In New York, the nation's leading textile importer and sales center, producers' materials were procurable at a better advantage in quality and price than anywhere else in the country. Up to the first decade of the twentieth century nearly all domestic materials handled by the wholesale dry-goods houses were manufactured in the mills of New York State and New England, the nation's unrivaled producers of cotton and woolen textiles; and a combination of circumstances made neighboring Paterson the nation's leading convertor of raw silk. Buyers coming to the country's greatest mart could stock ready-made clothing as well. The gateway city to Europe, long setting the fashions for the country, was attuned to every stylistic novelty emanating from abroad.[19]

With the coming of the East European Jews, the ready-made clothing industry revolutionized its pattern of organization. Under the contracting system that had prevailed in the mid-nineteenth century, Irish, English, and German immigrants toiled at home individually or in family groups, making coats, trousers, and vests for a contractor who received the cut goods from a merchant or manufacturer. In the 1870's outside manufacture had declined as factories sprang up, but the coming of largely unskilled workmen revived the contractor in a novel form of production, known as "section work," that aimed to exploit new recruits to the utmost through a minute division of labor. The contractors were no longer passive middlemen but entrepreneurs, skilled tailors—or at least skilled organizers of labor—who supervised in their own homes or shops the operators, basters, pressers, finishers, fitters, fellers, buttonhole-makers, and basting-pullers. In a city where factory and loft rents were high, the threadbare contractor provided the ideal solution to the savagely competitive economics of seasonal manufacture. To a far greater extent than in men's clothing, the merchant manufacturer in women's wear found him an indispensable intermediary upon whom might be thrust the production risks, the burdens of manufacture, and the responsibility for recruiting and supervising a labor force. The contractor could either rent or buy sewing machines on the installment plan, acquire loft space at a reasonable rental, and obtain materials on credit. In 1893 of some one hundred cloak and suit houses, only half a dozen maintained their own factories.

Contractors, vying to lower production costs by employing labor more and more efficiently, introduced the task system. Under this system the "team" engaged in section work—the ten or twenty workers, members of the family, relatives, *lanslite* (neighbors from the old country), or boarders—was assigned a work quota: individual workmen were no longer paid individually by the piece. An "infernal cooperative system . . . by which the contractor shares his misery with his dependent workmen," the task system was described as "the most ingenious and effective engine of overexertion known to modern industry." Yet it was not without its compensations. Virtually every immigrant was enabled to earn sufficient wages to keep body and soul together immediately upon landing in the city. Exploited as he was, this was a boon. For this reason, the "Boston" or "factory" system was slow to take root in New York.[20]

While cloak-manufacturing flourished during the 1890's, other branches of the women's ready-to-wear industry grew slowly, for thousands of independent seamstresses and dressmakers still catered to women's needs. Not until labor costs fell, techniques of design improved, and women gradually emancipated themselves from the home did the women's clothing trade create both an industry and a market. Expansion then proved phenomenal. By the first decade of the twentieth century, the industry embraced every item of women's apparel and attained first place in the city and the state. The tailor-made suits of the 1890's, smart and trim, with shirtwaist to match, reputedly America's first original contribution to the art of the *couturier*, were made world-famous by the Gibson Girl. Formerly a luxury, silk became a commonplace, as a variety of high quality trimmings came into mass use and fashion abandoned itself to a bewildering multiplicity of styles. From cloaks to infant's wear, from laces to feathers to artificial flowers, each branch developed its specialists to meet the new demands.[21]

Fur manufacture grew as an adjunct to the women's clothing industry. In the 1890's, improved machinery, electric power, and abundant skilled and semiskilled labor stimulated the production of fur garments. Jacoby's ingenious sewing machine that made a uniform firm stitch and a pliant even seam sewed high- and low-grade furs with uniform ease and at a cost unattainable in hand sewing. The 1200 fur workers of the mid-1880's rose to 4184 in 1899, to 7824 in 1909 and, with the equalization of the tariff on finished and unfinished furs, to 10,271 in 1913. In 1890 the industry had been manned by German nailers and finishers and Jewish cutters and operators. A few English, French, and German firms continued to serve the carriage trade, but by the first decade of the twentieth century, 75 per cent of the workmen and most manufacturers, former artisans themselves, were East European Jews.[22]

Ready-to-wear men's clothing, faster to develop than women's clothing, had become commonplace by the late 1880's. A member of the firm of Browning-King recorded that "men who had fancied they could never wear 'hand-me-downs' . . . soon found that neither in respect of style nor materials was the best ready-made clothing inferior to the handiwork of the merchant tailor." In 1889 a single Bowery firm sold 15,000 suits priced at $1.95 that were produced at a cost of $1.12½. By 1895, 90 per cent of American men were wearing ready-to-wear clothing and few could distinguish between higher grade ready-made clothing and custom-made models. By the eve of the First World War moderately priced ready-made clothing for both men and women was being exported to Europe.[23]

In no other industry could so many shops numbering so few employees be found. In 1913 the clothing industry in New York City numbered 16,552 factories and 312,245 employees. The factories, discounting an office force of less than one per plant, averaged eighteen employees. But the average was deceptive. Men's tailoring, the most highly capitalized branch of the clothing industry, with 45,842 employees in 2779 factories, counted 51 firms that employed over 100 persons, led by Browning-King, a non-Jewish firm with 801 employees. In the entire city only two other firms employed over 500 men; 559 firms employed between 20 and 100 persons but the remaining 2169 shops, or about 78 per cent, averaged 5 employees. If allowance is made for jobbers, listed as manufacturers, who gave out work to small contractors unaccounted for by the statistician, the morselized character of the industry becomes even more apparent.

This pattern was duplicated throughout the apparel industry. In men's caps and cloth and straw hats, only 6 of 301 firms engaged over 100 employees; 223, or 75 per cent, averaged 9 employees. In the women's clothing industry, of 2057 factories with 50,085 employees, only 62 engaged over 100 persons, 710 employed from 20 to 100 persons, and 1285 appeared to average less than one employee per workshop. Of 912 fur shops, 790 employed less than 20 workmen; only 5 employed over 100, the French firm Freres Revillon leading with 353 employees. The waste division had become a profitable independent branch of the apparel trades and 138 factories were devoted to "clip sorting." Although the leading factory counted over 300 employees, 128 firms, or nearly 93 per cent of those in the trade, averaged 6.

Over a span of three decades the clothing industry reshaped the city's social economy. In 1880, of 11,339 factories in New York City (the later borough of Manhattan), 1081, or nearly 10 per cent, were engaged in clothing manufacture, employing 64,669 persons, somewhat over 28 per cent of an industrial labor force of 227,332. Three decades later, of 23,479 factories in the borough of Manhattan, 11,172, over 47 per cent were engaged in clothing production and employed 214,428 persons, over 46 per cent of an industrial labor force of 413,615.[24]

By 1914 the industry's personnel had changed. Except in the older and more heavily capitalized men's clothing industry, employers were no longer of German Jewish stock, as they had been before the turn of the century, but now were overwhelmingly East Europeans. Employees too, once predominantly English, Irish, and German, except for the men's clothing cutters, were now East European Jews.

Initially, Jewish immigrants had been ready to accept almost any wage. An immigrant guidebook noted that impoverished Jews "who aspired to bread and pickles" earned 50 cents a day, spent 10 cents for coffee and bagels and saved 40 cents. "The Jew writes home that America is a land of gold and silver for he feels as rich as Korah." In the immigrant's mind, every dollar earned translated itself into two Russian rubles and a five-dollar weekly wage meant 10 rubles, a noble sum indeed. But the immigrant's sense of values quickly changed, a Senate Committee learned. "They soon become Americans and want to live as they see others live and then they find that they cannot make money enough to do that at the wages which they were first willing to accept." Greenhorns were often taken on as "apprentices" for what was at best a nominal wage and at worst no wage at all. However, for an over-all picture, their exploitation must be contrasted with the condition of many earlier comers who had risen from the same position to become contractors, jobbers, and manufacturers; who had advanced to the more skilled or supervisory branches of the industry; who had founded cleaning and dyeing establishments and pioneered steam laundries; who had turned to trade, service, and real estate energized by the vast growth in the Jewish immigrant and general population of the city.[25]

TOBACCO AND CIGAR-MAKING

During the same years that the clothing industry advanced, many Jews of diverse antecedents were employed in the expanding tobacco trades. Forced northward by the Civil War, cigar manufacture centered in New York City, where the variety of domestic and imported tobaccos could be conveniently assembled. Cigarmakers from Germany, where the cigar had attained the greatest vogue, predominated. But Dutch, Belgians, and English, a corps of Armenians, Cubans, Bohemians, Hungarians, and Poles, and a few of almost every nationality were attracted to the cigarmaker's bench. As the mold replaced the craftsman's fingers in shaping the cheaper cigars, semiskilled workmen entered the trade. In the opening years of the twentieth century 3000 of the 15,000 cigarmakers in the city who produced 25 per cent of the nation's cigars were East European Jews. While it was difficult to rise from employee to manufacturer, the cigar-store Indian proclaimed opportunity for self-employed tobacconists on every downtown street corner.[26]

But as the cigar gave way before the cigarette, the newer industry came to dominate the tobacco trades. The cigarette struck a fashion in the wake of the Crimean War and in the late 1860's attained commercial significance. Cigarettes were at first large, expensive, and hand-made from the Turkish leaf, but the development of "bright" Virginia tobacco led to the production of an inexpensive variety. While the production of cigars and other tobacco products remained stationary, between 1869 and

1914, cigarette production mounted ten thousand fold, and the cigarette became an article of mass consumption. Among the pioneer cigarette rollers were Jews who had mastered this skill in Russian factories. For a time in the 1880's the Kinney Tobacco Company employed as many as 2000 Russian immigrants; with the introduction of machinery, young women replaced men. In the late 1880's and 1890's production in New York City declined following the consolidation of the major companies, the acquisition by the Tobacco Trust of such Greek and Levantine Jewish firms as Anargyros and Schnassi, and the transfer of factories elsewhere. But in the first decade of the new century the trend toward mass production was arrested somewhat with the increasing popularity of Turkish cigarettes. Many small producers entered this highly competitive field hoping to profit from the expanded market and the varied tastes of the immigrants. In a bid for the immigrant trade even the American Tobacco Company featured "Volga," "Svoboda," and "Tolstoy" ("an aristocratic cigarette") brands with Russian mouthpieces.[27]

DAY AND FEMALE LABOR

Despite the roles that poverty and lack of skill forced them to assume, few Jews were to be found employed at day labor. These jobs were filled by physically more powerful immigrants of peasant stock, who flowed into the city. Certainly many young men, upon first landing in New York, put in a few weeks or months in day labor upon the docks, in factories, and on the railroad; some even idealized heavy physical labor, but their ardor soon passed when faced with reality. Others were employed on major bridge and tunnel construction projects. But as soon as they were able to regain their equilibrium they turned to more promising fields. A study based upon the occupational table of the United States Census of 1900 concluded that only 2 per cent of the Russians in New York were employed at common labor, while 10 per cent of the foreign-born and their sons were so employed.[28]

Because the ethic of survival in a strange city meant putting the entire family to work, women early played a major role in

New York's working life. An examination of the manuscript schedules of the Ninth Federal Census revealed that in 1870 young Jewesses already were employed as shirtmakers and tailoresses and as pants and vest makers. But prior to the 1880's they were not likely to have been employed in factories. Among the women recruited into industry were the pale-cheeked young students from the Ukraine who labored at shirts alongside their brothers, drowning weariness and disillusionment with nostalgic choruses of "O Dubinushka," "Tortured and Enslaved," and other Russian folk and revolutionary airs. In the early nineties an estimated 20,000 young Jewesses, largely American-born, were employed as saleswomen, milliners, typists, bookkeepers, stenographers, and public- and private-school teachers.

More usual for immigrant women was the exercise of their energies at homework. Employment as a tailor's assistant or modiste was especially desirable. As long as the contractor was able to maintain the family shop, the number of female workers remained high; but the antisweating legislation of the 1890's curtailed the opportunity for married women to work at home as finishers and in the minor operations of clothing production, and by 1908 homework had become the preserve of Italian wives. With the growth of new and lighter branches of the women's clothing industry and the establishment of large shops with their minute division of labor, young Jewish women in ever-growing numbers were recruited into what essentially became women's trades. Standing newspaper advertisements by shirt, whitegoods (underwear), and dress manufacturers promoted a high turnover as employers exploited the cheap and plentiful labor supply to the utmost.

The number of Jewesses in domestic service, so characteristic a calling for young girls in Eastern Europe, was small. Native Jews, eager to secure the services of nursemaids and household servants, were continually discouraged by the reluctance of Jewesses to enter these occupations. The menage with its servility could not compete with the comparative independence and enlarged horizons, even under sweated conditions, of shop and factory.[29]

THE PROFESSIONS, MAJOR AND MINOR

Harnessed to industry as the majority of immigrants were, glimmerings of professional paths remained a constant spur to achievement. The city lofts and cutting rooms paid them—but many looked forward to the day when they would walk out of the factory into more satisfying callings. Jews, reverent of learning, were to attain eminence especially in the professions.

Whenever possible, more talented and ambitious younger immigrants and virtually all native-born Jews renounced the shop and factory, even when it was to their advantage not to do so. Abraham Cahan's fictional hero, the millionaire cloak manufacturer David Levinsky, forever repented foregoing a City College education. "It is the sepulchre of my dearest ambitions, a monument to my noblest enthusiasm in America." A guidebook scribe testified to the virtues of the Astor Library, open from 8 A.M. to 10 P.M., with 20,000 volumes and over 450 newspapers and periodicals, surpassed only by nearby Cooper Union, "the most beautiful building upon which America can take pride."

For young immigrants who had come to America to satisfy thwarted ambitions for a professional education, the opportunities in the city proved welcome indeed. Bookish, with inquisitive minds, they were promising candidates for the independent professions to which they aspired. Medicine proved the favorite. Evening prep schools and private study hurried to qualify students for the coveted Regents' Medical Student Certificate (even this accreditation was not required before 1893), while by day they clerked in store or labored in factory. A didactic medical course lasting two school years at proprietary schools (each school year six months long) with low tuition fees payable in installments eased entry into the medical profession.

Indeed, so eagerly did East Siders flock to the healing professions that soon the Lower East Side developed its own medical world with its own medical societies, medical economic leagues, and even medical journals. At first, immigrant Jews in sickness turned to neighboring Irish and German physicians, to Dr. Harrie Abijah James, a bibulous obstetrician and others who soon became conversant with Yiddish and its dialects. Later,

Jews were more likely to rely on their own countrymen for the ordinary ailments, favoring non-Jewish specialists with wider reputations for the rarer afflictions. Only pioneer pediatrician Dr. Abraham Jacobi, one of the nation's most well-known physicians and the child-centered East Side's favorite consultant, eclipsed Dr. Hermann M. Biggs in this area's scale of reverence. Ludwig Kohn and Ignatz Rottenberg were popular with Austrian and Hungarian Jews, while Alexander Aaronson and H. B. Adler built up substantial practices among Russian and Polish Jews. Julius Halpern, David Robinson, Adolph Himowich, Max Girsdansky, Moses Mintz, and the saintly Paul Kaplan endeared themselves to patients by their selfless devotion. They became publicists, teachers, and candidates for political office, and joined lodges and benevolent societies. Like Doctor Rast in James Oppenheim's novel, East Side physicians, knowing that their patients relished prescriptions, dispensed simple remedies that often brought remarkable cures. The more bitter the concoction, the more it was appreciated. Doses before and after each meal, and a pill or two, preferably silver- or gold-coted, before retiring were especially prized. With the array of bona fide physicians in New York, the respectably placed *feldsher*, or practical surgeon, of Eastern Europe found few patrons.

Three European-trained Russian Jewish medical scientists received wide recognition. In 1888 twenty-six-year-old Max Einhorn, who had studied with Dr. Paul Ehrlich in Berlin, was appointed professor of medicine at the New York Post-Graduate Medical School; the first school of its kind, it had been founded six years earlier to raise the standards of American medical training. At the Rockefeller Institute for Medical Research, organized by Dr. Simon Flexner in 1901, the core staff of six included two Russian immigrants, the physiologist and pharmacologist Samuel J. Meltzer, and the medical chemist Phoebus A. Levene.[30]

By the first decade of the century, East European professionals were numerous indeed, "at the top of every social function, the attraction of every circle, and the ideal of every girl's dreams." Many Jewesses, inspired by the Russian women's rights movement, also prepared for the professions and were conspicuous as dentists, physicians, pharmacists, and lawyers. But married women generally harnessed their energies to their husband's careers, often driving their spouses to equip themselves for the professions. In 1903 a private census counted 1069 professional people on the Lower East Side. Between 1897 and 1907 the number of Jewish physicians had risen from 450 to 1000 in the borough of Manhattan and from 100 to 200 on the Lower East Side. Similarly, the number of Jewish pharmacists rose from 85 to 235 in Manhattan, from 45 to 115 on the Lower East Side, and the number of dentists rose from 59 to 350 in Manhattan and from 19 to 175 on the Lower East Side. Nicholas Aleinikoff, "the first Russian lawyer and notary," Louis Boudin, and Morris Hillquit became outstanding lawyers. But in law the American-born were at a decided advantage. The language obstacle, the lawyer's dependence on well-placed contacts, and the Russian immigrant's distrust of government discouraged immigrants from training for the bar, though law school fees were small. Engineering students were also relatively few.[31]

Many immigrants served their countrymen in religious and semireligious, intellectual and somewhat less than intellectual, capacities. In 1903, in addition to the 361 pedagogues on the Lower East Side, *shamosim* (sextons), *hazanim* (cantors), *mohelim* (circumcisors), and *shohetim* (ritual slaughterers) eked out a livelihood from their traditional functions and often exhibited an astounding versatility invisible to the eye of the statistician. Editors, writers, and translators were well represented. Insurance solicitors were everywhere. New York Life opened a Russian department and all the major insurance companies enlisted part-time agents. Burton J. Hendrick, a student of life insurance, wrote:

There is hardly a tenement home on the East Side of New York in which the Big Three have not each a representative. In every factory and every sweatshop have deferred dividends been sold. Bakers, grocers, butchers, and fishcart peddlers have done an insurance business on the quiet. Of the 5,000 [?] employees of one of New York's largest clothing establishments, at least 1500, it is said, have carried rate books.

The Yiddish theater offered employment to actors, choristers, musicians, and many others from costumers and bill posters to cashiers, ushers, and doorkeepers. The stage tempted many a singing young cigarmaker and comely young cloak finisher eager to exchange the drudgery at the bench for the flickering night lights of the theater. Many young immigrants sang in brief nocturnal careers for an attractive three- to four-dollar weekly wage and others enrolled at Max Moscovits' Tytacory Yiddish School of Acting. Around 1910 some 300 entertainers drew their livelihoods from the Yiddish theaters and music halls alone. Countless others were attracted to the amusement vocations in the wider world as the burgeoning vaudeville stage stimulated the talented and the hopeful. The names of Irving Berlin and Eddie Cantor symbolize the prominent role that these new immigrants long would play on Broadway and on the circuits.[32]

The growth of municipal functions vastly increased opportunities in government for the younger immigrants and the American-born. Too recently arrived and too politically independent to claim positions as a matter of seniority and political privilege, they strove for appointments to positions based upon merit. As President of the Board of Police Commissioners, Theodore Roosevelt, with a passion for "the Maccabee or fighting Jewish type," searched out young Jews of exceptional physical promise and encouraged them to join the police department. Whereas less than a score served with the police force in the 1880's, some 140 were so employed in 1901. A score of Jews served with the fire department by that time, a half-dozen acted as foremen or assistant foremen for the department of highways and a few others were scattered in supervisory and lesser positions in the sanitation department. The influx of young Jews into the teaching profession was especially marked. They were numerous in medical and laboratory positions in the nation's finest department of health and filled many minor legal positions in the city government.[33]

In 1905 the *New York Herald* published the results of a survey of the occupational distribution of the Jews of the city. Although the study failed to distinguish the variety of Jews, natives and immigrants, Germans and Russians, employees and employers, it appeared to reflect a reasonably accurate, if incomplete, portrait of the Jews of New York. The survey disclosed the drift toward new occupations and the social and economic dynamism unleashed by exposure to new opportunities.[34]

The cold statistics revealed economic mobility and fluidity. But few restraints bridled economic appetites "In the Great East Side Treadmill," described by Jacob Riis, and the costs of success often proved high. The cunning and unscrupulousness that were often incidental to material rise, the anxiety that accompanied the blistering pace of frontier industries, and the fear of poverty and unemployment took a heavy toll on physical and psychological well-being. Yet men seemed without choice. A popular immigrant guidebook advised in all seriousness:

Hold fast, this is most necessary in America. Forget your past, your customs, and your ideals. Select a goal and pursue it with all your might. No matter what happens to you, hold on. You will experience a bad time but sooner or later you will achieve your goal. If you are neglectful, beware for the wheel of fortune turns quickly. You will lose your grip and be lost. A bit of advice for you: Do not take a moment's rest. Run, do, work and keep your own good in mind . . . A final virtue is needed in America—called cheek . . . Do not say, "I cannot; I do not know." [35]

Whatever the qualities of the economic man, his were not the social virtues. The contrasts between the successful and those less fortunate produced chasms which law, the state, and society were slow to bridge. As the apparel trades grew to be without a peer in the industrial life of the city, the voice of protest would sound with ever-mounting resonance. The community of responsibility that had been shattered by the combined pressures of immigration, industrialization, and urbanization would be rewoven upon new looms. The scramble for position and place amid industrial chaos and social anarchy would be mitigated.

✒ 5 ✒

The Lower East Side

From their homes they come rosy-cheeked and with health
and Spring. They have had little fish, little meat, little
bread, and it is to get more that they come hither. But they
have had air and light. . . . Air and light, and water have
been from all time the heritage of man and even of the
animals. *Evening Journal* (1903)

By the first decade of the twentieth century, the Lower East
Side had become an immigrant Jewish cosmopolis. Five major
varieties of Jews lived there, "a seething human sea, fed by
streams, streamlets, and rills of immigration flowing from all the
Yiddish-speaking centers of Europe." Clustered in their separate
Jewries, they were set side by side in a pattern suggesting the
cultural, if not the physical, geography of the Old World. Hungarians were settled in the northernmost portion above Houston
Street, along the numbered streets between Avenue B and the
East River, once indisputably *Kleindeutschland*. Galicians lived
to the south, between Houston and Broome, east of Clinton, on
Attorney, Ridge, Pitt, Willett, and the cross streets. To the west
lay the most congested Rumanian quarter, "in the very thick of
the battle for breath," on Chrystie, Forsyth, Eldridge, and Allen
streets, flanked by Houston Street to the north and Grand
Street to the south, with the Bowery gridironed by the overhead
elevated to the west. After 1907 Levantines, last on the scene
and even stranger than the rest, for they were alien to Yiddish,
settled between Allen and Chrystie streets among the Rumanians with whom they seemed to have the closest affinity. The remainder of the great Jewish quarter, from Grand Street reach-

25 Public School 63
26 Music School Settlement
27 Asch Building
28 Astor Library
29 Cooper Union
30 Hebrew Technical School for
31 Labor Temple Boys
32 Rand School
33 Hebrew Charities Building
34 Metropolitan Life Building
35 Madison Square Garden
36 City College

Boundaries of sub-ethnic districts
······ Hungarian
+—+ Galician
o—o—o Rumanian
⌒⌒⌒ Levantine
— — — Russian

Shaded blocks indicate Tenth Ward

0   ¼ MILE

THE LOWER EAST SIDE

1 Newspaper Row
2 World Building
3 Chatham Sq. Library
4 Beth Israel Hospital
5 Israel Elchanan Yeshiva
6 Seward Park Library
7 Forward Building on Yiddish Newspaper Row
8 Educational Alliance
9 Henry St. Settlement and Clinton Hall
10 Machzike Talmud Torah
11 Hebrew Sheltering House
12 Hebrew Technical School for Girls
13 Home for Aged
14 Jewish Maternity Hospital
15 Young Men's Benevolent Association
16 Camp Huddleston Hospital Ship School
17 Beth Hamedrash Hagadol
18 Pro-Cathedral Mission
19 University Settlement
20 Grand Theater
21 Yiddish Rialto
22 Thalia Theater
23 People's Bath
24 Police Headquarters

ing south to Monroe, was the preserve of the Russians—those
from Russian Poland, Lithuania, Byelorussia, and the Ukraine
—the most numerous and heterogeneous of the Jewries of Eastern Europe.[1]

The leading streets of the Lower East Side reflected this immigrant transformation. Its most fashionable thoroughfare, East
Broadway, bisected the district. To the north lay crammed tenements, business, and industry. To the south lay less crowded
quarters where private dwellings, front courtyards, and a scatter-
ing of shade trees recalled a time when Henry, Madison, Rutgers, and Jefferson street addresses were stylish.

The Russian intelligentsia, for whom the Lower East Side was
New York, fancied East Broadway as New York's Nevsky Prospect, St. Petersburg's grand boulevard. In addition to the physicians and dentists who occupied the comfortable brownstone
fronts that lined its shaded curbs, an ever-growing number of
public and communal buildings came to endow it with a magis-
terial air. By the second decade of the twentieth century, the
ten-story edifice of the *Jewish Daily Forward,* set off by Seward
Park on Yiddish Newspaper Row, loomed commandingly over
the two Carnegie-built libraries, the Educational Alliance, the
Home for the Aged, the Jewish Maternity Hospital, the Machzike Talmud Torah, the Hebrew Sheltering House, the Young
Men's Benevolent Association, and a host of lesser institutions.

Only second to East Broadway was Grand Street. Long a leading traffic artery and a major retail shopping center of lower
New York, Grand Street fell into eclipse after the turn of the
century with the widening of the Delancey Street approach to
the Williamsburg Bridge and the comparative decline in ferry
traffic. Grand Street's popular department stores, Lord and Tay-
lor's, Lichtenstein's, and O'Neill's, moved uptown, and Ridley's
closed, leaving the way open for conquest by the newcomers.
Bustling Delancey Street, lined with naptha-lit stalls crammed
with tubs of fish; Hester Street, with its agents on their way to
becoming bankers after the example of Jarmulowsky's passage
and exchange office; and the Bowery, with the largest savings
bank in the world, symbolized the district's new retail character.[2]

Only after 1870 did the Lower East Side begin to acquire an immigrant Jewish cast. In the early years of the century a small colony of Jewish immigrants had lived there. Dutch, German, and Polish Jews had settled on Bayard, Baxter, Mott, and Chatham streets in the 1830's and 1840's. Shortly thereafter, German and Bohemian Jews took up quarters in the Grand Street area to the northeast and subsequently Jews of the great German migration augmented their numbers. Except for highly visible store fronts, Jews made little impress on the dominantly German and Irish neighborhood. But practically all East European immigrants arriving after 1870 initially found their way to the Lower East Side. Virtually penniless upon their arrival in the city, they were directed to the Jewish districts by representatives of the immigrant aid societies, or came at the behest of friends, relatives, or employers.[3]

The changes brought about by the great Jewish migration forced the district's middle-class Germans and Irish, living in predominantly two- and two-and-one-half story dwellings, to retreat to less crowded quarters. By 1890 the Lower East Side bristled with Jews. The tenth ward (loosely coinciding with the Eighth Assembly District), closest to the central factory area, was the most crowded with 523.6 inhabitants per acre; the adjacent wards, the thirteenth and seventh, numbered 428.6 and 289.7 persons per acre respectively. Exceeding 700 persons per acre by 1900, the tenth ward was the most densely settled spot in the city; residential block density was even more appalling as factories and shops crowded tenements. In 1896 a private census counted 60 cigar shops, 172 garment shops, 65 factories, and 34 laundries in the tenth ward. In 1906, of fifty-one blocks in the city with over 3000 inhabitants each, thirty-seven were on the Lower East Side. On Rivington Street, Arnold Bennett remarked, "the architecture seemed to sweat humanity at every window and door." Hardy, older, or improvident remnants of the region's earlier Irish residents and a floating seafaring population still clung to the river edges along Cherry and Water streets; at the turn of the century, Italian immigrants crossed the Bowery on Stanton and East Houston streets and crowded into the lower reaches of East Broadway. But in the second decade of the new century, the Lower East Side, from the Bowery to within a stone's throw of the East River, and from Market Street to 14th Street, had become a mass settlement of Jews, the most densely packed quarter in the city. In 1914 one sixth of the city's population was domiciled below 14th Street upon one eighty-second of the city's land area; most of New York's office buildings, and factories that employed over one half of the city's industrial workers were located in this district.[4]

Once the immigrants had come to rest on the Lower East Side, there was little incentive to venture further. Knowing no English and with few resources, they were dependent upon the apparel industries, the tobacco and cigar trades, and other light industrial employments that sprang up in the area or that were located in the adjacent factory district. Long hours, small wages, seasonal employment, and the complexity of their religious and social needs rooted them to the spot. It was essential to husband energies, earnings, and time. Lodgings of a sort, coffee morning and evening, and laundry service were available to single men for three dollars a month. Bread at two and three cents a pound, milk at four cents a quart, a herring for a penny or two, and apples at from one to five for a cent, depending on quality, were to be had. Accustomed to a slim diet, an immigrant could save much even with meager earnings and still treat himself to a bracing three-course Sabbath dinner (for fifteen cents). Thrift and hard work would, he hoped, enable him in time to search out more congenial and independent employment. Until new sections of the city were developed at the turn of the century only country peddlers were to stray permanently beyond the familiar immigrant quarters.[5]

There was a compelling purpose to the pinched living. Virtually all immigrants saved to purchase steamship tickets for loved ones and many regularly mailed clothing and food parcels to dependent parents, wives, and children overseas. The power of home ties buoyed up the spirits of immigrants wedded to the sweatshop and peddler's pack, whose precious pennies mounted to sums that would unite divided families. Among the early comers women were relatively few, but the imbalance between the sexes soon was remedied. In 1890 an investigation by the

Baron de Hirsch Society into the condition of 111,690 of an estimated 135,000 Jews on the Lower East Side counted 60,313 children and 22,647 wage-earners, with 28,730 unspecified, mostly women. Undoubtedly, the proportion of women and children in New York was far greater than it was elsewhere. In 1910 women exceeded men among Hungarians and Rumanians, were equal among Austrians, and made up 47 per cent of the Russians. As non-Jews from these countries were heavily male, Jewish women clearly outnumbered men, accentuating the group's domesticity. Among the major ethnic groups of New York, only the Irish, 58 per cent female, exceeded the Jewish ratio.[6]

A nondescript colony of Jews in the 1870's swelled into a center of Jewish life by the turn of the century, the drama of whose fortunes and passions was closely followed by fellow immigrants throughout the country as well as by those in the lands they left behind. A highly visible knot of Jews "huddled up together" around Baxter and Chatham streets had been engulfed by an influx that saturated the whole region with its flavor and institutions.[7]

THE TENEMENT BOOM

Ever since the 1830's New York's housing problem had been acute. Manhattan's space limitations exacerbated all the evils inherent in overcrowding, and refinements in the use of precious ground only emphasized the triumph of material necessities over human considerations. New York's division of city lots into standard rectangular plots, 25 feet wide by 100 feet deep, made decent human accommodations impossible. In order to secure proper light and ventilation for tenement dwellers twice the space was needed, a prohibitive sacrifice considering real estate values. No opportunity was overlooked to facilitate the most economical and compact housing of the immigrant population. To the improvised tenements that had been carved out of private dwellings were added the front and rear tenements and, finally, the dumbbell-style tenement of 1879.

With the heavy Jewish migration of the early 1890's, the Lower East Side, still relatively undeveloped compared to the Lower West Side, became the special domain of the new dumb-

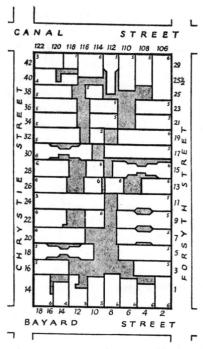

CANAL STREET

122 120 118 116 114 112 110 108 106

BAYARD STREET

18 16 14 12 10 8 6 4 2

A tenement block: smaller numbers indicate number of stories.

bell tenements, so called because of their shape. The six- to seven-story dumbbell usually included four apartments to the floor, two on either side of the separating corridor. The front apartments generally contained four rooms each, the rear apartments three. Only one room in each apartment received direct light and air from the street or from the ten feet of required yard space in the rear. On the ground floor two stores generally were to be found; the living quarters behind each had windows only on the air shaft. The air shaft, less than five feet in width and from fifty to sixty feet in length, separated the tenement buildings. In the narrow hallways were located that special improvement, common water closets. In 1888 a leading magazine described typical dumbbell tenements on Ridge, Eldridge, and Allen streets.

They are great prison-like structures of brick, with narrow doors and windows, cramped passages and steep rickety stairs. They are built through from one street to the other with a somewhat narrower building connecting them . . . The narrow court-yard . . . in the middle is a damp foul-smelling place, supposed to do duty as an airshaft; had the foul fiend designed these great barracks they could not have been more villainously arranged to avoid any chance of ventilation . . . In case of fire they would be perfect death-traps, for it would be impossible for the occupants of the crowded rooms to escape by the narrow stairways, and the flimsy fire-escapes which the owners of the tenements were compelled to put up a few years ago are so laden with broken furniture, bales and boxes that they would be worse than useless. In the hot summer months . . . these fire-escape balconies are used as sleeping-rooms by the poor wretches who are fortunate enough to have windows opening upon them. The drainage is horrible, and even the Croton as it flows from the tap in the noisome courtyard, seemed to be contaminated by its surroundings and have a fetid smell.

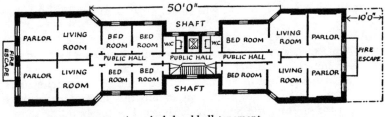

A typical dumbbell tenement

As if the tenement abuses were not degrading enough, the absence of public toilet facilities in so crowded a district added to the wretched sanitation. It was reported that "in the evening every dray or wagon becomes a private and public lavatory, and the odor and stench . . . is perfectly horrible." [8]

Conditions became almost unendurable in the summer months. Bred in colder and dryer climates, tenement inhabitants writhed in the dull heat. Added to the relentless sun were the emanations from coal stoves, the flat flame gas jets in lamps, and the power-producing steam boilers. Inevitably, roofs, fire escapes, and sidewalks were converted into sleeping quarters, while the grassed enclosure dividing Delancey Street and Seward Park supplied additional dormitory space. Late July and early August of 1896 were especially savage. Between August 5 and 13, 420 New Yorkers perished from the continuous heat, "the absolute stagnation of the air, and the oppressive humidity," noted Daniel Van Pelt, although the temperature averaged 90.7 degrees and never reached 100.

Fire and the possibilities of fire brought added terror to the inhabitants of overcrowded tenements. "Remember that you live in a tenement house," warned insurance agents. In 1903, 15 per cent of the tenements in the district still were without fire escapes. Of 257 fatalities in Manhattan fires between 1902 and 1909, 99 or 38 per cent were on the Lower East Side, all victims of old-law tenements.[9]

Few families could afford the privacy of a three- or four-room flat. Only with the aid of lodgers or boarders could the $10 to $20 monthly rental be sustained. The extent of overcrowding in the tenements, reported a witness before the United States Immigration Commission, was never fully known.

At the hour of retiring, cots or folded beds and in many instances simply mattresses are spread about the floor, resembling very much a lot of bunks in the steerage of an ocean steamer . . . The only way to properly determine the census of one of these tenements, would be by a midnight visit, and should this take place between the months of June and September, the roof of the building should not be omitted.

However trying tenement living proved to be for adults, for children it was stultifying, concluded a settlement worker. "The earlier years of the child are spent in an atmosphere which . . . is best described by a little girl, 'a place so dark it seemed as if there weren't no sky.' "

Evictions for nonpayment of rent and rent strikes were perennial. Uncertainty of employment, nonpayment of wages, unexpected obligations, dependents, and adversities contributed to the high incidence of evictions. In the year 1891–1892 alone, in two judicial districts of the Lower East Side, 11,550 dispossess warrants were issued by the presiding magistrates. In 1900 the absence of mass evictions was regarded as a mark of unexampled well-being.[10]

Earlier residents of the Lower East Side and hereditary property owners profited from the overcrowding. The rise in real estate values, exorbitant rents, and the low upkeep provided tenement owners with ample returns upon their investments. Even allowing for losses due to nonpayment of rent and an average occupancy of ten months in the year, landlords earned ten per cent. By more studied neglect, a resourceful agent might reap even higher returns. The Lower East Side tenements soon came to be recognized as the most lucrative investment in the city. Nowhere else did the speculator's market in tenement properties flourish as luxuriantly as it did here, where earlier immigrants had learned to exploit the misery of later comers.

In 1901 the further construction of dumbbell tenements was prohibited. The Tenement House Law of that year set new standards for future housing and attempted to correct the worst abuses in the existing buildings. All new tenements were to have windows that opened at least twelve feet away from those opposite. Toilets and running water in each apartment, unobstructed fire escapes, and solid staircases were required. In the old buildings modern water closets were to be installed in place of the outside privies. Finally, a Tenement House Department was established to supervise and enforce the provisions of the law. While the law never was effectively enforced, its initial achievements proved encouraging.

Many new tenements were quickly built according to the new specifications. In the fiscal year ending July 1, 1903, 43 per cent of New York's new tenements were located on the Lower East Side. Its inhabitants eagerly welcomed the brightly lighted rooms, bathtubs, and other improvements. At first, landlords on the Lower East Side were more prompt to make alterations in old-law tenements than landlords elsewhere in the city, for the heavy pressure of population made even remodeled properties attractive. The years 1905 to 1909 saw an unparalleled boom throughout the city with houses to fit every taste, from tenements to palatial mansions for chance customers, at unprecedented prices ranging up to $500,000. "It is doubtful if New York City, or in fact any other city of the world, ever before witnessed the expenditure of so many millions of dollars in the construction of tenement houses during a similar period." [11]

While new housing was on the rise, the fast developing clothing trades also were relocating and building. As the heavy settlement of East Europeans decisively affected the housing of the city's earlier residents, so the new growth of the apparel industry, manned by Lower East Side Jews, helped to transform the city's business districts. Once legislation and the advent of electric power combined to reduce Lower East Side sweatshops, thousands of garment shops and factories pushed up the axial thoroughfares of Lower Manhattan. By 1910 the continued march uptown found the garment industry intruding upon once fashionable Madison Square, the site of New York's tallest skyscrapers. Brownstones and brick residences were razed to be displaced by 16- to 20-story steel-girdered loft buildings trimmed with granite and marble and housing scores of clothing shops. In the course of this displacement, the city's central retailing district and its theater and hotel district were forced northward. The main retailing center, at 14th Street in 1880 and at 23rd Street in 1900, became anchored at 34th Street by 1910.[12]

DISEASE AND CRIME

Superficially, East European Jews seemed ill-prepared to contend with the demands that tenement living thrust upon them. "Their average stature is from five feet one inch to five feet three inches, which means that they are the most stunted of the Europeans, with the exception of the Hungarian Magyars." Shortest were the Galicians, tallest and sturdiest, the Rumanians. Undersized and narrow-chested, a high proportion were described as "physical wrecks." Centuries of confinement, habituation to mental occupations, chronic undernourishment, and a deprecation of the physical virtues ill-fitted them for heavy labor. Between 1887 and 1890 nearly five thousand immigrants were returned to Europe labeled physically "unfit for work." Seemingly helpless and emaciated, they were to exhibit exceptional capacity for regeneration; traditional moral and religious disciplines were to serve them in good stead.

Despite the trying conditions under which the immigrants lived, they showed a remarkable resistance to disease. With the highest average density of tenants per house in the city, the tenth ward had one of the lowest death rates. Indeed only a business ward and a suburban ward surpassed it in healthfulness. Dr. Annie Daniel, a pioneer in public health, volunteered her interpretation of this before the Tenement House Committee:

The rules of life which orthodox Hebrews so unflinchingly obey as laid down in the Mosaic code . . . are designed to maintain health. These rules are applied to the daily life of the individuals as no other sanitary laws can be . . . Food must be cooked properly, and hence the avenues through which the germs of disease may enter are destroyed. Meat must be "kosher," and this means that it must be perfectly healthy. Personal cleanliness is at times strictly compelled, and at least one day in the week the habitation must be thoroughly cleaned.

True, only some 8 per cent of Russian Jewish families had baths, according to a study of 1902, and these often without hot water. Yet the proliferation of privately owned bathhouses in the city was attributable largely to the Jewish tenement population. "I cannot get along without a 'sweat' (Russian bath) at least once a week," insisted a newcomer. In 1880, one or two of New York's twenty-two bathhouses were Jewish; by 1897, over half of the city's sixty-two bathhouses (including Russian, Turkish, swimming, vapor, and medicated bathhouses) were Jewish. If standards of cleanliness were not as faithfully maintained as precept required, the strict regimen of orthodoxy, even when weakened, contributed to the immigrant's general well-being.[13]

Nevertheless, close crowding and unsanitary conditions made all communicable diseases potentially contagious. Despite great apprehension between 1892 and 1894, Jewish immigrants did not carry to New York the cholera and typhus epidemics raging at the European ports of embarkation. But in 1899 the United Hebrew Charities became alarmed by the Board of Health's report of the mounting incidence of tuberculosis in the city. That Jewish immigrants might become easy victims of the "White Plague" was hardly to be doubted. "As many as 119 Jewish families have lived in one tenement house on Lewis Street within the past five years." Hundreds of flats had been occupied by fifteen successive families within a brief period. "Many of these houses are known to be hotbeds of the disease, the very walls reeking with it." Increasingly, the dread disease with its cough and crimson spittle took its toll. Ernest Poole, an investigator, frequently heard the plea of the afflicted. "Luft, gibt mir luft—Air, give me air." Especially susceptible were the intellectuals, whose often shattered spirits, overwrought minds, and undernourished bodies fell prey to the killer. Yet so great was the immigrant's concern for health that the mortality rate from tuberculosis was lower on the East Side than in the city's prosperous districts. Venereal diseases, previously almost unknown among Jews in Eastern Europe, became progressively more common among young men, as restraints were weakened by exposure to new temptations.[14]

Alcoholism, a prime contributor to poverty, ill-health, and mortality among other national groups, was unusual among Jewish immigrants. As Jews replaced the earlier inhabitants, the many saloons of the Lower East Side, trimmed with shields that proclaimed them "the workman's friend," declined. Those that survived drew few clients from a neighborhood addicted to soda water, "the life-giving drink"; they depended on the throng of transients that passed through the district. Jews did not abstain from drink. Yet only upon religious festivals and during the Sabbath ritual when the Kiddush cup was emptied did alcohol appear in the diet of most immigrants. In 1908, $1.50 a year for holiday and ritual wine seemed adequate for a family of six. "The Day of Rejoicing of the Law and the Day of Purim are the only two days in the year when an orthodox Jew may be intoxicated. It is virtuous on these days to drink too much, but the sobriety of the Jew is so great that he sometimes cheats his friends and himself by shamming drunkenness," Hutchins Hapgood noted. Jews habitually imbibed milder beverages. Russians were notorious tea drinkers. Hungarians were addicted to coffee. The less austere Galicians and Rumanians tippled mead and wine respectively. But in the New World all fell victim to the craze for seltzer or soda water with its purported health-giving powers. In his long experience, reported the president of the United Hebrew Charities in 1892, he had known only three chronic Jewish drunkards.[15]

Neurasthenia and hysteria, however, took a heavy toll of victims. Their sickness was the result of a history of continual persecution and insecurity, intensified by the strains of settlement in unfamiliar surroundings. Diabetes, associated with perpetual nervous strain, was common. Suicide, rarely recorded among the small-town Jews of Eastern Europe, also found its victims in the tenements of New York. Despair, poverty, and the fears generated in the imagination led some immigrants to take their own lives. "Genumen di gez" (took gas) was not an uncommon headline in the Yiddish press. Yet in the late 1880's only the city's Irish showed a lower suicide rate than did Russian Jews.

However desperate the straits in which Jewish immigrants found themselves, confirmed paupers among them were few. The rarity of alcoholism, the pervasiveness of the charitable impulse, the strength of ties to family and *lanslite*, and a deep current of optimism preserved the individual from such degradation.[16]

Prior to the 1880's only the Rubinstein murder case spotted the record of New York's Jews. Upon the testimony of doubtful witnesses, Rubinstein was sentenced to death for the slaying of his girl cousin, but cheated the hangman by taking his own life. The first crime of violence attributed to a Jew in the city's annals, its very novelty gave rise to the popular street song, "My name is Pesach Rubinstein." So unassailable was the peaceful reputation of the Jewish districts that it was a matter for continual commendation. In 1878 Jews numbered 7 in a workhouse population of 1178; 8 among 485 prison inmates; and 12 among 1110 house-of-correction inmates.

The obloquy attached to the strident Jews of Baxter and Chatham Streets; to the Canal Street clothing shop puller-in and the Division Street millinery shop pulleress; to Michael Kurtz, better known as "Sheeney Mike," reputedly the "champion burglar of America"; and to "Marm" Mandelbaum, unmatched receiver of stolen goods, did not detract from the high repute of the city's Jews. The two dozen Bowery pawnshops were owned by Americans or earlier immigrants who catered to the needs of a heterogeneous population and were not part of the immigrant community.

The major crime and violence in the area did not stem from the immigrants. They were its victims. The Lower East Side had always attracted much of the city's criminal element to its margins. By the last decades of the nineteenth century, it had shed the ferocity of earlier years when the "Bowery B'hoys" and

the "Dead Rabbits" terrorized the area. But Mayor Hewitt's reform drive in 1887 inadvertently reinforced the district's frailties by forcing criminals and prostitutes from their accustomed
uptown resorts into the less conspicuous tenements of the tenth
ward, where they remained, undisturbed even by the Parkhurst crusade. The Raines Law, which provided that only hotels could serve liquor on Sundays, worsened the situation. In
1896, of 236 saloons in the tenth ward, 118 were Raines Law
hotels, while 18 were outright houses of prostitution. In the
first decade of the twentieth century, crusading District Attorney William Travers Jerome kept open house in his special office on Rutgers Street, at the hub of the Lower East Side, and
the most salient features of criminality were forced underground. By 1905 the "peripatetic sisterhood" had been driven
from the Bowery, and Captain Godard's Anti-Policy Society's
campaign banished gambling from the thoroughfare. But the
criminal elements soon returned.[17]

Crime was endemic to the Lower East Side. The close collaboration between police officers, politicians, and criminals, revealed in detail in the Lexow and Mazet investigations of the
1890's, had turned the district into a Klondike that replaced the
uptown Tenderloin as a center of graft and illicit business. Invariably the culprits in these activities were not immigrants, but
Americanized Jews learned in street-corner ways and shorn of
the restraints of the immigrant generation. "It is not until they
have become Americanized, have adapted themselves to the en-
vironment of the district and adopted its ways and vices, that
they become full-fledged wretches," commented Dr. I. L. Nascher. In the early years of the twentieth century the effect of
such conditions upon the young deeply disturbed those anxious
for the public weal. In 1909 some 3000 Jewish children were
brought before Juvenile Court and in the next few years Jewish criminals regularly made newspaper headlines. The appearance of an ungovernable youth after the turn of the century
was undeniable and excited apprehension.[18]

The violations of the law that characterized the immigrant
community differed from the crimes of the sons of the immigrants. The former were an outgrowth of occupational over-

crowding, poverty, and religious habits. Straitened circumstances contributed to the large number of cases of family desertion and nonsupport. Concentrated in marginal commerce and industry, Jews were prone to transgress the codes of commercial law. "The prevalence of a spirit of enterprise out of proportion to the capital of the community" gave rise to a high incidence of felonious larceny, forgery, and failure to pay wages. Peddlers and petty shopkeepers were especially vulnerable to police oppression for evading informal levies as well as formal licensing requirements. Legislation controlling business on Sunday found Jewish immigrants natural victims. In so congested a district, the breaking of corporation ordinances was unavoidable and the slaughtering of chickens in tenements in violation of the sanitary code proved to be a distinctly Jewish infraction.[19]

The Bowery, way-station of derelicts, transients, and unsuspecting immigrants, attracted the less stable and wary of the immigrant girls. The dancing academies that sprang to popularity in the first decade of the twentieth century snared impetuous, friendless young women. Lured by promises of marriage, they soon were trapped by procurers for the notorious Max Hochstim Association and other white slavers who preyed upon the innocent and the unsuspecting. The appearance of prostitution, previously rare among Jewesses, alarmed the East Side.[20]

The Lower East Side, girded by the Bowery with its unsavory establishments and Water Street with its resorts of ill-fame that catered to the seafaring trade, was surrounded by violence. Bearded Jews often were viciously assaulted by young hoodlums, both non-Jews and Jews, the area adjacent to the waterfront being especially dangerous. In 1898 and 1899, the newly organized American Hebrew League of Brooklyn protested a rash of outrages in the wake of the Dreyfus affair. Nevertheless there was only one instance of mass violence: the riot of July 30, 1902 at the funeral of Rabbi Jacob Joseph. This incident, the only one of its kind, can be attributed to the stored-up resentment of the Irish who were being forced out of the area by the incursion of Jews.[21]

SIGNS OF CHANGE

Gradually the miseries and trials of adjustment were left behind. For those who had inhabited the hungry villages of Eastern Europe, the hovels of Berditchev, and the crammed purlieus of Vilna and Kovno, the factories and sweatshops of New York provided a livelihood and possible stepping-stone. Despite unsteady and underpaid employment, tenement overcrowding and filth, immigrants felt themselves ineluctably being transformed. The Lower East Side, with its purposeful vitality, found no analogue in the "leprous-looking ghetto familiar in Europe," commented the visiting Abbé Félix Klein. Physical surroundings, however sordid, could be transcended. Optimism and hope engulfed every aspect of immigrant life. For a people who had risen superior to the oppressions of medieval proscriptions, the New York slums acted as a new-found challenge. Each passing year brought improvements that could be measured and appraised. Cramped quarters did not constrict aspirations. "In a large proportion of the tenements of the East Side . . . pianos are to be seen in the dingy rooms." And soon the phonograph was everywhere. "Excepting among the recent arrivals, most of the Jewish tenement dwellers have fair and even good furniture in their homes." [22]

The East Europeans began to venture beyond the boundaries of the Lower East Side into other areas where employment was available on terms compatible with religious habits. Brooklyn's German Williamsburg district, directly across the East River, where Central European Jews had been established for some decades, was settled early. In the late 1880's a few clothing contractors set up sweatshops in the languid Scottish settlement of Brownsville, south and east of Williamsburg. The depression delayed further expansion for a decade despite the extension of the Fulton Street El in 1889. Then the tide could not be stemmed. Between 1899 and 1904 Brownsville's population rose from ten thousand to sixty thousand. Land values soared as immigrants came at the rate of one thousand per week. Lots selling for two hundred dollars in 1899 brought five to ten thousand dollars five years later. As the real estate boom revolutionized land values, many a former tailor was suddenly transformed into a substantial landlord or realtor who disdained all contact with shears and needles of bitter memory.[23]

The mass dispersion of Jews from the Lower East Side to other parts of the city was in full swing in the early 1890's, as the more prosperous pioneers hastened to settle among their German coreligionists in Yorkville between 72nd and 100th streets, east of Lexington Avenue. For many a rising immigrant family in this period of swift change, it was judged to be a ten-year trek from Hester Street to Lexington Avenue.

The unprecedented flow of immigrants into the old central quarter, exorbitant rents, and the demolition of old tenements incidental to the building of parks, schools, and bridge approaches drastically reduced the area's absorptive capacity and spurred the search for new quarters. The construction of the Delancey Street approach to the Williamsburg Bridge in 1903 displaced 10,000 persons alone. The consolidation of the city and the growth and extension of rapid transit facilities connected what were once remote districts with the central downtown business quarters. In the new developments, cheaper land made possible lower rents that compensated for the time and expense of commuting. On Manhattan Island, the construction of underground transit opened to mass settlement the Dyckman tract in Washington Heights and the Harlem flats. The new subway also opened the East Bronx to extensive housing development. In Brooklyn, in addition to the heavy concentrations in Brownsville, Williamsburg, and South Brooklyn, Boro Park with "tropical gardens" and "parks" became increasingly accessible. Even distant Coney Island was brought into range by improved transit facilities.[24]

With 542,061 inhabitants in 1910, the Lower East Side reached peak congestion. Thereafter, a decline set in. By 1916 only 23 per cent of the city's Jews lived in the once primary area of Jewish settlement, compared to 50 per cent in 1903 and 75 per cent in 1892. By the close of the first decade of the twentieth century the Lower East Side had lost much of its picturesqueness. In tone and color, the ghetto was perceptibly merging with the surrounding city. East European Jews had scattered to many sections of the city and were swiftly becoming an integral, if not as yet a fully accepted, element in the life of the community.[25]

In 1870 the Jews of New York were estimated at 80,000, or less than 9 per cent of the city's inhabitants. By 1915 they totaled close to 1,400,000 persons (nearly 28 per cent) , a number larger than the city's total population in 1870. Before 1880 the Jews of the city were hardly more than a subject for idle curiosity. But thereafter, the flow of East European Jews quickened the city's industrial life, helped to transform its physical shape, and contributed a varied and malleable people to the metropolis. Despite poverty and great numbers, these immigrants created no new problems. But their presence accentuated New York's shortcomings in the face of unprecedented demands upon its imagination and resources. In the early years of the new century, their voice would be heard. The problems of industrial relations and urban living accentuated on the Lower East Side were to become the focus for major reforms.[26]

✢ 6 ✢

Germans versus Russians

The thoroughly acclimated American Jew is oftentimes almost as peculiar among Jews generally as the race is singular
among mankind. . . . He stands apart from the seething
mass of Jewish immigrants . . . and looks upon them as in
a stage of development pitifully low.

The Hebrew Standard (1894)

AT a time when established Jews were becoming acutely sensitive to the opinions of their fellow New Yorkers, they were
faced with the prospect of a mass migration of coreligionists
from Eastern Europe, whose coming seemed to threaten their
hard-won respectability. German Jews had shed the tradesman's
mien and were acquiring the higher mercantile manner. As
they became Americanized, their ties with the German community in New York became less pronounced and they, along with
Jews of American origin, were discovering a common identity
as Jews that they had not known earlier.[1]

Yet in the years of the great Jewish migration, to be identified as a Jew became more and more irksome. The hosts of uncouth strangers, shunned by respectable New Yorkers, seemed
to cast a pall upon all Jews. Disturbed native and German Jews,
heirs to the age of reason and science, condemned everything
that emanated from the downtown quarter.

It had not been so earlier, when disparities had been less
marked and less consequential. East Europeans, few and far
between, blended into the immigrant city and created no problems. Place of origin, family pride, clan solidarity, and intellectual tastes loosely defined business and social relations, but dif-

ferences were in degree rather than in kind and fleeting contacts minimized friction. Gruff-mannered East Europeans tended to hover on the edge of more elegant "German" society despite mutual animosities. The Russian-Polish Jew, assuming German airs, became the "Kavalrier Datch." Selig became Sigmund, eager to dwell in the shadow of German respectability, at last to claim, "Mayn waib is gevoren ah datchke un ich bin gevoren ah datch" (My wife has become a lady and I a gentleman). As the East European colony took shape, the German model persisted; but it lost its primacy, for Russian pioneers could now turn to their own circles to satisfy their social needs.[2]

Established New York Jews made every effort to become one with progress. In 1870 the *New York Times* saluted Temple Emanu-El in its new Moorish edifice as one of the globe's leading congregations, "the first to stand forward before the world and proclaim the dominion of reason over blind and bigoted faith." Clearly an age was dawning when all men, regardless of race or ancestral faith, would come together in universal communion. "In the erection and dedication of the Fifth Avenue Temple, it was not only the congregation that was triumphant, it was Judaism that triumphed, the Judaism of the heart, the Judaism which proclaims the spirit of religion as being of more importance than the letter." In 1873 German Emanu-El turned to Manchester, England, and called Gustav Gottheil to its pulpit to preach Judaism's universal message in impeccably English accents, comprehensible to all New Yorkers.[3]

European events sustained in German Jews the conviction of the supreme merit and eventual acceptance of all things German—all, regrettably, but language. With the rise of a new Germany, New York Germans, even as they became more American, compensated for earlier rebuffs with a rising flamboyance. Jews shared in the elation and further celebrated the removal of lingering disabilities upon their kin in the new empire. They took new pride in their roots and vicariously partook of German imperial prestige, assured that the German Empire meant "peace, liberty, progress, and civilization." German Jews, insisted Rabbi Kaufmann Kohler, free of the "shackles of medievalism," their minds "impregnated with German sentiment . . .

no longer Oriental," stood convinced of their superiority to East Europeans and regarded all vestiges of a segregated past with discomfort.[4]

The fears of uptowners, colored with racist phraseology, smoldered in the Anglo-Jewish press. There anti-Russian sentiment assumed a withering metaphysical rationale as "a piece of Oriental antiquity in the midst of an ever-Progressive Occidental civilization" called forth the ghost of a happily forgotten past. Uptown Jews, sensitive to the reverberations of the new German anti-Semitism, were far more distressed by the "un-American" ways of the "wild Asiatics" than were non-Jews. "Are we waiting for the natural process of assimilation between Orientalism and Americanism? This will perhaps never take place," exclaimed the *American Hebrew*. *The Hebrew Standard* echoed these misgivings: "The thoroughly acclimated American Jew . . . has no religious, social or intellectual sympathies with them. He is closer to the Christian sentiment around him than to the Judaism of these miserable darkened Hebrews." Even Emma Lazarus in her sonnet inscribed to the Statue of Liberty, "Mother of Exiles," called the immigrants of the 1880's "the wretched refuse of your teeming shore." [5]

Nothing in the newcomers seemed worthy of approval. Yiddish, or Judeo-German, "a language only understood by Polish and Russian Jews," though intelligible to non-Jewish Germans, was denounced as "piggish jargon." Immigrant dress, ceremonials, and rabbinical divorces were anathema. Yiddish theaters were barbarous; Yiddish newspapers, collectively stigmatized as "socialistic," even worse. Furthermore, "dangerous principles" were "innate in the Russian Jew." Mounting newspaper publicity proved especially distasteful. "The condition of the Jewish quarter . . . has too often been the subject of extravagant word-painting." Lincoln Steffens' reports of East Side life in the *Evening Post* and *Commercial Advertiser* were resented equally with Abraham Cahan's realistic fictional essays.

Our newspapers have daily records of misdemeanors, marital misery, and petty quarrels that may largely be attributed to the same source. The efforts of intelligent brethren to raise the standards of Judaism have been frustrated by the efforts of misguided people who regard all teaching and criticism, as an outrage on their suddenly acquired and misunderstood liberty.

Most intolerable of all was that "anomaly in America, 'Jewish' trades unions." Germans, embarrassed by Russian business competition, dismissed their rivals, whose names often ended with "ki," as "kikes." So Russians often were forced to Germanize their names in order to escape the stigma among German credit men. "Uptown" and "downtown" separated employers from employees, desirable from undesirable, "classes" from "masses," "Americans" from "foreigners," and icily confirmed the most categorical judgments.[6]

MAKING NEW AMERICANS

Yet, uptowners of means spared no effort to assist downtowners. "The uptown mansion never forgets the downtown tenement in its distress." Uptowners, taken unawares by the heavy immigration of terror-stricken refugees in 1881 and fearful of a pauper problem, attempted to restrain further immigration. But as the tide could not be stemmed, the Jewish charities of the city, aided considerably by West European Jewry, chafingly accepted their new responsibilities. The *American Hebrew* urged: "All of us should be sensible of what we owe not only to these . . . coreligionists, but to ourselves, who will be looked upon by our gentile neighbors as the natural sponsors for these, our brethren."

The established Jewish charities proved unequal to the new demands. The United Hebrew Charities, formed in 1874 during the economic crisis, had efficiently administered extrainstitutional relief, but so moderate had been the claims made upon it, that in 1880 its treasury showed a balance of $14,000. Mass migration transformed the scope of Jewish charity. The Hebrew Emigrant Aid Society, improvised for the crisis, raised $300,000 to succor the first contingents of refugees. In a single year, the HEAS expended as much as had the United Hebrew Charities in its seven-year existence. "Assistance was no longer claimed as a fraternal right, nor extended as a kin-like obligation," recalled Professor Jacob H. Hollander two decades later at the Fifth Biennial Session of the National Conference of Jewish Charities.

It was the imperious demand of stricken humanity. But, as the situation lost its bitter novelty and the burden settled in onerous pressure, benevolence waned and something akin to patronage grew. The charitable association became no longer a semi-social device whereby the more prosperous members of the community relieved the misfortunes of neighbors and associates, but a tax-like charge for the indefinite relief of misery and dependence of a distinct class, different in speech, tradition and origin, unsought in arrival and unwelcome in presence, whose only claim was a tenuous tie of emotional appeal and an identical negation in religious belief.[7]

Help continued nevertheless. Local groups and individuals, aided by the Independent Order B'nai B'rith, the Baron de Hirsch Fund, and the Union of American Hebrew Congregations ministered to the needs of immigrants. The Forty-Eighter Michael Heilprin of the *Nation* came to a premature end as a result of his exertions to settle immigrants on the land. When refugees overflowed Castle Garden and the lodging houses nearby, the State Commissioners of Emigration opened the Ward's Island buildings to the newcomers and Jacob H. Schiff contributed $10,000 for the erection of auxiliary barracks. The United Hebrew Charities provided free lodgings, meals, medical and midwife care, and, for countless unfortunates, free burial. The UHC's employment bureau did its best, even when "the market was overladen with the kind of work offered" and "applicants were nearly all without special trade or calling and . . . physically unable to comply with the conditions demanded in this country." In 1885, despite depressed trade conditions, the UHC's employment bureau turned away only 744 of 3036 aplicants as unemployable.[8]

German Jews devised comprehensive schemes to divest downtown brethren of the marks of oppression and to remodel them in the uptown image. Mrs. Minnie D. Louis' sixteen-verse poem outlining uptown's Americanizing mission, "What it is to be a Jew," opened with the image of the ghetto Jew,

> To wear the yellow badge, the locks,
> The caftan-long, the low-bent head,
> To pocket unprovoked knocks
> And shamble on in servile dread—
> 'Tis not this to be a Jew

and closed with a portrait of the American Jew, fully realized,

> Among the ranks of men to stand
> Full noble with the noblest there;
> To aid the right in every land
> With mind, with might, with heart, with prayer—
> *This* is the eternal Jew!

First and foremost came vocational preparation, training not available to immigrants under other auspices, and tutelage in American customs. With these goals in mind, the United Hebrew Charities had organized special classes in the domestic and sewing arts for girls as early as 1875, and a few years later the Hebrew Free School Association had opened the Hebrew Technical School for girls. After 1890 the Baron de Hirsch Fund supervised and supported an array of educational facilities that included the Hebrew Technical Institute for boys, an evening technical school, and evening English classes, initiated by the YMHA to supplement the public evening schools. "Jargon journalists, Hebrew teachers, musicians," anxious to qualify for admission to professional schools, were given special instruction; in 1896, of a class of 18, 8 were admitted to medical school, 3 to law school, and 4 to special technical schools. Earlier as later, insufficient classrooms postponed for many months admission to public education and a preparatory school was organized to drill the fundamentals into children who waited to be admitted to the bulging city schools. Between 1905 and 1910 school buildings on the Lower East Side were so strained that the Camp Huddleston Hospital Ship at the foot of Corlears Hook was converted into a city school where ten thousand children received instruction.[9]

The zeal to Americanize underlay all educational endeavor, from kindergartens first organized in 1882, on up through the grades. The Hebrew Free School Association, originally founded to discourage Christian missionizing among the children of the poor, recast the course of study of its afternoon schools. Training in the amenities, cleanliness, and the practical home and industrial arts crowded aside the curriculum of Jewish history, Jewish religion, and the Hebrew elements. The Reverend Clifton Harby Levy's advice to the trustees of the Baron de Hirsch classes that the addition of Hebrew to the curriculum would enlist parental support was ignored. The Federation of Temple Sisterhoods, originating in 1887 with the Emanu-El Sisterhood, sponsored classes of like pattern and maintained day nurseries as well. But in 1905 only one Jewish-sponsored crèche, the Brightside Nursery, served the entire Lower East Side.[10]

Uptown reached the summit of its Americanization program in the Hebrew Institute. This Jewish-sponsored community house, hailed by its founders as a "center of sweetness and light, an oasis in the desert of degradation and despair," was organized jointly in 1889 by the Hebrew Free School Association, the Young Men's Hebrew Association, and the Aguilar Free Library Society. In 1891 it was housed in an impressive five-story structure at the northeast corner of Jefferson Street and East Broadway, and in 1893 it was renamed the Educational Alliance. From 9 A.M to 10 P.M. class and meeting rooms, an auditorium seating 700, library, gymnasium, shower baths, and a roof garden entertained a wide range of activities. While adults learned "the privileges and duties of American citizenship," youngsters received the benefits of its many advantages. Vocational courses, classes in English, civics, American history, and English literature, and Edward King's especially popular classes in Greek and Roman history were augmented by sermons, public lectures sponsored by the Board of Education, and flag-waving exercises on the national holidays.

Not until the first decade of the twentieth century was the Educational Alliance to bridge the gap between modern, urban New York and the psychological world of Torah and ghetto by conducting its courses in Yiddish. But its initial program remained an outstanding unifier. A host of clubs, each with patron author, poet, scientist, statesman, or philosopher—including the George Eliot Circle for girls—crowded the calendar and vied for the never-adequate meeting rooms. In a city growing more sensitive to the collective pleasures given by music, musical training especially was encouraged. Piano, violin, mandolin, and singing classes met regularly and the melodic din of rehearsing trios, quartets, orchestras, choral groups, and a children's symphony echoed through its halls. If drawing classes elicited a poor response, art exhibitions jointly sponsored with the University Settlement, assisted by the public schools, set unprecedented attendance records. A ten-cent admission charge to Saturday evening concerts and entertainments discouraged only the mischief-makers from attending. The first English performances in the Jewish quarter, "As You Like It" and "The Tempest," added Shakespearean fare to Purim and Hanukkah plays. Physical exercise, slighted by serious youngsters, was promoted by a full and vigorous athletic program. Dr. Jane Robbins, a founder of the College Settlement, spoke to young women on personal health and feminine hygiene in 1898, and leading physicians lectured to young men on "The Marriage Question: Its Physical and Moral Sides." A few years later the Henry Street Settlement welcomed similar talks, presaging the introduction of such education into the public schools. In the first decade of the new century, a few hundred paid and voluntary workers descended upon the Alliance, its annex, and its two subbranches to direct and supervise a beehive of activity that weekly attracted some 37,000 adults and youngsters.[11]

Deeply influencing the children, the Educational Alliance remained alien to the adult East Side, more so perhaps than the public schools and settlements, for these at least did not represent themselves as Jewish. At the Alliance, English was the official language and at the Alliance's People's Synagogue Dr. Adolph Radin conducted religious services in Hebrew and German. Yiddish, in immigrant eyes the touchstone of Jewishness, was taboo. Although the Alliance's successive Russian-born directors, Isaac Spectorsky and David Blaustein, could do little to affect the major lines of institutional policy, they were sensitive to the needs of their countrymen. The reading room, visited by a thousand persons daily, bulged with over one hundred Hebrew, Russian, and Yiddish journals. The Zionist Hebrew

Literary Society, where youngsters sampled their first Hebrew idyl or renewed a romance with a reborn Hebrew literature, "is certainly in the line of moral culture," noted David Blaustein apologetically in the Alliance's annual report. The Russian-American Hebrew Association, founded in 1890 by Dr. Radin, its president and sole officer, "to exercise a civilizing and elevating influence upon the immigrants and to Americanize them," broke precedent to permit Zevi H. Masliansky, the East Side's magnetic Zionist preacher, to lecture in his native Yiddish. No less than Hebrew and Yiddish, Russian, the language of the intelligentsia, was unwelcome at the Alliance, although on occasion Russian-speaking societies met on the premises. Radin, a Posen Jew, felt moved to explain that "Russian" simply designated the place of origin of the immigrants, not the "half-barbarous civilization often signified by that name." [12]

PHILANTHROPY VERSUS SELF-HELP

Despite their failings, German Jewish charitable institutions aroused the admiration of all New Yorkers. Echoing Andrew Carnegie, Jacob H. Schiff, writing in the *Independent*, reaffirmed the stewardship of wealth with Jewish overtones. "Philanthropy as the aim and ideal of Judaism," succinctly described the path taken by the religious impulse.

Few human needs were overlooked. Old institutions were modernized and expanded and new ones were established to meet unanticipated requirements. Mount Sinai, formerly the Jews' Hospital, admitted more free clients than any other private institution in the city; nearly nine tenths of its patients in the 1880's were treated without charge. The Hebrew Orphan Asylum Society and the Hebrew Sheltering and Guardian Society generously provided for orphans, while the Clara de Hirsch Home for Working Girls provided adolescents with recreational facilities. The Association for the Improved Instruction of Deaf Mutes—the oldest oral and only Jewish school for the deaf in the country—and societies for the blind and the crippled aided the handicapped. In 1893 a Jewish Prisoners' Aid Association was formed reluctantly to minister to the relatively small but growing number of Jewish prison inmates. Before the turn of the century offending Jewish lads had been sent to the state-maintained House of Refuge or to the Catholic Protectory, as Jews proved laggard in providing for their youthful transgressors. But a precipitous rise in juvenile delinquency led to the founding in 1907 of the Hawthorne School of the Jewish Protectory and Aid Society. The Lakeview Home for Jewish unmarried mothers followed; and a few years later, the Jewish Big Brother and the Jewish Big Sister associations were formed to supervise youngsters on probation. Rounding out the major Jewish social agencies organized primarily to care for immigrant needs was the National Desertion Bureau, founded in 1911 to locate missing husbands.[13]

Uptown institutions, however proficient and commendable, did not satisfy downtowners. East Europeans, treated as mendicants, were hardly grateful for the bounty bestowed. Efficient charity, with its documents and inquests, seemed incapable of performing the religious obligation of *Zedakah*—on its highest plane, pure loving kindness. Prying strangers outraged the sense of decency of folk who in their home circles were often persons of consequence. As soon as it was possible, self-respecting immigrants made every effort to assist their own.

In the philanthropic institutions of our aristocratic German Jews you see beautiful offices, desks, all decorated, but strict and angry faces. Every poor man is questioned like a criminal, is looked down upon; every unfortunate suffers self-degradation and shivers like a leaf, just as if he were standing before a Russian official. When the same Russian Jew is in an institution of Russian Jews, no matter how poor and small the building, it will seem to him big and comfortable. He feels at home among his own brethren who speak his tongue, understand his thoughts and feel his heart.[14]

From their earliest coming, immigrants in need instinctively turned to their fellow townsmen. "The amount of small charity given directly from the poor to the poorer will never be known." The many-sided *lansmanshafts*, uniting the features of the Old World burial, study, and visitors-of-the-sick societies, bound the immigrant to his *shtetl* and birthplace. At first these societies had been coextensive with synagogues. But with the onset of the great migration each town and village asserted its individuality. As early as 1892 a contemporary directory listed 136 religious societies on the Lower East Side and doubtless there were more. Ninety-three were registered as Russian-Polish; the rest, classified as Austro-Hungarian, embraced Austrian, Hungarian, Rumanian, and some German congregations. The Beth Hamedrash Hagadol on Norfolk Street alone welcomed all Jews.[15]

After 1880 *lansmanshafts* independent of synagogue ties began to supersede the religious societies. The better managed benevolent societies furnished insurance, sick benefits, and interest-free loans, as well as cherished cemetery rights. In time, women's auxiliary aid societies were founded whose members were tutored in the parliamentary amenities by their male sponsors. In 1914, 534 benevolent societies, with from 50 to 500 members each, embraced virtually every immigrant household in New York City. When *lansmanshafts* affiliated with fraternal orders, they were transformed into familiar American lodges. Since the established German associations discouraged the entrance of newcomers, East Europeans formed their own. In 1887 Hungarians organized the Independent Order Brith Abraham, which conducted its business in German, but welcomed all comers; this organization soon became the largest of all Jewish fraternal orders. In 1900 the Workmen's Circle, and in 1912 the Jewish National Workers' Alliance were founded by Jewish trade unionists dissatisfied with the quasi-religious ritual and tone of the existing orders.[16]

By the late 1880's, East Europeans had already begun to organize their own communal charities. Russians and Austro-Hungarians founded their respective free burial societies. The cathedral Russian congregation established the Passover Relief Committee of the Beth Hamedrash Hagadol and prided itself on its catholicity: "In dispensing money and matzos to the poor, all are recognized as the children of one Father, and no lines are drawn between natives of different countries." The *Hevra Hachnosas Orchim* (the Hebrew Sheltering Society), formed in 1890, undertook to feed, lodge, and clothe friendless immigrants and to aid them in finding employment or in seeking out *lanslite.* In 1909 the Hebrew Sheltering Society was united with the Hebrew Immigrant Aid Society, founded in 1902 to ease the entrance of newcomers into the country. The expanded HIAS was to serve the needs of immigrants for over half a century.[17]

The self-help principle took characteristic communal form in 1892 in the *Gemillat Hasodim* Association, the Hebrew Free Loan Society. The Society, relying solely on the endorsement of merchants of standing, made interest-free loans of from $10 to $200 to immigrants eager to set up independently in business. Within little more than a decade, the society's funds soared to over $100,000 as grateful borrowers, recalling the source of their success, contributed to its capital.

East Europeans also founded their own hospitals. Beth Israel, beginning in 1889 as a dispensary on Birmingham Alley, "the shortest and most dismal street in the whole city," grew to become the Lower East Side's leading hospital. Lebanon Hospital, Beth David, and the Hungarian People's Hospital followed, and in 1904 Galicians and Bukovinians undertook to found Har Moriah. Despite the opposition of the United Hebrew Charities, East Side physicians organized the Jewish Maternity Hospital in 1906 so that East Side mothers no longer had to depend on the New York Lying-In Hospital. These East Side institutions could be trusted to be kosher and to treat East European patients and physicians as equals. (Although ninety per cent of Mount Sinai's patients were East Europeans, East European physicians were not admitted to that hospital's staff.) In 1897 institutional care for the aged poor also was inaugurated with the founding of the Home of the Daughters of Jacob.[18]

Levantine Jews maintained an existence independent of Yiddish New York. As early as 1884 Gibraltans, culturally akin to the Levantines, founded Congregation Moses Montefiore in East Harlem. However, the number of true Levantines did not become significant until over two decades later when unrest within the Turkish empire brought a mixed multitude of ten thousand to the city. Dominantly Judeo-Spanish (Ladino) in speech, they included several hundred Greek-speaking Jews, and one thousand Arabic-speaking Jews from Aleppo in Syria. At first they were aided especially by the sisterhood of the city's oldest congregation, the Sephardic Shearith Israel, distant kin indeed to the newcomers. But in 1913 these latest immigrants organized a mutual benefit society, and the Oriental Ozer Dalim Society to care for their own needy.[19]

The religious urgency to provide a genuinely Jewish educa-tion for their sons drove downtowners to trust to their own re-sources. Half the Lower East Side children receiving a religious education in the 1890's attended the classes of the Hebrew Free School Association, but most of them were girls, for these classes did not answer the needs of East Europeans (many of whom even suspected that the cookie-laden Mrs. Minnie Louis of the Downtown Sabbath School was a Christian missionary). Parents gladly sacrificed to send their sons to the traditional Hebrew schools; the registration in 1903 at the Lower East Side's 307 *heders* (religious elementary schools) was 8616 boys and only 361 girls. There the *rebi* (religious teacher) linked the generations in intimacy of mood, ritual, and language, and slaked the consciences of parents who welcomed the opportuni-ties thrown open to their children by the public schools, but who dreaded the impiety and the emptiness created between generations.

Late afternoon and early evening, pedagogues in basements or tenement flats, above saloons and dance halls, drove young-sters through the mechanics of prayer-book reading, rarely un-derstood in the Old World, but in the New not even feared or respected. More ambitious and systematic were the Talmud Torahs which at first dispensed shoes and clothing along with a traditional religious education. In 1886 the Machzike Talmud Torah acquired its own building on East Broadway and soon shed its charitable aspect. In the same year the Yeshiva Etz Chaim was founded as an all-day school where a small number of youngsters pursued Talmudical learning. In 1901 the Ameri-canized Jacob Joseph Yeshiva was organized "to prepare He-brew boys for life in this country." Finally, the Yeshiva Rabbi Isaac Elchanan, organized in 1896 for pursuing advanced Tal-mudical studies, completed the educational ladder for traditional Jewish learning. While most parents strained to pay the small fees, many were neglectful or unable to meet their obligations. The announcement in 1908 that three out of every four children received no religious education was doubtless exaggerated. Even so, it did reflect poverty, indifference, and weakened parental control. A dismal literal translation of the Talmud testified to the hopelessness of inspiring respect for traditional knowledge among the American-born.[20]

A few enthusiasts, disgusted with formalistic Jewish studies, pioneered modern Jewish schools in an effort to link son to father, to breathe meaning into an ancient heritage in the modes of a new age. Zionists opened modern Hebrew schools in the 1890's while Jewish nationalists founded Yiddish folk schools around 1910, both groups searching for bridges over the chasm separating the generations that would unite the most advanced democratic ideals to a transvalued Jewish tradition. Random trials also were made with socialist Sunday schools, sponsored by the Socialist party, where lessons in "capitalist ethics" were replaced by lessons in "socialist ethics." At Emma Goldman and Alexander Berkman's Ferrer Center and School, two dozen youngsters were regaled with the lessons of anarcho-communism and listened to lectures by Clarence Darrow, Edwin Markham, and Lincoln Steffens that pointed to the free development of the individual. However humanitarian in intent, these experiments remained on the fringe of the immigrant community and acquired but a small and uncertain following.[21]

THE LARGER GIVING

Traditions of Jewish communal responsibility left little need for outside aid. Despite seasonal unemployment and acute poverty in the mid-nineties and during the 1907 and 1914 depressions, the resources of city, state, and non-Jewish private agencies were lightly taxed. In crisis years, aroused private citizens lent a hand, and examples of nonsectarian charity were many. In 1882 non-Jewish merchants and bankers contributed to the Hebrew Emigrant Aid Society, while in 1891, at a banquet honoring Jesse Seligman, non-Jews contributed to the Russian

Transportation Fund for the Moscow refugees. In the depressed nineties Mrs. Josephine Shaw Lowell's East Side Relief Work "put our poor 'Hebrew Jews' at work to clothe the poor Negroes of the Sea Islands," and John B. Devins, pastor of Hope Chapel, transformed the East Side Relief Workers' Committee into the Federation of East Side Workers that included Protestants, Catholics, and Jews. In 1907 Mrs. Russell Sage and Warner Van Norden made substantial gifts to the United Hebrew Charities; Henry Phipps, too, proved a generous and steady supporter of the Legal Aid Bureau of the Educational Alliance.[22]

Where municipal, state, and private institutions felt the pressure of the newcomers, they shared the burdens with the Jewish agencies. The City's Board of Estimate annually allotted a small sum to the United Hebrew Charities; and the state earmarked more substantial amounts for the Hebrew Orphan Asylum Society, the Hebrew Sheltering and Guardian Society, the Aguilar Free Library Society, and the Jewish hospitals. The Charity Organization Society, the New York Association for Improving the Condition of the Poor, the Children's Aid Society, and the Society for the Prevention of Cruelty to Children cooperated with the United Hebrew Charities. The Sloane Maternity, the New York Lying-In, and the Mother and Babies' hospitals aided expectant mothers in out-patient departments. The *Tribune* Fresh Air Fund, the *Herald* Ice Fund, the spectacular fund-raising of the *World* and the *Journal,* and Nathan Straus's sterilized milk for the children of the tenements also contributed to the well-being of the immigrant East Side.[23]

Two nonsectarian agencies proved especially useful. The Deutscher Rechts Schutz Verein, founded in 1876 by German immigrants, became the Legal Aid Society in 1894. By then most of its litigated cases were recorded on the East Side and in 1899, an East Side branch was opened at the University Settlement. The Society's panel of prominent attorneys, cooperating with the Legal Aid Council of the United Hebrew Charities and the Legal Aid Bureau of the Educational Alliance, arbitrated petty disputes without charge and kept thousands of cases from reaching the court dockets. The Provident Loan Society, authorized by a select committee of the Charity Organization Society, also performed a special service. Operating as a small loan association, it proposed to reduce the high interest rates of pawnbrokers, permitted to charge 3 per cent per month, by charging 1 per cent. By 1911 there were three Provident Loan Society branches on the Lower East Side and one each in the Bronx, Williamsburg, and Brownsville, the major foci of East European Jewish settlement.[24]

PROMISE OF COMMUNITY

At the turn of the century all East Europeans, despite their diversity, were characterized as "Russians." Russian immigrants, with their numbers, variety, intellectual drive, and sense of historical exigency, defined and redefined the quarter's horizons of heart and mind. Despite their nostalgia for the scenes of their childhood and youth, having fled a despotic homeland to which there was no returning, they were quick to embrace America as their first true homeland. Galicians, however, harbored a genuine affection for the benevolent Austrian empire and could easily return. While idealistic Russians formed the Lermontoff Benevolent Society and a host of liberty-loving clubs, celebrating the Russia to be, wistful Galicians founded the Crown Prince Rudolph Verein, the Franz Joseph Kranken Unterstutzung Verein, and the Franz Ferdinand Benevolent Society, honoring the Hapsburg empire as it was. In 1884 Hungarians organized the Magyar Tarsulat (Society) and in the same year lonely Rumanians banded together in the Roumanisch-Amerikanischer Bruderbund. The huge Russian colony, agitated by the winds of the world to come rather than by monuments to attained liberties, overshadowed the lesser enclaves. In 1904 immigrants isolated from the main currents of the quarter formed the Federation of Galician and Bukovinian Jews to promote intercourse with culturally more energetic Russians.[25]

The low intermarriage rate, even between individuals of the diverse East European Jewries, reflected their group solidarity. After 1900 the equipoise between the sexes in each group and a clan-centered social life especially limited contacts. The barriers that separated East European Jews from non-Jewish New

Yorkers militated against marriage outside the fold. After 1900, however, the association of Jewish women with Italians and non-Jewish Russians in the apparel trades led to some marriages. The highly publicized nuptials of Americanized "emancipated" Jewish women and social reformers were unusual. Yet, in these years, such alliances were only slightly less frequent than marriages between uptowners and downtowners.[26]

In time, bridges of communication formed between Germans and Russians. Yet only a complex transformation wrought on both groups by American and world experiences over more than half a century was to boil away the mutual incomprehension and intolerance that kept Jews apart. In these years, cooperation was rare and halfhearted in the lone area of social encounter between uptown and downtown—charitable endeavor. In 1901 the downtown Auxiliary Society of the United Hebrew Charities disbanded, no longer content with a subordinate, mere fund-collecting role. In the same year the Downtown Burial Society, *Chesed Shel Emes*, assumed full responsibility for the Lower East Side, and the United Hebrew Charities dissolved its Free Burial branch. After 1904 requests for aid to the UHC declined; inadequate relief discouraged those in desperate need, while the galaxy of mutual aid societies provided for those less seriously distressed. Yet, even as Germans and Russians pulled apart, the rise of an American-trained generation of Russians spelled the onset of a new equilibrium. Indeed, as early as 1901 downtowners envisioned a United Hebrew Community, "to effect a union of Jewish societies and congregations in New York City." [27]

In the early years of the twentieth century, the beginnings of accommodation between Germans and Russians were discernible, as the spirit of American reform penetrated both groups.

Part Three

JUDAISM SECULARIZED

❧ 7 ❧

Voices of Enlightenment

"Science, civilization and justice."
Volksadvocat (1888)

TRADITIONAL social forms, religious brotherhoods, and charitable associations gave immigrants their bearings and provided as well for their practical needs. A revitalized Yiddish, enlarged to a legitimate language, introduced a world beyond the previous imaginative stretch of the immigrants. Jews, armed with new resources of language, were to see cultural institutions of their own making evolve in the New World experience, institutions which were to articulate the rude excitement of self-discovery, the clash and accommodation of civilizations.

YIDDISH: YAWP OF THE PEOPLE

At first East European intellectuals in New York found themselves without tongue. Humbled and mute before demands unanticipated by the folk imagination, they were troubled by a sense of inadequacy that was ironically at odds with traditions of moral and intellectual excellence. The Yiddish vernacular, although colonized with intellectual allusions drawn from ancient Hebrew and Aramaic texts, was yet a dialect. Devoid of intellectual precision, the folk tongue was spurned by the enlightened and the traditionally learned alike as "jargon." Yet in a democratic age, the vernacular was to prove itself the compelling means of discourse. To meet the challenge of a social revolution, intellectuals perforce would call forth new resources of language. They would develop the Yiddish word into an agent of enlightenment and Americanization and bring folk divorced from the mainstream of western civilization into conversation with their times.

Early newspaper and stage Yiddish, in accord with the whole drift of East European culture, simulated German and eagerly drew upon the resources of the language of Moses Mendelsohn and the Haskala. In New York the vast German settlement and the high repute of German Jews reinforced this philo-Germanism. Even the orthodox Yiddish press reprinted Goethe and the German classic writers. Early literary Yiddish, grounded in the Teutonic Yiddish of immigrants stemming from the German rim lands, was compounded of Hebrew characters, German vocabulary, and Yiddish syntax. This "deitchmerish," as it was called by disconcerted Lithuanians, gave system and a common denominator to the chaos of Yiddish subdialects, and served as an entry to German and western culture.[1]

In the late 1880's Lithuanians came to outnumber other Yiddish-speaking folk and inspired efforts for a less arthritic rendition of the folk tongue. At this time Alexander Harkavy, animated by the democratic and folk impulses that agitated the Jewish labor and socialist movements, embarked on a tireless career to redeem the vernacular. In 1886, in *Di yiddish-daytche shprach,* this pioneer lexicographer proclaimed Yiddish a member of the family of languages. A year later he contributed a series of articles on Yiddish grammar to the *New York Idishe Illustrierte Zeitung* for the edification of aspiring writers. A New York Yiddish weekly further bolstered the claims of Yiddish by printing one of the earliest expositions of the history of the "jargon." And in 1891 the vernacular acquired high sanction when Harkavy published the first "English-Jewish" dictionary. This volume contained "long and comprehensive definitions" of scientific words on every subject that "might interest a civilized people," and even updated American dictionaries by including such words as "electrocution." Within less than two decades the *Complete English-Jewish Dictionary* had passed through eleven editions. Again, "gathering the stray words of the language," Harkavy in 1898 compiled an impressive and only somewhat less popular complementary volume, the first advisedly Yiddish, rather than Judeo-German, dictionary, "the product of six years' indefatigable labor."

Matching Harkavy's exertions, fellow Lithuanians Abraham Cahan and George Selikowitch gave literary currency to the spoken Lithuanian idiom. Yet these pioneer journalists placed small stock in the vernacular's literary capacity, viewing Yiddish as no more than a makeshift on the road to Americanization and modernization. Yiddish grammar and orthography continued to balk at discipline, but the momentum of Yiddish literary culture, the transplantation of one third of East European Jewry, and the moral involvement of Yiddish in a great folk upheaval, invigorated the vernacular beyond all expectation.[2]

Despite popular usage, the Yiddish written word, self-conscious and rigid, was slow to absorb the American idiom. In the 1870's the earliest Yiddish-American doggerel included such English words as "boy," "supper," "dinner," and "boss." But official Yiddish abjured Americanisms. Although Harkavy from the outset included such new terms as "politic," "industry," and "guarantieren," not until the third decade of the twentieth century did his dictionaries welcome "American Yiddish." By 1900, however, the average immigrant mingled one hundred English words and expressions in his daily speech. "Never mind," "alle right," "that'll do," slipped readily from the tongue; and "politzman" and "ein schon kind, ein reg'lar pitze" (picture) elicited polar emotions. The Yiddish of the daily press also quickly reflected the naturalization of the idiom and the fading prestige of receding German models. Seasoned and Americanized editors adopted English phrases that appealed to their readers. Abraham Cahan even introduced phonetic spelling and called for a Yiddish Yiddish, for "mama gab," devoid of pretensions.[3]

THE FIRST PERIODICALS

Yiddish, in attaining literary status, became the medium for far-reaching forms of communication. But throughout the last three decades of the nineteenth century the Yiddish periodical wrestled with the elementary mechanics of journalism. Editors and publishers were without experienced writers, literary traditions, journalistic models, linguistic resources, or an audience accustomed to reading newspapers or magazines; furthermore, the traditional-minded resisted distractions that snatched all too precious moments from prayer and study.[4]

Early Yiddish periodicals, edited by Lithuanians who were fired by the Hebrew enlightenment, were invariably short-lived. The first Yiddish paper, Buchner's lithographed *Yiddishe Zeitung* (1870), offered articles on politics, religion, history, literature, and science, culled from German and European Hebrew periodicals. At the height of the Franco-Prussian War, the successor to the *Yiddishe Zeitung*, Hirsch Bernstein's *Yiddishe Post* (1870–1871), attained a circulation of 4000. But when the keen interest in European affairs subsided, it suspended publication. Bernstein then joined forces with Jacob Cohen, a politician, and published the *Hebrew News* (1871). This thirty-two page weekly, quartered into English, German, Hebrew, and Judeo-German, reflected a polyglot audience and endured only through the three-month election campaign. In 1872, Kasriel Sarasohn embarked on his extended publishing career with the *New Yorker Yiddishe Tsaytung*, printed in German with Hebrew characters and catering to readers from German Poland. Its successor, the *Yiddishe Gazetten* (1874–1928), for lack of talent or resources, in its early years reprinted the Judeo-German *Israeli*, of Mainz, Germany, under its own masthead. But the *Gazetten* succeeded in becoming the leading Yiddish weekly in the final decades of the century and annexed its competitors one by one. These included the *New Yorker Israelite* (1875), the *Idishe Volks-Zeitung* (1878–1880), with 1500 subscribers (its title inspired by the German socialist daily *New Yorker Volks-Zeitung*), and the *Israelitische Presse* (1877–1884), with 3000 subscribers. In 1885 the circulation of "the largest and cheapest Hebrew paper in the world" stood at 8000. At the turn of the century, the *Gazetten* proclaimed itself the product of "the consolidation of twenty newspapers" and the representative of "the interests of over a million Hebrews of America." In 1890 the *Gazetten* had not yet crystallized its later orthodoxy and conservatism but courted readers in every quarter.

The *Jewish Gazette* is not sold to any political or religious party. Its duty is to hear all sides on every important issue. It will print anything worthwhile, be the writer a rabbi, a doctor, a poet, a socialist, a philosopher, or a crank. Let each one say what he feels; this hurts no one and is sometimes very interesting.[5]

The production of Yiddish periodicals in New York City, the hub of the Yiddish-American universe, was accelerated by the rising immigration. Between 1885 and 1914 over 150 daily, weekly, monthly, quarterly, and festival journals and yearbooks appeared. The yearnings for free expression, suppressed in the Old World, erupted in the New. Self-discovered authors, journalists, and humbler enthusiasts bewitched by the printed page, turned groggy with printer's ink and the perturbations in their own brains. The passion to educate and uplift, political and literary zeal, appetites for literary immortality and momentary fame, ideological divergencies, and the commercial instinct drove the presses at a furious pace. Periodicals—traditional and antitraditional, humorous and philosophical, commercial, recreational, and literary, anarchist, socialist, or Zionist—plunged into the market place. These were ready to serve, instruct, inspire, but never merely to distract a curious and skeptical, yet credulous public. By the early years of the twentieth century even the Russian-educated who had disdained the "jargon" press were attracted by the energetic Yiddish fare.

In the late 1880's Russian intellectuals, inflamed with hatred for tyranny, injected a lasting vitality into the Yiddish weeklies. Social ethical suasionists who shunted between anarchism and socialism, they played a role out of proportion to their numbers in efforts to sting fellow immigrants into self-reform. The Haymarket riot and the Henry George mayoralty campaign spurred the earliest of the radical weeklies, Abraham Cahan's *Naye Tsayt* (1886) and the more durable *New Yorker Yiddishe Volks-Zeitung* (1886–1889).

Although the socialist *Naye Welt* (1888) and the anarchist *Wahrheit* (1889) were short-lived, the radical independent

Volksadvokat (1888–1925), edited by George Selikowitch, formerly editor of the St. Petersburg Hebrew *Hamelitz*, became the weekly edition of three successive daily newspapers. The United Hebrew Trades' *Arbeiter Zeitung* (1890–1902), superseding Ephraim London's independent socialist *Morgenstern* (1890), became the leading weekly of its kind in the 1890's. The libertarian socialist *Freie Arbeiter Shtimme,* launched on July 4, 1890, and edited and written by the tubercular David Edelstadt, suspended publication upon his death in 1893, but was revived by Saul Yanovsky in 1899. Monthlies, such as the socialist *Zukunft* (1892–　　　), the most long-lived and distinguished of all Yiddish periodicals, the anarchist *Freie Gesellshaft* (1895–1914), that appeared when funds availed, the weekly *Zeitgeist* (1905–1908), published by the *Forward,* and Dr. Zhitlowsky's *Naye Lebn* (1908–1914), were especially literary and philosophical. The *Arbeiter* (1904–1911) served as the revived Yiddish voice of the Socialist Labor Party.[6]

Independent labor journals appeared on occasion in the 1890's, even though the *Arbeiter Zeitung,* representing the United Hebrew Trades, dominated the field. At the height of the 1890 tailor's strike, Israel Barsky edited the *Schneider Verband.* In 1894 the United Trade Unions, upon seceding from the United Hebrew Trades, put out the *Union Zeitung* in opposition to the *Arbeiter Zeitung.* In 1904 the United Hebrew Trades attempted to publish its own independent weekly, the *Arbeiter Welt,* as a successor to the *Arbeiter Zeitung* but fell short of its objective. The *Garment Worker* (1893–1903), occasionally carrying Yididsh columns; the bilingual *Capmakers' Journal* (1903–1906), ably edited by William Edlin; the *Cloakmacher* (1905) and its successor, the *Ladies' Garment Worker* (1910–1918); the *Papier-Zigaretten Macher* (1907); the *Idisher Baker* (1910–1913); the *Neckwear Macher* (1910); the *Painter* (1911); and the *Knitters' Hoffnung* (1913) served a widening circle of Yiddish-speaking unionists.[7]

There were ventures in every imaginable field of publication as enthusiasts searched for an audience or attempted to coax one into existence. Shaikewitz's *Vegveiser in der Amerikaner Bizness Velt* (1892), Kranz and Sharkansky's *Shtadt*

Anzeiger (1893), "A Monthly Magazine of Literature, Art, Science and Trade," and the *Grocer's Guide and Modern Biznessman* (1908), tried to provide practical instruction in American business ways. But their literary predilections reflected a certain unclarity of purpose and their quick demise cast doubts on their fitness as commercial counselors.

The dramatist Abraham Goldfaden experimented with the first illustrated fortnightly, the *New Yorker Illustrierte Zeitung* (1887–1888), while Morris Wechsler and David Apotheker published the Judeo-Hungarian *Weibershe Zeitung* (1888), the earliest women's periodical in the vernacular. There were special subethnic periodicals as well. Wechsler's *New Yorker Idishe Zeitung* (1885–1904), the *Yiddisher Gayst* (1910), and Jacob Pfeffer's *Yidishe Wochenblatt* (1905, 1909–1910) and *Volksblatt* (1910) catered respectively to Hungarians, Rumanians, and Galicians. Joel Entin's *Di Freie Idishe Volksbine* (1896) and Jacob Gordin's *Theatre Journal and Familien Blatt* (1901–1902), the *Dramatishe Welt* (1904), and the *Idishe Bine* (1909–1910) attempted to gain the patronage of better theater "patriots" while the *Theatre and Moving Picture Review* (1913) added the new film to Yiddish New York's cultural purview. The *Schach Jurnal* (1906) catered briefly to chess zealots, the *Shadchan* (1908), to the unmarried, and *Unzer Gezunt* (1910–1914), to the health-minded. Harkavy's *The Hebrew American Weekly* (1894), with its parallel English and Yiddish columns, provided weekly English lessons, while *Unzer Shrift* (1912), in Latin script, attempted to teach Yiddish to the American-born and English to immigrants.[8]

A profusion of humorous periodicals mirrored the sense of absurdity that rarely deserted immigrants. Beginning in 1888 austere small-town sons of Lithuania warred with the irreverent metropolis in a succession of comic journals. *Der Yudisher Puck* (1894–1896), the most outstanding, adopted the title of the popular American and German comic weeklies. Especially prominent in these productions was the enterprising hand of Shomer, the Yiddish romantic novelist; Abraham Sharkansky, Moses Seifert, and Morris Rosenfeld, rhymster, litterateur, and bard respectively, also added their talents.

An interval of a dozen years without a single try at comedy was broken in 1908. Prosperity, melting satire into irony, saw jesters poke fun with a new accuracy and sharpness. In the new idiom, crusty Lithuanian wits, by now somewhat mellowed, collaborated with lighter-spirited Galicians such as Jacob Adler, who adopted the pseudonym B. Kovner to counter the Lithuanian prejudice. These humorists, aided by cartoonists Saul Raskin and Lola (Leon Israel), entertained even as they admonished an audience ready to chortle at its own foibles. The lively irreverent wag, *Der Groiser Kibitzer* (1908), which became the widely read *Der Groiser Kundes* (1909–1927), was unsparing of swelled heads, inflated bank rolls, and "all-rightnicks" (parvenus).[9]

Miscellaneous literary weeklies, monthlies, and annuals regularly sprang up. These were devoted to popular science, criticism, sketches, verse—some original—and translations and adaptations from foreign literature. *Der Hoizfreind* (1889–1890) and Shomer's *Der Menschenfreind* (1889–1891) were the pioneers. Harkavy's *Der Nayer Gayst* (1897–1898), the most distinguished of its kind for the period, aimed for cultural variety and included columns on uptown theatrical and musical events and on chess. Abraham Raisen's *Dos Naye Land* (1911–1912) and *Di Literarishe Welt* (1912–1913) and David Pinski's *Di Yiddishe Wochenshrift* (1912) were fresh with the vitality of newcomers.

Zionist publications appeared fleetingly, beginning with *Hovev Zion* (1886), supplement to the *New Yorker Yiddishe Zeitung,* and Dr. Joseph A. Bluestone's *Shulamith* (1889). The Dreyfus affair, the publication of Herzl's *Der Judenstaat,* and the first Zionist convention at Basel echoed upon American shores in Menahem Dolitzky's *Di Tsayt* (1897–1898), *Der Zionist* (1898), and *Mevasseres Zion* (1898). A few years later *Di Naye Shtunde* (1904), *Di Yiddishe Zukunft* (1908), the labor Zionist *Der Yiddisher Kemfer* (1907–   ), *Dos Yiddishe Folk* (1909–1931), and the socialist-territorialist *Volksstimme* (1910–1912) reflected mounting sympathy with the modern Zionist cause in the face of renewed massacres and political reaction in tsarist Russia.[10]

THE NEW JOURNALISM AND ABRAHAM CAHAN

With the growth of a daily Yiddish press, weeklies and month-lies became less important. Yet before 1894 all attempts to pub-lish genuine dailies had been futile. In 1881 and again in 1883, Sarasohn's *Yiddishe Gazetten* briefly issued a daily edition. Sara-sohn's *Yiddishes Tageblatt* (1885–1928) proclaimed itself "the only Jewish daily in New York," but like the *Teglicher Herold* (1891–1904), it appeared thrice, at best four times, weekly.

In 1894, however, a combination of circumstances made a true daily press possible. The heavy Jewish immigration in the early nineties exceeded the total for the previous decade. Mass unemployment and economic crisis, added to the stir of labor struggles and the campaign for political and civic reform cen-tered on the East Side, helped crystallize the daily reading habit. The fall in the price of newsprint from twelve cents in 1870 to two cents per pound in the mid-nineties and the adoption of linotype machines by the Yiddish newspapers encouraged mass production. Yiddish newspapers, originally sold casually at gro-ceries, were vended with gusto on street corners in the midst of the depression when grown men grasped at the chance to earn a few pennies. While the penny weekly *Yiddisher Recorder* (1893–1895) collapsed despite a reputed circulation in the tens of thousands, three of the four Yiddish penny dailies, the *Tage-blatt,* the *Teglicher Herold,* and the *Abendblatt* (1894–1902) held their own; the *Teglicher Telegraph* (1895) alone failed. In the mid-nineties when Hearst's *Journal* and Pulitzer's *World* battled for a new mass patronage, Yiddish newspaper circulation was assured. For a time at the turn of the century as many as six dailies competed for readers. The socialist *Forward* (1897–   ), the *Tegliche Presse* (1898), the *Tegliche Volks-zeitung* (1899), the *New Yorker Yiddishe Abendpost* (1899–1905), the *Yiddishe Welt* (1902–1905), the independent *Warheit* (1905–1918), and the anarchist *Abendzeitung* (1906) appeared in quick succession and vied for circulation with the dailies founded earlier. In 1901 the first and only successful Yid-dish morning paper, the *Morgen Journal,* appeared. Published by Jacob Saphirstein and edited by Peter Wiernik, it prospered on its want-ad columns. Its only competitors in this limited field, the *New Yorker Morgen Blatt un Yiddishe Welt* (1905) and the socialist *Morgenzeitung* (1906), each lasted but a few months.[11]

All the Yiddish dailies resorted to sensationalism. But the new journalism received its most eloquent expression in Abraham Cahan's *Forward*. Cahan had come to New York in 1882 at the age of twenty-one, eager for freedom and determined to write. In the ensuing two decades he served an apprenticeship in American living that was to prepare him for his role as editor of the nation's outstanding Yiddish daily. This perceptive Russian intellectual shared in all the experiences of his fellow immigrants: he was factory hand, lecturer, teacher of English, labor organizer, law student, and socialist preacher. But from the outset he cultivated literary ambitions. In his first year Cahan mailed an article describing the coronation of Tsar Alexander III to the *New York World* and it was promptly published. By the mid-1880's Cahan's journalistic career encompassed the Russian, Yiddish, and English fields. He acted as American correspondent for Russian periodicals, edited the *Naye Tsayt*, the *Arbeiter Zeitung*, and the *Zukunft*, wrote editorials for the socialist *Workmen's Advocate* and contributed features, stories, and literary criticism to the *Sun*, the *World*, the *Century*, and the *Forum*. In 1896 his first novel, *Yekl, A Tale of the Ghetto*, was published by Appleton's. But in the following year Cahan severed his connections with the newly founded *Forward*, which was torn by politics and strife. At the same time he was dismissed from his position of eleven years standing as a teacher in an adult evening school on the complaint of a trustee who had heard him deliver a socialist speech. Physically exhausted and penniless, Cahan found himself without any means to earn a livelihood. His novel, despite the high praise of William Dean Howells, brought him no royalties. Women, who constituted the major market for novels, devoured knightly romances but had no interest in immigrant stories; furthermore, an unmoral love story that alluded to sex was taboo. Convinced that no career awaited an author of realistic novels portraying Jewish life, Cahan turned to the English press. First, he secured a commission to write a weekly article for the *Sun*. Then Lincoln Steffens, the assistant city editor of the *Evening Post* and an admirer of *Yekl,* accepted a few of his articles and introduced him to the editor of the *Commercial Advertiser*. As a result, three months after leaving the *Forward,* Cahan was contributing human interest features and character sketches to three distinguished American newspapers.

Cahan's chance encounter with Steffens led to a lasting friendship and proved to be the turning point in his career. In November 1897, when Steffens became city editor of the *Commercial Advertiser,* he placed Cahan on the regular staff. The former Yiddish journalist had an intimate knowledge of the Jewish world. But he wanted to explore the cosmopolitan metropolis and to familiarize himself with all its human aspects. He was given the job of police reporter, receiving his first lessons at police headquarters from Jacob Riis, chief reporter for the *Sun*. In the next four years Cahan's assignments ranged from the reporting of murders and fires to the interviewing of Boss Croker, Buffalo Bill, and William McKinley. Each assignment opened a new world to his curiosity and imagination.

During these years Cahan became an influential figure on the *Commercial Advertiser*. The newspaper's unusual staff of college graduates respected him as a novelist and as a literary critic who passionately admired the great Russian writers. Goaded by Cahan, the *Commercial Advertiser* devoted many columns to interpreting the Lower East Side to its readers, while Cahan provided that informed luminous charm that could not be matched by the other newspapers. Steffens joyfully accused him of bringing the spirit of the East Side into the offices of his paper. Indeed, Cahan guided his colleagues to the Canal Street cafés where the question of realism in the arts was eagerly debated and to the Bowery theaters where the audiences divided into factions. Hutchins and Norman Hapgood became especially charmed with the Lower East Side and "Hutch," encouraged by Cahan, wrote a series of articles that were assembled in 1902 into a minor classic, *The Spirit of the Ghetto*.

Upon the resignation of Lincoln Steffens in 1901, Cahan left the *Commercial Advertiser*. He rejoined the immigrant commu-

nity vested with the aplomb and dignity acquired through success in the greater American sphere. Nearly four eye-opening
years stripped him of many of the prejudices of the Russian Jew
and chastened his view of American life. Cahan returned to the
Forward an accomplished journalist and polished literary craftsman. In the eyes of the immigrant community Cahan had become a real American whose advice was to be heeded. He had
achieved an English literary style of distinction, and his colleagues on the *Forward* assured him that his Yiddish had been
improved in the process.

With his natural talent for journalism, Cahan transformed
the *Forward* almost single-handedly from an obscure sectarian
newspaper with six thousand readers into the pacemaker of
Yiddish journalism. An obsessive interest in human problems,
an ear attuned to the aches and aspirations in his readers' hearts,
and a conviction in the infallibility of his judgments led Cahan
away from the dogmatic paths pursued by the socialists of the
book and formula. The "socialism" of Lincoln Steffens made it
clear to Cahan that social and political convictions were to be
defined by actions rather than by slogans. Despite his loyalty to
Marxian terminology, Cahan did not trample on the sensibilities of the *Forward's* readers. In practice, his socialism was a fervent almost personal concern with all human problems and a
sympathy for the miserable and oppressed of all lands, races, and
creeds.

Despite his own and his readers' joy in polemics, Cahan dog-
gedly kept his ear to the ground. Just as he brought the excitement of the East Side into the offices of the *Commercial Advertiser,* so he carried back with him to the *Forward* the refreshing
liberal American spirit that animated that newspaper. This
adept student of the popular mind found his greatest challenge
in Yiddish journalism. He came to be regarded as the spokesman for Yiddish New York, and the Yiddish Arthur Brisbane.

Simple and direct in style, the *Forward* supported labor, socialism, humanity, and distinguished Yiddish and foreign literature. But it also enticed the women with serialized romances,
made prominent places for human interest features, and in its
Bintel Brief (Bundle of Letters) column combined social case-

work with advice to the lovelorn. In 1909 the *Forward's* first article on American sports, "The Fundamentals of Baseball Explained to Non-Sports," apologetically but scientifically interpreted the national "madness" to its readers with the aid of a three-column diagram of the Polo Grounds.

By 1910 the two nominally socialist dailies, the *Warheit* and the nonprofit *Forward,* were so securely established that even the arch press rivals, Louis Miller and Abraham Cahan, exchanged pleasantries on occasion. Mass immigration drove the combined New York circulation of the four Yiddish dailies, led by the *Forward,* over the 455,000 mark in 1914, a figure exceeded only during the war years. By then, the *Forward,* always ready to aid the underdog with purse and voice, had become a monument to the unquenchable individualism of Abraham Cahan, outdistancing its competitors as it instructed them in the popular art.[12]

As in all else, Levantines maintained their own periodicals but reflected the Yiddish milieu. Unable to secure adequate financial support, the Ladino daily *El Aguila* (1912) failed within a month, but the weekly *La America* (1910–1925) proved more stable, printing a Yiddish column to attract advertisers in the greater East European community.[13]

Dedicated spirits, stirred by the grandeur of Hebrew poetry, delighted by the intricacies of Hebrew grammar, and convinced that style and art were attainable only in a classical idiom, attempted to win readers for Hebrew journals. Yet of the more than a score that appeared in New York before 1914, few outlasted their first year. Enthusiasm for a renascent Hebrew literature, a rapturous awakening to the tongue of the patriarchs and prophets, and dreams of a modern Zion were insufficient to sustain journals written in euphuistic prose and comprehensible only to the learned.

Yet, the first Hebrew periodical, Z. H. Bernstein's *Hatsofe Baaretz Ha-hadasha* (1871–1876) showed vitality. *Hatsofe,* enlivened by the fresh liberating mission of the Hebrew enlightenment and superior to the as yet crude Yiddish journals, drew for copy upon the roving East European voices of Haskala, *Ha-Maggid* (1856–1903), *Ha-Melitz* (1860–1903), *Ha-Tse-*

firah (1863–1904), *Ha-Lebanon* (1863–1887), *Havatzelet* (1870–1910), and *Ivri Anochi* (1873–1890), which over the years found a haven in Odessa, St. Petersburg, London, Jerusalem, Paris, Berlin, and in lesser cities. *Hatsofe* supplied foreign news, reported on the activities of fellow immigrants, advised upon American conditions, and printed Hebrew idyls; it also introduced its readers to dreams of socialism. West European immigrant readers also were attracted to *Hatsofe,* for Hebrew still linked all traditionally educated Jews.

But the hope that neoclassical Hebrew would join the diverse Jewries was indeed romantic. Literate Hebrew readers, if they had not done so initially, soon turned to the better American, German, and Anglo-Jewish periodicals, while those who still yearned for the Hebrew idiom might choose from among the half-dozen superior European Hebrew journals.

Gerson Rosenzweig's weekly *Ha-Ivri* (1892–1902), alone among the later Hebrew periodicals, defied sudden death. But its 4000 listed circulation of 1899 was attributable to the business talents of the Yiddish newspaper magnate Kasriel H. Sarasohn, not to its own drawing power. Even traditional Hebrew supplements to the Yiddish press proved powerless to retain reader interest under American skies. Poets, like Menahem Dolitzky, with a gentle ardor for the biblical tongue, stood aloof from the life around them. Without a popular message, they sank into elegiac verse and mourned the fate of culture and learning in their adopted land, while seeking a vexing livelihood in the Yiddish press. In 1909 and again in 1913 newly arrived immigrants, inspired by a more democratic Zionist enthusiasm than their cloistered predecessors, founded and refounded the daily *Ha-Yom.* Passionately espoused dreams lingered on, but *Ha-Yom* quickly succumbed to the realities of American journalism.[14]

Before the Yiddish press attained standing, better educated East Europeans patronized the German press. In 1890 over 7000 Jews on the Lower East Side, including many East Europeans, claimed German as their mother tongue. Even Jews barely literate in German attentively scanned the want-ad columns of the

Staats-Zeitung; and Herman Rosenthal, a Russian intellectual, regularly contributed articles on Russian affairs to the columns of the nation's leading German daily. Many Hungarian Jews, who comprised over half the city's Hungarian colony, shared the culture and interests of their non-Jewish compatriots and were represented among Hungarian journalists. Marcus Braun, a reporter with the *German Herold* and the *Morning Journal,* in the 1890's published the *Hungarian-American* and the *Oesterreichisch-Ungarisch Zeitung;* Michael Singer published and edited *A Bevandorlo (The Immigrant).* Jews were the chief customers for *Ecoul Americci,* a Rumanian weekly published in the early years of the twentieth century.

But it was in Russian journalism that Jews were most con-spicuous. As early as 1890 some 5000 immigrants on the Lower East Side listed Russian as their native tongue, and the earliest Russian periodicals, edited by Jews, relied almost wholly on Jewish patronage. Louis Miller's pioneer *Znemia* (1889–1892), saturated with hatred of tsarism, printed the writings of Peter Lavrov, Gregory Plekhanov, and other leading Russian political exiles; appearing fitfully, it was kept alive by its patron, the chief assistant architect of the new Carnegie Hall, Waldemar Stark (Staleshnikov), a non-Jew. The short-lived *Progress,* edited by the versatile Jacob Gordin and the scholarly Isaac Hourwich, attained high literary excellence. George M. Price's and Jacob Gordin's *Russkaya Novosti* (1893)—subsequently *Russkaya Zhizn in Amerika,* edited by Boris Bogen—like Herman Rosenthal's weekly organ of information, *Russko-Amerikansky Viestnik* (1893), introduced immigrants to their adopted land and acquainted them with the affairs of the Russian colony; both soon acquitted their purpose. After 1905, with increased migration, Russian journalism revived with Gordin's *Russki Golos* (1907–1910); *Russko-Amerikanski Rabotchi* (1907–1908), monthly organ of the Russian Social Democratic Labor Party of New York; *Russkoye Slovo* (1910–   ), which in 1913 became a daily, *Novy Mir* (1910–   ); and *Golos Truda* (1911–1917), an anarchist monthly. But by then Russian periodicals had gained a wide readership and no longer depended on Jews. However, veterans such as Elias Rosenthal and Leo Deitch, among the more recent immigrants, continued to play a leading role in Russian journalism.[15]

LITERATURE

In New York few restraints curbed the immigrants' craving for the written word. This hunger found its most commonplace satisfaction—especially among women—in Yiddish romantic fiction. Nahum Meier Shaikewitz, the most prolific adapter and producer of this genre, had come to New York in 1888, already well known as Shomer, the pseudonymous author of romantic novels adapted from popular German and Russian works. Shomer's novels, animated by the spirit of enlightenment and deriding obscurantism and superstition, accustomed small-town folk to the reading habit and opened new worlds to their imagination.

Excited by the popular German serial paperback or *shund-roman*, in 1892 Sigmund Kantorowich and his partner Jacob Saphirstein began to publish Yiddish versions of these thrillers that attained immediate popularity. By 1898 some 65 novels had been adapted, as a score of writers labored to satisfy the demand. Beginning with the perennial bestseller, *The Secrets of the Tsarist Court or the Graveyards of Siberia,* based on the assassination of Tsar Alexander II, translators attuned to the sensibilities of their readers, bowdlerized with a will, wrapping piquant episodes with pointed homilies. *The Count of Monte Cristo* and *Don Quixote* were lasting favorites. Readers gobbled *Eighty Days around the World* and other science fiction in Abner Tannenbaum's limpid translations. *Man Eaters* held its audience breathless through 266 penny installments. Newspaper publishers, made frantic by falling circulations in the face of the *shundroman* craze, commissioned novels for their columns. By 1900 romantic fiction had become a journalistic staple, the *Tageblatt* proclaiming its tales "the most beautiful," and the publication of serial paperbacks virtually came to a close.[16]

Original Yiddish writings, inspired by Russian literary

models, exerted a profound influence but were no match for tales of adventure and romance. Libin's portraits of tenement and sweatshop, and realistic sketches by Gordin and Kobrin were featured in the radical journals and little magazines. They were exceeded in pathos only by Morris Rosenfeld's threnodies. Translations from Turgenev, Tolstoy, Flaubert, Zola, and Howells, and even critiques of Henry James, also educated the tastes and perceptions of younger immigrants and introduced them to the best contemporary writings. The Sunday *Forward's* thick literary supplement proved too costly to continue. But Abraham Cahan, champion of "the thrill of truth," took pride in his paper's devotion to serious modern literature; under his editorship, the *Forward* cultivated creative Yiddish writing and encouraged Abraham Raisen, Sholem Asch, and Jonah Rosenfeld in Eastern Europe, and lesser talents in New York. Indeed, the *Forward's* editor even turned the *Bintel Brief* column into a literary forum. "Under your tenement roofs are stories of the real life-stuff; the very stuff of which great literature can be made. Send them to us. Write them any way you can. Come and bring them, or tell them to us."

Yiddish literature, rising to heights of genuine self-discovery, soon penetrated all the Yiddish dailies. As a dialect flowered into a literary tongue, its richness and individuality brought flashes of self-understanding to immigrants who saw their un-phrased thoughts aglow on the printed page. Readers who craved Shomer's marvelous tales deferred to what they sensed to be higher standards. If Mendele and Peretz seemed as obscure as a folio page of the Talmud, untutored folk could contemplate these writings in occasional study groups, ponder columns of literary commentary, and at the least, bask in the reflected glory of their storytelling preachers. But all could take instant delight in the homely tales of Sholem Aleichem.[17]

Hebrew literature, like the Hebrew periodicals, remained esoteric. Limited to a small circle of devotees, the Hebrew fare consisted of rabbinical and homilectical tracts, discourses on ritual, and a few works of apologetics. A number of scrappy pieces by religious skeptics and Spinozists—such as the redoubtable S. J. Silberstein—bits of verse, and Rosenzweig's bitter-

sweet, epigrammatic satire, *Masechet Amerika* (1891), completed the Hebrew output. Ivriah, a society founded in 1906 "to
spread the knowledge of Hebrew literature, chiefly in Hebrew
publications," faced almost insurmountable obstacles. The ten-
volume Hebrew encyclopedia, *Otser Yisroel* (1906–1913), was
derived largely from the *Jewish Encyclopedia* (1901–1906), by
its dedicated editor, Judah D. Eisenstein.[18]

Book publishing developed slowly in an era when newspapers
and periodicals served as libraries absorbing the pennies of immigrants who impatiently awaited succeeding installments of
the writings of their favorite authors. (Even the pedestrian *Yiddisher Zhurnal* serialized Graetz's classic *History of the Jews*.)
Bibles, prayer books, Talmudic folios, and scrolls of the Law
commanded a steady market, but these were imported at low
cost from reliable sources in Central and Eastern Europe. Before 1900 printers, booksellers, and newspaper publishers confined their efforts to printing guidebooks, almanacs, language
manuals, study books, dictionaries, occasional collections of
theater couplets, and serial paperbacks. In 1888, 2000 copies of
Morris Rosenfeld's first volume of collected lyrics, *Di Glocke*,
published by a recklessly enthusiastic printer, went largely un-
sold.

After 1901, however, the merger of a number of bookseller-
printers into the Hebrew Publishing Company augured better
times for Yiddish book publishing. In addition to adaptations
of romantic novels and pirated reprints of Peretz and Sholem
Aleichem, nonfiction was published. Dr. Caspe's *Idishe Vis-
senshaftliche Bibliothek* specialized in popular science, and the
New York Radical Publishing Company, in free thought literature. The International Library Publishing Company became
the first firm to publish serious works in Yiddish. Philip Kranz
edited its distinguished list of titles, which included adaptations
of the works of the great thinkers from Aristotle to Herbert
Spencer, the novels of Tolstoy and Zola, and histories of the
French Revolution and pre-Columbian America. Virtually every topic, from the etiology of tuberculosis to opera plots, had
its Yiddish expositor.

For well over a decade the East Side's Max Maisel, a distributor of English, German, and Russian philosophical works by advanced writers, had resisted inferior Yiddish literature, but in 1906 he too became a champion of Yiddish books. Jacob Saphirstein's Jewish Press Publishing Company, book department of the *Morgen Journal,* climaxed a career of Americanizing texts with Peter Wiernik's hymn to the New Canaan, *History of the Jews in America* (New York, 1912, 1914), in English and Yiddish editions, and Paul Abelson's illustrated *English-Yiddish Encyclopedia Dictionary* (New York, 1915). Earlier, in a race for subscribers, the *Forward* had distributed 25,000 copies of Harkavy's *English-Jewish Dictionary* as a premium. In 1912 in the first two volumes of a projected multivolume Yiddish history of the United States, Abraham Cahan drew on the tenement imagery of the Yiddish quarter to describe the Pueblos of the Southwest; his tenement readers responded by buying up twenty thousand copies. Finally, on Prince Kropotkin's seventieth birthday, the Kropotkin Literary Society was launched to publish anarchist and socialist classics on an annual subscription basis.[19]

THE RITES OF THEATER

Like Yiddish journalism, the Yiddish theater arose as a product of a folk upheaval that brought small-town East European Jewries in touch with the greater urban and non-Jewish world. It was without a peer as a popular medium. The Yiddish theater, bounding with life and greater than life, fulfilled a variety of functions. It was educator, dream-maker, chief agent of charity, social center, and recreation hub for the family. All could share in its simple pleasures, adore the glorious players, and have a good cry.

At the turn of the century, eleven hundred performances were given annually before an estimated two million patrons. Purchasing tickets that cost from a quarter to one dollar, they filled the theaters to capacity on weekends and underwrote a continual round of benefits during the week. To the delight of

Lincoln Steffens, immigrants threw their entire bodily energies into the artistic and ideological controversy that surrounded the stage spectacle.

Unique as it was to America, the Yiddish theater had its beginnings overseas. In the late 1870's an incipient theater sprouted in the war-booming cities of Jassy, Bucharest, and Odessa. There Abraham Goldfaden fashioned tragicomic historical "operas" that were performed in New York by the early fugitive acting companies which fled the tsarist empire in 1883 when the Yiddish theater was closed. These diversions interwove the buffoonery of the traditional Purim play, the festivities of the wedding day, and the boisterous excitement of the Feast of the Rejoicing of the Law with rhyming couplets, song and dance, the antics of the *badchan* (minstrel), and sheer horseplay.[20]

Goldfaden's *Bar Cochba* and *Shulamith*, with their biblical and love-of-Zion motifs, and *Shmendrick* (The Ne'er-do-well) and the *Tsvay Kuni-Lemel* (Two Innocents), both savage indictments of religious hypocrisy, were vigorous fare. Dominated by tuneful melodies, these held the early Yiddish stage. Less talented imitators quickly followed suit. *How Moses Gave the Law on Mt. Sinai, Esther and Haman, The Father's Curse, Ezra, Bathsheba, Daniel in the Lion's Den, The Fall of Jerusalem, Rachel and Leah,* and *Joseph and His Brethren* were played for audiences for whom parable and homily were integral parts of all public recitations, and who brought religious expectancy to the crudest morality and miracle extravaganzas. Even stern Russian critics were forced to admire the magnificent pageantry, however unpalatable they found such "historical dramas" as *Sabetai Zvi,* subtitled "a folk comedy from Galician life."

The "greenhorn" mélanges, bursting with the absurdities of immigrant bewilderment, the incongruities of mispronunciation, the heartbreak of parting, and the tears of reunion with loved ones, were constant favorites. These performances, momentarily dissolving the loneliness outside, schooled folk in the rough surfaces of city living, and knowingly familiarized them with the tenement wilderness. The success which inevitably came to stage immigrants in Rumanian-born Joseph Lateiner's romantic musical carnivals generated confidence in the American dream.

To romantic musicals, "historical operas," and "greenhorn" favorites were added topical dramas, which provided blood-curdling peeks into a horror-filled universe. Galician-born Moses Horwitz, the dean of the daily news melodrama, gory with homicides and murders, portrayed subjects of larger interest as well. The Homestead strike and the Johnstown flood were social catastrophes drawn from the American scene, while *Tisza Eszlar, Hurban Kishinev,* and *Mendel Beilis* depicted the revival of medieval persecutions in Eastern Europe. As menacingly real as Russian pogroms loomed the historic oppressions in Egypt, Persia, Babylon, and Spain, and playwrights, adept at tear-draining and past masters of the moods of their audiences, rarely omitted the brooding theme of Israel's martyrdom.[21]

Even the Russian intellectuals admired the magnetic Mogulescu and prized Goldfaden's jaunty tunes. But they scorned the Yiddish theater's frivolity and parochialism. When, therefore, in 1891, a champion of serious theater appeared in New York, the enthusiasm of Russian intellectuals knew no restraints. Jacob Gordin, a son of Gogol's native town and a disciple of Tolstoy, was possessed by the modern spirit in its severe Muscovite garb. In turning his hand to the drama, Gordin felt called to enlighten his audiences, to raise them to higher levels of perception, and to lend universality to their daily experiences on a high artistic plane. Gordin accepted the limitations of the Yiddish theater and peopled his plays with homely Jewish characters and situations rooted in folk life. His adaptations from the classics pointed to the dilemmas of a world where irrevocable social and economic forces tested all traditions and raised identical moral problems for all men.

Gordin's adaptations only obliquely resembled the dramas of Goethe and Shakespeare, Ibsen, Gorky, and Hauptmann, and the realism proved more pretended than actual, but spectators were not likely to be perturbed by such details. "Criticism is absent here for drama is still a form of worship," recorded the German historian Karl Lamprecht, after visiting the Yiddish theater. Gordin frequently lectured his audiences on the connection between the *Jewish King Lear* and other plays and their Shakespearian prototypes. *Rosie,* an adaptation of Schiller's *Kabale und Liebe,* consisted of four acts of tragedy and then for those who desired, one act of comedy. *Mirele Efros, or The Jewish Queen Lear* and *God, Man, and Devil,* a synthesis of Job and Faust adapted to Jewish life, presented Gordin at his best, while *Minna, or the Yiddish Nora* probed Ibsen's delicate *Doll's House* theme.[22]

At the turn of the century serious Yiddish theater reached its peak influence and prestige. Thereafter the Lower East Side began to lose its coherence as it merged with the city. The moral authority wielded by Russian intellectuals in the grim nineties weakened in the face of prosperity and the spell of Old World sets and moods snapped as ten-cent vaudeville and ten-cent movies invaded the district. In a single year, twelve "Idishe varieties" appeared, offering one-acters, sparkling with ostensibly Yiddish melodies. In 1910 the Bowery became indisputably the Yiddish Rialto. The Atlantic Gardens was converted to Yiddish vaudeville, Miss May Simon was billed as the Yiddish Leslie Carter, and all the Bowery theaters housed Yiddish-American entertainment. From there it was but a step to English vaudeville where Jewish comic types had strutted the boards for over a decade.

Two events in 1904 symbolized the decline of the serious stage. Jacob Gordin failed as the director of his own theater and Jacob Adler, the leading exponent of Gordin's dramas, opened the Grand Theater—the first structure built specifically for the Yiddish stage. In 1912 Thomashefsky's new National Theater on Houston Street even surpassed the Grand in the magnificence of its appointments. The National compared favorably with Broadway palaces and offered similar enjoyments subject to the same commercial will-o'-the-wisp.[23]

The plays of Gordin and the more realistic dramas of his less literary disciples, Kobrin and Libin, continued to be given, but they were not highly successful. Although in 1913 the première of Sholem Asch's *God of Vengeance* proved a special event, serious theater was forced to depend largely on earnest amateur groups, the Yiddish "Little Theater" movement. As early as 1894 the Socialist Dramatic Society proudly had performed *Doctor Love*, Kranz's adaptation of Molière's *L'Amour Medecin*. In 1896, inspired by German example, the Russian-speaking admirers of Jacob Gordin had founded the *Freie Juedische Volks-Buehne*. Reorganized in 1902 as the Progressive Dramatic Club, for over a decade it faithfully presented performances and readings from the experimental and contemporary tragedies of literary Russian and Yiddish dramatists. The Hebrew Dramatic League, "Not to Amuse, Only to Teach," was but one of many other groups of amateurs pledged to advanced theater.[24]

Finer Yiddish theater, much admired by serious uptown critics, also received a hearing on Broadway. In 1902 Jacob Adler played a sympathetic Yiddish-speaking Shylock with an English-speaking cast in a fresh performance of *The Merchant of Venice*. While gifted players like David Kessler and Bertha Kalisch were abducted temporarily from the Yiddish boards by uptown theater managers, youngsters like Fania Marinoff made a complete break. In 1906 Harrison Grey Fiske directed an English production of Gordin's *Kreutzer Sonata*, tribute indeed to Tolstoy, the Russian Revolution, and East Side drama.[25]

Firsthand Russian influences, however limited, also centered in the Jewish quarter. In the spring of 1905, astir with revolution and the promise of a free new Russia, a dramatic company led by Pavel Orleneff and Alla Nazimova of the Moscow Art Theater arrived in New York from London and opened with Tchirikov's *The Chosen People*. In this protest against Russian pogroms, the non-Jewish dramatist invoked the redemptive powers of Zionism as a solution to the Jewish plight. The patronage of Mesdames Astor, Vanderbilt, and Whitney gained a brief hearing for the troupe before an audience of society women and Broadway theater people. But with the renewal of tsarist pogroms everything Russian became anathema on the East Side, and there was a precipitous decline in attendance at the Russian Art Theater on Third Street, causing an end to regular performances. Nazimova soon turned to the English stage and in Ibsen's Hedda Gabler, launched a distinguished American career.

These years also witnessed the appearance of the earliest exponents of the Russian school of dance and ballet. But these emissaries of Russian culture went directly uptown. In 1907, three years after arriving in New York, Louis H. Chalif founded the Chalif Russian Normal School of Dancing, where he instructed society in the graces of the rigorous Russian art. Upon the invitation of Otto H. Kahn in 1910, the first interpreters of Russian ballet in America, the Pavlova-Mordkin company, made its debut at the Metropolitan Opera House.[26]

CANTORS AND STRINGED INSTRUMENTS

Music, although without authority or tradition, was woven into the texture of Jewish life. Even in hard-bitten Lithuania, prayer motifs colored dimly formed arias and recitatives, study oscillated to a measured nasal chant, and work hummed with folk tunes. All three idioms often intermingled in unpremeditated medley. In New York, synagogue and theater formalized musical expression.

To religious and folk melodies, the theater added Italian operatic and European folk airs, and even assimilated "Daisy Bell," "Do, Do, My Huckleberry Do," and "The Bowery Girl." In 1896 the Windsor Theatre's chorus master, Jacob Sandler, composed the grand lament, beginning "Eili, Eili, lomo azavtoni" (My God, My God, Why hast Thou forsaken me!) for a Thomashefsky Passover season production, drawing upon the original psalmist for inspiration for the most moving of New World Jewish melodies. The popularity of Yiddish theater songs encouraged an extensive sheet music trade, especially cultivated by the firm of Katznellenbogen and Rabinowitz, that paralleled the American fad.

Liturgical music, often launching its younger practitioners onto the music hall stage, was stimulated by the ambitions of rival synagogues eager to redeem debt-ridden properties by attracting capacity congregations on the annual Penitential days, for which seats traditionally were sold. Odessa's Pinhas Minkowsky and choir, hired at $5000 by the Eldridge Street Congregation, and other lesser priced imported cantors intoxicated worshippers with awe-inspiring hymns punctuated with sustained trills, bravuras, and free vocal fantasia. For a time, in the late eighties, competition among synagogues and virtuosi attained scandalous proportions, but as economic conditions improved, rivalries became less strident.[27]

Some Jews brought with them works of a rising Russian musical school which was gaining world-wide attention. Indeed, Andrew Carnegie admired Russian compositions even above the songs of his native Scotland, and in 1891, at the opening of Carnegie Hall, Tchaikovsky graced the podium as the first guest conductor. In the nineties students of Anton Rubinstein and Leopold Auer of St. Petersburg's Imperial Conservatory, impelled by the expulsion of Jews from the great cities arrived in increasing numbers. By 1903 Modeste Altschuler was able to organize the Russian Symphony Society of New York dedicated to the "mission of acquainting the American public with the works of the Russian composers." On January 7, 1904, in the first of six concerts at Cooper Union, an orchestra of sixty-five, consisting of Jewish graduates of the Imperial Conservatory, performed works by Tchaikovsky, Glinka, Rachmaninoff, and Wieniawski, with Michael Svedrofsky as violin soloist. Immediate acclaim led the conductor to expand his complement of musicians to ninety-five and to move uptown to Carnegie Hall, where for over a decade the orchestra annually introduced the latest Russian musical compositions, including the then radical works of Stravinsky, to New Yorkers. At a more popular level, touring Russian balalaika orchestras, some of whose members were Jews, serenaded the Russian colony in 1910 and 1911 and also attracted musically curious uptowners.[28]

In these years the American debuts of Ossip Gabrilowitsch, Mischa Elman, Leo Ornstein, and Efrem Zimbalist foreshadowed the rich harvest of Russian-born Jewish virtuosi who were to become a byword on the American concert stage. The violin became intimately linked with Jewish musicianship; in 1908 Irving Berlin's "Yiddle on Your Fiddle—Play Some Rag-Time," seized upon this image. The Russian Choral Union, the later Russian-American Singing Society, directed by Boris Steinberg, and the Russian Musical Society were "Russian" in the antecedents of their members, but not in their repertory. The Halevi Singing Society presented Hebrew melodies, and the Rubinstein Symphony Orchestra dedicated a number of evenings to music by Jewish composers, such as Meyerbeer, but these concerts were integral parts of a cosmopolitan choral and instrumental program. Only a handful of scholarly devotees of the Choral Society for the Study of Ancient Hebrew Melodies, founded in 1905, searched the distant past for musical inspiration.

One Russian immigrant ventured to compose serious music. The versatile Platon Brounoff, conductor, teacher, pianist, singer, music critic, and lecturer, described himself as "the only representative of the Russian modern school of composers in America." Brounoff was inspired equally by Russian, Jewish, and American themes. His American Indian grand opera, "Ramona," based on Helen Hunt Jackson's novel, anticipated the works of Charles Wakefield Cadman. But like others who strained to compose serious music based on Indian, Negro, cowbow, and idyllic themes, Brounoff's efforts could hardly compete with urban ragtime.[29]

ARTISTS, ORATORS, KIBITZERS

Unlike music, art was a stranger. Tradition and the context of East European life combined to restrict artistic statement to the conventionalized techniques of printing, engraving, and calligraphy, sanctified by their immediacy to the word. Significantly, at a popular East Side art exhibition, Meyer von Bremen's "Mother and Child" alone touched the heart; the rest remained remote and un-Jewish. Saul Raskin, who had studied in Parisian ateliers, pleaded the humanitarian and democratic values of art rooted in folk themes in the earliest articles on art to appear in Yiddish, but with little effect. Jacob Epstein's sketches for *The Spirit of the Ghetto* and Abraham Walkowitz's drawings, like George Luks's oil painting, "Hester Street," failed to arouse a Jewish audience. For a people whose esthetic joys sprang from the Hebrew word, who detected the flavor of Isaiah in ordinary family correspondence, plastic forms seemed irrelevant and unworthy. Indeed, so rare was the drafting facility among Jewish immigrants that the *Forward* at first relied on a non-Jewish Rumanian for its drawings.[30]

For serious youth, the lecture platform was without peer. A direct encounter with the higher life of learning and ethics presented joys for which an older generation looked to traditional moral and Talmudic discourses. A rare evening passed that did not offer a half-dozen formal lectures, meetings, and protest rallies. Readings from Shaw and Ibsen, Thoreau and Tolstoy, proved a treat. And curbstone homilists, rarely flustered by rain or snow, could be counted upon for unheralded disquisitions on social justice and the good society.

More formalized societies for enlightenment also fed the appetite for learning. Jacob Gordin and a coterie of physician-philosophers founded the Educational League in 1900 to convey "knowledge for its own sake," from elementary arithmetic and spelling to Attic tragedy and the philosophy of Nietzsche "in a medium familiar to the Jewish immigrant." Lectures at the Young Men's Educational League, the Workmen's Circle branches, and the Voice of Labor societies were equally dedicated to the diffusion of learning and its delights.[31]

The intellectual and cultural life of the immigrant community found its most genial refuge in the coffee house or "Jewish saloon." In the late eighties, wine cellars, cafés, and restaurants sprang up, popularized by Jacob J. Kampus, the blintz-maker of Delancey Street, and other Rumanians, accustomed to them at home. In the evenings lunchrooms became frugal "Kibitzarnias." There, over steaming Russian tea and lemon, thin slices of cake, and Russian cigarettes, "confused minds," disturbed by life's complexities, found respite and tonic in talk. On Rutgers Street and East Broadway, cafés entertained through the night as the journalists of Yiddish Newspaper Row defended their signed columns against the sallies of their challengers. Here Jacob Adler, "the Yiddish Salvini," greeted his admirers and Jacob Gordin, "the Yiddish Shakespeare," declaimed his plays. Here the admirers of Marx and Kropotkin, Zola and Tolstoy, debated abstruse turns in philosophy and political economy, the purposes of art, and the standards of the theater. Even elderly

Talmudists with untrimmed beards and long black coats drank honey cider, chewed lima beans, and disputed the finer points of the Law in their favorite cafés. By 1905 some 250 to 300 coffee houses, each with its *Tendenz* and special clientele, congregated on the Lower East Side. By then a dozen fashionable restaurants had sprung up as relative affluence encouraged more luxurious tastes and less overflowing, if more precise, talk.[32]

Other recreations mixed the Old World with the New and even the serious East Side enjoyed the Sunday picnics, bicycle trips, and steamboat excursions which were among the initiatory rites that turned greenhorns into Americans. Some fifteen public halls served as the East Side's "winter picnic grounds." The New Irving Hall, "the largest, most convenient, and most beautiful place on the Lower East Side," was an imposing structure. Accommodating nearly 1200 persons this "true temple of Eden" packed traditional seven-day wedding festivities into a single evening. Less commodious halls functioned primarily as schools where dancing-masters like Abraham Cahan's "Professor Peltner" introduced many a heavy-footed pair into the higher refinements. "Von two tree! . . . Zents to de right an' ladess to the left!" From early September to late June, the Lower East Side rang with the convivialities of benefit balls. After the turn of the century, with the march uptown, Tammany Hall, Madison Square Garden, and Grand Central Palace became the sites of elaborate masked ball benefits where expectant *lanslite* might spy out a familiar countenance amid strange multitudes, and aid a worthy cause besides. Even "Professor" A. Hochman, "the renowned Psalmist and Mindreader" of Rivington Street did not search for clients in vain. With prosperity, card playing became infectious. Yet even frailty was hitched to a higher purpose; card parties rivaled theater benefits as mainstays of charitable and religious enterprise.[33]

The varied cultural forms which immigrant Jews helped to build reflected their impulse to creativity and self-improvement, generated by new worlds and new visions. In this energetically social process, diverse Jewries were linked to the greater society and to one another, smoothing over intramural provincialisms even as they were more clearly defined. Strangers, sharing a passion for the universal coin of the spirit, joined in a larger communion. Immigrants, vexed by uncertainty at every turn, attempted to appreciate in their own terms the problems that faced them in the new land.

In approaching the greater society, they brought with them the intellectual vitality, the moral perplexity, the religious optimism, the sound and the fury of a great awakening. In the process, Jews attained a cultural and intellectual richness in New York greater than any in Eastern Europe.

∾ 8 ∾

The Great Awakening

I had ears but could not hear, because of my ear-locks; I had eyes and could not see because they were closed in prayer . . . I am Rabbi Nehemiah no longer, they call me Nehemiah the atheist now.

"The Apostate of Chego-Chegg" (1899)

O lost am I, O lost
In pandemonium's alley
My brow aflame with brooding
My. eyes but tears do tally.

Morris Rosenfeld (1912)

No quarter in the city throbbed with such inner turmoil as did the Lower East Side in the final decades of the nineteenth and early years of the twentieth centuries. No other district in New York sensed the agitation to its life rhythms so sharply or harbored aspirations so out of joint with its tenement milieu. Deadening sensibilities, the New World developed psychical instability, even liquidity of character among the Jews. Chasms of misunderstanding embittered family relations. In novel roles among Jews of strange Jewries, men often seemed beyond Old World measure. "Names are changed as easily as shirts"; Greenbaum was tailored to Greene, Levy to Lamar, and Warschawsky to Ward. Overnight *shister* (cobbler) turned mister and mister turned *shister*. Everywhere the unlearned took precedence over scholars. Indeed, all life's conventions and expectations seemed topsy-turvy. "The patriarchal family life of the Jew is his strongest virtue," noted Jacob Riis. "It is the one quality which redeems and on the Sabbath eve when he gathers his household about his board, scant though the fare be, dignifies the darkest slum of Jewtown." Yet where wordly-wise children guided their elders, adult patterns, shaken in their equilibrium, trembled beneath pitiless scrutiny, and filial affection often vanished.[1]

In the New World as in the Old, the fear of poverty and of tyranny affected group attitudes. " 'They cry before they are hit;' not only individually, but also as a class." Pervaded by a deep-seated optimism, Jews were nevertheless apprehensive, haunted by the specter of persecution, ever on the defensive. "The word Christian suggests to them proselytizing and cruelty, and they are suspicious of all Christians." [2] Outrage saturated group memories and conditioned their ambitions, their judgments, and their behavior. Yet in America as in Europe, great forces were at work, remodeling. Everywhere pulses stirred to hope unprecedented.

TRADITION AT HALF-MAST

The religious regimen with which Jews crammed their days relaxed even among older folk. However bountiful the blessings of the new land, "American piety was as tasteless as American cucumbers and American fish," concluded an immigrant in one of Cahan's stories. For youngsters and for those who had spent some years in Europe's larger cities, the breach already had been made, the accustomed harmony had been shattered. With the passing of each week daily observance and prayer diminished in regularity and duration. A full day was skipped and another. Even prayers for the dead were blinked. Then one day the need was no longer felt. Worn-out "four corners" (fringed cloth worn by males beneath their outer garments) were not replaced; phylacteries fell into discard; the prayer shawl was unfurled only on the most solemn occasions; and the prayer book, so seldom used, gradually dropped from sight. Men shed their Old World garments, skullcaps, untrimmed beards, and sidelocks, and exchanged the surtout for the Prince Albert (styled the Prince Isaac by the pious) ; women doffed their perukes and kerchiefs. In the doing, sacred rites seemed violated. Starched collar and necktie alone undermined the immigrant self-image and suggested a new mode of behavior. Observant greenhorns contrasted with "Yankees," and made all old country customs appear retrograde and uncouth, the dreaded symptom of the "greener."

Unhinged from the old associations, the calendar guideposts to feasts and fasts appeared less reliable. Religious festivals, with their spontaneous, even pastoral charm, went limp, drained of communal relish, out of touch with the seasons. The pounding machines and city rush even diluted the once longed for Sabbath repose. What meaning was there to Sabbath bread twists displayed on weekdays, to Passover matzo on sale the four seasons long? Even on the Jew-swollen Lower East Side, Purim and the Feast of the Maccabees might pass almost unnoticed, for every night was festive at the theater, every day profane upon the street. How could Succoth (Feast of Tabernacles) be savored, a booth erected, or rushes for the roof be gathered in a packed tenement? Where could fragrant green twigs be found for the Feast of Weeks, when only "garbage barrels rearing their overflowing contents in sickening piles" lined "the streets in malicious suggestion of rows of trees"? Everywhere the present mocked the past, and turned yesterday's pious wise man into an old country bumpkin.[3]

The *Beth-hamedrash* was no longer the same. This house of prayer and study, literary and dramatic center, home of musical worship, office of mutual aid and brotherly communal devotion, gradually was bereft of its attractions. Bit by bit its grip was loosened by lodge and benevolent society, newspaper and lecture platform, theater and dance hall, library, school, and trade union. Soon it loomed bare, dutiful, and ancient. Daily regularity dropped off and even Sabbath attendance thinned out. At the century's turn, the decline of the sweatshop and mounting economic pressures dealt Sabbath observance a heavy blow. In 1912 the two great Jarmulowsky banks still remained shut on the Sabbath, but only 25 per cent of the city's Jewish workmen rested on the sacred day of rest, and of these a majority were employed by contractors. Even Hester Street storekeepers shamelessly exhibited their wares on the Sabbath and some dared to do so on the Penitential days. A 1913 survey of two police precincts at the Lower East Side's heart revealed that

1770 of 2975 stores, nearly 60 per cent, were open on the Sabbath. No effort, however organized, was able to stem the tide. The Keepers of the Sabbath Society failed dismally in an attempt to boycott Yiddish New York's leading nonobservant newspapers, for life's new tempo impelled even the devout to purchase the *Forward* or the *Warheit* on Saturday to keep abreast of the news. At the Yiddish theaters, Friday night and Saturday matinee performances were sellouts and Bowery music halls lured giddy youngsters even on the high holidays.[4]

Yet virtually all immigrants solemnized the three Penitential days. In this season even the least observant paused momentarily, frightened by the casualness of their oversights, by the fracture between past and present. In tenement lofts and dance halls, in theaters and storefronts, in saloon meeting rooms and at Tammany Hall, and wherever space could be hired profitably, religious entrepreneurs annually contrived a rash of provisional prayer halls. These were packed to capacity so as to yield the highest return on investment, but the ever present danger of fire lent an aura of eerie retribution to the high holiday Judaism of the marginally devout.

In an unrestful sea, even romantic-eyed visitors detected only patches of surface calm.

His black coat, his long black beard, his rounded shoulders, the Hebrew curls at his temples, indelibly mark his place in the heterogeneous life of the streets. He can be seen walking with serene countenance in the midst of this seething caldron of modern life as unscathed as Shadrach, Meshach and Abednego in the fiery furnace of Nebuchadnezzar, and with as profound a faith in the watchfulness of a personal God.

But the silhouettes of old Jews in long straight surtouts and high fur caps that charmed East Side reporters beat a perpetual retreat.[5]

Melancholy indeed was the state of the rabbinate. Loosed from its moorings, the function of the honored magistrate and interpreter of the Law was at best attenuated and limited largely to ritual questions. Even when the will availed, the New World mocked all efforts at transplantation. Instead, self-styled religious functionaries proliferated. These professionally observant "reverends," essentially "performers of matrimony," were ridiculed in the theaters as "rabbis for business only," Hutchins Hapgood observed. "Mere adventurers get into the position—men good for nothing . . . They clap a high hat on their heads, impose on a poor congregation with their up-to-dateness and become rabbis without learning or piety." Enlightened scholars like Moses Reicherson, the Hebrew grammarian, and Abraham H. Rosenberg, the compiler of a projected multivolume *Cyclopedia of Hebrew Literature*, hobbled along unhonored and unknown. Where the premises of life were so changed, comely Old World wisdom wore thin.

Rabbi Jacob Joseph's sad fate provides the most striking example of the fall of the rabbinate. In 1887 an association of downtown congregations invited the Vilna rabbi to fill the grandiosely conceived office of Chief Rabbi at a handsome annual salary of $2500 with an additional $1000 for rent, furnishings, and utilities. The association chose Joseph primarily to oversee the chaos of ritual slaughtering and to lend religious prestige to downtown's conglomerate Jewries. But recollections of the hated *korobka* (Russian meat tax), the slander of rabbinical rivals, zealots, and journalists, the animosities of conflicting Jewries, and the resentment even of mild authority brought disaster. The fancy title of Chief Rabbi was powerless to conceal the sterility of Joseph's role. Bewilderment, crippling illness, and indifference soon relegated the scholarly rabbi to an obscurity relieved only by the great show of public mourning at his funeral in 1902. Only in 1911 did a concerted effort bring a semblance of order to *kashrut* (dietary laws) supervision. By then, the immigrant community was beginning to regain its balance.[6]

THE SOCIAL IDEAL

As once reliable guides lost in influence, and traditional sources in consolation, Russian-speaking students, in the throes of emancipation, assumed leadership of the immigrant community. As New World air ruffled Old World confidences, and evasions of religious prescriptions demoralized, these folk preachers

and teachers of the new replaced the "ever moaning pious Jews
who continually complain of their fate but do nothing about
practical matters." To perplexed folk, fearful of the world
about, these soothsayers spoke with arresting voice. They ranted,
inspired, and moralized in newspapers and periodicals and on
theater and lecture platforms. They ventured into politics, organized Jewish unions, and ennobled life by affording the dis-
inherited a glimpse into the heritage of the ages. They saw in
the labor movement an instrument for redeeming Jews from
humiliating occupations, for straightening ghetto-bent backs,
and for refashioning the downtrodden into men equal in spirit
as well as in law with other men. "Neither wealthier nor more
pious but more of a man," was the cause they championed for
their fellow immigrants.[7]

The student reformers formed the sole link to a new world of
learning and social righteousness. They felt themselves at the
brink of a new era. In one swoop as it were, men stood liberated,
naked of yesterdays, aching for tomorrows fertile with limitless
possibilities for human fulfillment in a world quit of ignorance,
superstition, and despotism. Extolling individual rights, they
welcomed new forms of social action and expression. They unfurled the banners of common brotherhood on the highest
plane of social idealism and pledged heart and mind to the
promise of a new life, to the betterment of mankind and the
world. Detached from familiar patterns, many enlightenment-
obsessed pioneers, like their eighteenth century archetype, Solomon Maimon, underwent harrowing inner crises in their soli-
tary wanderings across strange lands before reaching the New
World. Driven by hunger, self-doubt, and loneliness, a few lost
balance, and in the abyss between past and present, slipped into
the embrace of Christian missionaries. Vilna-born political exile and early social visionary Aaron Lieberman, crushed and
alone in Syracuse in 1880, died by his own hand. At his side lay
his last despairing *feuilleton*, "Der Dollar," dedicated to his
spirit's New World nemesis.

More fortunate were those students who came in company in
the 1880's. Like the Russian Narodnik intellectuals, they idealized the United States and believed that the agricultural com-

mune could best be realized on American soil. But after disastrous experiences that ranged from Sicily Island, Louisiana
to New Odessa, Oregon, Herman Rosenthal, Paul Kaplan, and
their fellow Am Olam (Eternal People) colonists forsook the
agrarian life for New York's tenements. There these idealists,
still wearing their blue student blouses and caps, formed Russian-speaking communes; they were joined by stray Bilu adherents who had endured the trials of pioneer farming in fevered Palestinian marshes, would-be students squeezed out of
Russian schools by quotas, and young folk who had tarried in
European universities before migrating. These genteel sons and
daughters of Odessa, Kiev, and Vilna experimented with cooperative living and even formed a cooperative laundry. For a
time the Tolstoyan anarcho-communist William Frey, a member of the New York Russian colony and a leader of the New
Odessa commune, inspired a vogue for vegetarianism and the
religion of humanity. Frey's saintliness and dedication to paci-
fism evoked genuine admiration. But immigrant idealists, ever
warm with the Russian struggle for freedom, looked to more
immediately relevant social ideals.[8]

Drunk with the vision of liberty, restless minds fumbled with
wisps of socialism and anarchism, positivism and the religion of
humanity, Ethical Culture, and a medley of social ideals that
promised a key to the universe. Emptied of the religious securities of their fathers, they inhaled the bracing vapors of ethical
and intellectual controversy. Devoutly they clutched for the
hope of modern ideas and the promise of a regenerate society.

Intellectuals turned to German sources of inspiration. They
identified European civilization and the advances of modern society with German culture, and accepted Karl Marx, modern
Germany's greatest prophet, and his disciples as their own. "As
Moses' teachings spread to the Jews of the world from Jerusalem, so Berlin radiated socialist tuition to all the nations," recorded Abraham Cahan. At hand on the German East Side, big
Justus Schwab's 1st Street saloon gathered radicals of all hues
and many nations. The Socialist daily *New Yorker Volks-Zeitung,* edited by the Russo-German aristocrat Serge Schevitch,
and Johann Most's anarchist *Freiheit* supplied lively contacts

with the most advanced European social ideas. In the new Russian colony, the exiled Schevitch at last found an audience to which he might lecture in his native tongue.

The nascent Yiddish labor and socialist movement drew upon this congenial Central European milieu for its ideas, practices, and nomenclature. Their party branches were called "sektions"; their trade unions, "gewerkschaften"; the party members, "genossen." The names of newspapers and periodicals also paid tribute to German models. And the fraternal Workmen's Circle faithfully copied the constitution of the Arbeiter Kranken und Sterbe Kasse (Workmen's Sickness and Death Fund). Although German in form, the appeal of socialism lay in its universalism, in the moral majesty of its social critique, in the messianism of a message that welcomed all men regardless of race or creed into the community of mankind. The impressiveness of its learning, the spirit of brotherhood that it communicated, the optimism and ethical appeal that promised "an enlightened and blessed time," were irresistible.[9]

The socialists felt an urgent need to master English in order to fulfill their educational mission among native Americans. As early as 1883 two former Russian university students, though hardly conversant with either Yiddish or English, compiled the first Yiddish-English study book by transcribing the English and transliterating the German of Ollendorf's standard German-English manual. In the same year, Nicholas Aleinikoff and Abraham Cahan were hired to teach English to immigrants at the Young Men's Hebrew Association reading room. Somewhat later, Morris Hillquit, Philip Kranz, and Louis Miller welcomed a three-dollar weekly stipend for conducting twice-weekly two-hour sessions at the city's Vandewater School. To Yiddish immigrants, English was more than the language of their adopted land. It was the gateway to the modern spirit. The English word tugged at freshly awakened Talmudic students "with a kind of impure force" that promised to unloose forbidden continents of knowledge, bewitching non-Jewish mysteries. They were "in a fervor of impatience to inhale the whole of the Gentile language—definitions, spelling, pronunciation and all —with one desperate effort. It was the one great impediment" which seemed to stand between "them and the enchanted new world that had revealed itself" to their vision.[10]

Immigrants for whom the portals of enlightenment remained shut because they were unable to make the leap into the higher English world of the mind could turn to the printed word in the Yiddish vernacular. The modern spirit informed Yiddish magazines and newspapers with a zest for learning. A vestibule to broadened horizons, the *New Yorker Yiddishe Volks-Zeitung* proclaimed its motto, "science, liberty, organization"; the *Volks-advocat* dedicated its pages to "science, civilization and justice"; the *Zukunft* emblazoned "science, literature and socialism" on its masthead; and the *Nayer Gayst,* "a monthly for science, literature and art," announced itself "a school for every reader who wants to look at the world with open eyes."

The pioneer *Zukunft,* aiming to reconstruct the social mind of a people, proved the most ambitious venture in the democracy of the higher learning. The credo of the first Yiddish monthly dedicated to the new knowledge spoke to the mission that animated its editors.

We announce quite frankly, we will not conceal this fact from anyone. We are undertaking to publish a scientific journal in jargon —a novelty in the indigent jargon literature—only as an experiment. The Jewish labor movement is growing very rapidly and is developing workmen who want to learn about the social question of our time and to become cultured generally; but alas, they can not do so because until recently only old wives' tales and doggerel were written in jargon and they are unfamiliar with other languages or know too little.

Socialism was to be the handmaiden of enlightenment, the *Zukunft* declared:

The workman must know more than how he is oppressed economically and swindled politically and what to do in order to cast off the capitalistic chains. He must also understand how mankind attained its present level, how it lived earlier and how it developed. We want him to understand Darwin's teachings about the struggle for existence equally with Karl Marx's theory of surplus value; we want him to understand the origins and development of religion equally with the origins of private property; we desire . . . that he also know all matters relating to it and correctly understand why the ABC is so designed and not otherwise.

Upon its fifth anniversary, its editor proudly announced that although only thirty-two issues of the *Zukunft* had appeared, it was still the world's only popular scientific Yiddish periodical, amazing enlightened Jews in Russia hitherto unable to conceive that physics, astronomy, and Marx's teachings could be explained in the "vulgar mother tongue." [11]

As Liberty Hall and Liberty pharmacy proclaimed the East Side's dominant passion, so Psalm 113 in Feigenbaum's parody became a hymn to the liberty of the spirit:

Hallelujah—Praise, O ye honest people, praise the name of Liberty. Blessed be the name of Liberty from this time forth and forevermore. From East to West the name of Liberty is to be praised. She hath risen high above all nations, unto the heavens hath she reached. She hath ascended heaven and driven away the Gods, hath come down on earth and broken the chains. She raiseth up the friendless out of the dust, the needy she lifteth up from the dunghill.[12]

Article-length biographies with pen-and-ink drawings of the heroes who struggled for freedom through the ages flashed through succeeding issues of the *Zukunft*. First came Karl Marx and Frederick Engels. Then followed Robert Owen and Charles Fourier, Francis Babeuf and Peter Lavrov, William Liebknecht and William Morris, Ferdinand Lasalle and Aaron Lieberman. Month after month, in frontispiece and leading article, marched the architects of a new world order—Wendell Phillips and John Brown, Giuseppi Mazzini and Victor Hugo, Henry Hyndman and Thomas More, Baruch Spinoza and Thomas Paine, Lewis H. Morgan and Saint Simon, Pestalozzi and Lessing, Shelley and Shakespeare. And interspersed among them, the growing number of martyrs and prophets of a free Russia and a free world.

Literature and literary criticism went hand-in-hand, instruments dedicated to a social morality that aimed to enlighten man. "To candidly criticize a work that ought to educate men is the most sacred duty of every honest publicist," affirmed an early Yiddish literary journal. Abraham Cahan, in introducing Mendele and Sholem Aleichem to *Zukunft* readers, assessed their works in terms of their social relevance and authenticity to life, and found them wanting. "True art and true logic coincide . . . As scientific psychology is still undeveloped, the truly good novel takes the place of science in relation to man's soul and character." [13] Verse without a social purpose was alien to the morally intense modern East Side. The song of propaganda, of agitation and lamentation, was front page copy in the radical press. In rasping hymns, Abraham Cahan and the pseudonymous "psalmist" Morris Hillquit denounced capitalism and the world's many evils. Morris Winchevsky's faithful Yiddish rendition of "The Song of the Shirt" that preceded him across the Atlantic from London, and Morris Rosenfeld's tenement-heartbreak balladry entered the precincts of poetry.[14]

Radicals, in their efforts to loosen the grip of custom and to free men for thought and action in the everyday struggle for the world of common brotherhood, cast the naked light of modern biblical criticism, evolutionary theory, and comparative religion upon miracles, the biblical timetable, and Pentateuchal prescriptions. "Religions are empty fantasies," Philip Kranz wrote. "We have none of the accepted beliefs regarded as religious. We do not believe in the God who negotiated with Moses our preacher." Simple Reb Nehemiah in Cahan's story, "The Apostate of Chego-Chegg," experienced a fierce awakening. "I had ears but could not hear, because of my ear-locks; I had eyes and could not see because they were closed in prayer . . . I am Rabbi Nehemiah no longer, they call me Nehemiah the atheist now." [15]

So-called anarchists were especially dedicated to the task of unfrocking traditional beliefs. In 1889, on the eve of the awe-inspiring Jewish New Year, the Pioneers of Freedom, a small Russian-speaking group founded in 1886 (on the eve of the Day of Atonement following the sentencing of the Haymarket martyrs) , distributed antireligious tracts in the form of mock penitential prayers. These proclaimed that prior to the Babylonian exile, Jews knew of no "Judgment Day," that monotheism evolved from fetishism, that from the conflict of competing gods arose the "Trust God." Indeed, these tracts insisted that God had never existed and, drawing upon Robert Ingersoll's "Mistakes of Moses," that Jehovah was an Egyptian God and Moses an Egyptian priest. Uptown Jews tried in vain to dissuade from intemperate outbursts the disenchanted revolting against the weight of the past. Youngsters, separated from family and kin, to whose sensibilities they would have deferred, openly travestied the Day of Atonement. A ticket to a Yom Kippur ball read:

Grand Yom Zom Kippur Ball with theatre. Arranged with the consent of all new rabbis of liberty. Kol Nidre Night and Day in the year 6851 (5651), after the invention of the Jewish idols, and 1890, after the birth of the false Messiah . . . The Kol Nidre will be offered by John Most. Music, dancing, buffet, Marseillaise and other hymns against Satan.[16]

David Edelstadt, a former Russian university student and editor of the *Freie Arbeiter Shtimme*, assailed religious traditions and institutions for dividing men. His "Anti-Religion," dedicated to the "Defenders of Darkness," closed with a call to liberation:

Börne, Lasalle, Marx
Will deliver us from the diaspora
The world will recognize no distinctions
All will be free, whether Turk, Christian or Jew
Every age has its sacred message
Ours is freedom and justice.

Another early anarchist insisted that barriers among men would vanish only when "the general social question" was resolved, when "a society is established where the designations: Jew, Christianity, nation, and belief will disappear . . . when the bright sun of civilization will liberate all mankind . . . when national and racial differences will become problems for the scientists." [17]

Yet, Jewish ethical perceptions went uncontested. Reacting fanatically against his narrow Hasidic Warsaw youth, Benjamin Feigenbaum sought humanist sanctions for Jewish ethics. This ardent Jewishly learned pamphleteer, unlike his religiously un-

lettered facile fellow radicals, saw no necessary connection between morality and religion. Yet, however, radical were Feigenbaum's ideas about God, the universe, and the economic basis
of society, this archantagonist of Jewish religious conceit championed the Pentateuch's social laws as vital for mankind's ethical
development. He acknowledged the proverbial integrity of Jewish family life, but attributed its virtues to long experience
rather than to religiously prescribed moral codes. However critical of Jewish marriage and divorce customs, however insistent
that ideally only love and affection between true equals sanctified marriage, Feigenbaum warned that in an imperfect world,
forebearance and consideration for others were still the ultimate
virtues. Furthermore, this antireligious firebrand did not doubt
the wisdom of Jewish sexual codes when compared with those of
Christianity.

At times the more ingenuous entertained wild notions about
the relations between the sexes. But radicals, surrounded by
representatives of a secure moral order and imbued with the
Jewish family ethos, consummated their passions in talk and projected the ideal state of human relations into the distant future.
Indeed, in the late 1880's a medical student's clinical discourse
on the procreative organs shocked a mixed audience of young
iconoclasts. Respectful of learning yet unable to face one another for shame, they grimly held their seats to the end for fear
of appearing old-fashioned. Emma Goldman stood alien to
the Russian radical community in her defiance of delicate conventions as in her anarchic individualism. At the New Odessa
commune in Oregon, radicals looked askance upon the few
dalliers in free love. So tenacious were men's habits of behavior
in a tradition that did not admit apostasy, that even avowed free
thinkers abstained from breaking the proscription against utter-
ing the Hebrew word for God.[18]

Intellectuals, enamored of the Marxist analysis, conceded that
the socialist message, in its noble simplicity, might easily be
memorized by all. But to be a full-fledged socialist, insisted the
Zukunft, required learning and an understanding of such ab-
stractions as "class," "capitalist exploitation," and "political
struggle." Yet if the terminology of socialism evaded Jewish folk,

they responded to its beatitudes and apocalyptic vision. A workman in quest of a full Sabbath day's fare recorded:

One Friday, going home from work and considering what paper to buy, I noticed a new Yiddish paper with the name *Arbeiter Zeitung*. I bought it and began to read it, and remarkable, this was the thing I wanted. It was the first Yiddish, socialist newspaper. Although till then I never heard about socialism and its doctrine, still I understood it without any interpretation. I liked it because its ideas were hidden in my heart and in my soul long ago; only I could not express them clearly . . . That paper preached, "Happiness for everyone"; this has always been my ardent desire; it preached "peaceful development," excellent. I always liked peace. It said that "new changes for the betterment of the people could be reachd by free and decent speech, and free and decent press." This I could sign with my both hands. What person with common sense could deny them? [19]

Invariably, the popular Yiddish socialist press packaged its message to suit the habits of mind of its readers. Scriptural invocations and preambles and the prophecies of Isaiah and Jeremiah gilded didactic texts, almost Talmudic in their tortuousness. In the *Arbeiter Zeitung,* the "sedra," the "proletarian preacher's" mock discourse equivalent of the weekly portion of the Pentateuch, appealed to ordinary folk for whom prayers had been numbed by ritual reiteration, yet who yearned for rejuvenated affirmations of social justice uttered in the name of God and Moses and the prophets. The earliest Yiddish socialist brochure, *Di geula,* "Redemption," translated by the author as "remedy," fixed the tone of the socialist message on the Lower East Side. It closed with Isaiah's message of universalism: "Then there will be no rich and no poor, no poverty and no diaspora, no Jew and no Christian . . . only equal, blessed and contented folk."

In the holiday season, the prophetic message sounded with preternatural intensity. On Pentecost eve 1886 Abraham Cahan compared the socialist message to the giving of the Law on Mount Sinai. A Passover eve colloquy identified the Day of Deliverance, the Messianic coming, with the social Revolution. Israel's liberation from the Egyptian yoke symbolized the liberation of humanity, as predicted by Isaiah. Hence, Jews were urged to join with "oppressed mankind" in "the sacred struggle." [20]

On the eve of the Penitential Days in 1890 the imminence of a new era for mankind was proclaimed with apocalyptic starkness:

The Day of Atonement nears . . . Dark clouds hang low. Soon the terrible storm will begin that will destroy the rulers with their ugly cart and liberate the harnessed slaves; the storm clearing away the mountains of human bones will make way for the gleaming edifice of brotherly love, of eternal liberty, of equality, of endless bliss. The angel of death of capitalism stands poised. On the threshold waits the angel of light.

"All Israel has a share in the world to come" was given a worldly gloss by the "Talmudical Socialist." "All Israel" meant "the fighters who were struggling for the destruction of the oppressors." "The world to come" was interpreted as "progress."

In 1894 in the midst of the depression, the international May Day dawned with the thunder of the Tishbite.

It is five years now since the new prophet Elijah, the May Day fete, has appeared on the world scene with his grand *shofar* [ram's horn], with the rousing revolutionary song, the Marseillaise. It is five years since the prophet Elijah has come forth to proclaim to the world that very soon the day of liberation, the judgment day will come, the day that will straighten out all that is crooked, that will raise the despised, wipe the tears from the miserable, refresh the languishing. [21]

For the political labor movement, East Side socialists envisioned the highest ethical mission, "to create the history of civilization in its true sense . . . to disseminate the principle of cooperation—of social communal work in all sectors of human life." Upon learning of the great St. Petersburg strike in 1896, the United Hebrew Trades of New York sent its warmest greetings "to our Russian brothers."

In this strike we see the beginning of the end of Russian tyranny and of the Russian chains; the beginning of the struggle which will abolish in Russia the difference between a Hebrew and a Christian,

Russian and German, which will destroy the wall that separates man from man and class from class; which will forever make an end to the rifle and the dagger, and establish forever Freedom, Equality and Fraternity.

Many a sweatshop laborer embraced the socialist message with the piety with which he performed his devotional exercises. In the depths of the depression, workmen sold 10,000 copies of an invocatory issue of the *Arbeiter Zeitung*. At the founding of the *Forward* at Walhalla Hall in 1897, workmen filled collection plates with love offerings of prized pocket watches, watch chains, and personal jewelry. Abraham Cahan recalled: "If ever there was a paper supported by the holy spirit—upon holy inspiration —it was ours." [22]

Yet in the late 1890's social speculation, soaring to spheres of unreality and messianism brought disillusion in its wake. Radical sectaries, wedded to intellectual positions bled of life, became engaged in a war of words that dissipated energies, divided loyalties, and alienated sympathies. The Yiddish DeLeonist daily denounced the Spanish-American War as a "capitalist war" and viewed the fate of Captain Alfred Dreyfus, a "capitalist" and a "bourgeois," as a matter of no concern to socialists. But Jewish workmen regarded the land of the Inquisition and the auto-da-fé as unworthy of their sympathy; the Cubans, an oppressed folk like themselves; and the war, a grand humanitarian venture, testing their newly acquired American patriotism. At the Educational Alliance nine hundred recent Russian immigrants enrolled as [army] volunteers, and East Side lads were prominent among New York's "Rough Riders." Alfred Dreyfus stood as a symbol of man's intolerance to man. Verily the *Abendblatt* had fallen on evil days when it strove to undermine the *Forward* by denouncing Dr. Isaac A. Hourwich as a Russian *agent provocateur*. [23]

Although sectarian fanaticism and self-righteousness smoldered after enthusiasm had vanished, the turn of the century brought vast change. Broadened horizons relaxed the extremist Russian mental set. With growing prosperity tempers softened. The demands and exertions of everyday business activity in the immigrant community left little time for speculation. Many of the most articulate, having completed their professional studies, became absorbed with their daily routines. Joseph Barondess, formerly a popular labor leader and now a busy insurance agent, no longer was interested in dispensing "science before an audience." "Until the Ideal Society will be realized, I have certain duties to perform towards my clients, for which they pay." Older visionaries, chastened by experience, adjusted their ideals to realities and conceded that the evils of the existing system obscured the accompanying blessings.[24]

Abraham Cahan, the editor of the *Forward,* summed up the essentials of the new socialism. "The *Forward* is the workingmen's organ in their every righteous fight against their oppressors; this struggle is the body of our movement. But its soul is the liberation of mankind—justice, humanity, fraternity—in brief, honest common sense and horse sense." Cahan, fresh from his experiences with Lincoln Steffens on the *Commercial Advertiser,* temporarily sidelined the most eloquent and unreconstructed orators and phrasemakers, tapering Marx's postulates to measure. In principle, labor was still the source of all value and rent was robbery. But in practice, the *Forward* acknowledged that so long as the capitalist system prevailed, it was advisable to deal with "honest landlords" and admittedly there were some. Indeed, in October 1901 the Yiddish press, including the socialist *Forward,* carried a full-page advertisement beckoning readers to invest in the Utopian Land Company and other capitalistic ventures.

Oil land in California—Treasures more precious than gold. Mines abounding with treasures . . . an opportunity for every man to participate in the venture which made the Standard Oil Company. Oil and land as an investment. Dividends the first of January, 1902. You need no broker . . . If you do not read English you may . . . speak your mother tongue . . . You will be answered in Yiddish and all details will be given you in Yiddish.[25]

The dogmatic categories that ascribed all virtue to the workman and all wickedness to the employer were scanned with a jaundiced eye. "We idealize the working class a bit too much," confessed a *Forward* editorial. Labor-backed San Francisco

Mayor Schmitz's enthusiasm for boxing and the behavior of "the aristocrats of labor," the Hoe machinists, at Rabbi Joseph's funeral, were proof enough of labor's failings. The *Forward* advertised the "capitalist" Constitution in a ten-cent Yiddish translation as "the little torah," (Pentateuch) , "the highroad to citizenship, employment, and success." If the class theory did not apply to individuals, nevertheless, justice and righteousness resided with labor. Workmen remained "the teachers of the people" and a socialist employer was honor-bound to treat his employees more generously than did his fellows. The *Forward* presented a gold fountain pen to the workman who submitted this definition of a "scab": "When God created a scab, he took the legs of a horse, the head of an ass, the face of a dog, the hair from a hog, the heart of a hare, combined them, and out came a scab." [26]

At the turn of the century philosophical anarchists, "a gentle and idealistic body of men," viewed their youthful fulminations with nostalgic unbelief. "Which comrade's heart does not beat more rapidly when he recalls the flaming enthusiasm of those times, when the neediest would give away his last cent to support" our newspaper. The editor of the revived *Freie Arbeiter Shtimme* avowed that anarchists had become more practical. "They realized that the world was laughing at their Don Quixotic demands." Now, all that anarchists pleaded for, he insisted, was "just a bit of honesty." Horrified by the assassination of McKinley by a fellow radical, the anarchist editor protested that anarchism's first principle called for "peace among men." Aghast at the hysterical press outcry and the virtual destruction of the *Freie Arbeiter Shtimme* office by Jewish rowdies, Saul Yanovsky, the anarchist paper's editor, refused to share the same platform with Emma Goldman. The anarchist message, however, did not lose its savor for the disciples of Peter Kropotkin. "Read these words with love . . . Plant these truths wherever you can. Every slave is a man, and every man is a hero when his weapon is love and truth . . . With these weapons there must be a free new world." [27]

SOCIALISM AND JUDAISM

Since its founding, the Russian-speaking colony had shared vicariously in the struggle for a free Russia. As early as 1880 Narodnaya Volya had despatched Leo Hartmann, a non-Jew, to the United States to create good will for the "Russian abolitionists." Hartmann and the earliest Jewish Narodnik, Leo Goldenberg, subsequently editor of *Free Russia* for the Friends of Russian Freedom, founded the Russian-American National League in 1887 and along with Robert Ingersoll and Father McGlynn protested the pending Russian-American Extradition Treaty. The Samarazvitia—a Russian educational society—the Red Cross group, the Grinevetsky society, the Russian Labor Club, the *bruderliche hilfe fur di russishe politishe,* and the Russian Social Democratic Society assisted Russian revolutionaries and political exiles in Western Europe.[28]

Yet by the early years of the twentieth century the Russian struggle had receded to the fringes of the Russian colony's concerns. In the colony's calendar of sacred days, November 11, commemorating the martyrs of Chicago's Haymarket Riot, shared a special place with the March 13 anniversary of the Russian revolutionists of 1881. Russian-speaking immigrants helped fill the Great Hall at Cooper Union to overflowing in 1896 to honor the memory of Sergius Stepniak, founder of the Friends of Russian Freedom, and revolutionary martyr. And throughout these years, members of the Russian colony posted their social and business notices in the Yiddish press in the Russian that proclaimed them the East Side's spiritual elite. At annual New Year's Day balls, nostalgic for the days of yore, they sang Russian songs, made socialist speeches, toasted the Russian struggle for freedom, and made the rafters ring with huzzahs for the martyrs in Schlusselberg prison and Siberia. Then, in the early hours they slipped back to their workaday pursuits for another year.[29]

Then in 1903 the dream of revolution began to take on an almost unbelievable reality as nightmarish episodes roused the Russian colony to an unprecedented pitch of excitement. The Yiddish newspapers, their front pages bristling with banner headlines, daily reported on the Russian struggle for freedom and the havoc wreaked upon fellow Jews, their own families and fellow townsmen. The press, detailing massacre upon massacre and outrage upon outrage, memorialized the dead and the maimed and lauded the courage of revolutionaries. "Our holy land has become sacred through the martyrdom of Russia's fighters for freedom. Siberia is our holy land," blazed a *Forward* headline. An annual memorial service paid tribute to the martyred Vilna cobbler, Hirsh Leckert, while Sasanov's assassination of the ruthless von Plehve seemed to augur the final destruction of Russian tyrants. In July 1905 a Yiddish Sappho saluted her Old World cousins for their heroic stand and in November the Yiddish press exulted in banner headlines: "Constitution . . . Russia Becomes Completely Free." Following upon each barbaric outrage, as the human toll was recorded, processions of thousands marched with black-draped flags in bereaved protest on the Lower East Side. On December 4, 1905, 100,000 Jews paraded up Fifth Avenue to Union Square and Christian churches tolled their bells in sympathy for the mourners.

The Russian Revolution of 1905 saturated Russian-Jewish organizational life. Friends of the Bund, *lanslite* societies, Red Cross societies, Social Democratic groups, aid societies of the Social Revolutionary and Polish Socialist parties, and Self-Defense associations exerted every effort to aid endangered brethren overseas.[30]

An awakened new Russia, seeking aid, dispatched emissaries to the great New York Russian colony. In 1903 the first representatives of the Bund, Arkady Kremer and Michael Berg, arrived. In 1904 Catherine Breshkovskaya, "Grandmother of the Russian Revolution," and Chaim Zhitlowsky came as delegates of the Social Revolutionary Party, and newly arrived Bundists held their first American convention in New York, highlighted by Jacob Adler's presentation of Gordin's drama, "The Bundist," at Grand Central Palace. In 1906 Nicholas Tchaikovsky, pioneer Russian revolutionary, and the novelist Maxim Gorky came to speak for a free Russia. The ovation accorded Gorky "rivaled the welcome given to Kossuth, Hungary's champion of freedom, and Garibaldi, the father of a United Italy," reported the *New York Times*. Maxim, Liber, and Medem recounted their hair-raising escapades to overflow crowds at Cooper Union and in East Side assembly halls. Thousands listened with rapt attention to Gershuni's account of his escape from a Siberian dungeon, as romantic a tale as *The Count of Monte Cristo,* the East Side's favorite novel. At the first anniversary celebration of Red Sunday, Mother Jones and Jack London were among the speakers who addressed a vast Union Square throng.[31]

In these years the antireligion battle lost its sting. For a time, anarchist-sponsored "Yom Kippur Balls" continued to draw crowds of the curious and the newly disenchanted. But the Kishinev pogrom and succeeding massacres of Jews soon muted the tongues of iconoclasts and expounders of free thought and decimated their audiences. The *Forward* pleaded for respect for the genuinely pious. Following the Kishinev horrors, even a kaftan-attired guest clasping the Scrolls of the Law to his bosom was favorably considered for a door prize at the *Forward's* annual masquerade ball at Grand Central Palace, although "proletarian" garb was prescribed. The higher criticism lost its militancy. Even the anarchist *Freie Arbeiter Shtimme's* editor called his popular lecture "The Bright and Dark Side of Religion." The author of an article on Jewish mythology, frankly acknowledging his inability to read the Bible in the original Hebrew, asserted that his purpose was but to inform. Benjamin Feigenbaum insisted that his analytical tract, *Kosher un treif* (The Jewish Dietary Laws), was not antireligious but that every enlightened person ought to have a scientific knowledge of the subject, indeed that it was a necessity in "every enlightened home," a "shulchan aruch" (religious manual) for free thinkers.[32]

Time as well as catastrophe brought an understanding of American conditions to radicals bred to Russian extremism, "a broader comprehension . . . a humane relationship to one's self, to one's own feelings," as a *Forward* editorial put it in 1909. The *Forward* even acknowledged that problems of community responsibility made some form of cooperation among New York's Jewries desirable. Even Michael Zametkin, veteran socialist lecturer and publicist, rejected the simple socialist formula and acknowledged the delicacy and complexity of the spiritual adjustment to American life. The whole range of past emotional conditioning, attitudes to government, nationalism, and the relations between Jew and non-Jew, had to be relearned, he said. Benjamin Feigenbaum contrasted the situation in Europe, where Jews were forced to remake themselves into another nationality, with the dignified integration of Jewish workmen in the United States. Comradeship and association, rather than separation, would promote mutual respect between Jews and non-Jews. Like the various religious sects, insisted this iconoclast, Jews could remain steadfast in their Judaism, yet share in the amenities, customs, dress, politics, business, and language of other Americans.[33]

Although veteran socialists continued to adhere to the broad humanitarian ideals of socialism, expositors of Marxian intricacies relinquished their role to newcomers. In 1906 Abraham Cahan abandoned his role as a Marxist exegete after rendering a textual word-by-word commentary and translation of the first chapter of *Kapital* in the early issues of the *Zeitgeist*. In 1909 veteran socialist Jacob Milch, who had risen to become a prosperous sugar refiner, founded the *Naye Welt*, "devoted to the study of American life and institutions" from the viewpoint of "historical materialism." But he confessed the exceeding difficulty of popularizing Marx, and after two or three issues Milch gave up the ghost.[34]

After the turn of the century the rising nationalisms of Eastern Europe re-echoed upon American shores in Jewish form. The spirit of utopian socialism and redemptive nationalism cohabited in every conceivable ideological combination. Brandishing the torches of diverse millenarianisms, Bundists, Zionists, and Territorialists, Zionist-Socialists and Socialist-Territorialists, Poale Zion and Social Revolutionary-Territorialists, vied for adherents. Dr. Chaim Zhitlowsky, Social Revolutionary emissary, urged that Yiddish be proclaimed the Jewish national tongue and advocated a socialistically oriented Jewish autonomism in a hypothetical commonwealth formed by the "United Peoples of the United States." Unlike Zhitlowsky, earlier radicals had regarded Yiddish as a necessary makeshift and group differences—except for those based on religion—a transient state arising from distinctions between the "green" and the "yellow," the newcomers and the Americanized. Even the emigré Ber Borochev viewed the United States as a "nationally-indifferent state." Seasoned radicals who recalled the temper of Jewish election that had possessed the socialism of the nineties, found Zhitlowsky's ideas startlingly un-Jewish. Yet for a time, Zhitlowsky's *Naye Lebn* stood second in prestige only to the *Zukunft* among the cognoscenti. Zhitlowsky's distinguished bearing, personal magnetism, intellectual gifts, oratorical power, and publicistic talents gained him many admirers, if few disciples. In 1910 Zhitlowsky published the first book on philosophy in Yiddish, as if to quash doubts as to the vernacular's dialectical capacities.

More pervasive in influence, however, was the purely literary nationalism that received its finest expression in the labors of Solomon Bloomgarden, known as "Yehoash." In 1910 Yehoash, who had rendered Longfellow's "Hiawatha" into lyrical Yiddish four years earlier, completed sensitive Yiddish renditions of Isaiah, Job, the Song of Songs, Ruth, and Ecclesiastes. In so doing, he began a life work that led to the translation of the Bible into a masterful Yiddish, that gave dignity to the vernacular and that opened the sacred books to the unlearned. In collaboration with Dr. Charles Spivak in 1911, Yehoash compiled a dictionary that collated the Hebrew elements of Yiddish, in part product of, in part preparation for, his lifelong labors.[35]

For most Jewish socialists, although often unaware of it, socialism was Judaism secularized. To Abraham Cahan socialism was a religion, "the poetry of the oppressed miserable workman." Lyricized the *Forward's* editor in 1910: "The spiritual cheer which this ideal creates . . . is a divine reward . . . a reward that Judaism promises the righteous in the world to come but which laboring humanity attains in this world." The new socialist *Evening Call,* underwritten by the *Forward,* was hailed by the Yiddish socialist daily as a true harbinger of a free press. As the *Arbeiter Zeitung* had beseeched its Yiddish-reading audience to support the *People* seventeen years earlier, so the

Forward implored its subscribers to purchase this new English Socialist paper as their "sacred duty"; if they knew no English, they were duty-bound to persuade their children to read the *Call*. In the same vein, the *Forward* greeted the new Rand School, "the socialist yeshiva . . . where the rabbis and teachers of our movement" were being prepared, as a beacon of social enlightenment.[36]

Humanitarianism, brotherhood, and progress with its socialist and Judaic glow flowed on in Yiddish New York. To the holidays of the Jewish calendar were added Labor Day and May Day, the Fourth of July and the exciting weeks before Election Day. With festivities and marching bands, the recitation of hymns of hope and elegies of despair, history became earnest and real. Each passing year recorded the forward march of progress, the anniversaries of the French Revolution, and Paris Commune, and the martyred assassins of Alexander II. At home and closer in time, the Haymarket victims, the Hazelton and Colorado miners, Moyer, Haywood, and Pettibone, and the "Children of Lawrence," aroused an instinctive philanthropy, compassion, and identification. When in August 1908 anti-Negro violence reached a climax of blood-letting at Springfield, Illinois, the Yiddish dailies responded with banner headlines and editorials ringing with indignation and disbelief, terming the riots "the Pogrom in Springfield."

Every incident and event in the struggle for freedom had to be dramatized and extolled, marked by a song, an essay, or a debate that greeted the unfolding world of human brotherhood rising out of an anguished present and an even darker past. Even local merchants' advertisements echoed dissent and dissatisfaction with the dismal state of the world. Read an advertisement in the *Forward* in November, 1897: "A Protest Meeting—All are invited to gather at 81 Delancey Street. Express your protest against the present cold by purchasing good warm gloves." At Cooper Union and Union Square, at rented East Side halls and upon unrented sidewalks, the world's prophets of progress and representatives of the downtrodden passed in endless procession. Emissaries of revolution and the victims of injustice pleaded their causes to overflow audiences. Finally, annual rent strikes, led by the Ladies' Anti-Beef Trust Association, and seasonal labor revolts kept the Lower East Side in continual turmoil.[37]

In the Fourth of July, the *Forward* found the highest expression of liberty's promise. "It is our holiday. And it gives us confidence and hope. It shows us that that which is not can be and what even drags out can come. It shows us that the thought of freedom is the beginning of true freedom." [38]

Magnificent righteous discontent that rocketed to spheres of absurdity was inevitable under the pressures of so great an awakening on the tenement-sweatshop frontier. These were the unavoidable excesses of noble aspirations. The Lower East Side's reverence for life and learning and the dignity of man's spirit were finding broad channels for self-expression that were recasting the minds of small-town Jewries. In so doing, Jewish immigrants forged their spirit and experience into the American pattern.

Part Four

LEARNING A NEW SOCIAL ETHIC

∽ 9 ∽

Labor's Dilemma

What is a strike if not a battle among people who should be
living like brothers? Is not every strike a sign that our society is deathly sick?   *Arbeiter Zeitung* (1890)

In the final decades of the nineteenth century organized labor
was only beginning to find a means to survival. Varied living
standards and craft vanities, added to the antipathies of skilled
and unskilled, native and immigrant, made labor cooperation
a continual trial. East European Jews shared organized labor's
predicament in the 1880's and 1890's and responded to labor's
ideals and enthusiasms. But their segregation in the apparel industries and their individualism placed them on the periphery
of labor's triumphs until the close of the first decade of the
twentieth century.

SURVIVAL OF THE FITTEST

Labor rights, in the early 1880's were virtually unknown in
law and were beyond the concern of public opinion. Before
1883 New York's labor laws proved worse than valueless.

Every legislative measure calculated to improve the condition of
the working people has been stubbornly resisted at every step from
incipiency to completion. Never was a labor bill allowed to pass in
the form which its originators had deemed essential to the object in
view. When it could not be killed outright, it was so amended as to
defeat its chief purpose, or even so emasculated as to render it not
only useless, but possibly harmful and odious to those for the benefit
of whom it was primarily intended.

At best, trade unions persisted on sufferance. With wages, hours, and working conditions fixed by custom and the market, the workman's bargaining position remained weak. The vicissitudes of the economy, industry's changing character, the immigrant flow, and the heavy penalties inflicted upon union men curtailed labor organization. Of 232 New York City labor unions in 1900, many essentially benevolent societies, only 45 antedated 1880.[1]

In the early 1870's veterans of the North American Central Committee of the International Workingmen's Association, after failing to unite German and English-speaking unionists, organized a central trades assembly of skilled workmen. But the depression and bitter employer opposition sent union membership in the city careening down from 44,000 to 5000 dues payers and destroyed the assembly. Union activity revived as economic conditions improved and in 1882 workingmen founded the all-embracing Central Labor Union at a Cooper Union protest gathering called to voice sympathy for Ireland's oppressed peasantry. On Sundays, at the CLU's Donnybrook gatherings, valiant spirits strove "to organize the day laborer with the skilled mechanic, ignoring those prejudices which are more deeply rooted in the working people as a class than in almost any other body of people in the nation," testified Edward King before a committee of the Senate. In 1885, when the Knights of Labor was at its peak, the impulse to organize all workmen caught hold; New York's District Assembly 49 of the Knights, with 60,000 members, accounted for half the delegates to the Central Labor Union. In that turbulent year, the CLU succeeded in persuading the state legislature to make Labor Day a legal holiday.[2]

In 1886, depression, mass unemployment, and strike failures propelled labor into politics, driving the CLU to disregard a resolve of the previous year that "our experience in Independent Political Action has not only been ridiculous but disgraceful." The eight-hour-day demonstrations, the Haymarket massacre, the defeat of Gladstone's Irish Home Rule bill, and the imprisonment and conviction of the boycotters of Theiss' beer garden in New York plunged the Central Labor Union into a frenzy. At a Cooper Union mass meeting, labor leaders John

Swinton, Edward King, and John McMackin called for political action. Germans and Irish, trade unionists and socialists, skilled and unskilled, Single Taxers and Greenbackers, Samuel Gompers and Terence Powderly, fastened on the United Labor Party's magnetic Henry George, who appealed "to representatives of all classes of men who earn their living by the exertion of their hand and head." In the November election fraud alone thwarted the Single Taxer's bid for the mayoralty of the nation's greatest city.

The United Labor Party, however, was built on sand. Ethnic and ideological conflict soon destroyed the entente between Irish and Germans. Even amid the excitement of 1886, the Irish bond to Tammany precluded more than a feint in the direction of independent labor politics. Father McGlynn's Anti-Poverty Society generated enthusiasm, but the society's temper and auspices and McGlynn's fall from papal grace led to its decline. Socialist and anticlerical German unionists, "distinguished for their cohesiveness . . . for their disposition to gather together and hold together," made uneasy allies with the emphatically American Irish. Such exceptional Irishmen as Thomas Moran, "the most sagacious and finished debater" of the socialist Excelsior Labor Club; Patrick Doody, "one of the best known and sterling champions of every honest reform"; and Peter J. McGuire, socialist president of the Carpenters' Union and cofounder with Gompers of the American Federation of Labor were powerless to fill the gap.[3]

In the late 1880's District Assembly 49 of the crumbling Knights and the shaky AFL unions contended for members, while factious local unions maintained affiliations with both for the sake of peace. In 1889, amid charges of political corruption, the German unions seceded from the CLU and formed the Central Labor Federation. An attempt at reunion was unsuccessful, despite the CLU's compromise in adopting a socialistically worded constitution. The AFL's denial of a charter to the CLF because it harbored a Socialist Labor Party section, led a few unions to withdraw in protest and form the new Federation of Labor of New York, which in 1892 merged with the Central Labor Union.[4]

The general upheaval and George's near election brought token redress of labor's grievances, if little change in public attitudes. By the early nineties, the statute books required the labeling of convict-made goods; prohibited yellow dog contracts; and regulated female and child labor, tenement house manufacture, and the hours of labor on street, surface, and elevated railroads. An improved mechanics' lien law was passed, and a State Board of Mediation and Arbitration was set up. The first factory act also provided for the appointment of a single, meagerly paid inspector and an assistant to oversee tens of thousands of factories in the nation's greatest manufacturing state. Yet, there was "a glaring discrepancy between this abstract recognition and the actual treatment of labor organizations in the administration of the law." The antiblacklisting law remained unenforced. The courts regarded a strike for reduced hours, better treatment, sanitation, or safety appliances as a "criminal conspiracy"; only a strike for higher wages was viewed as legal. "In order to arrive at an interpretation so utterly at variance with the spirit of the age, our courts had to search the records of the early part of the century for precedents." [5] The prohibition of sympathetic strikes, according to the labor leader Frederick Sorge, drove Germans, especially those who were engaged in service trades, to resort to the boycott. "Boycott here, boycott there, boycott everywhere." In such times, the law only could be viewed by workmen as "the poor man's enemy, bestowing on him all its severity and reserving its blessings for the wealthy." [6]

In organized labor's attempts to find itself, two Jews, English-born Samuel Gompers and Hungarian-born Adolph Strasser, emerged as leaders. In the 1870's they piloted the cigarmakers' section of the International Workingmen's Association into the stormy waters of social idealism by recruiting women, unskilled bunchbreakers, and tenement workers; organizing German, Bohemian, and Hungarian sections; and establishing a cooperative store. But the dream of solidarity fast vanished. The disastrous 1877 tenement strike by ten thousand workmen, broke the union's back. In subsequent years the chastened cigarmakers proceeded cautiously. The International Cigarmakers' Union of America, revived in 1879, adhered to strict craft lines, took the English Amalgamated Society of Engineers as a model, and insisted on high dues, benefits, and mutual aid. When 3000 newly arrived German socialist cigarmakers followed Samuel Schimkowitz into Progressive Union No. 1 of the Knights of Labor in 1886 with the intent of organizing tenement labor, Strasser ended the dual union threat by persuading the Central Labor Union to amalgamate the upstart union with the International. The cigarmakers' union, with its sure sense for the arithmetic of idealism, traced out the American trade union pattern and nurtured American labor's outstanding leader and spokesman.[7]

JEWISH UNIONS

Unlike earlier Jewish immigrants, East European Jews remained isolated in the city's industry, and their isolation conditioned their relations with other workmen. They were concentrated in light manufacturing or in Jewish food and service trades, and did not compete directly with organized labor. Only for a time in the swiftly changing apparel, furniture, and cigarmaking industries did their presence lead workmen to murmur "spoiled by the Jews."

East European Jews stemmed largely from villages and towns where industry and commerce were intertwined, where economic individualism was as pervasive as social and religious cooperation. These strangers to collective economic action, inoculated with the American dream, impatiently tolerated their degradation to mere workmen. "The Jews were fairly ravenous for education and eager for personal development . . . all industrial work was merely a stepping-stone to professional or managerial positions," recalled Samuel Gompers. Yet, East European Jews proved inordinately receptive to labor's message, if not to labor organization.

On the Lower East Side the Jewish labor movement emerged out of the utopian hopes that animated the small colony of former Russian students who found themselves, in tenements and factories, "a hand of the machine, a thing, a commodity, but by no means a man with his own will, sympathies and dislikes."

For the soul's deepest stirrings
Too frail hangs our speech
Copious by far are our tears
With these alone can we preach.[8]

In 1885 these young people united with kindred spirits among Galicians and Hungarians nearby, whom they happened upon in the columns of the German socialist *New Yorker Volks-Zeitung,* and formed the Jewish Workmen's Society. The society, encouraged by the Knights, the Central Labor Union, and the United German Trades, founded an antisweating league and fourteen independent unions, including a peddlers' union. Within a year, however, the Jewish Workmen's Society and the unions had disappeared.[9]

Again in 1888 the intellectuals who led the Russian and Yiddish sections of the Socialist Labor Party mustered enthusiasm for labor organization. Rallying three frail Jewish unions, they met with delegates of the SLP, the *Sozialist* (the party's official organ), and the United German Trades at the German Labor Lyceum. There they founded the United Hebrew Trades, on the model of the United German Trades. In 1890 German unions contributed half the $2000 fund collected to launch the *Arbeiter Zeitung,* the United Hebrew Trades weekly. The Hebrew Labor Federation of the United States and Canada envisioned even wider horizons, but it proved stillborn. By 1892 the United Hebrew Trades claimed forty affiliated unions. The UHT did not found separate organizations where the number of Jewish craftsmen was small, but instead eased the entrance of Jewish immigrants into the German unions which admitted workmen who could pass a none-too-strict muster as Germans. Where Jewish workmen were numerous, the German unions, cooperating with the UHT, chartered Yiddish-speaking locals of bakers, waiters, bookbinders, upholsterers, carpenters, and architectual iron workers.[10]

The UHT played a decisive role in the garment trades where at first no distinction was made between contractors and workmen. In 1890 the United Hebrew Trades defined contractors as employers, barring them from the unions. In 1891 the United Brotherhood of Tailors, organized by the UHT two years earlier, welcomed the American leadership of the AFL-chartered United Garment Workers' Union of America. But when, in 1893, the socialist UHT attempted to found an inclusive Jewish Clothing Trades Council, relations between immigrants and Americans became strained to the breaking point.[11]

Jewish unions, in these years, were aided by emissaries from the German labor and socialist movements, the Knights, and by free-wheeling Scottish reformers. Edward King, hailed by the *Forward* as "our noble and learned friend," filled the gap between generations by combatting street-corner Americanism with his lectures and discourses, tirelessly evangelizing for labor. This tiny Scottish positivist, for a time the Central Labor Union's key figure, repeatedly brought East Side Labor's plight to the attention of the churches. John Swinton, a fellow Scotsman and former New York *Sun* editorial writer, in the 1880's published and edited the outstanding labor paper that carried his own name. Swinton continued to lend his voice to the cause of labor and the "alien starvelings," as he called the newcomers, despite failing eyesight and the loss of his life's savings in the decidely individualistic *John Swinton's Paper*. A third Scot, the adventurous "Professor" Garside, who vanished as suddenly and as mysteriously as he had appeared, proved invaluable in gaining wide public attention and support for the 1890 cloakmakers' strike.[12]

Native and West European Jewish union men, fearing for their own status, resented the "Russians," but acted as intermediaries nevertheless. George Bloch, *Volks-Zeitung* reporter and editor of the *Bäcker Zeitung*, organized and became president of the first Jewish bakers' union. Henry White helped found the United Garment Workers' Union and for over a decade served as its general secretary and edited the *Garment Worker*. In the early 1890's Samuel Kopenheim acted as secretary of the short-lived International Cloakmakers' Union of America. Edward Finklestone, a barber and editor of the *Official Journal of the Central Labor Union*, S. H. Jacobson of the United Clothing Cutters and "midget of the Central Labor Union," Ludwig Jablinowski, Samuel Prince, and Adolph Strasser of the cigarmakers were all leading unionists although not in close contact with the newcomers. Without doubt, Samuel Gompers led all the rest as a mediator for Jewish labor. In principle, Gompers decried separatism and he opposed the admission of a Jewish local into the Cigarmakers' International Union. Yet in practice, he accepted the exigencies of East European isolation and volunteered his assistance to the United Hebrew Trades in founding Jewish unions. After his only defeat for the AFL presidency in 1894, Gompers devoted a year to organizing the garment trades. Striking tailors awaited a Gompers address with highest expectations: "They look forward to . . . an intellectual feast," noted the *New York Journal*.[13]

In early summer 1893 depression dawned on the Lower East Side. By September it was estimated that 32,000 of the city's 100,000 unemployed were clothing workers. The *Arbeiter Zeitung* cautioned calm and patience and the counsel was generally heeded. A trade union relief committee led by Samuel Gompers met with Mayor Gilroy to discuss ways and means to relieve unemployment but accomplished nothing. Early in 1894 an unemployment conference, chaired by the University Settlement's Stanton Coit, met before an audience of 20,000 workmen at Madison Square Garden. There, Dr. Felix Adler, Seth Low, Dr. William Rainsford, Samuel Gompers, and Daniel DeLeon discussed public works projects as palliatives for the acute distress, but without effect.[14]

Although there was little public sympathy for labor's rights in the 1890's, there was much compassion for labor's plight. The *Daily News* and the *Morning Journal,* especially, and their German editions, the *Tages Nachrichten* and the *Morgen Journal,* devoted considerable space to labor news. In 1890 the desperate leaders of the cloakmakers' strike had resorted to a monster hunger demonstration by the strikers' wives and children and, without exception, the newspapers opened subscription lists. The sweatshops of the Lower East Side, in the shadow of Newspaper Row, aroused the indignation of the *Tribune* and the *Sun* and reminded *Herald* reporter Ida Van Etten of the slavery of the pharaohs. "Upon the Jewish proletariat of New York is forced the problem of freedom from a servitude worse than that of Egypt." [15] Even in the Fall of 1894, when the Pull-

man strike turned public opinion against all strikes, striking
Jewish tailors drew sympathy and praise, primarily because of
their religious habits. At Thanksgiving, kindly uptowners provided free holiday dinners for the children of strikers. Indeed,
doled out by the COS, and allotted and distributed through the
Charity Organization Society, was responsible for a garment
union membership that was not to be surpassed for nearly a generation. Peddlers, porters, and the sundry unemployed eagerly
paid fifty-cent monthly union dues, anticipating job tickets
doled out by the COS, and allotted and distributed through the
union. In that year, an anonymous donor, rumored to be the
banker, Jacob H. Schiff, contributed $10,000 to the United He-
brew Charities to sustain striking cloakmakers. On the Lower
East Side the Yiddish press unanimously supported labor's grievances. The orthodox *Gazetten* hailed Joseph Barondess as "the
talented leader of the cloakmakers" and regularly printed his
announcements and strike reports. Indeed, the orthodox *Tageblatt* insisted that it published labor's statements without charge
while declining substantial fees for printing manufacturers' reports. "The *Tageblatt* is now and always ready to support the
workmen in their just struggle." [16] During the depression the
Jewish Labor Lyceum became the chief center for dispensing
aid. In a five-week period, its relief committee aided 25,000
people, as employed workmen, storekeepers, and professional
folk pitched in with money, provisions, and services. The United
Hebrew Trades' *Arbeiter Zeitung* appealed to Jewish communal spirit and enlightened self-interest:

Businessmen! Contractors! Capitalists!

Forget now who you are and what you are! Forget your bitter feelings! Forget all old accounts—if your heart is not stone—be human!
Help, help your workers, your customers . . . in their time of need!
Help them to overcome their need—remember, one hand washes the
other!—They will again become your workers, your customers and
your patrons and with their help you will retrieve the bread which
you have cast out upon the waters.

During strikes, local restaurateurs distributed free meal-tickets
and Jewish congregations offered five-cent dinners to union card

holders. Indeed, after the turn of the century, the Workmen's Circle, socialist fraternal order, was embarrassed by the charge that aid to strikers was a humanitarian act and not a distinctively socialist one, for, it was pointed out, even conservative *lansmanshafts* allowed strike benefits to members. During a bakers' general strike, the *Forward* appealed not to class solidarity but to the sense of Jewish communal responsibility.

> It is wholly a domestic matter with us. The workmen are ours and the bosses are ours, and we alone are the customers . . . Let us show the world that when a struggle like this occurs in our midst, we settle the question in a feeling of justice and human sympathy—that we settle the issue in favor of the workmen and their just demands.[17]

During these years labor's problems were compounded by the image of the foreign anarchist. A series of incidents that grew out of the cloakmaker union's sudden rise to prominence in 1890 incited the New York press to extravagant reporting. The *Evening World* falsely identified the leader of the cloakmakers as an exiled Russian nobleman, "Baron" Joseph Barondess, "whose desperate traits" had driven him into exile. Indeed, the newspaper even alleged that Barondess was Johann Most's successor as chairman of Revolutionary Section No. 1 of America and that he had called on his two thousand cloakmaker followers

> to resist to the last even if the streets of New York should be dyed with their blood. It is in this way that he holds his place and excites the admiration of those "progressives" who have no religion but the doctrine of anarchy, no home but the gin-mill, no country but their Revolutionary Section.

Thereafter, Barondess became an easy target. Press sensationalists blew up a minor strike altercation in Jamaica in which he was remotely involved into an "outrage" and "orgy" of "desperados" and "border ruffians," an example of "anarchistic tyranny." Barondess, freed of charges of complicity in the Jamaica incident, received a twenty-one-month prison sentence on a technical charge of extortion which even the redoubtable legal talents of Howe and Hummel were powerless to prevent. In the face of hysterical condemnation by the press, the *Journal of the Knights of Labor* defended the union leader: "Foreigner as he is, Barondess has shown a far truer appreciation of the principles of industrial freedom than the majority who pride themselves on their American birth and ancestry." Even before popular clamor led Governor Flower to pardon Barondess, Central Labor Union leader James Archibald, through Tammany's Boss Croker, had gained the governor's ear.[18]

In the chaos of the mid-nineties, the Jewish unions fell victim to the ambitions and the rhetoric of Daniel DeLeon. The Socialist Labor Party leader, excluded from the AFL, turned to the Knights of Labor. There his trusty lieutenant, Patrick J. Murphy, secretary of District Assembly 49, maneuvered the United Hebrew Trades into line in 1893 to help elect DeLeon a delegate to the Knights convention. But DeLeon, failing to capture the Knights, founded his own Socialist Trade and Labor Alliance in 1895. Few German or American unions succumbed to his invective. But the Alliance managed to capture the United Hebrew Trades (despite DeLeon's diatribes against Russian Jews), thereby forcing anti-DeLeonists to form their own Federated Hebrew Trades Union of Greater New York. Meaningless as unions, these central assemblies and their affiliates prospered as intellectual debating societies.[19]

The hopelessness of the Jewish unions was to be seen in the annual strike which had become an institution by 1900 with "annual victories."

In July there is a strike. In August it is settled . . . A walking delegate is chosen to collect dues. In October it becomes known that there are more unsettled shops than union shops. In November wage rates are reduced. Then they begin to scold the bosses for breaking the agreements. In December it becomes apparent that the agreements are not worth a whiff of tobacco. In January dues are no longer paid. In February the walking delegate is tossed out of the shop. In March mass meetings are called to revive the union. In April the union ceases to exist . . . and in June they decide to strike. And strike they do.

Unions remained outside agencies to which workmen paid assessments to conduct strikes and negotiate settlements. Since the strikers aimed to restore the busy season wage rates reduced in the slack season, victories were won easily. Indeed, on many occasions, unions did not represent the workmen but served as impartial judicial tribunals.

The notion of collective bargaining remained elusive. Despite persistent indoctrination by labor leaders, strikers continued to think in traditional modes. Striking vestmakers, upon concluding the sixth tractate of the Talmud, celebrated the occasion with the customary libations and, reported Abraham Cahan, drew a moral from their reading that bore but remotely on the labor problem..

Saith the Law of Moses: "Thou shalt not withhold anything from thy neighbor nor rob him; there shall not abide with thee the wages of him that is hired through the night until morning." So it stands in Leviticus. So you see that our bosses who rob us and don't pay us regularly commit a sin, and that the cause of our unions is a just one. What do we come to America for? To bathe in tears and to see our wives and our children rot in poverty? Tears and sighs we had in plenty in the old country.

Unions were meaningful as a focus for discontent and protest, but as permanent associations they found little grass roots support. Jacob Riis wrote: "Over and over again I have met with instances of these . . . Russian Jews deliberately starving themselves to the point of physical exhaustion, while working night and day at a tremendous pressure to save a little money." To folk accustomed to a lean diet, the 14-hour day, the 84-hour week, and the sweatshop offered prospects for independence. However moved by the blueprint of the ideal society and labor's mission, immigrants were inclined to rely on individual and family diligence to extricate themselves from the ranks of the depressed.[20]

Furthermore, throughout this period the ties that linked fellow townsmen obstructed labor organization. While Jewish workmen paid respectable dues to *lansmanshafts* and benevolent societies, unions melted away from lack of funds. Workmen, compartmented in patriarchal *lansmanshaft* or family work units, were replenished continually by newcomers, and these in turn were bound to potential immigrants in the *shtetls* of their birth. Contractors solicitously made place for relatives and fellow townsmen, often providing their passage money. "Everything bearing the name of my native place touched a tender spot in my heart," mused David Levinsky. As patron and benefactor, the "boss" shared the joys and sorrows of his workmen, attending circumcisions, *bar mitzvahs*, weddings, and funerals, and often acting as banker and personal adviser. Although resentment against exploitation in *lansmanshaft* shops flared into strikes, these outbreaks did not destroy the paternalistic pattern.

In the 1880's men's tailors came principally from Poland's Suvalki province. Puchevitz exported furriers, and Warsaw pursemakers. Bakers were generally Hungarians and non-Russian Poles. In the late 1880's vestmakers consisted of skilled Hungarians and semiskilled Russians laboring respectively in the Hungarian and Russian areas of the East Side. Ninety per cent of the pantsmakers in the 1890's were Rumanians, drawn to the trade by the first *lansman* (fellow townsman) contractor. Islands of Germans, Galicians, Hungarians, and Plotzk and Warsaw Russians were to be found in the necktie industry. At the turn of the century, the newly established children's cloak industry was manned entirely by *lanslite* from Puchevitz, Smilevich, Dukar, and Berezin, outside of Minsk. Raincoat waterproofers were virtually all transmigrants from England who, beginning in 1897, were imported to work in the young American mackintosh industry. Perhaps only husky Bessarabian teamsters, smiths, and porters, drafted directly from Castle Garden and Ellis Island into heavy labor as pressers, entered unperturbedly into the impersonal factory routine.

Despite recurrent failure, the labor movement succeeded as educator and inspirer. The lives of individual Jewish unions were brief and their triumphs fleeting but the transcendent ideals and the broadening social experience aroused a new sense of personal and social dignity. The unions broke through the darkness of material toil and brought light and hope to tenement and sweatshop. Few immigrants would forget the exhilaration of the first shop strike, vivid testimony to the grandeur of American freedom.[21]

CRAFT UNIONS TRIUMPHANT

While the Jewish labor movement was foundering, earlier immigrants were attaining a place in the social order. Out of the depression, the craft unions emerged as organized labor's undisputed leaders. In 1895 J. W. Sullivan of the sturdy International Typographical Union sounded the American Federation of Labor keynote: "We run the largest local business enterprise in the American continent. This enterprise is to bull our labor market." In 1897 the unprecedented conference of the president of the board of police commissioners, Theodore Roosevelt, with Central Labor Union officers signaled the new acceptance of organized labor.

German and English-speaking trade unionists were coming together despite jurisdictional conflicts. In 1888 the German bakers' union began to publish its journal in English, its editor noting that "misapprehensions between German and other nationalities would have been scarcer and the mental feeling which now binds the German organization to the national trade organization would have bound the English-speaking elements as faithfully and effectively." In 1894 the twenty-one-year-old German-American Typographia affiliated with the International Typographical Union, retaining its autonomy and reserving the right to choose the ITU's third vice-president and ex-officio secretary-treasurer. In 1902 the Inside Architectural Bridge and Structural Iron Workers' Union adopted English for official business. Eight painters' unions which had united in 1897 to form the Amalgamated Painters and Decorators Union of New York City merged with the rival Brotherhood of Painters, Decorators, and Paperhangers a decade later. Ethnic and jurisdictional differences continued to divide German cabinetmakers and Irish-American building carpenters and created contention between inside Germans and outside Irish in the United Brewery Workmen's Union. Yet, with few exceptions, unionists subordinated their differences to a spirit of cooperation. At the turn of the century New York's rival central assemblies, the German Central Labor Federation and the Irish Central Labor

Union, merged to become the Central Federated Union, a sounding board for all points of view, inimical to none.[22]

The strengthened trade unions reflected a rising prosperity, a willingness by employers to treat skilled labor with equity, and the fusing of "old" immigrant and second generation Americans into a privileged labor class. In New York, as elsewhere, more strikes were won in 1899 and 1900 than at any previous time. In 1902 more than half of organized labor in the city, concentrated in the building trades, with 62,000 members, worked an eight-hour day at wages 20 per cent higher than those of a few years earlier. In that year the rival building trades councils amalgamated to form the United Board of Building Trades, which represented 22 unions of skilled and 15 unions of unskilled workmen. Furthermore, the trade agreement that had taken form in the 1890's recognized the legitimate interest of a third party—the public—in every labor conflict, and provided a constitutional framework that enabled master builders to cooperate with unions in the seasonal, highly competitive, and decentralized building trades.

Despite the growth of trusts and the resort to the court injunction, the craft unions stood on firm ground. German and Irish unionists with their higher standard of living were regarded by older Americans as superior to Italians, Russians, Austrians, and Bohemians and therefore entitled to greater consideration. Organized labor also received political recognition. Both Democratic and Republican legislators consulted union representatives and vied for the labor vote. John McMackin, once a leading supporter of Henry George, in 1899 had become state commissioner of labor. In 1902, the New York courts affirmed labor's right to strike for the closed shop; in 1905, in the face of the open shop drive, the judiciary reaffirmed the legality of the closed shop.[23]

Veteran leaders of the Jewish labor movement quickly perceived the new status of the AFL unions. In 1898 Joseph Barondess denounced DeLeon and extolled the achievements of the "pure and simple" unions which had secured the eight-hour day by "vulgar unscientific" strikes and boycotts unendorsed by the

Socialist Trade and Labor Alliance. "This is what the conservative pure and simple, unscientific faking trade union movement has accomplished," the socialist *Forward* insisted. "The best way for workmen to insure themselves against future need, the best insurance company, the best lodge and benefit society . . . is a trade union," the newspaper continued. Unemployment, sickness, and death benefits became the foundation blocks for the newly organized Manhattan Knife Cutters' Union and the revived United Brotherhood of Tailors, but other Jewish unions proved too weak to follow their example.[24]

In the early years of the twentieth century, stable unions remained almost as difficult to maintain in the Jewish trades as earlier. This was true despite the eclipse of sweatshops, the weakening of the *lansmanshaft* economy, and the rise of large factories. In the clothing trades, for example, workmen still were required to provide their own sewing machines and even to pay a fifty-cent freightage charge for transporting the cursed "katerinka" (sewing machine) from one shop to another. Graduated subcontracting, irregular wage payments, charges for thread and electricity, and fines for cloth spoilage, broken needles, and worn-out leather belts persisted. Immigrant acceptance of employment at any wage, the free movement from one shop to another in the many semiskilled sectors of the apparel trades, and the attraction to new lines made for continual instability. The labor turnover, the high earnings of skilled veteran workmen, the openings for foremen, subcontractors, and designers, and the dogged will to independence further discouraged labor organization. In these prosperous years, better-paid workmen were able to rent summer quarters for their families in the mountains and at the shore. "The great trouble in the cap trade, I will say in all trades controlled by my co-religionists, is that the Hebrew wage earner is only in the trade temporarily, hoping and praying that one day he will become a boss." As Workmen's Circle members became employers, the labor fraternal order was abashed by the change in its "class" character. The *Forward* ruefully conceded that men with administrative and managerial talents were attracted to business, leaving only agitators behind in the union. To browbeat the "little sweaterel" for leaving the union for business—"you have sold your birthright for a bag of lentils"—availed not at all.[25]

Two Jewish unions, however, attained stability. Hebrew American Typographical Union No. 83 was revived as a charter affiliate of the United Hebrew Trades in 1888 and profited from its association with the International Typographical Union. The premium placed on the printer's skill enabled No. 83 to weather the 1890's, and by 1898 its members earned $18 weekly, double the wages of 1890, and worked an eight-hour day. By then the union was ready to withstand the strain of technological unemployment created by the introduction of the linotype machine. Following the example of German Typographia No. 7, Hebrew American Typographical Union No. 83 halved the prevailing wage-hour standard by instituting a four-hour work day and an $11 week. By 1907 the expansion of the Yiddish press increased employment opportunities, bringing a six-hour day. The United Hebrew Trades condemned the union for craft complacency, but the *Forward* exulted: "The printing trade is better than an experiment with a socialist colony." [26]

In the apparel trades, the capmakers alone welded a strong union. In the early 1890's the coming of East Europeans and the Nellie Bly (a new style cap named after the globetrotting journalist) rage had energized this small industry which was free of the features of contracting and dominated by a handful of German manufacturers concentrated in New York. Skilled artisans, almost all East Europeans, were regularly employed and proved amenable to organization. The reorganized United Cloth Hat and Capmakers' Union of North America, which acquired an AFL charter in 1901, prided itself upon its adherence to the highest ideals of trade unionism and internationalism. "The only international union in this country which carried out in spirit the decision of the American Federation of Labor and the International Congress of Labor" honored both May Day and Labor Day. The *Cap Makers' Journal* announced:

> Labor Day has no particular significance outside of it being a time for the general glorification of human activity, expressed in the forms of things produced by the hand and the brain. But May Day stands for the struggle of the organized working class all over

the civilized world for economic independence and for the inauguration of a happier epoch for mankind.[27]

In 1903 all five union locals struck simultaneously for the first time, young women were organized, and the union membership passed 3000; the following year, the first woman served on the union's executive board. Late in 1904 the union, locked out by the large manufacturers, who were encouraged by the nationwide open shop drive, was forced into a thirteen-week general strike that taxed its resources to the near breaking point. The *Forward,* the United Hebrew Trades, and the AFL unions contributed generously to the $34,000 strike fund, while the new New York Women's Trade Union League promoted badly needed press publicity. The AFL threat of taxing its members to support the strikers finally intimidated employers and brought a reasonable settlement.[28]

In the early years of the century the zeal of the United Hebrew Trades did not abate. No trade, however proud, lowly, or intractable, proved alien to an organization eager to give dignity to all men. Laundry workers, bank and retail clerks, glaziers, janitors, tombstone engravers, Yiddish writers, antique coppersmiths, old clothes cleaners, and rag pickers, all were clasped to its bosom. If the UHT barred installment peddlers, it was on the grounds that they were not, properly speaking, workingmen—indeed that installment peddling was a degrading occupation. It eschewed the music-hall actors, agreeing with the *Forward's* injunction that these workmen were unworthy of the "pure name of a union," until they demonstrated that their trade was as clean as carpentering or tailoring. Only the Hebrew-American Newsboys Union, ages six to twelve, the Levantine bootblacks in Hester Street Park, and the Baxter Street pullers, evaded the United Hebrew Trades.[29]

The AFL craft unions, having gained acceptance, jealously hugged their new status. The Amalgamated Painters' Union admitted 1000 East European Jews in 1901, but thereafter the building trades unions excluded newcomers. Consequently, in 1906 the United Hebrew Trades proceeded to found alteration building trades unions. When, by 1914, the industry had become a major focus of Jewish labor, the UHT formed a Central Federation of the Alteration Building Trades, counting many thousands of workmen.[30]

In spite of the ethnic rivalries, economic competition stood out as the basic cause for labor discrimination. The few unions in which Jews had achieved status were equally avid to preserve the job market. In 1899, after a long struggle, the United Hatters admitted the Hebrew Hatters' Union, with 1500 members, to its ranks. The Hebrew Hatters thereupon instituted a high initiation fee and made entrance for newcomers difficult. The AFL Jewish Actors' Union did likewise in a field where jobs were notoriously fewer than aspiring thespians. In the slow fall season of 1904, even the United Cloth Hat and Cap Makers' Union devised an examination plan to shield its members from competition.

Economic and ethnic rivalries reinforced one another in the clothing industry. In men's clothing, the officers of the United Garment Workers' Union, representing the veteran skilled cutters, had little in common with the members of the affiliated United Brotherhood of Tailors and kept their distance. A majority of the UGW executive board members and organizers were Jews but they were Germans. Devoid of missionary zeal, they were governed by pride of craft and status that limited their activity to the perfunctory negotiation of strike settlements, leaving strike leadership and organization to the United Hebrew Trades. Only on one occasion, in 1904, when the open shop drive menaced their own position, did German cutters strike alongside Russian tailors.[31]

Another factor further complicated the situation: the manufacturers in the men's clothing industry were extremely well organized. The National Association of Clothiers, organized in 1897 and claiming to represent 97 per cent of the leading manufacturers in the twelve great clothing markets, determinedly pursued a paternalistic policy and denounced that "un-American institution," the closed shop. "According to the spirit of our institutions, the laws of the land are of general and equal application and should be enforced without regard to class or condition." The association, through its National Labor Bureau, promised to shorten hours and increase wages by agreement be-

tween manufacturers as trade conditions permitted. But trade
conditions were not likely to permit improvements, the *Daily
Trade Record* exclaimed: "Why, tailors! There is no scarcity
of tailors; they are thicker than the hair on a dog. . . . If there
is one thing that Russians can do better than the Japanese, it is
to make pants. There is not a boat that comes to these shores
that does not bring a thousand possible tailors."

Labor in the women's clothing industry was relatively homogeneous. Yet, there too, the English-speaking cutters remained
aloof from the rank and file of the International Ladies Garment Workers' Union. Although the ILGWU achieved a respectable membership by 1904, in 1905 it seemed on the verge
of dissolution. Yet within five years, this union was to become
the remarkably successful leader of great strikes.[32]

PRELUDE TO RECOGNITION

With the Jewish unions in the doldrums, cooperatives
achieved a precarious popularity. Formed in 1901 on a model
inspired by transmigrants from England, the New York Industrial Cooperative Society operated ten retail shops. The cloakmakers' union opened a women's clothing shop, striking bakers
founded a cooperative bakeshop, striking capmakers planned
a cooperative, and for a time the seltzer workers' union succeeded in maintaining two cooperatives. Bad management and
waning enthusiasm led the New York Industrial Cooperative
Society to dissolve in 1906, but the cooperative idea lived on.
In 1908 a cooperative magazine appeared, and in 1910 the cooperative league founded at the Rand School organized a union
hatter corporation and other short-lived enterprises. The Universal Cooperative Society, renamed the Industrial and Agricultural Cooperative Association in 1912, administered boarding
houses and restaurants as well as a hat and shoe business. But
in these years, the cooperative movement remained experimental.[33]

Weak Jewish unions invited the intervention of the newly
founded Industrial Workers of the World. The IWW, drawing
support from the immigrants who came after the Russian Revo-

lution of 1905 for whom every strike heralded the "social revolution," organized dual unions, but made no effort to attract the unorganized. Socialistic union men and intellectuals initially sympathized with the industrial union cause and in 1905 the United Cloth Hat and Cap Makers' Union even sent a delegate to the inaugural IWW meeting in Chicago. But the IWW's destructive tactics, reminiscent of the Socialist Trade and Labor Alliance, convinced enthusiasts that the United Hebrew Trades, socialist in spirit if not in letter, represented "the industrial workers of the East Side." In 1907 the IWW's Jewish Industrial Sub-Council dissolved along with its largely paper affiliates.[34]

The nativist indictment of labor that coupled trade unions with immigrants leveled no special reproach at Jews. In the wake of the Paris Commune, Charles Loring Brace, with still fresh memories of New York's Draft and Orange riots, had warned that there were "just the same explosive social elements beneath the surface of New York as of Paris." But "the Prolétaires of New York," counted among "the Dangerous Classes," failed to erupt those "social volcanic forces" that "continuously exist in great cities." Even in 1886 alarm seemed unwarranted on the New York scene and the eagerness to build armories in midtown was not matched by opportunities for their employ. The "Oriental" district with its moments of "anarchist noise" received more than its due in newspaper notoriety. But Jewish labor leaders and radicals were not distinguished from other immigrants coming from less favored zones. Professor Burgess' localization of socialism in Eastern Europe proved almost as general as the indictment of simpler nativists: "There is scarcely a waiter in a large hotel or restaurant in New York who does not betray his foreign birth by his accent." [35]

The Jewish trades had remained singularly free of violence. During strikes, hats were crumpled, hair tousled, and pickets were manhandled; occasionally, brass-knuckled blows were struck. But with the advent of the IWW, and the coming of the postrevolutionary immigration, the incidence of physical violence mounted. Soon hoodlums invaded the garment scene and employers and unionists alike drew upon the services of "Big Jack" Zelig and other strong-armed worthies. Yet as late as 1905,

Jesse Pope, pioneer student of the apparel trades, remarked upon the exceptional freedom from intimidation and the rarity of property damage in the clothing industry.[36]

Police violence was another matter. New York's labor leaders had become wary of the law ever since the unprovoked police assault upon an orderly Tompkins Square unemployment gathering in 1874. But newcomers were less cautious. On the Lower East Side perennial strikes and picketing "without bounds" made "Russians" synonymous with disorderly behavior and aroused police vigilance. The Yiddish labor press, fresh with memories of tsarist massacres, labeled municipal ordinances "ukases"; the police, "Black Hundreds"; and police discipline, "pogroms." "Forbidden to strike—not in Russia—but here in the land of freedom," blared a headline in the *Abendblatt*. In 1908, the peaceful Unemployment Conference in Union Square, called by the socialists to bring public attention to the condition of the unemployed, unexpectedly was broken up by a massed charge of mounted police. The subsequent detonation of a bomb by a half-crazed youth that resulted in his self-destruction and the death of his companion aroused almost unanimous press hysteria. The *Evening Post,* alone among New York's newspapers, protested and charged the police with trespassing upon a peaceful assemblage. In 1909 the election of Mayor Gaynor, however, heralded a new era that brought a degree of freedom of speech and assembly to the city and a hitherto unknown exemption from interference at labor meetings.[37]

By the second decade of the century the stage was set for a new age of labor relations in the apparel trades. The career of Joseph Barondess, "King of the Cloakmakers," epitomized the long trek up the road of human dignity. Landing in New York in 1888, Barondess successively peddled, worked in a paint factory, and labored at the Arbuckle sugar refinery, before stepping up the garment ladder, from pants to shirts to cloaks. Becoming a labor leader in the 1890's, Barondess was identified with every phase of the immigrant's struggle for justice. He spoke in a homilectical Yiddish, studded with Talmudic allusions, alternated wit with pathos, and was as able to scold his followers into line as to debate a rabbi's right to kosher boycotted bread.

"Women and children followed . . . as he went from house to house, kissing his hands and calling him their deliverer," reported the *New York Journal*. This labor reformer hero of Edward King's novel *Joseph Zalmonah,* like his idol John Swinton (for whom he named one of his children), was a moralist and humanitarian. In the late 1890's, weary of rivalry and strife, he retired from labor leadership to enter the insurance business, but, mindful of "oppressed humanity," Barondess remained ever loyal to his youthful ideals. This one-man philanthropic federation, employment agency, and civic lecture bureau, stood ever ready to serve labor's cause. In 1900 Barondess, as the Lower East Side's erstwhile labor spokesman, was invited to join the National Civic Federation. A decade later a man once jailed and denounced as an "anarchist" was appointed to New York's Board of Education and was proposed for state commissioner of labor.[38]

Under different conditions, traits that made Jewish workmen reluctant union members would make them able labor leaders and rank and filers in humanly complex and morselized industries. A study of workmen's leisure habits revealed that Russians led all other nationalities in club and lodge activity and stood first in night school and public lecture attendance, library visits, private study, the reading of books, and friendly intercourse. In answer to the request of the Bakers' Union, the Board of Education provided that union with an instructor in English. Other unions followed suit. The *Capmakers' Journal* hardly needed to remind its readers of their duty in the fall and winter season:

The long evenings have arrived, and it behooves all intelligent workmen to spend their leisure time in equipping themselves mentally for the life task before them. Standing on the corners, playing cards, or drinking in the saloons does not tend to develop one's moral and mental makeup. But education does. Therefore, read and think.[39]

The flow of new immigrants dedicated to the labor movement as a folk mission was to inspire a massive labor revival at the close of the first decade of the twentieth century. The cities, the factories, and revolution in Eastern Europe produced men capable of communicating their enthusiasm for liberty. These immigrants were to unite their revolutionary romanticism with the practical experience of veteran unionists and bring status to the Jewish labor movement. The "divine spirit" that spoke to the Bund in the alleys of Vilna was to prove contagious on the plazas of Union Square.

∽ 10 ∽

Reform in Full Stride

The imagination of New York is not sufficiently alive to the fact that it is about to become one of the greatest cities in the world; our mind is still apt to become accustomed to the condition of New York in the past.

Felix Adler (1894)

IN the late eighties, while organized labor was struggling to survive, a new vitality seized New York. The image of a modern municipality remained elusive, but wealth, ostentation, aristocratic pretensions, and the persistent little-Old-New-York mentality of leading Gothamites could no longer check enthusiasm for civic renascence.

The faith of reformers in New York's social destiny replaced the accepted rationale for the city's faults. These progressives rejected the idea that "Darkness and Daylight," "Sunshine and Shadow," "Velvet and Rags," were the inevitable penalty for metropolitan greatness. New York contained "in microcosm all the contrasts of our modern life—its worst and its best aspects," and reformers were anxious to reduce the worst and enhance the best. Ernest Howard Crosby, successor to Theodore Roosevelt in the New York Assembly, set the tone of *fin de siècle* optimism in a poetic plea that merged echoes of Emerson and Whitman with accents of George and Tolstoy.

O sprawling, jagged, formless city! City without voice! . . .
Conceive something worthy of expression . . .
Become now at last conscious of the germ of soul that is in you
And stake your overweening energy on that! [1]

The reform that sustained this vision never quite shed its cast of gentility, philanthropy, and detachment from the plight of the unfortunate. Not that condescension was intended. But unlike the labor movement, colored by the vehemence of the radicals, the reformers' call at times seemed as remote as a Washington Square drawing room. Felix Adler and Bishop Potter, Charles B. Stover and Lillian Wald, Jacob Riis and Charles Sprague Smith, Frank Damrosch and Thomas Davidson, reflected the tone of an era in which the educated, socially advantaged, and financially privileged confronted the realities of New York and attempted in conscience to efface the evils with good works. In so doing, they founded the core social institutions of the modern city. If an easy comradeship with tenement dwellers eluded reformers, it was not for want of effort.

Civic duty could not be blinked in a decade that saw journalist-photographer Jacob Riis and the Byrons pioneer the latest camera techniques "to catch instantaneously all the details of a scene with the utmost fidelity," bringing realistic portraits of the city's worst features to public attention. Leading clergymen, newspapermen, and the new social workers fixed their gaze on the gross inequalities fostered by a sundered commonwealth divided between classes and masses, wealth and poverty, Americans and immigrants. They recognized the "labor question" or the "social question" as vital, and committed themselves to action. They studied sweatshops, slums, child labor, and the crowding of the poor, and dedicated themselves to restoring a measure of humanity. They denounced corruption in government, proclaimed the middle-class political virtues, and spoke out on all the issues that comfort bred them to avoid. "It is not sufficiently realized by many of our fellow citizens that the American government means one thing in the poor quarters of the city and quite another in the quarters of the rich." [2]

Without questioning fundamental assumptions, economic or political, reformers aspired to remedy current social evils by honesty, philanthropy, and scientific method. Within a generation their piecemeal efforts were to find growing expression in law and public opinion. By the early years of the twentieth century, Godkin's admonition in the *Nation* (in a review of Jacob

Riis's *How The Other Half Lives*) against "the propensity to regard social therapeutics as consisting of a change in material conditions" appeared anachronistic.

Reformers found a potent if often unwelcome ally in the sensational press. The big circulation dailies, featuring the contrasts between poverty and wealth, focused public attention on the plight of the other half. Pulitzer's *World,* and more particularly Hearst's *Journal* and *American,* trumpeted popular causes and actively exposed malefactors in business and government. The *Journal* and *American,* fed by Hearst's political ambition, fortified by editor Brisbane's solicitousness for "Poor Old Moses," called for cheaper milk, ice, and transportation; supported labor; and favored the municipal ownership of public utilities.

Yet Protestant patricians, men of wealth, seniority, and executive place, retained reform leadership. Protestant churchmen were the first to unfurl the standard of reform. By accepting the theory of evolution, they liberalized religious thought; and by taking on the challenge of the city, they embraced the social gospel and endowed Protestantism with a vitality that up to then had been ebbing before the onslaught of unprecedented social and intellectual pressures.[3]

The passionate reformism that stirred the Irish in the 1880's was aborted and did not accomplish much. Although Catholics were about to become the largest single religious group in the city, Irish Catholic reform, culminating in the Henry George campaign and Father McGlynn's Anti-Poverty Society, quickly subsided in the face of Archbishop Corrigan's disciplinary measures and the urge to solidarity for the advance of Irish America. McGlynn's disciple, Father Thomas Ducey, continued to interpret Pope Leo XIII's "Rerum Novarum" forcefully by enunciating "the true gospel of labor." But his remained a lone voice. The Catholic Church, tolerant of human frailty, was inhospitable to human speculations when these threatened order and disputed authority. Its largely immigrant and proletarian constituencies, torn by ethnic strife and dominated by the newly risen Irish, were loyal to Tammany and instinctively hostile to reformers, whose social and moral perfectionism was past understanding. Only Protestant heretics, aristocratic Anglophiles, and Republicans could be capable of such fantasies and hypocrisies.[4]

Immersed in the moil of the market place, most German Jews were lukewarm to reform sentiment. The reform temper, nurtured by evangelical zeal, proved alien to them, and Puritanism conflicted with their habits and their interests. When even the liberal Unitarian, the Rev. Henry Bellows offhandedly asserted at joint Thanksgiving Day religious services at Temple Emanu-El in 1879 that Judaism had not yet attained to the level of Christianity, Jews tended to avoid associations that detracted from their dignity. Prosperous Jews, as a matter of course, contributed generously to the Charity Organization Society and to other general charities. But these charities were Protestant in tone, their management the prerogative of the old families; Felix Adler of the Ethical Society, Edwin R. A. Seligman of Columbia University, and Jacob H. Schiff, a German immigrant who combined financial acumen with a keen sense of social responsibility, served as officers. Like Catholics, Jews counted the care of their own less fortunate a religious obligation.[5]

As reform grew more imaginative and became divested of its sectarianism without a sacrifice of its zeal, American sons of German Jewish immigrants joined the reformers. "No moral system has much weight against vested rights," asserted the president of the United Hebrew Charities in 1894 at a session of the Tenement House Committee. "It requires new laws . . . possibly some of which would be not entirely republican, in order to improve the system." The climate of social and political activism of the late 1890's and early years of the twentieth century, and the rising respectability of civic and humanitarian movements furthered the enlistment of second generation Jews in reform causes.[6]

THE IDEAL SLUM

Reformers directed their efforts to the "other half" as a whole, but singled out the city's East European Jews as a tattered remnant to be brought within the fold of comfort and community. The newspapers invariably pointed to the Lower East Side as primarily in need when they opened their columns for a popular subscription to aid sick babies, requested donations of Christmas gifts for needy children, or publicized harbor and river excursions during the summer months. The great Jewish quarter, situated near the heart of the city, was easily accessible, and its miseries were concentrated. For proof, skeptics could turn to the frontispiece of DeForest and Veiller's classic study, *The Tenement House Problem*, which celebrated "The Most Densely Populated Spot in the World—The Lower East Side of New York."

However receptive to the attentions of American "aristocrats," older Jewish immigrants suspected reformers of conversionist motives—and not without cause. From a row of Bowery storefront missions, missionaries eagerly grasped for unredeemed souls. Bishop Henry Codman Potter made his headquarters at the two buildings of the Pro-Cathedral Mission on Stanton and on Essex streets, Dr. Elsing held forth at the Dewitt Memorial Church on Rivington Street, and a handful of Christian Jewish missionaries attracted onlookers, but tempted few converts. To the untutored eye, missionaries were indistinguishable from reformers.[7]

Many reformers found the American faith in the tenements. Jacob Riis rejoiced over the Russian Jews' "all consuming passion" for liberty which set them apart from most immigrants. Another observer recorded that Yiddish theater audiences embraced the refrain of George M. Cohan's catchy tune, "Amerika ist ein frei land," singing it over and over until exhausted.

More remarkable was the intellectualism of the children that evoked from Police Commissioner McAdoo admiration mingled with pity for so austere a childhood. "Think of it! Herbert Spencer preferred to a fairy story by boys and girls." East Side teachers discovered these youngsters to be more than they had bargained for. "Fifty-eight little children of Israel entrusted to her care" challenged the "Ideals of Education" of the typical normal-school-trained teacher of Myra Kelly's East-Side stories. Miss Constance Bailey's "earnest effort to set the feet of the

First Reader Class firmly in the path which leads 'through the years, maybe,' as Mrs. Mogilewsky used to say, to American citizenship" was "an education for both youngsters and teacher."

I think no one can come in contact with these people—really try to know them; to understand their difficulties and their struggles; their sufferings and their patience—without remembering all their lives long. These impressions do not fade. Rather, they grow clearer and deeper as one learns more about other lives.

The larger problems of maturity passed far from Room 8, but their shadow crossed its sunshine. This was inevitable in a community where all the life of a family, eating, sleeping, cooking, working, illness, death, birth, and prayer is often crowded into one small room.

The seriousness, bookishness, industry, and common sense of these youngsters stirred comparison with a vanished New England where a mystic idealism stood harnessed to hard-headed practicality. In a city where education from the rudiments through college could be had without cost, study ordained by religion but keyed to modern knowledge promised to open boundless opportunities for the diligent, even from among the poorest. In 1891, of some 60,000 East Side children, only 1000 received no education and most of these soon would be in classrooms; on the Lower East Side, a school absenteeism rate of 8 per cent was caused almost entirely by sickness. By the turn of the century youngsters of East European origin had become a majority at the city's free institutions of higher learning.[8]

The sprouting of a labor movement, the travail of the sweatshop, the quest for the exotic and the picturesque, added to a compassion for the obvious underdog, inspired the interest and excited the imagination of reformers in the Lower East Side, "as unknown a country as Central Africa." Nursed upon the Old Testament, many reformers experienced a sense of religious kinship with the descendants of the Israelites. To write solely of the uptown Jews "is as if we should attempt to write the history of the ancient Jews and leave out the captivity of the children of Israel, their triumphant passage through the Red Sea in their marching to the desert under the leadership of Moses."

In the early nineties, George Kennan's revelations of Siberian prison horrors and Harold Frederic's reports of renewed barbarism in *The New Exodus* heightened sympathy for the victims of Russian atrocities. American writers in particular rose to support the struggle for a free Russia. Joining the American Friends of Russian Freedom, Ernest Howard Crosby, William Dean Howells, and other admirers of Russian literature cherished the spirit of freedom in the works of Chekhov, Dostoevsky, Tolstoy, and Gorky that promised an end to tsarist darkness. Sniffing the scent of a live struggle for liberty in 1905, Arthur Bullard and Ernest Poole gaily slipped overseas to fight the Russian Revolution. In 1906 a distinguished writers committee, led by Mark Twain, welcomed a propagandist of the Russian Revolution and fellow writer, Maxim Gorky, to the United States. To a prominent Gothamite, the Russian Revolution loomed as "the romance of today." Caught up in this wave of idealism, New Yorkers converted their ardor for universal democracy into building stones for their own civic institutions.[9]

CHURCHMEN IN THE ARENA OF LABOR

New York's first advocate and practitioner of social Christianity was Dr. Felix Adler, a Jew. Heir apparent to his father, the scholarly Rabbi Samuel Adler of Temple Emanu-El, the young, German-schooled Adler rejected formal Judaism as being incompatible with the modern spirit and even found a Jewish-style Unitarianism untenable. In 1876, aided by the country's best-known Jew, Joseph Seligman, president of Emanu-El, Adler founded the nonsectarian Society for Ethical Culture and henceforth dissociated himself from all specifically Jewish endeavors.

Adler, concerned from the outset with public as well as with private morality, was outraged by the indifference of his liberal Unitarian colleagues of the Free Religious Association to the human problems facing an urban industrial society. "Deed, not Creed," his motto for Ethical Culture, spurred efforts to enlightened aid for the workingman. The resources of the Society followed suit. Formed in 1877 and molded by Adler's vision, the United Relief Works of the Society for Ethical Culture administered the first free kindergarten in the city, a district nursing department, and a workingman's school for children.

Led by his own commitment into the civic market place, Adler worked zealously for social reform. His efforts prompted the tenement house investigations of the early 1880's and the enactment of the first antisweating legislation. His lectures inspired the founding of a company headed by Joseph W. Drexel and Oswald Ottendorfer, dedicated to replacing rickety tenements with exemplary ones. By 1887 the Tenement House Building Company had erected on Cherry Street six model buildings costing $155,000, and housing Russian Jews engaged in the making of shirts, ties, and cigars. As civic reform projects multiplied, Adler responded to the call. The Ethical Society leader served as secretary of the Citizens' Union, became the guiding spirit behind the Committee of Fifteen's investigation into prostitution, and for many years chaired the National Child Labor Committee. Working tirelessly himself, Adler was to see his disciples found the Madison House Settlement on the Lower East Side to advance the Ethical program of social service.

When labor's well-wishers were few, Adler consistently showed himself to be a friend and frequently arbitrated and mediated labor disputes. Adler sponsored Henry George, although unsympathetic with the Single Tax idea, on the grounds that George focused public attention on the crucial labor question. Adler's Sunday public lectures on the issues of the day at Chickering Hall, and after 1892 at the new Carnegie Hall, attracted a considerable labor following—so much so that Samuel Gompers, whose sole connection with religion was maintained through his membership in the Ethical Society, could record that the Ethical Society leader was in the forefront of those who "were trying to work out ethical standards that would have meaning in the affairs of everyday life." Few men of his time took on a more comprehensive role in effecting these ideals than did Adler, to adherents of the Ethical Society, a prophet; to the many who looked to him for help, a spokesman.[10]

As New York's most pragmatic clergyman, Felix Adler set the pace of reform, but others were not far behind. Lyman Abbott, successor to Henry Ward Beecher as pastor of the Plymouth

Congregational Church and as editor of the *Christian Union*—the city's leading religious weekly—wrote in 1885:

Up to a recent date industrial competition even when producing suffering and death, was the best condition which existing circumstances would permit. It represented the normal tendency of commerce and society. It evolved invention and discovery, and made the unnumbered improvements upon which modern life is based. Under its auspices the growth of civilization has gone on from the rudest social state to its present development . . . We cannot move a foot, stir a step, to purchase or to sell, but we find the great genius of capital, the friend of man under our feet, by our side, at our back.

But, he counseled, wealth now had lost its power for good:

The very fact that wealth has accumulated and concentrated to such an extent as to injuriously affect the well-being of society, demands the application of new principles to industrial life, in order that competition may cease and diffusion begin. For, with all the good that competition has wrought, the principle is now a destructive one.

The trade unions, Abbott felt, by limiting competition and instituting cooperation, were destined to advance a new order of industrial relations.

In these years the *Christian Union* proved an effective sounding board for Abbott's program. In its columns, local clergymen published articles on "The Home Heathen" in the great cities. Josephine Shaw Lowell's "The Bitter Cry of the Poor in New York—Some of its Causes and Some of its Remedies," Booth's *In Darkest England* abridged, and Riis' *How the Other Half Lives* also were serialized in its pages. If *Christian Union* readers, "men of brains and leisure," were slow to respond to Abbott's exhortations, they were not unwilling to listen.[11]

The wealth and social standing of its leading members, its polity, its adaptability to the tenements, and its close ties with England, made the Episcopal Church an even more effective exponent of social Christianity. The Rev. R. Heber Newton spoke out earliest, but by virtue of his position, Henry Codman Potter, Episcopal Bishop of New York, came to be most influential.

In 1886 the spiritual guide to the Four Hundred publicly rejected the accepted economic view that labor was a commodity. Thereafter the bishop campaigned against the evils of sweatshops, slums, and child labor and effectively sustained, despite raised eyebrows in his congregation, his more radical colleagues in the church.[12]

Bishop Potter and his fellow churchmen pioneered in labor relations by organizing the Church Association for the Advancement of the Interests of Labor in 1887. The CAIL, in its monthly organ, *The Hammer and the Pen,* and in the public press, proclaimed labor the standard of social worth, asserting that "the divinely intended opportunity to labor" ought to be assured to all men. Crusading in top hat for labor, CAIL urged the use of the ballot, distributed printed literature, and sponsored lectures and public meetings at Annex Hall and Cooper Union. It urged fair treatment for saleswomen in retail stores during the 1889 holiday season, initiated special church services on the eve of Labor Day the following year, and circulated a petition that exhorted church members to assign all their printing orders to fair employers and to seek a shorter legal work day for printers. Special CAIL committees cooperated with labor and other reform groups. Its Labor Committee campaigned against the sweatshop and for the union label in the baker's trade, and, along with the Committee of Organized Labor of the Social Reform Club, participated in joint conferences with the Baker's Union. The CAIL Committee on Sweating, along with the Committee on Organized Labor of the Social Reform Club, the United Garment Workers' Union, and the Consumer's League was instrumental in printing a list of the "fair" retail houses.

But the CAIL's most dramatic work was to focus on strike settlement. In 1893 it appointed a Board of Arbitration headed by Bishop Potter, which the following year was reorganized as the New York Council of Meditation and Conciliation. The council rounded up representatives of capital and labor and representatives of the public, such as Bishop Potter, Felix Adler, Seth Low, and Mrs. Josephine Shaw Lowell, and successfully arbitrated the electrical workers' strike and the marble workers' strike in 1895; in the following year, the council also settled the lithographers' strike. The striking cloakmakers also found CAIL support. Invited to air their grievances at St. Michael's Church, the cloakmakers found that none less than Bishop Potter himself had come to preside. Through the decade of the nineties the CAIL, despite limited successes, brought a philosophic poise to the arena of labor that was not to be matched for a generation.[13]

THE GOOD NEIGHBOR

Of the many institutions that showed the social concern of upper-class reformers, few carried the commitment of the settlements. Unlike the austere Felix Adler and the stately Bishop Potter, who remained afar, settlement workers took up full-time residence in the tenements, sharing the food, the filth, the noise, and the heartache. Problems of health and home care, schooling and recreation, culture and politics, fused into the reform work of the settlements. Settlement reformers, less Olympian in judgment than the CAIL, but equally ardent in purpose, applied Felix Adler's "Deed, Not Creed" teachings to the home neighborhood where so much needed to be done.

The major settlement houses aimed to bring estranged New Yorkers together rather than to keep them apart and were deliberately nonsectarian. In this respect, they were unlike the earlier institutional churches. The Educational Alliance, formerly the Hebrew Institute, and the Jewish Emanu-El sisterhood settlement on Orchard Street, inspired by Miss Grace Dodge, followed the lead of the nonsectarian settlements; the Episcopal House of Aquila, which undertook to demonstrate both kosher and American cooking to Jewish housewives, did likewise.

The first settlement house in the United States, inspired by London's Toynbee Hall, was founded in tenement rooms on the Lower East Side in 1886 by Dr. Stanton Coit, an Ethical Society leader. The Neighborhood Guild's regenerative mission knew no bounds.

Irrespective of religious belief, or non-belief, all the people, men, women or children, in any one street, or any small number of streets in every working-class district . . . shall be organized into a set of clubs which are by themselves, or in alliance with those of other neighborhoods, to carry out or induce others to carry out, all the reforms, domestic, industrial, educational, provident, or recreative, which the social ideal demands.

In 1891, with Seth Low of Columbia University as president, the Neighborhood Guild became the University Settlement; seven years later it acquired its own well-equipped five-story building at the corner of Eldridge and Rivington streets. By then "a picket line of settlements, planted only a few blocks apart," stretched up the East Side from Henry Street to 104th Street. The College Settlement, founded in 1889 by Smith College women, the Nurses' or Henry Street Settlement, the Educational Alliance, and the University Settlement were the pride of the Lower East Side.[14]

Overwhelmed by the magnitude of their task, settlement workers were apt to undervalue the effectiveness of their efforts. James K. Paulding of the University Settlement described their influence as "individual rather than general, intensive rather than widespread." Yet these influences were deeply felt. The settlements, second only to the public schools in alerting youngsters to the greater American world, served to "Americanize" the children—and some parents too—and to advance the civic well-being of the crowded quarter. A variety of classes, clubs, lectures, entertainments, and well-stocked libraries contributed to this end.

Enlarging the scope of their projects, settlement workers soon spearheaded civic reform. They served on the district committee of the Charity Organization Society, cooperated with the City Vigilance League, the Good Government Clubs, the Trade and Labor Conference, and the Federation of East Side Workers. The Sanitary Union, composed largely of uptowners, remained in close touch with the police, fire, street cleaning, health, and public works departments to "secure law tempered with kindness and fairness towards the people." The University Settlement staff kept up intimate contact with the needs of the district, guided by developments throughout the city, and with

Mayor Strong's administration in 1895 acquired a mandate for specific reforms. Trips to Albany to secure the support necessary for such projects as police reorganization, the improvement of working conditions for women in mercantile houses, and the restriction of female labor in tenements were part of sustained, often tedious, efforts to effect practical results. Cooperation of the Board of Health and Police with their work brought marked improvements, as asphalt replaced cobblestones on the Lower East Side. "The filthiness which was found a year ago, and which in the preceding summer made this quarter almost unendurable, has been succeeded by a cleanly condition of the streets." [15]

As settlements brought cleanliness out of litter, so they coaxed into being community service for the sick. Founded by the Misses Mary Brewster and Lillian Wald, the Henry Street Settlement initially dedicated its resources to the founding of a nursing service, "most considerate of the dignity and independence of the patients, free from denominational or political influence." Miss Wald's success led to the incorporation of a nursing service into the city school system during the Low administration, the first of its kind in the world. In 1901, Miss Wald organized the Social Halls Association to provide wholesome amusement spots for tenement residents. In 1904 she saw the first unit, Clinton Hall, completed. Its two restaurants, kosher kitchen, lodge and club rooms, bowling alleys, billiard rooms, roof garden and dance hall (which also served as an auditorium seating 750 people) made Clinton Hall one of the Lower East Side's great social centers.[16]

The settlements fought as a unit for their programs. Small parks and recreation piers, the building of badly needed and more attractive school buildings, the wider use of school facilities, roof playgrounds, and school gymnasiums, were among the first goals of the settlements. School buildings were opened evenings and served as play centers for the galaxy of children's clubs that flourished in the district and that formerly had met in candy-stores. Nearly all open schools were located on the Lower East Side, as a demand for them in other parts of the city was slow to develop. Responding to the plea of the reformers, Public

School 63 transformed its classrooms evenings and emerged as the most active social center in the city.

Settlements, quick to espy a civic lack, put in a bid for small parks. In 1887 not a single park existed on Manhattan Island below Tompkins Square. In 1890 Charles B. Stover of the University Settlement founded the Society for Parks and Playgrounds with ex-Mayor Abram S. Hewitt as president. By the turn of the century the municipal administration had substantially, if tardily, implemented the Small Parks Act of 1887 and the Society for Parks and Playgrounds had grown into the Outdoor Recreation League. To the ten and one-half acres of Tompkins Square Park was added Corlears Hook Park with eight and one-third acres, Hamilton Fish Park with somewhat over three and one-half acres, Seward Park, at Canal and Jefferson streets, and a small triangular ground plot at Grand Street and East Broadway. In 1903 the most fully equipped public playground in the country was opened at Seward Park amid the world's most crowded tenements.[17]

The settlements spurred the building of municipal baths as well, although their program proceeded slowly. In 1891 the New York Society for the Improvement of the Condition of the Poor had erected the People's Bath in Center Market Place near Broome Street, and the trustees of the Baron de Hirsch Fund had constructed a bathhouse on Henry Street. Under pressure from the settlements, an act of 1895 that authorized the building of municipal baths was implemented six years later when the New York City Free Baths were opened on Rivington Street.

The University and Henry Street settlements developed into labor centers, with their residents intervening in the labor disputes of the district. The Waistmakers' Union, organized in 1899, and consisting primarily of young women, was invited to meet at the University Settlement after a vain search for a gathering place away from a saloon. In 1900 eleven unions that represented almost as many phases of the labor movement, including the Central Federated Union and the United Hebrew Trades, regularly assembled there. At the Henry Street Settlement capital and labor met on neutral ground, while Clinton Hall functioned as an informal labor center.[18]

Hester Street: The pushcart market on Friday morning at the height of the Sabbath trade.

Carpenters' and tinkers' exchange.

Sweatshop: A family at work.

Immigrants waiting their turns at the offices of the United Hebrew Charities.

Abraham Cahan (1860–1951), spokesman for Yiddish New York.

Bertha Kalisch as Ophelia in the Yiddish *Hamlet*.

Jacob Gordin and his fellow Yiddish playwrights discussing the drama in an East Side café.

A class in the condemned Essex Market School.

On the tenement circuit: A Henry Street Settlement nurse makes
her rounds over the rooftops in order to save miles of stair climbing.

"You're a bunch of scabs."

Samuel Gompers addresses three thousand shirtwaist-makers at Cooper Union.

Striking shirtwaist-makers selling copies of the *Call*, the New York Socialist daily.

A commentary on the Triangle Fire, 1911.

"מיט פֿולע הענט גיט"

!גאַסט אין קאָנגרעס אַ ווילקאָמען : מײַסטער לאָנדאָן גיט אָנקעל סעם—װעלקאָם!

Uncle Sam welcomes Meyer London to Congress.

Limited as their efforts were, the settlements also assuaged the hunger for books. At the University Settlement, the librarian was especially jealous of the imputed literary tastes of her young Jewish patrons.

In trying to guide their reading we must not have a Procrustean standard based on our own race sensibilities and individual preferences. We must not forget that these are the children for whose parents were written such distinctly non-Anglo-Saxon books as "Anna Karenina," "Crime and Punishment," and "Taras Bulba."

But she was not entirely right, for the longing for the American scriptures was unsurpassed. "Shall we ever be able to satisfy the demand for United States histories? We have now 182, and usually there are none on the shelves fitted to the capacity of the younger boys and girls." Bryant and Emerson, Longfellow and Lowell, were cherished by the junior East Side, who assigned them to the most starry heights of their literary firmament.[19]

BEYOND NEIGHBORHOOD

The contagion of reform that swept through the settlements spread into every department of civic life. The city itself was slow to recognize the craving for books as a basic human need, for many New Yorkers failed to see "why the city should provide a large appropriation for the reading of its citizens, any more than it should provide games." Not until 1879 did private citizens found the New York Free Circulating Library, the first in the city. Oswald Ottendorfer, publisher of the *New Yorker Staats-Zeitung,* Grace Church, and George Vanderbilt followed suit. Jewish groups combined to found the Aguilar Free Library Society, whose East Broadway unit, housed at the Educational Alliance, was by far the most assiduously used library in the city. In 1900 the New York Free Circulating Library's eleven branches were transformed into the circulation department of the New York Public Library and Andrew Carnegie's $5,200,000 donation for buildings placed New York's libraries on a new footing.[20]

While the settlements pursued their diverse mission, specially constituted reform groups turned their attention to the plight of laboring women. In 1888 the Misses Grace Dodge and Ida Van Etten organized the Workingwomen's Society. The society, in its fight for legislation to regulate the hours of work of women and children in factories, undertook an antisweating campaign in the clothing and cigar industries that led to the appointment of the state's first women factory inspectors. In 1903 the Workingwomen's Society became the Women's Trade Union League, adopted the slogan "The Eight-Hour Day; A Living Wage; to Guard the Home," and began to develop leaders directly from among the workingwomen. In 1892, following the Workingwomen's Society's investigation into the working conditions of saleswomen and cash girls, representatives of the three major faiths formed the Consumers' League. "All workers should receive, not the lowest wages, but fair living wages," became the League's credo, as it endorsed only those retail mercantile establishments with "Standards of a Fair House." Upon Edward King's advice, the League adopted a "white list" in preference to a "black list," a positive rather than a negative boycott so as to circumvent the judiciary's definition of a boycott as a conspiracy. By 1896, 53 of the city's leading retail houses had qualified for the white list.[21]

An era of municipal reassessment saw associations for political reform emerge and become permanent, as the aristocrat who aspired to become a democrat entered politics. Theodore Roosevelt, at 28 the Republican mayoralty candidate, set the keynote for a whole generation of reformers. The scion of one of New York's oldest families denounced the retreat from the active life by the "leaders of the so-called social world" and called for leadership by men of birth, breeding, and wealth. "A leisure class whose leisure simply means idleness is a curse to the community, and so far as its members distinguish themselves chiefly by aping the worst . . . traits of similar people across the water, they become both comic and noxious elements of the body politic." Roosevelt cautioned young men of education to "beware of associating only with the people of his own caste and of his own little ways of political thought." [22]

The first of a series of groups that was to place civic reform on a permanent footing, the People's Municipal League, was organized in 1890 by the Rev. R. Heber Newton, who was succeeded by the Rev. Charles H. Parkhurst, president of the New York Society for the Prevention of Crime. But by 1892 lay reformers had assumed the reins of civic leadership mindful that "no evil is so potent, and none works so much to undermine the best efforts of social and religious reformers as the political corruption that has flourished so long in our city." Successor to the moribund City Reform Club, the new City Club, through its committees and Good Government clubs with six thousand dues paying members, proposed to divorce municipal issues from state and national politics. In September 1894, subcommittees of the Committee of Seventy were appointed by the Chamber of Commerce to study the municipal problems of street cleaning, garbage disposal, waterfront improvement, civil service, public baths and lavatories, small parks, tenement house reform, and the state of the municipal payrolls. Formed in 1897, the Citizens' Union, improving upon its predecessors, in its first year distributed over 2000 circulars dealing with civic problems in German, Yiddish, Italian, and English. Whatever its faults, the Citizens' Union became a permanent factor in the life of the city dedicated to civic education and to raising standards in government. R. Fulton Cutting, father of the Citizens' Union, in 1908 founded the Bureau of Municipal Research that foreshadowed an era of unprecedented civic planning.[23]

Among the intellectual elite discussion groups also helped to crystallize reform sentiment. The select Nineteenth Century Club, founded in 1876 by Courtland Palmer to encourage free intellectual exchange in the conflict between science and theology, gradually turned its attention to civic and social matters. In its chambers, the labor question, socialism, and the recognition by public bodies of the doctrine of a living wage were roundly debated. In 1890 R. Heber Newton and Charles B. Stover organized a Christian Socialist group that met jointly with the Bellamy Nationalist clubs and listened to talks by Lyman Abbott, Walter Rauschenbusch, and other apostles of the social gospel. The Fabian-minded Altrurian League, formed in 1894, projected systematic investigations in social economics.

Organized in the same year upon the suggestion of Felix Adler, the Social Reform Club, led by Ernest Crosby and Father Thomas Ducey and composed equally of trade unionists and social reformers, was especially interested "in the elevation of society by the improvement of the condition of the wage-workers." [24]

The public lecture, reaching a wider audience than the civic organizations and reviving the pre–Civil War lyceum in a new form, became a distinct vehicle for communicating with New Yorkers. In 1889 at the *New York World's* suggestion, the Board of Education inaugurated a free lecture system that complemented the free evening schools, "the best evening schools of any city in the country" with "special schools for special nationalities." In 1897 well over four hundred thousand people attended over one thousand lectures in the city's schools, at Cooper Union, and at the Metropolitan Museum of Art. This program, under the direction of Henry M. Leipziger, pioneer in adult education at the YMHA, included such outstanding speakers as Theodore Roosevelt, Woodrow Wilson, and President William R. Harper of the University of Chicago. That same winter the public lectures at the Educational Alliance were almost entirely concerned with labor and social problems; Professor John B. Clark, Samuel Gompers, Mrs. Josephine S. Lowell, and Dr. Isaac A. Hourwich spoke on strikes, arbitration, trade unions, labor and politics, tenement house evils, and cooperation and competition. [25]

COOPER UNION: TUTOR OF EQUALITY

The crowning expression of the impulse to interpret a metropolitan civilization to its citizens was attained in 1897 with the founding of the People's Institute at Cooper Union. Established in 1859 by Peter Cooper for the education of the working classes, Cooper Union had become instead a technical mecca and had failed to live up to its broad promise. Yet Cooper Union was ideally situated to house "a perpetual mass meeting." It was located at the vortex of Little Italy, on the border of the Lower East Side, and surrounded by a great factory district that extended across the East and Hudson rivers to Long Island and New Jersey.

Charles Sprague Smith, formerly Gebhard Professor of German at Columbia, a "scholar in forgotten languages" and first teacher of Icelandic in the United States, was the initiator and first director of the People's Institute. In 1895 he founded the Comparative Literature Society for the mutual comprehension and conservation of the city's many ethnic cultures. Out of it arose the People's Institute. At first prospects for success seemed dim indeed, Smith recalled in *Working with the People.*

The attitude of the laboring class as a whole and also of a large number of active social reformers, up to the very beginning of our public work, may be defined as one of doubt and watching, with the expectation that this attempt would be one in another of the many half-hearted efforts to bring different sections of our society together —efforts doomed to failure by their very insincerity.

Yet within a few weeks, Smith gained the support of leading reformers, philanthropists and trade union leaders, and the People's Institute was launched.[26]

Before overflow audiences, inaugural lecturers Sidney Webb, Samuel Gompers, Thomas Davidson, Father Edward McGlynn, and Dr. R. Heber Newton spoke on the theme of democracy. Thereafter, nightly lectures on American and European history, literature, contemporary social problems, ethics, and sociology filled out a budding social science program. Talks on labor problems brought the city's leading trade unionists to Cooper Union's Great Hall, while discourses "directed mainly toward tracing the laws of social progress and applying them to present problems" foreshadowed the "new history." In 1899 the Honorable Hugh Lusk of New Zealand lectured on the history of democracy in Australia; Boston's Mayor Josiah Quincy spoke on public baths and gymnasiums; Edward Everett Hale invoked the spirit of Emerson; Booker T. Washington held forth on America's race problem; and Michigan's Governor Hazen S. Pingree discussed the trusts. Jacob Riis, John R. Commons, and "Golden Rule" Jones were among the galaxy of leading reformers to hold the platform, as the People's Institute aspired to become an evening school in a living social science, "a people's forum that summons to its bar officials of State and city to give accounts of their stewardship, and whose summons is heeded."

Earlier as later, the socialist theme ranked first in popularity. A debate staged between Columbia's Professor Edwin R. A. Seligman and millionaire California socialist Gaylord Wilshire packed the Great Hall. "Crowding aisles, entrances, and all vacant spaces, even clambering upon the platform, leaving only room there for the speakers," nearly 3500 people jammed the 1600-seat auditorium and hundreds of others milled about outside. "No policemen were present to enforce order and none were needed."[27]

Proclaiming religion without dogma, the Sunday night People's Church, affiliated with the People's Institute, was especially popular; even skeptics and nonbelievers did not balk at the admission charge. Professor Charles A. Briggs of the Union Theological Seminary, Lyman Abbott, and the young Stephen S. Wise were among the array of clergymen who volunteered to face the throng of 1600, about half of them, including one hundred women, from the Lower East Side. Discussion unfailingly became animated but rarely approached disorder. After 1910 the new Labor Temple, nearby, organized by the Presbyterian minister Charles Stelzle, drew off the chronic expounders of socialism. At the Labor Temple, socialists and other radicals made up 75 per cent of the audience and, here too, at least 50 per cent were heterodox-minded Jews who reveled in attacking their favorite target, organized religion. Yet the "metaphysical crank" —"the person that insists that he cannot 'see or smell or feel God!' and therefore cannot accept him; and the man who will have his little joke"—who wrote his questions out by the yard still stood his ground in the people's church, noted Jacob Riis good-humoredly.[28]

Through the People's Lobby, the People's Institute mobilized sentiment for the municipal ownership of subways, industrial arbitration, tenement legislation, and laws promoting public parks and schools. In 1909 the People's Lobby, cooperating with the Women's Municipal League and the College Settlement, persuaded the state to regulate dance halls. The weekly *People's*

Institute Bulletin, later to be the *Civic Journal,* published reports by the Institute's Legislative Committee on pending bills at Albany, ran columns on civic and social matters, and featured articles on the Jews of the Bible and the Lower East Side.

For a time, some New Yorkers envisioned the expansion of the People's Institute into a People's Palace with a separate edifice to house its varied activities. But the People's Palace never rose beyond the blueprint stage. However appealing the idea, to most reformers the very name seemed shamefully patronizing and un-American. The People's Institute ever retained the democratic spirit that inspired its founders. Here labor's friends received their last honors. Henry George, Father McGlynn ("the People's Priest"), Ernest Crosby, Bishop Potter ("the People's Bishop"), and in 1910, Charles Sprague Smith himself, were paid tribute before being laid to final rest.[29]

Unfortunately, the People's Institute never fulfilled Smith's expectations as a center of culture for all levels of society. The aura of condescension clung to it and to its director as it did to other reform ventures.

The millionaire and the tramp jogged elbows, and every section of our community was represented, though the tramp was naturally more in evidence than the millionaire. But the men in rags and tatters, the great unwashed, associated on terms of equality with the men clothed in fine raiment, and for a time the Angel of Peace spread his wings over the Assembly, and the spirit of brotherhood ruled apparently every heart in a delightful Pentecostal way. But that all passed quickly.

Lecturers at the People's Institute were often ill-at-ease before the heavily Lower East Side audiences; a disconsolate professor of literature commented: "the people . . . care nothing about literature as such . . . They are somewhat daft . . . on questions ethical, social, sociological . . . and apparently have no room in their minds for any other interests." Sympathetic teachers, however, welcomed such students. "This has been an experience that I can only call exhilarating. The audience is the most thoroughly alive crowd that I ever had the pleasure of addressing. They listen well, are most responsive, and join in discussion with an eagerness that is positively exciting."[30]

The People's Institute, in an effort to come closer to the Lower East Side, briefly rented the Educational Alliance auditorium in 1898 and treated East Siders to a lecture series entitled, "The Problems which the Nineteenth Century Hands over for Solution to the Twentieth." So began an all too brief association between sensitive East Side youngsters and Thomas Davidson. This "Knight Errant of the Intellectual Life" had crossed and recrossed the Atlantic in search of knowledge, inspiration, and above all, the ideal spiritual society. In 1889 this evangelizing Scot, who attributed the infirmities of American political institutions to ignorance, had founded the short-lived New York Society for the Promotion of Good Citizenship to educate Americans in the "history and dignity" of their heritage. Davidson, disillusioned with Christian theology, the "unbrotherly, supernatural, world-despising religion of the churches," hungered for a truly Christian society where "the cruel distinction that has so long been drawn between civic and religious life, between the service of man and the service of God, will be blotted out, and it will be recognized that a noble civic life, which seeks the good of all, is the most religious of all lives." He was convinced, he wrote further in the *International Journal of Ethics,* that "the Jewish religion is far more rational than the Christian, and indeed, Christians, as they advance, come nearer and nearer to Judaism." [31]

But Davidson perplexed his young admirers, imbued with the slogans of Marxian socialism, by denouncing all collectivist schemes as begetters of paternalism, fatal to the development of spiritual integrity and personal independence. Despite his opposition to the socialist enthusiasm, Davidson endeared himself to his young disciples, among them Morris R. Cohen, the later renowned City College philosopher, by his personification of the full-blooded life of the mind, his unquenchable idealism, and his virile asceticism. They believed as he that knowledge made men free. The Breadwinners' College, also known as "Branch B of the Educational Alliance" or "the Davidson Club," perpetuated the memory of its beloved founder, who from the glens and mountains of his youth brought to the youth of the Lower East Side a devotion to the educational ideal. [32]

NEW PATRONS OF THE ARTS

The opening of the doors of the Metropolitan Museum of Art on Sundays in 1891, in response to Charles B. Stover's campaign, announced the spreading of the spirit of democratic reform to the arts. A projected East Side Museum and Art Gallery to stimulate the artistic consciousness of tenement dwellers, however, was never seriously considered. Soon music was to become even more accessible to the masses. While strolling German bands and itinerant Italian street musicians played an important role in the city's informal musical life into the late 1880's, more refined music continued to be the preserve of the fashionable and the well-to-do. Germans, with more cultivated musical tastes, proved especially sensitive to this civic shortcoming.

Recognizing that music contributes more than any other art to brighten and beautify our lives, and that it is the art that can be practiced by the greatest number of people, since nature has furnished nearly every person with a correct ear and a singing voice, I have decided to open a course of lessons in reading music and choral singing,

announced Frank Damrosch, who with his father Leopold, his brother Walter, and his sister Clara, comprised the city's most distinguished musical family. In 1892 Damrosch organized the People's Singing Classes for young adults. Teachers donated their services, music was provided free, and a ten-cent charge per session eliminated all traces of charity. By 1905, 2000 young people, including many East Siders, were enrolled. On Sundays, under the conductor's personal supervision, the People's Choral Union for more advanced students met to study the choral masterpieces. In 1904 Damrosch founded the Institute of Musical Art of the City of New York (later the Juilliard School of Music) and James Loeb's half-million dollar donation to that institution assured free musical training to talented youth.

The Henry Street and University settlements did not neglect musical training. And Miss Emily Wagner's efforts to provide free musical instruction to the children of the Lower East Side, beginning in a church basement on Rivington Street, led Frank Damrosch and David Mannes to found the Society of the Music

School Settlement for the musically talented. In 1907 1200 youngsters received weekly lessons at the Music Settlement buildings on East 3rd Street; by then its considerable staff included eighteen settlement-trained assistant teachers.[33]

Popularly priced symphonic concerts were inaugurated in 1899 at Cooper Union, when the People's Institute yielded five evenings to Franz X. Arens and the People's Symphony Concerts Association, which aimed to create the "musical atmosphere" wanting in the city. The People's Symphony Concerts, starting inauspiciously with a half-filled hall, by their fourth year were completely sold out before the season's opening. Subsequently the concerts were transferred to Carnegie Hall where the overflow could be accommodated.

Serious drama also became part of the People's Institute program. The People's Theater presented Shakespearean recitals before audiences of over 2000 people. But the overcrowding of the Great Hall at Cooper Union, as with the symphonic concerts, led to the enforcement of the building codes. "The bad tidings spread over the Lower East Side among the thousands who have rejoiced in the Cooper Union dramas and music more than in the opportunity of listening to their most daring socialists. Seldom has the speed with which tidings travel had a better illustration," reported the *New York Times*. As part amend, perhaps, for the blow to popular serious drama, the Misses Alice and Irene Lewisohn directed an annual Spring Festival in a special theater for the people at the Henry Street Settlement that presaged the Neighborhood Playhouse, pioneer of the little theater movement.[34]

HAND IN HAND

Apprenticeship in the 1890's led, after the turn of the century, to partnership between the young graduates of the settlements and reformers. In 1890 Richard Watson Gilder, editor of the *Century*, prematurely had urged that a group of young East Siders be induced to publish a newspaper devoted to civic matters. In 1901, in the wake of the successful Low campaign and the enactment of the tenement house law, local Jewish and

Protestant clergymen, disaffected politicians, and young settlement graduates founded the East Side Civic Club. The club, modeled on the Civil Service Reform Association, aspired "to organize the public opinion of the East Side, and . . . to provide a deeper basis for the public growth and expression of this public opinion through civic education."

The East Side Civic Club waged its most effective campaign in defending the Tenement House Law of 1901 against amendment and even managed to unite the Yiddish press on this issue, the only instance of cooperation in Yiddish journalism. Club members, aided by the English and Yiddish newspapers, gathered 40,000 signatures to a mammoth petition. At the People's Institute, a resolution on the tenement question was carried by a vote of 1700 to 1, and rumor had it that the one dissenter was a tenement house speculator. Marshaled by the club, twenty-two East Side organizations were represented at hearings before Mayor Low; a large delegation from the Citizens' Union, Tenement House Commissioner Robert W. DeForest, R. Fulton Cutting, Richard Watson Gilder, Lyman Abbott, the editors of the Yiddish press, and members of the club journeyed to Albany to meet with Governor Odell. East Side Civic Club representatives, lobbying for a district that "will stand any sort of treatment without complaint or protest," devotedly attended Board of Estimate meetings. Club members linking their efforts with other reform groups, petitioned for additional school buildings, improved transit service, adequate street cleaning, small parks, playgrounds, and push-cart markets.[35]

In the early years of the twentieth century socialism, domesticated, became indistinguishable from social reform. Indeed, on the Lower East Side, socialism acquired a native American air. Looking to Union Square, the Rand School, endowed in 1906 by Mrs. Carrie Rand, mother-in-law of the Christian Socialist George D. Herron, annually inducted two hundred students into the temple of the new American socialism. Largely East Siders, they listened to Charles Beard, Robert Bruere, Morris Hillquit, and John Spargo lecture on socialism, government, economics, American history, and municipal problems. Courting Lower East Siders, Harriet Stanton Blatch led the suffragette invasion of the district in 1906 "to try and rouse working women on the question of the suffrage." Personal contact revealed the common source of the ideals that inspired social reformers and East Siders alike, reported the *Evening Post* in 1908.

One thing that is taking a hold on the radical Socialists this fall is the speaking of the Christian Socialists from the campaign platforms. Socialists . . . are not much on mixing the doctrine of the Bible with their theories and practices, but the ministers and church workers who have gone on the Socialist stump have made a "hit" with their audiences by the stories of the prophets and the lessons in leadership derived from Solomon and Moses. This new brand of campaign argument has "caught on."

At the Church of the Sea and Land, at Hester and Market streets, the Rev. Alexander Irvine, Presbyterian social gospeler and socialist, consistently drew upon the Holy Scriptures for his text. "Sunday evening in the Spring and Fall, I spoke to large congregations of Jewish people from the steps of the church, on the spirit of Jewish history—as to what it had done for the world and what it still could do." [36]

The era's transcendent note was heightened by the widely publicized nuptials of East Siders Rose Pastor and Anna Strunsky to millionaire socialists James G. P. Stokes and William E. Walling respectively. To some the earthly millenium envisioned in Zangwill's current drama, "The Melting Pot," seemed at hand as Christian and Jew, rich and poor, American and immigrant, joined in bonds of matrimony. [37]

The fresh gusts of social reform advanced the welfare of the city's less privileged inhabitants and significantly affected the lives of Russian Jews and their children. Mediators between the Lower East Side and the incomprehensible world beyond radiated kindliness and humanitarianism, however cool and subdued. Inevitably the outstretched paternal hand often was uncomprehending, the grand gesture patronizing, and the plans of reformers, despite much accomplishment, as frequently romantic as realistic. Yet views were broadened and human sympathies deepened. Building on these foundations, patrician and democratic reformers were drawn to a common meeting ground of socially meaningful activity unequaled in the city's annals.

∾ I I ∾

The Political Wilderness

If new fresh energies do not betake themselves to politics, the country will certainly be doomed to decline and dissolution.   Morris Hillquit (1895)

LACKING in fundamental issues, politics in the years following the Civil War proved incidental to the activities of the city's uptown Jews, who were strenuously absorbed in business and professional routines. Jewish political conduct was guided by ethnic and family loyalties, humored by the idiosyncrasies of personal and business ties. Old New York Jews generally were Democrats, as were most Jews of post-bellum Southern origin. Realtors, liquor purveyors, and saloon keepers, led by Morris Tekulsky, brawny president of the State Liquor Dealers' Association, as well as many Jewish workmen, were prudentially drawn to the amiable sachems of St. Tammany. German Jews shared the dominant politics of their fellow Germans, Republican in national, independent in state and local, affairs; in recognition of their loyalties, in the 1890's Edward Lauterbach, a son of Bavarian immigrants, was chosen chairman of the Republican County Committee of New York. East European immigrants of the 1870's and earlier, idolizing Lincoln, of whom two appreciative biographies had appeared in the East European Hebrew press, followed the lead of their German coreligionists and supported the party of the Great Emancipator. But by the late 1880's, the Lincoln image had faded. For the new immigrants, the Civil War was less than a dim memory.[1]

Russian Jewish immigrants, fresh from the Old World, suspected all government and were untrained in its forms. Only gradually did they learn to use the tools of politics. They were bound to neither the Democratic nor the Republican party by interest, habit, or sentiment, and their humble place in the city's economy only buttressed their alienation. Groping toward political identity, they tripped into the pitfalls of the innocent. They wandered in a haze of impotence from Tammany to reform to revolution trying to express themselves through the politics of the tenement.

The newcomer's first encounters with government differed little from his trials with tsarist officials. For the Russian Jew, "law," "police," and "prison" conjured up Siberian tortures. Victimized at every turn, he found it hard to associate liberty with law. To the striking garment worker, the policeman's poised billy loomed as a hideous weapon. To the peddler, the first lesson in Americanism was to placate "the brass button" whenever possible, "to come to Limerick," and "five dollars protection money for the policeman" was the recognized business fee. Furthermore, Sunday laws, seemingly contrived to despoil poor Sabbath-observant Jews, provided grounds for systematic police extortion. A brush with the law over some irregularity meant a drive to the Clinton Street Court, where justice of a kind was meted out in an atmosphere reeking of everything but solemnity.

Every day a bewildered, ignorant, pitiable mass is jammed into the benches, rushed to the bar, and sent home—with as little decency and less formality than one commonly finds in a Bowery Museum. Cases are overlooked, adjourned and dismissed simply because the litigants are unable to understand when they are wanted, or are unable to make their presence known.

Even more repellent was the Essex Market Court, headquarters of Martin Engel, kosher chicken czar and Tammany district leader. Facing into the stench and tumult of a live poultry mart and abbatoir, it stood opposite "Silver Dollar" Smith's saloon, where cases were fixed and law tempered for a consideration.[2]

"DE ATE": TENEMENT LOYALTIES

From the Battery to St. Mark's Place, politics in the latter decades of the nineteenth century, was the province of Tammany subalterns associated with the unsavory vocations lining the Bowery and its tributaries, and beholden to "Big Tim" Sullivan. Building permits, extensions on commercial paper, bail, and pardons for offenders could all be arranged for those on friendly terms with the Tammany chieftain. When Big Tim passed the good word, tenement and health department inspectors looked the other way; and for favors conferred, Big Tim expected Election Day gratitude.

In the 1890's the handy-fisted Baxter Street Jews, schooled in Irish political ways, dominated the four Republican and six Democratic clubs of the Eighth Assembly District, known as "De Ate." Although in the heart of the Tammany-controlled tenements, De Ate, the city's principal Jewish assembly district, with voters of sixteen different nationalities and a considerable German bloc, voted Republican. And "Stitch" McCarthy, born Sam Rothberg, Republican captain and saloonkeeper, often bested Tammany at its own game.[3]

But a newly enrolled electorate, combined with new issues, decisively upset this Republican stronghold in 1892 and the Ate's assemblyman, "Silver Dollar" Smith, a nominal Republican, hastily donned Tammany attire. At a time when Jewish immigration reached a new peak in the wake of the Moscow expulsions, the Republican administration in Washington assumed control of immigration, tightened regulations, made efforts to exclude refugees on the grounds that they were assisted immigrants, and drafted restrictive immigration legislation. In the fall of 1892 the fear that immigrants might become carriers of typhus and cholera induced President Harrison to proclaim a special quarantine that practically brought immigration to a standstill. In October and November of 1892 only 537 Jewish immigrants were admitted at the port of New York, compared to 9047 in the corresponding months a year earlier. The polls of the Eighth Assembly District tolled protest and dismay. Henceforth, legislative attempts to restrict immigration, and Russia's oppression of Jews would continue to be major political issues in Yiddish New York. From 1888 to 1912, in seven presidential elections, no party carried the Eighth Assembly District twice in succession; these special questions, charged with deepest personal emotion, contributed to the district's political inconstancy.[4]

If foreign concerns affected immigrant ballots at decisive turns in national elections, domestic matters proved more steadily compelling to an overwhelmingly labor constituency. In 1886 new immigrants were treated to a rare slice of political drama. In that year the most able candidates ever to vie for the mayor's office engaged in the most hotly contested campaign in the city's annals. Henry George kindled labor unrest into political revolt and captured the hearts of Jews of the new exodus with "The Land Laws of Moses," an address which the Single Taxer first delivered at the San Francisco YMHA. Jewish immigrants enthusiastically enrolled in the Tenth Ward Hebrew Association for George, the Henry George Tailors' League, and the Henry George Tobacco Workers' League. De Ate proved the only district in the city to register a greater vote for the defeated candidates, Henry George and Theodore Roosevelt, than for the victorious Tammany-backed Abram S. Hewitt. If contemporary observers were prone to exaggerate the George vote in the Eighth District, taking voices for ballots, the election returns assured doubters of the district's independence.[5]

BALLOTS OF DESPAIR

The Henry George campaign opened a new era of labor evangelism on the Lower East Side. There socialist candidates were to find their most fervent constituencies. But in 1891 the largely Jewish Hungarian and Russian SLP clubs counted only 140 members, and the New York City–centered Socialist Labor Party persisted "a German colony, a branch of the German social democracy." The New York press forebearingly depicted socialists relaxing in the quiet refuge of their beer garden headquarters, "a bit of Old Germany transplanted in some mysterious manner to modern New York." The editors of the *Times* thought the socialist *New Yorker Volks-Zeitung,* "imbued with the American thirst for news," much like any other newspaper after readers "grew tired of having dished up for their daily intellectual meat—Socialism without condiments." Socialist leaders Alexander Jonas and Serge Schevitch, gentle and scholarly, were portrayed sympathetically and the party's platform was presented in detail in the *Tribune.* The stately Mrs. Pamelia Leonard, mother of Lillian Russell and a disciple of Mary Baker Eddy, presided over the tiny American SLP branch and reading club for Americanized Germans, which also drew assorted female spiritualists, Greenbackers, Single Taxers, temperance crusaders, associates of the neighboring *Truthseeker,* the curious and lonely of many persuasions, and those with no convictions at all.[6]

In 1890 this politically timid German party acquired in Daniel DeLeon a spokesman with an unusual command of the English language and its vituperative range. This brilliant Curaçao-born son of a Jewish military surgeon, who had campaigned for Henry George, flirted with Bellamy Nationalism, and lectured on international law at Columbia University, at last found a home in the labor movement. DeLeon inveighed against "Lager Bier Sozialismus" and "Deutschtum," and replaced German with English as the party's official language. He edited the weekly and daily party organ, the *People;* ran repeatedly for political office; and sought to inspire and lead a political labor movement, his own Socialist Trade and Labor Alliance. In the midst of the nation's worst economic crisis up to that time, DeLeon became the Socialist Labor Party's undisputed leader.[7]

With the advent of DeLeon, the Jewish labor movement, torn between politically minded socialists and apolitical anarchists, finally accepted political leadership. For a people in the throes of a great awakening on the urban frontier, politics carried a religious intensity and social urgency to which neither major party was prepared to respond. The *Arbeiter Zeitung* hailed Election Day in 1892 as "Judgment Day" and likened the Socialist Labor Party to the Abolitionists. The "joy that an honest man gains on fulfilling a sacred duty" was sufficient reward for voting for its candidates. To Abraham Cahan, writing in the

Zukunft, the Democratic, Republican, and Populist parties were not true parties. "Pitiful souls, bought souls . . . but not parties . . . Is this a party that changes its program, its very soul every Monday and Thursday!" Reform was hopeless, pronounced the *Arbeiter Zeitung,* upon the election of Mayor Strong in 1894. "There is no need to celebrate over Strong's 42,000 majority but rather over Grant's 42,000 minority. We must not cheer the victory of the aristocratic good government clubs but the defeat of Tammany." At the pit of the most acute depression in the nation's history, Morris Hilkowitz (Hillquit) predicted, "if new fresh energies do not betake themselves to politics, the country will certainly be doomed to decline and dissolution." [8]

In the depths of the crisis, Daniel DeLeon ran for Congress from the city's most hard-hit district, the Lower East Side. The Socialist Labor Party standard-bearer polled 10 per cent of the vote in 1894, rising to 18 per cent two years later, the most impressive total by far for any SLP candidate in the city. Although the Yiddish press identified DeLeon as a Jew, he never acknowledged his Jewish origins and to his disciples the beginnings of this apostle to the despairing were neither clear nor relevant. In the late 1890's DeLeon consistently received 30 per cent of the ballots cast for assemblyman in his own Lower East Side district. Thereafter he continued to run for public office and to edit the *Daily People* until its demise, two months before his death in 1914. But the changed scene in the early years of the twentieth century left DeLeon a political anachronism. His voice was still heard but failed to command. [9]

DeLeon's ambition to create a labor movement in his own image burst the illusions of party unity among the socialist factions bound together by depression and bewilderment. Personal abuse and deliberate falsehoods in the German and English schismatic press, peppered by legal suits, were matched by the scurrilous feud for control of the Yiddish Arbeiter Zeitung Publishing Association. The riot of verbiage and "polemic" registered the Socialist Labor Party's low estate and the talent for vilification and slander confirmed its political fatuousness. [10]

In this atmosphere, grace, tact, and gratitude were unknown.

Dismayed by the 1896 election results, when a Republican presidential aspirant carried New York City for the first time, Louis Miller raged: "Socialism seems so clear, simple, and logical to us that only a dunce or a scoundrel could fail to understand it." Yet the gap between the logical intellectuals and their errant flocks did not go unfilled for lack of trying. In 1897 upon the publication of the Socialist Labor Party platform "in accurate and clear Yiddish," the *Forward* urged: "it is the duty of those who as yet do not understand socialism, to read and study it. The excuse that it is difficult is not valid. Every point is explained and translated . . . With simple care the stated principles easily can be understood." [11]

Leading radical polemicists Benjamin Feigenbaum and Louis Miller argued the causes for the Socialist Labor Party's disappointing showing in the *Zukunft's* seven final issues before its suspension in 1897. Feigenbaum, mixing allusions to Bryce, Marx, and Nicholas Paine Gilman, attributed the party's misfortune to an American "cultural lag," that obstructed the operation of the economic laws of scientific socialism, and counseled patience. He closed with a quotation from Hypolyte Taine: "We must wait out the transition period which the Anglo-Saxon must take between thought and deed." Miller, on the contrary, urged a complete change of tactics—the abandonment of the trade unions and the adoption of the pragmatic American reform socialism advocated by the American Nicholas Paine Gilman. [12]

At the turn of the century socialist politics lost its appeal to German trade unionists. The passing of the depression, the legalization of the Social Democratic Party in Germany, the precipitous fall in German immigration, and the dismemberment of the Socialist Labor Party, all contributed to a mass defection of German members. The integration of German unionists into the expanding AFL left only a grey-haired socialist remnant still interested and active in New York. Russian names thronged to the party ticket as the weight of the socialist appeal swung to the East European districts. When a leading Russian Social Democrat and Plekhanov disciple, Dr. Sergius Ingerman, became editor of the German Socialist opposition newspaper,

Gross New York Arbeiter Zeitung, Russian clearly had replaced German in the social democracy of New York.[13]

BALLOTS OF HOPE

In 1901 the Fusion Party turned the spotlight on the Lower East Side following the exposure of prostitution by the Committee of Fifteen, Bishop Potter, and the Women's Municipal League. Young George W. Morgan, attorney for the Committee of Fifteen, rented an office on Delancey Street, organized a staff of open-air speakers, and canvassed the Lower East Side house by house. The Fusion Party candidate for district attorney, William Travers Jerome, opened his campaign headquarters in two bare rooms above a saloon, stumped the district night after night, and between 10 and 5, Sundays included, saw anyone who wanted to quiz him on his plans. A son of one of the nation's leading textile men, Fred Stein, unversed in Yiddish, founded the eight-page *Kol fun der Ghetto* (Voice of the Ghetto), and for eleven consecutive days distributed tens of thousands of copies of this reform campaign daily free. The election of Seth Low, president of Columbia University and the University Settlement, at the head of a balanced ticket that included a German Catholic for president of the Board of Aldermen and a Jew for Manhattan borough president gratified the aspirations of newly risen ethnic groups for political recognition and was accountable in part to the vigor of the East Side campaign.[14]

Republican reformers, working in municipal campaigns in the 1890's had become aware of potential support among Jewish immigrants. In some Tammany-controlled lower Manhattan wards, Jewish immigrants came to hold the balance of power, forming a counterweight to the regular Democrats. In the early years of the twentieth century, Republican progressivism, and Rooseveltian magnetism and knight-errantry in defense of persecuted Russian Jewry carried a number of East Side Jews into high Republican councils. Theodore Roosevelt, a former New York police commissioner and governor, had been sensitive to new sources of urban Republican support, and upon reaching the White House did not forget his friends. In the presidential campaign of 1904 Yiddish community leaders enrolled 4000 voters in the Independent Roosevelt Committee. For the first time in thirty years the Austro-Hungarian Sixteenth Assembly District, a banner Tammany district, elected a Republican assemblyman. What is more, the Roosevelt landslide nearly carried a Republican into Congress, a feat never before approached on the Lower East Side. The poet Menahem Dolitzky feted the defender of Russia's Jews against tsarist barbarism in a "Psalm to Roosevelt," beginning: "Father of our country, how shall we honor thy name." The Sixteenth District's Hungarian-born state legislator, combining with Hearst forces against Tammany, was re-elected in 1905. The continued Republican showing furthered the fortunes of Jewish political hopefuls. In 1906 an East Side Jew of the great migration was nominated and elected to a high state judicial post; in 1908 the Hungarian-born clothing salesman Samuel Koenig, a Sixteenth District leader known as "Little McKinley" for his vigorous support of the tariff in 1888, was elected secretary of state; and in 1911, at the high noon of Republican progressivism, Koenig succeeded Herbert Parsons as New York Republican county chairman.[15]

In these years, too, William Randolph Hearst reached the pinnacle of his fame as the champion of the tenement dwellers. And on the Lower East Side the politically ambitious publisher of the *New York American and Journal* became quite a vote-getter. In 1903, when American newspapers gave scant attention to Russian news, Hearst dispatched special correspondent Michael Davitt, "Great Irish Patriot and Writer," to report on the Kishinev atrocities firsthand; in 1905 the *New York American* featured an on-the-scene account of the Red Sunday massacre in St. Petersburg, cabled on commission by Maxim Gorky. Hearst thundered against Russian barbarisms in the name of Americanism, even threatening war. He led the fund drive to aid pogrom victims, printed pogrom reports in Hebrew type, and helped launch the campaign for the repeal of the Russian Commercial Treaty of 1832. In 1904 Hearst entered Yiddish journalism directly. His *Yiddisher Amerikaner* soon failed, but when a candidate for mayor in 1905 and for governor in 1906, he published Yiddish campaign dailies. In the bitterly contested mayoralty race, Hearst carried the Lower East Side, falling 3600 votes short of taking the election. Hearst, endorsed for the governorship by a shaken Tammany in 1906, overwhelmed his victorious Republican opponent by tremendous majorities on the Lower East Side. Even in 1909 the publisher, in a final independent bid for the mayoralty, retained a considerable East Side following.[16]

In the opening years of the twentieth century the American-born sons of the great migration became an important force in politics. Although Jews counted but one Tammany district leader in 1907, the volume and fluidity of ballots forced Irish sachems to yield some desirable places to the newcomers in its ranks who clamored for recognition, even if they were unable to deliver the vote with professional regularity. For many years an eloquent friend of the Jews, Ohio-born Samuel S. Cox, had represented the Lower East Side in Washington. At last in 1900 Tammany gave the nod to Henry M. Goldfogle, a municipal court judge and a regular son of the old East Side. A giant screen on Yiddish Newspaper Row announced in Hebrew characters that Goldfogle was to become the first Jew to represent the great Jewish district in Congress. In 1905 former socialist Louis Miller founded what became the East Side's first pro-Democratic Yiddish daily, the *Warheit*. And in 1913, the East Side's Aaron Jefferson Levy, born on the Fourth of July (1881), became New York State Assembly majority leader and potential Grand Sachem of the Hall.[17]

Socialists—both German and Russian in intellectual heritage —in the early years of the twentieth century discovered the Lower East Side. The *Forward* urged East Siders to form their own Committee of Fifteen rather than to rely upon "uptown" and reprimanded socialists for declaiming about the future society while ignoring practical reforms. The socialist daily praised the work of the East Side Civic Club and enjoined its readers to unite with reformers in all efforts at civic betterment, bearing in mind that "our motives are not their motives." In 1903 all four Yiddish dailies joined with reformers to oppose attempts to thwart the Tenement House Law of 1901. Quoting the Talmudic dictum, "Pleasant quarters broaden man's understanding," the *Forward*, urged its readers to sign the petition being circulated by the East Side Civic Club. By 1909 the *Forward*, mellowed even in its opinions of Tammany, acknowledged that the recently deceased "Little Tim" Sullivan, faithful aide to his namesake, boss of the East Side, had well acquitted the role of the benevolent Tammany father, but reminded its readers of Borough President John Ahearn's misuse of city funds.[18]

The coming-of-age of the East European Jewish vote in the city coincided with mounting Russian tyranny, growing anti-immigrant sentiment, and the call for domestic reform. National politics continued to respond to the issues that troubled Yiddish New York. Elections, called the "magnificent American phenomenon" by the *Yiddisher Zhurnal*, had made tens of thousands of immigrants into Americans, jealous of their newly won status. Although the Lower East Side districts recorded the smallest proportion of registered voters in the city in 1912, reflecting the recent immigration and political inexperience of its electorate, the total number of Jewish voters in New York was estimated at 113,000. Overwhelmingly newcomers, Jews comprised over 23 per cent of the electorate in Manhattan. Candidates for office, from the presidency down, appealed to the interests of their Jewish constituents. In 1908 William Howard Taft's campaign speech at the East Side's Thalia Theatre was devoted solely to the immigration and Russian passport questions. For the first time in 1911 and again in 1912 immigrants celebrated the Fourth of July by marching in huge parades and listening to music and patriotic speeches. On the eve of the 1912 elections, the Yiddish press was a political billboard. The Progressive Party, in a series of ads, took its stand on the Russian question and on labor and immigration legislation, and all parties heatedly contended for the immigrant vote.[19]

A three-cornered race for the governorship of New York that insured Democratic victory in 1912 allowed East Siders to pay tribute to the nation's most distinguished Jew in public life, Oscar S. Straus, the fortuitous Progressive candidate. Along with Jacob H. Schiff and Cyrus Sulzberger, Straus had headed the National Committee for the Relief of Sufferers by Russian Massacres in 1905 at the time of the second Kishinev pogrom. In

1906 even the socialist *Forward* had hailed Roosevelt's appointment "of this independent Democrat and earnest Jew" as Secretary of Commerce and Labor. In 1912 the nationalist Yiddish daily, the *Warheit*, hailed Straus as a truly great Jew, "a famous Jewish diplomat, scholar, and communal worker," and a symbol of the Jew's right to high office. A vote for Straus expressed a true Americanism that would make for a bond between non-Jew and Jew. A vote for Straus would redeem the Jewish name now besmirched by the front-page notoriety of Jewish criminals. As a final fillip, the *Warheit* declared: "our enemies in Russia are opposed to Straus's election." A *Warheit* write-in and Yiddish theater straw poll disclosed that nearly 79 per cent of Yiddish New York intended to vote for Straus.[20]

Most Jewish immigrants, as predicted, cast their ballots for Straus. It was not an easy choice, for they were torn between their admiration for their coreligionist and their sense of gratitude to East Side Congressman William Sulzer. Jews could not forget that it was Straus's Democratic opponent, the Chairman of the House Foreign Affairs Committee, who had introduced the resolution calling for the abrogation of the Russian Treaty. In six predominantly Jewish districts, Straus's presence on the ballot as a Progressive offset Wilson's attractive candidacy and compensated for Roosevelt's diminished popularity. In three districts where Straus received overwhelming majorities, Roosevelt clung to his coat tails, but in three others, where Straus's pluralities were slight, Wilson outran the Bull Mooser.

As was expected, Sulzer was elected governor, but his term of office came to a swift close. In 1913, for defying Tammany's instructions, the New York Assembly impeached the governor on the charge of misemploying campaign funds. A few months after Sulzer's conviction, John Purroy Mitchell lead a Fusion Party ticket to victory over Tammany in all five of the city's boroughs. In that election a still grateful and incensed Lower East Side district elected Sulzer to the Assembly on an anti-Tammany Progressive ticket by a three-to-one margin over his Republican opponent, who ran ahead of the Democrat. So persistent was the anti-Tammany sentiment that in 1914 in a four-cornered race for the governorship, Sulzer garnered a considerable vote as the nativist American Party gubernatorial candidate. The Lower East Side districts surpassed all others in this protest vote.[21]

In an era of reform, prosperity, and a new international-ism, the Socialist Party lost much of its distinctiveness and merged into the urban progressive stream. Into its ranks came Joseph Medill Patterson, Upton Sinclair, J. G. Phelps Stokes, W. E. Walling, Robert Hunter, and Charles Edward Russell. In 1906 the Hillquit Congressional campaign placed socialist electioneering on a practical footing. The "capitalist" press gave serious attention and much space to the socialist program. *The New York Times* and the *Evening Post* interviewed Hillquit and the *New York Journal,* where Hearst mixed socialism with every available nostrum calculated to attract a popular follow-ing, invited Milwaukee socialist Victor Berger to write a series of articles.

In 1906 *Forward* editor Abraham Cahan joyfully welcomed the American invasion of the Lower East Side. Just as ten years earlier he had hailed the increasing frequency of the "Yankee accent" at SLP conventions as a portent of socialism American-ized, so he now exulted in the renewed intimacy. "Readers! The finest Americans are interested in our congressional campaign; they await the election of Morris Hillquit with impatience; they look upon this as the beginning of a revolution in the po-litical life of America." At a Hillquit banquet arranged by the Professional League of the East Side, reformers Hamilton Holt, editor of the *Independent,* Edwin Markham, Charlotte Perkins Gilman, Eugene Wood, and Professor Franklin H. Giddings, endorsed the socialist candidates. Wood, pointing to Hillquit, closed his remarks with an eye-twinkling allusion to the Messianic hope: next year in Washington. Hugh Pentecost, Charles A. Beard, John Spargo, and Alexander Irvine stumped the district for Hillquit, and thousands paraded to Rutgers Square to hear twenty-five speakers call for Hillquit's election. In 1908, University Settlement headworker Robert Hunter and millionaire socialist James G. P. Stokes entered the political fray and ran for the assembly in East Side districts on a socialist platform that urged protection for pushcart peddlers, sanitary tenements, clean streets, and better factory conditions.[22]

The romantic novelty of politics, the social and intellectual distinction of socialist candidates and speakers, and the vision of the good society provided an emotional outlet in the years following the Russian Revolution of 1905 that few recent immigrants could resist. The Socialist Party alone welcomed the newcomers into parades and public assemblies at which all were equal, edified them with stirring speeches, and recalled the revolutionary inspiration of their oppressed homeland. The *Forward's* characterization of Hillquit as potentially "the first Russian Jew, the first Socialist, and the first truly cultured man in Congress," appealed to ethnic, moral, and intellectual pride.

Yet the *Forward* ruefully admitted, following the election of 1906, that after sixteen years of political campaigning the party had been unable to gain the support of the "Americans" who did the voting. In 1908 Hillquit's charge that Daniel DeLeon's congressional candidacy had contributed to his own defeat was but the cry of the sectarian, for DeLeon received a bare 1 per cent of the district's vote on the Socialist Labor Party ticket. Infinitely more formidable were the two Yiddish dailies the *Tageblatt* and the *Warheit,* which conducted a special anti-Hillquit campaign charging that the socialist candidate did not really represent his fellow Jews and that he even opposed free immigration. In 1909, the *Forward,* confessing that few party members over thirty years of age were to be found on the Lower East Side, bemoaned the high mortality rate among "socialists." The leading Yiddish humor weekly, the *Groiser Kundes,* cartooned the Socialist Party as a corpse struck down by "Bluffitis," "Demagogitis," and "Tammanyitis." Indeed, so-called socialists proved slow to relate the struggle for freedom in their homeland to the American political process and refrained from voting. From 500 members on the Lower East Side in 1906, the party had fallen to 60 by 1911. Only the attraction of the Hillquit-Haywood debate in 1912 drove *Forward* editor Abraham Cahan to pay up his long-delinquent party membership dues as the price of admission to Cooper Union.[23]

The election to Congress in 1914 of Meyer London, the first Socialist to be elected to any office in New York City, rang out as a triumph for labor and a personal tribute. London ads appealed to men of all parties. The emotional labor lawyer acquired virtually all of the votes that in the four-cornered 1912 race had been deflected to the Progressive Henry Moskowitz, downtown leader of the Ethical Culture Society and campaigner for Oscar Straus. The *Forward's* house-to-house electioneering in three consecutive Congressional campaigns (with its pages listing the names and addresses of every one of the district's 12,000 registered voters) finally brought victory to the East Side's beloved labor tribune whose devotion to the cause of the workingman was matched only by his passion for knowledge. Condemning the *Forward* for not printing a single socialist argument, the Yiddish organ of the small Socialist Labor Party commented bitterly and correctly that the votes for London were "London votes" and not "Socialist votes." They were also votes for "one of ours," the first Congressman of Russian birth, replacing the representative of the prevailing office-holding class indifferent to labor affairs.[24]

To the extent that the Socialist Party in New York continued to represent the interests of Jewish labor, which could find neither comfort nor voice in the major political parties, it was to serve as a social and educational force both for the larger community and for its constituency. If the Socialist Party's messianic temper limited its political effectiveness, it increased its inspirational balm and spurred its intellectual vitality. The beloved Eugene V. Debs, from whose lips had poured in 1897 "a Niagara of poetic pearls . . . with penetrating . . . earnest simplicity," reassuringly stood at the head of his flocks in the wilderness in 1912. "Like a holy prophecy of a godly man rings the acceptance speech of Eugene V. Debs. It scintillates and glows . . . The sparks flame up together and become a mighty pillar of fire which will enter our campaign and guide the way," thundered the *Forward*. The grand social vision reminded New Yorkers that much needed to be done that had never been done before, if the American promise was to expand to meet the human as well as the technical challenge of an urban society.[25]

∽ 12 ∽

Dawn of a New Era

Out from the ghetto will go the lessons of Judaism:
"Brotherly love—universal peace."
H. Idell Zeisloft, *The New Metropolis* (1899)

THE rise of the Jewish labor movement in the early years of the century testified that at last the city's largest immigrant group had become not only workmen with rights, but citizens without shame. Never before were labor's battles won so conclusively by such great numbers in a single industry. Almost overnight, East Europeans were to win status as the operators of the now industrialized needle trades. Demanding to be heard, they fought their way to victory.

The hard-won advances of Jewish labor, though rooted in past struggles, were the natural outcome of the progressive years. They capped the decade of the muckrake when New York's new mass circulation magazines confronted an entire generation of citizens with the harsh penalties exacted by progress and wiped the smile of complacency off the face of American life. In 1902 Hutchins Hapgood's *Spirit of the Ghetto,* and Hamilton Holt's seventy-five profiles of such "undistinguished Americans" as the bootblack and sweatshop girl, added artistic fidelity to the brush strokes of the muckrakers. In 1906 the popularity of O. Henry's *Four Million* confirmed the shift in social interest.[1]

In the early 1900's social experiment was the order of the day. Championed with missionary zeal, such pioneer urban causes as tenement reform had entered the city fabric. Former settlement workers and their writing friends shot up to prominence and influence as editors, publicists, educational statesmen, social agency and foundation directors, heads of municipal departments, officeholders, and governmental confidants at every level. Protestant and Jewish social service, crashing denominational lines in the quest for social justice, merged in name as they already had in fact. In 1906 *Jewish Charity* united with *Charities and Commons*, which in 1909 became *Survey*, fusing practical Christianity with practical Judaism.

During these years Columbia University was closer to the heart of New York's civic problems than it ever had been before or has been since. A new Columbia, flowering into a university on its new Morningside Heights campus, paced the nation in re-educating Americans for urban living. Led by Nicholas Murray Butler, successor to Seth Low, who set the course of the educator as civic leader, Columbia expanded to meet the needs of the nation's greatest city. John Dewey descended from the philosophic empyrean to revolutionize the common schools, Franz Boas linked pioneer anthropological investigations to social controversy, Devine and Lindsay brought practical social problems out of the tenements into the classrooms. Felix Adler, in the novel chair of political and social ethics, and historians James Harvey Robinson and Charles A. Beard were also shaping new perspectives.[2]

From the White House, the city's most exuberant son radiated a broad-berthed nationalism and an awakened social conscience that proved infectious. Optimism, self-criticism, and an awareness of world responsibilities inspired American statesmanship, as the New World ventured forth to redress the balance of the Old.

SHALOM FOR AMERICANS

Progressivism, the rising interest in foreign affairs, and events in Russia contributed to a growing accord between Germans and Russians in New York. Jews of wealth and position, aroused by the butcheries and persecutions in Russia after 1903, founded in 1906 a permanent, New York–centered national agency, poised to meet with executive dispatch any danger that menaced fellow Jews abroad. The American Jewish Committee, as the organization was called, concentrated upon two major issues that troubled Yiddish New York. It led a successful public campaign for repeal of the Russian Reciprocity Treaty of 1832 discriminating against American Jews, and it fought renewed impulses to restrict immigration. In the latter struggle, the American Jewish Committee was joined by the National Liberal Immigration League, sparked by Jews, and a host of immigrant societies.

Inter-Jewish relations acquired a different face as the Yiddish-speaking newcomers placed their stamp upon the city and reduced native Jews to a small minority. The cleavage between Russian and German persisted, but the growing importance and vitality of the East Side and its satellites overflowing into the city mainstream eased group tensions. Immigrant youngsters passed through the common schools, matriculated at the city's higher institutions of learning, graduated from the settlements, and were in business. They mingled in the city's varied life, and discovered their points of contact with other New Yorkers. They earned recognition in many walks of life, and with an enthusiasm for freshly seen vistas, sparkled as evidence of America's liberating and transforming power. The rise to leadership in Jewish affairs of German Americans and younger Russian immigrants promoted communication between hitherto remote sectors of the community. German Jews, embarrassed by the distinctions of an earlier day, publicly recoiled at the perpetuation of social barriers and saw their own pretensions in a somewhat ironic light.

I think I know what constitutes a normal Jew in New York. A normal Jew . . . is one who either himself or whose father speaks English with a German accent. An abnormal Jew . . . is one who speaks English with a Russian accent . . . A man who speaks English with a German accent is a native, but a man who speaks English with a Russian accent is a foreigner.[3]

Conflicts between Germans and Russians did not abate, but now they were staged on an American plane. Heretofore "they came to view us as monkeys with earlocks," commented a *Forward* editorial in 1902 in reviewing the changes that had come to the Lower East Side. But if Russians continued to look askance upon the thin Jewish culture and "un-Jewish" religious practices of their uptown brethren, even the socialist press praised the high-mindedness of Madison Avenue coreligionists. Uptown Jews continued to snipe at downtown ways. Julia Richman, the first woman to be appointed a district superintendent of schools, and a Jewess, insisted that the police rigidly enforce the city ordinances against pushcart peddlers, leading East Siders, headed by Joseph Barondess, to petition the Board of Education, although without success, to transfer "this self-constituted censor of our morality and . . . patron saint of the slum seekers" to another district.[4]

Still, New York's Jewish institutional life reflected the new status attained by Russia's immigrants. Between 1897 and 1899 the New York Public Library added Jewish and Slavonic divisions. In 1901 Rumanian-born Solomon Schechter accepted the presidency of the reorganized Jewish Theological Seminary that aimed to build a bridge between East European tradition and the twentieth century. By 1906 the twelve-volume *Jewish Encyclopedia,* the first and best of its kind in the modern world, was completed, giving unprecedented coverage to Russians in their European and American settings. In the year of the Russian Revolution of 1905, the 250th anniversary program that celebrated the settlement of Jews in New Amsterdam, and the collectively penned *Russian Jew in the United States,* both paid sensitive tribute to the idealism, intellectual alertness, and latent abilities of Russians.

Even more telling was the new dignity accorded to Yiddish. It acquired a historian in Harvard professor Leo Wiener, and attained a place, if still grudgingly, among the family of languages. Wiener's English rendition of Morris Rosenfeld's first volume of collected verse was widely praised. Sensitive non-Jewish educators and social workers who puzzled out the language, the better to understand the newcomers, now were joined by Louis Marshall, who aided in the founding of the Americanizing *Yiddishe Welt.* With pragmatic zest, this distinguished constitutional lawyer waded into the Yiddish tongue. At immigration commission hearings, uptowners valiantly defended Yiddish New York on its demonstrable merits.

They Americanize so fast that you can not hold them back . . . You can not prevent their Americanization. They go along at the most wonderful rate. So far as their reading foreign newspapers is concerned, it does not seem . . . that that at all interferes with their Americanization. A man's thought may be thoroughly sympathetic with our American thought and yet he may express it in another language.[5]

Shortly after the turn of the century, the uptown-sponsored Educational Alliance lifted the ban on Yiddish and helped Russians to become Americans in terms of their own Yiddish culture. *Sholem Aleichem tsu immigranten,* a guidebook prepared by the Alliance staff, greeted newcomers to a strange world in familiar accents. In the *Yiddishe Welt,* uptowners welcomed a Yiddish reading of the Declaration of Independence for its "sonorous periods enriched with the striking idioms" of the Hebrew tongue. Paul Abelson, the first young Russian to earn a Columbia Teachers' College doctorate, energetically pioneered in immigrant education. Abelson single-handedly transformed the Alliance's Evening School of English and Civics, classifying adult students into twelve grades and placing them according to background. The young educator devised a basic English vocabulary, used Yiddish primers as the tools of communication, and to assist him in his labor, enlisted the talents of Charles B. Stover and James Hamilton of the University Settlement, and the East Side's Alexander Harkavy, Zevi H. Masliansky, and Peter Wiernik. With a daily attendance of 500 and a waiting list of 1000, English classes conducted in Yiddish proved inordinately popular. For those unable to attend on weekdays, Saturday and Sunday evening classes alternated simplified English and Yiddish lectures and used Franklin's *Autobiography,* the Declaration of Independence, and the Constitution as basic scriptures. This adult curriculum, contrasting with earlier "Bobolink, Bobolink, spink, spank, spink" pedagogical overtures, even included Yiddish lectures on child care for mothers. Soon the curriculum was adopted by the Board of Education's adult evening school division, both humanizing and easing immigrant adjustment.[6]

In these years, pioneer Russians sought to fulfill their Jewish responsibilities in American terms. Merchant-scholar Judah D. Eisenstein, earliest historian of the Russians of New York, and translator of the Declaration of Independence and the Constitution into Hebrew, in 1899 helped found the American Congregation the Pride of Jerusalem to collect funds for poor Jews in Palestine. In 1906, the Jewish Self-Defense Association, originally formed to aid Jews resisting massacre in Russia, proposed to organize a New York Congress "to unite Jews of state without regard to political or religious opinion, . . . to secure for Jews equal rights all over the world," and "to repel defamation and spread true information." The Federation of the Jewish Organizations of New York State, dedicated "to inculcate principles of true and pure Americanism," aimed at uniting Jews irrespective of political or religious opinion so as to promote the welfare of Jews at home and abroad; however slight its accomplishments (its 400 affiliated organizations yielded but $219 in dues), it expressed the growing aspiration for social responsibility upon the part of the newest comers. In the same year, A. S. Schomer, son of the novelist, lauded German Jews for their efficient fund-raising for pogrom victims, and censured Russian Jews for the impotence of their organizations in the face of crisis. He called for an "International Congress for All-Israel" which would "be recognized by the Jewish people . . . [and] by the powers as the mouthpiece of twelve million Jews." This East Side Republican politician promised that "a new era will dawn in Jewish affairs." The American Jewish Committee's preliminary deliberations, the broad social makeup of the romantically conceived Kehillah, the Committee's municipal adjunct, and the attempted federation of Jewish philanthropies—the Federation of Contributors to the Jewish Communal Institutions of New York—further reflected the new accord between Russian and German.[7]

PULPITS FOR JUSTICE AND UNITY

Leading young American-born rabbis began to speak out for a civic-oriented, revitalized Judaism. Reform Judaism, courageous and vital in its early years, had paled by the twentieth century into a universal ethical mission pronounced by German-accented rabbis and echoing to empty pews. Now, Stephen Wise and Judah Magnes, whose formative years had spanned the breadth and grandeur of the American continent, yearned for congregations big and sprawling as the nation's greatest city. Tall, handsome, and eloquent, both envisioned themselves in the active prophetic tradition, Wise inclining to a Hebraic Unitarianism, Magnes to a Jewish high church. Significantly, Magnes and Wise, of Polish and Hungarian stock respectively, represented social and cultural elements midway between Russian and German. They were bound to the German by marriage and position, to the Russian by an insurgent Americanism, and they aspired to link uptown and downtown in bonds of fellowship.

Young Stephen Wise, emulating Henry Codman Potter, the "People's Bishop," and Edward McGlynn, the "People's Priest," aspired to become the People's Rabbi. In 1906 Wise, after six years of eye-catching public activity in socially experimental Portland, Oregon, was called to bring the breath of the new century to Temple Emanu-El. But he regarded the terms for leading the nation's cathedral synagogue as prejudicial to a free pulpit and refused to accept. In 1907 this admirer of Felix Adler ("the one prophetic Jewish voice in the life of the city"; "Emerson in form, but his spirit that of Isaiah"), came to New York and founded his own chapel. After three years of theater stumping, Wise succeeded Adler as Sunday morning lecturer at Carnegie Hall, where he inherited a considerable Ethical Culture following. "It should be possible to accomplish through the Free Synagogue movement, within Judaism what the Ethical Culture movement has done without the ranks from which it has sprung," intoned Jacob H. Schiff, diligent and informed supporter of all worthy causes and institutions, at the Free Synagogue's founding. Upon Lillian Wald's invitation, Wise founded a downtown Free Synagogue branch at Clinton Hall, and here renewed his friendship with East Side youngsters whom he had instructed in the late nineties at the Educational Alliance. Like Adler before him, Wise plunged into the public arena, but with Rooseveltian gusto. In 1912, his efforts led to the appointment of the United States Commission on Industrial Relations, and helped lead a Republican bolt to Woodrow Wilson. Glorying in his tactlessness, the rabbi embraced all liberating, noble, and just causes, denounced all breaches in the moral law, and strode forth to elevate America, Judaism, and mankind.[8]

Unlike Wise, twenty-nine year old San Francisco–born Judah Magnes accepted Emanu-El's call. But Magnes' summons for counterreform found no more response among Emanu-El's congregants than did Wise's ambition to turn the temple into a civic forum. Magnes had helped found the Jewish Self-Defense Association, had been chosen president of the new Zionist fraternal order, B'nai Zion, and like Wise had taken part in the first international Zionist conventions. He too turned for fulfillment to the greater urban throngs. Police Commissioner Bingham's sensational charges of Jewish criminality in October 1908, echoed by Jewish magistrates, led to Magnes' civic debut. Summoning leading East Siders to a Clinton Hall meeting in February, 1909, the young rabbi, with a grand flourish, projected a kehillah (communal council) into being "to wipe out invidious distinctions between East European and West European, foreigner and native, Uptown and Downtown Jew, rich and poor; and make us realize that the Jews are one people with a common history and with common hopes." Although Magnes' accomplishments fell short of his aspirations, in the ensuing decade a kehillah with bureaus of education, social morals, industry, and philanthropic research, alleviated distress in areas of felt social dislocation.[9]

THE NEW NEEDLE TRADES

Bursting with Jewish immigrants, the apparel trades, "the city's largest productive force and the greatest contributor to its manufacturing wealth," stirred with great changes in the offing. By 1910, the Russian-born were the most numerous single immigrant group in the city, passionately alive to the breach between ethical practice and profession. More so than any other group in the city, they were aggrieved, assertive, and consciously implicated in the problems of an urban-industrial commonwealth. Beneath the searchlight of metropolitan dailies and the probing eyes of social reformers, the advance of intramural Division- and Orchard-street disputes to Fifth Avenue and Broadway was to catapult a civic eyesore into a national disgrace. An industry with 15,000 to 20,000 employers, 300,000 employees, and some 1,000,000 persons directly dependent on its well-being stood on the threshold of a new self-respect.

The triumph of political reaction and the cessation of pogroms in Russia left immigrants free to combat the evils that surrounded them. Energies formerly committed to the Jewish emancipation struggle and the fight against tsarist absolutism were poured into domestic channels, seeking to bring dignity and status to labor. "We can play a greater historic role than the Bund in Russia," thundered the *Forward* in vain in 1906. But to the hundreds of thousands of instreaming immigrants, similar appeals soon would set spirits soaring. The Bund, Russian symbol of social regeneration translated into American terms, was to sound the call to social and industrial democracy.[10]

Ever since the early nineties social reformers had interceded in East Side labor affairs. In 1892 the injustice done Joseph Barondess had aroused the interest of the Women's Industrial League. The University Settlement's James B. Reynolds had monitored sweatshops, intervened in strikes, aided strikers, encouraged the formation of trade unions, and acted as a one-man social service agency in the garment trades. The CAIL periodically had heard reports on sweatshop conditions from garment workers' lips, had endorsed the union label, had aided strikers in the cigarmaking, baking, and apparel trades and, in *Hammer and Pen,* had denounced "those who . . . abuse and maltreat their poorer brethren." Lillian Wald had aided young women to organize a frail precursor of the waistmakers' union and Jacob Schiff, though arguing against its propriety, had aided strikers anonymously through the good offices of the Henry Street Settlement.[11]

Yet, pioneer strides in industrial arbitration had made no impression in the chaotic apparel trades. The overtures of the New York State Board of Mediation, the CAIL's Board of Mediation and Conciliation, and the unquenchable Mrs. Lowell and Father Ducey, had met with uniform failure. In 1895 Schiff's proffer of an adjustment committee consisting of Seth Low, James B. Reynolds, William J. Schieffelin, Edwin Seligman, and himself to settle the cloakmakers' strike had proved unacceptable. After the turn of the century, Joseph Barondess, a member of the National Civic Federation and spokesman for the public, on occasion had succeeded as a strike arbitrator. The Rev. Bernard Drachman had interceded in the 1901 bakers' general strike; Rabbi Wederowitz of the Henry Street Synagogue had issued a call for financial aid to the striking tailors in 1907; and striking East Side dress clerks had threatened to call on the synagogues and Bishop Potter in their struggle for a Sabbath day's rest. But no pattern had been set.[12]

By the early years of the twentieth century, fundamental social change in the apparel trades had prepared the way for a lasting basis for orderly labor industrial relations. Crippling strikes in the 1890's and the heavy depression that trapped the leading merchant manufacturers with a huge unsalable overstock had encouraged unemployed cloak contractors to launch out on their own. "The Moths of Division Street" maintained no offices or showrooms, employed no supervisors or designers, and produced goods in slack times at half wages. Content with slight profits, they stitched out garments at 25 per cent of their cost to the "Giants of Broadway." Within a decade the economies of Division Street had remodeled the cloak industry. Proprietors of the handful of leading German houses prudently abandoned the field and entered more advantageous branches of commerce. They became department store magnates, wholesale cloth and credit men, brokers, and bankers. By 1910 Alsatian-born Max Meyer was virtually the only one of the earlier generation who remained a big manufacturer. The thousands of women's garment manufacturers, led by Reuben Sadowsky's Sabbath-observing Broadway cloak factory, with thrice-daily prayer services for its 1500 employees, were almost all former East Side contractors.

Although differences were inherent in the position of employers and workmen, talk was possible between them, for they were cut from similar patterns. They spoke the same language, were reared in the moral law of Torah, responded to the same rhetoric and imagery, and employed the same gestures. Many a 1910 cloak manufacturer had been in labor's vanguard little more than a decade earlier, and union leaders were quick to remind an "all-rightnick" socialist employer of his earlier labor militancy. All were subject to the publicity of a community of opinion that wielded a withering social and moral pressure, and all recognized the relevance of ethical standards to economic problems, however undermined these perceptions were by human frailty.[13]

The dramatically staged great general strikes after 1909 were previewed two years earlier in the new reefer, or children's cloak, industry, where a strike victory and union recognition seemed attainable. The 1500 workmen, trusting *lanslite* aflame with revolutionary ardor, had entered the new industry with its shoestring-financed shops as the first rung on the ladder to cloakmaking. In 1907, when *lanslite* employers answered union demands with an anticipated lockout, the stage was set. The strike was planned for the height of the cloak season when seasonally unemployed cloakmakers could not flood the tiny industry's labor market. In this compact and humanly homogeneous Lispenard Street industry, the International Ladies' Garment Workers' Union's New York Joint Board, led by tried veterans Abraham Rosenberg, Meyer London, and Benjamin Schlesinger, brought labor's full resources to bear. The *Forward* through its columns, the Workmen's Circle (a growing labor fraternal order), and the United Hebrew Trades raised $10,000. A *Forward*-sponsored theater benefit, and serenading musicians for the pickets, added moral to material support. After seven weeks the employers' association, prompted by Schlesinger's entreaties, yielded to Gompers' urging and the orthodox *Tageblatt's* editorial counsel, and came to terms with the union. The strike settlement freed workmen from paying for needles, straps, and shuttles, and specified that employers provide sewing machines. The settlement also abolished inside pressing contracting, instituted the closed shop, and reduced the work week from 59 to 55 hours. The victory, however limited in scope, was unprecedented.

Following this strike, a lull fell over the garment trades. The

1908 depression, idling one third of organized labor in the city, affected the unorganized even more severely. The calling of an East Side Crisis Conference, the Unemployment Conference at Union Square, and the heavy demands upon Jewish charity registered the affects of the short depression in the immigrant Jewish industries.[14]

In 1909 reform became the order of the day. A succession of events, starting in the waist industry, where a few shop strikes rallied Women's Trade Union League support, precipitated the great strikes that were to spotlight the city's greatest industry. In that year, long quiescent feminists and suffragettes snapped into stride. On Labor Day, Charlotte P. Gilman, Morris Hillquit, and Rabbi Stephen Wise, addressed marching columns of plainly clad, teen-age girls marshaled by the Women's Trade Union League, as grim-faced women unionists paraded for the first time. In October, at a city-wide convention, 800 delegates representing all the city's assembly districts formed the Woman Suffrage Party, launching an eight-year campaign for woman's enfranchisement in the nation's wealthiest and most populous state. In November, the keepers of the conscience of Reform Judaism, the Central Conference of American Rabbis, met at the Educational Alliance in the heart of the Lower East Side and listened for the first time to an address on "The Workingman and the Synagogue." In that month William J. Gaynor, who advocated that Union Square be set apart as a free forum on the model of London's Hyde Park, was elected Mayor of New York. Then on the evening of November 22nd at Cooper Union, Abraham Cahan, Benjamin Feigenbaum, Meyer London, Samuel Gompers, and Mary Dreier, president of the New York Women's Trade Union League, addressed a waistmaker's mass meeting. Suddenly, the audience was electrified by the impassioned Yiddish plea of Clara Lemlich, a slip of a teen-age girl, for a general strike. At the chairman's call to take the Jewish oath, "If I turn traitor to the cause I now pledge, may this hand wither from the arm I now raise," 20,000 waistmakers went out in the first great strike of women in American history. The *American Hebrew,* generally silent on labor matters, printed Stephen Wise's salute to a new era in industrial relations.

The synagogue may hope to speak to the workingman only if it first speak for the workingman . . . The time has come when instead of waging fictitious warfare about the question of the closed shop with labor organizations, there should be an honest and serious attempt to bring about an understanding between capital and labor so that there shall be a recognition on the one hand of the right of trades unionism, and on the other hand such adoption of methods of agreement and conciliation as shall virtually make strikes and lockouts and every manner of industrial dispute impossible.[15]

The Yiddish press, led by the *Forward*, kindled indignation in Yiddish New York; Socialist Party spellbinders, United Hebrew Trades organizers and other veteran unionists recruited from the sidewalks, and fashionable reformers extended the strike's scope; and the mass circulation muckraker magazines brought it to national attention. In the inaugural year of the revived woman's suffrage movement militant, the waistmaker "uprising" roused universal appeal; all New York hummed Charles K. Harris's tune, "Heaven Will Protect the Working Girl."

Spearheaded by the social elite, the strike dramatized woman's industrial plight. Mrs. Henry Morgenthau, wife of the president of the Free Synagogue, Mrs. O. H. P. Belmont, Mrs. Bolton Hall, and Miss Carola Woerishoffer posted bail for arrested pickets set upon by street-walkers and harried by the police. Conscience-ridden college women took turns at strike duty. On foot and at times daringly perched behind the wheels of Mrs. Belmont's automobiles, they made their presence felt. As violence mounted, nationally renowned attorneys, led by Samuel Untermeyer and Columbia University Law School Dean George W. Kirchwey, came to the defense of arrested pickets, joining their pleas with labor lawyers Morris Hillquit and Meyer London. The Political Equality Association sponsored mass sympathy meetings at the Hippodrome and at Rutgers Square. Anna Howard Shaw, president of the National Woman's Suffrage Association and one of the nation's finest woman orators, denounced the employers, while Archbishop Farley found occasion to bless the strikers. At a meeting of the exclusive Colony

Club presided over by Miss Anne Morgan, Mrs. Belmont, and Mrs. J. Borden Harriman, striking waistmakers, led by John Mitchell, chairman of the Trade Agreement Department of the National Civic Federation, and tiny Rose Schneiderman of the Woman's Trade Union League, appealed in behalf of the exploited waistmakers.

The Women's Trade Union League successfully blared forth its plea for support. On December 3, League women led columns of strikers in a suffragette-style protest march on Mayor McClellan's City Hall office. Two League members edited special strike editions of the *New York Call* and the *New York Evening Journal*, while others distributed 30,000 postcards, raised 20 per cent of the $100,000 strike fund, picketed, and exhorted. Despite these prodigious efforts, National Civic Federation representatives failed to budge the large manufacturers, the union went unrecognized, and only the small shops accepted settlement. Yet the dramatically staged strike captured the public's sympathy and set the stage for an industrial revolution in the garment trades.[16]

The strike's contagious idealism, overriding the divisions among immigrants, also encompassed the few hundred Negroes employed in the clothing trades.

It's a good thing, this strike is, it makes you feel like a real grown-up person . . . But I wish I'd feel about it like them Jew girls do. Why their eyes flash fire as soon as they commence to talk about the strike—and the lot of talk they can put up—at times they make a body feel like two cents.

For the first time since 1882, when Italians and Jews joined the freight-handlers union, the waistmakers' strike brought members of these two groups together in a union. By then many Italians had come to shed their suspicion of outsiders, including their Jewish neighbors. Some Italians even acquired a speaking knowledge of Yiddish, and their East European Jewish associates and employers served for many as models of Americanism. The appearance of union leaders schooled in Italian socialism, such as the Bellanca brothers and Salvatore Ninfo, the debut of Fiorello H. LaGuardia on the labor scene, and the organization of foreign language federations by the Socialist Party, spelled a new American unity among the more recent ethnic groups in labor's ranks.[17]

The confidence of ILGWU leaders was mounting in the spring of 1910, bolstered by the strike success and widespread public sympathy. Within five months, the ILGWU, encouraged by the return of the ladies' garment cutters' union to the fold, the affiliation of the Ladies' Tailors' Union, and the support of the AFL executive council, resolved to call a general strike. For the first time, Jewish workmen struck in response to a referendum and quit their machines in a great planned strike. Another precedent was set when a labor organization hired Madison Square Garden for a meeting in its own behalf, a meeting described by the *Forward* on June 30 as "the greatest Jewish labor meeting the world has ever seen." Although Abraham Cahan, the United Hebrew Trades, and the Socialist Party hesitated to the last, fearing a miscarriage, the well-ordered response of some 60,000 workmen at the appointed hour blotted out lingering doubts. New York's vast cloak industry closed down completely; the greatest strike in the city's annals had begun. The *Forward,* styling the strike a "folk movement," on July 9 called upon strikers to maintain their "sacred" oath. Morris Rosenfeld, veteran sweatshop bard, composed a song of inspiration and the *Evening Journal* published 50,000 free copies of a special strike edition. Blessing the strikers, the orthodox *Tageblatt* urged them to repudiate the "socialist demagogues" and to learn the practical ways of American trade unionism. As in the past, the moral and material assistance of the immigrant community rushed to support the 75,000 strikers. Strikers kept abreast of the latest strike developments through the cloakmakers' trilingual (English, Yiddish, Italian) *Naye Post,* the Yiddish daily press, and the *Giornale Italiano.*

Through its influential following, the Ethical Culture Society led the way in seeking a settlement. Henry Moskowitz, taking the initiative, called upon A. Lincoln Filene, fellow member and prominent Boston business and civic leader, to intercede. In turn, Filene, whose department store trade was being adversely affected by the strike, prevailed upon his fellow Bostonian Louis Brandeis, brother-in-law of Felix Adler and known as the "people's attorney," to lend his prestige and skill as chief arbitrator. Max Meyer, leader of the Manufacturers' Protective Association, responded by enlisting the legal talents of his fellow Ethical Culturist Julius H. Cohen. At the end of July negotiations began.[18]

Union and employer representatives convened at the new fifty-story Metropolitan Life Insurance skyscraper, overshadowing Madison Square and towering unchallenged over the city. Julius H. Cohen, attorney for the employers, opened the joint conference.

We come in a meek and humble spirit, because we are realizing the big social problem that we are facing at this table here; that it is not a mere matter of this strike, whether you win this strike or we win this strike; that is a subordinate issue. The big question in this matter that we want to dispose of is how can the people for whom you are speaking live just a little better than before, and how can we help them to do it, and how can we prevent this fearful waste in the future, and we are humble because we realize that is a big problem, and because it is going to require the best brains and the best heart we can give to it, and we are going to make that contribution on our side, and we are going to expect you to make yours on your side.

Meyer London, representing the union, showed a similar conciliatory spirit.

We do not come to control your business; we do not come to control your trade. I, personally would have liked to see a state of affairs where mankind should control everything in a co-operative effort, but I realize in the year 1910 and in the cloak trade it is hardly possible of realization, and I have so advised my clients, and they have agreed with me in that view.[19]

Through the hot summer days, as orders piled up and strikers tightened their belts, negotiations dragged on. At a critical juncture, Sampel Gompers, intervening at first through the good offices of John B. Lennon of the Journeymen Tailors' Union and then directly, effected a compromise on an issue that might have caused a breakdown. At long last, Brandeis hurdled the manufacturers' objection to the closed shop by substituting his

pet "preferential shop." But in using the phrase "equally competent," to describe the qualities sufficient to require employers
to prefer union men, he incurred Meyer London's displeasure.

I bow with reverence to your great command of the English language, but the difficulty is this: If you will attempt to draw fine distinctions in any paper you will submit to our people, the more refined is the distinction the less they will understand it, and think
they will be deceived, and therefore I ask you to strike out the word
"equally."

Terminological difficulties arose again when rival attorneys
clashed over the settlement's designation. Cohen's "treaty of
peace" upset union leaders as much as London's "collective
agreement" disturbed employers. Finally, Jacob Schiff, ever
jealous of the reputation of the Jewish community, summoned
Louis Marshall to break the deadlock. Marshall solved the
semantic difficulty by suggesting the word "protocol." On Labor
Day eve, preceding the Jewish Penitential days, the greatest
strike in the city's history ended in festive parade and thanksgiving.[20]

The "Protocol" became a landmark in industrial relations.
The Joint Board of Sanitary Control, directed by Dr. George M.
Price, with W. J. Schieffelin, president of the Citizen's Union,
Lillian Wald, and Henry Moskowitz representing the public,
laid the foundations for a comprehensive health and safety program. The Protocol created a Board of Arbitration to settle
major disputes, and also set up a Board of Grievances for the
continuous adjudication of minor disputes between unions and
an employers' association whose members employed 60 per cent
of the workmen in the trade. Despite evasion and ultimate
breakdown, the Protocol, with employers, union, and public
representatives accepting joint responsibility, explored new
paths for industrial peace. All subsequent labor conflicts in the
garment industries were to draw upon the Protocol experience.[21]

For the third time in slightly over a year, on March 26, 1911,
public attention riveted upon the garment district. This time
it was not a strike. Late Saturday afternoon when all union shops

had shut for the day, a fire suddenly broke out on the upper floors of the Asch building in the nonunion Triangle Waist factory off Washington Square. In the city's largest waist factory, 850 employees, mostly young girls, were trapped behind locked doors. Within ten minutes, the flash holocaust had done its work, snuffing out 146 lives, leaving many more burned, maimed, and disfigured. A fireman at the scene reported: "They hit the pavement just like hail. We could hear the thuds faster than we could hear the bodies fall." Among the fatalities were the wife and two sons of one of the partners of the Triangle Waist Company, for industrial disaster failed to distinguish between employer and wage-earner. The tragedy cut deep. "For half a year I was unable to enjoy the taste of food. Through those days and nights, I had no rest neither in the shop nor at home, day and night I saw their forms living and dead," recorded a horrified clothing worker in his autobiography many years later. There were few in Yiddish New York who were without relatives or friends working under similar conditions, few who had not tasted from the bitter cup. Charred, often unrecognizable, the victims were interred in a common plot at the Workmen's Circle Cemetery following a mass memorial parade of fifty thousand silent marchers solemnized by the whole Lower East Side. At Cooper Union Morris Hillquit urged that these dead shall not have died in vain. Uptown at the Metropolitan Opera House, Stephen Wise pronounced "the life of the lowliest worker . . . sacred and inviolable," and demanded immediate action to prevent the recurrence of such tragedy. In addition to providing immediate aid, the American Red Cross raised a $100,000 relief fund and made outright awards that exceeded $80,000 to families left helpless by the loss of their breadwinners.[22]

Early the following fall, the special State Factory Investigation Commission meeting at City Hall heard Abram Elkus, vice-president of Stephen Wise's Free Synagogue and the commission's counsel, declare: "The so-called unavoidable unpreventable accidents which, it has been said, were once believed to be the result of the inscrutable decrees of Divine Providence, are now seen to be the result in many cases of unscrupulous

greed or human improvidence." Out of the Commission's investigation into hours of labor, safety laws, and working conditions
came recommendations that the state legislature, led by Alfred E.
Smith and Robert F. Wagner of New York's East Side, enacted
into law. In 1913, after amending the constitution, the legislature passed a second workmen's compensation law to replace
the law of 1910, which had been declared unconstitutional. In
that year, the New York State Federation of Labor commended
the legislature for passing in a single session the most comprehensive and most valuable labor measures that ever had been
placed on any state's statute books.[23]

In 1912 a second general strike rocked the garment industry.
This time, some 10,000 workmen in New York's fur trade, despite the hesitancy of union officials, stepped into the picket
line. Although employer representatives refused to enter the
same room with union officials and only Rabbi Magnes' inter-
cession brought a settlement, advances were made. The union
failed to gain recognition, but the settlement's terms specified
wages and hours, and provided for an industry-wide joint board
of sanitary control and a joint conference committee for the
adjudication of disputes equally balanced with employer, union
and public representatives. In 1913, thus heartened, the union
joined with workmen in other cities to form the International
Fur Workers' Union and affiliated with the AFL.[24]

Memories of the Triangle disaster were still fresh in the early
months of 1913 and strikes in the waist, whitegoods, dress, and
related industries that employed mostly women attracted wide
public sympathy. The city's leading preachers, John Haynes
Holmes, John Howard Melish, Charles Parkhurst, and Stephen
Wise attempted to establish a strike fund by public subscription. Women's Trade Union League veterans entered the fray
and, after interviewing strikers, Theodore Roosevelt called for
the authorization of a second state factory investigation. Now,
experienced employers readily agreed to terms. Following the
strike settlement, Dr. Nahum I. Stone's detailed study of piece-
pricing, authorized by Protocol administrator Belle Moskowitz,
sought to chart a blueprint for negotiations in a chaotic industry.[25]

Unlike the women's clothing industry, the men's clothing industry proved less amenable to unionization and less accessible to public opinion. The American-born United Garment Workers' Union executive had little sympathy with the immigrant Brotherhood of Tailors and the latter had few meeting points with their employers. Consisting largely of first and second generation German Jews, the nationally organized men's clothing manufacturers, with a brisk business élan, could not easily be persuaded to underwrite social change. Theirs was an old standardized industry, substantially capitalized, and, in its upper ranks, little troubled by style winds. Although corporate ownership was uncommon, the incorporated firms in the men's clothing industry far outproduced those in the ladies' field. In 1914 the incorporated 17 per cent in women's wear manufactured 29 per cent of the product by value, while the incorporated 15 per cent in men's wear produced 48 per cent of the product by value. Furthermore, unlike the New York–centered women's clothing industry which manufactured 72 per cent of the American product, the men's clothing industry in the city contributed only 35 per cent of the national output. Indeed, between 1909 and 1914, while the value of women's clothing produced in the city rose 28 per cent, the value of men's clothing declined 12 per cent.

The union's feeling that conditions in the industry were hardening precipitated a tailors' general strike in December 1912, involving some 50,000 workmen. Although the Brotherhood of Tailors was poorly prepared for a long struggle and was supported only half-heartedly by the UGW, the strike brought gains. Labor's Meyer London, seated on the three-man settlement committee alongside the public's Judah Magnes and the employers' Marcus M. Marks, once more put the principle of arbitration into practice. The union's position was strengthened, even though the leading manufacturers prevented the union from attaining recognition.

To dramatize the era's spirit of conciliation, in 1914 the Businessmen's Group of the New York Society for Ethical Culture sponsored an exhibit of "Better Industrial Relations." After viewing the display, John Lovejoy Elliott recorded: "The thought became deeply impressed that among some economic groups in the community a moral relation was springing up, and the beginnings of justice could be found where before there had been no thought of justice in the relationship." The Jewish labor movement at last could rest assured of its permanence.[26]

In January 1914, Clarence Darrow and Samuel Gompers were honored guests at the United Hebrew Trades' silver anniversary banquet. Gompers, carried away by his own eloquence and the spirit of the occasion, philosophized, and not without insight.

The changes that have been wrought in these Hebrew trade unionists have transformed to a great degree not only the outward lives but the character of the workers. Many of them came to our city, outcasts . . . helpless, wounded in body, mind, and soul; hopeless they accepted that there would be nothing better for them except the great beyond. They have been turned toward hope in the present and they have been made to realize the possibility of securing better conditions now. This is the work of the American trade union movement . . .

Nor has this transformation been an easy one. The Hebrew race is one whose character has been scarred by cruelty, injustice, and mental and physical persecution that have lasted for centuries. The blind unreasoning prejudice against the race has been of such a character and such a degree that its effects are part of the very fibre of the people . . .

Yet all of the old racial characteristics, the deep awareness of reality and the spirit of mystical understanding that have given the world its greatest religions, are still dominant in the Hebrew race. Their love for their national ideals . . . is what one of the race has called 'fibre love', a feeling which nature intertwines with every fibre of the being and which keeps its strength even between those who scarcely have one thought in common.

Gompers may have been unprecise and undoubtedly overvalued trade union influences, but he knew the changes that had come to his Yiddish-speaking coreligionists. With five thousand members in 1909, by 1914 the United Hebrew Trades claimed 250,-000 in 111 affiliated unions, unions of diverse Jewries and many non-Jews as well.[27]

As the apparel unions achieved position and power between

1909 and 1914, able immigrants found in these semi-industrial unions an outlet for their socially creative energies. The strike victories enabled them to test their abilities in the close management of pioneer industry-wide settlements. In the men's as in the women's clothing industry, the newcomers seized the helm, eager to play a progressive independent role in the labor movement. In 1914 they formed the Amalgamated Clothing Workers' Union. In the same year, thousands of Jewish immigrants, excluded for over a decade, were admitted to the ranks of the AFL Brotherhood of Painters. The lament of Jewish workmen that "it is no longer possible to speak Yiddish at the executive meeting of a large union," best summed up the wider demands made upon the newest leaders in New York's industrial life.[28]

Epilogue

Trampled upon, banished as they have been for centuries
under the ban of religious persecution, at last they find a
land in which they have rights equal with all their fellow
countrymen.   *Puck* (1878)

IMMIGRANT Jews, who had won arduous battles and cemented
their roots into the factories and tenements, schools and synagogues of New York, looked ahead to that larger acceptance
that was the American promise. But for nearly two generations
this fulfillment was not to be theirs.

World War I, shattering old securities, crystallized a new set
of national attitudes. The antiforeign hysteria swept even New
Yorkers into a forgetfulness of the American tradition, a hysteria that did not end with the war. Hospitality for the stranger
turned into rejection and a new climate of intolerance mocked
the immigrant's faith in his adopted land. In the years of the
great migration fellow citizens did not turn on Americanized
Jews as bearers of an immigrant and foreign tradition, but the
attitudes which conditioned the later anti-Semitism already had
taken shape.

RACIST STIRRINGS

New York in 1914 claimed over half of the nation's Yiddish
immigrants. In this heyday of the Lower East Side, the island
city loomed more than ever before as the national metropolis
and its kaleidoscopic community elicited the envy and the
homage of visitors and sojourners alike. The Lower East Side,
refracting the cultural crosscurrents of the Jewish and western
worlds, heeded the call of a buffeted Yiddish diaspora, and unfailingly responded to the cry of humanity. "Every outrage, upheaval, or economic distress in almost any part of the world is
evidenced here by newcomers," observed Police Commissioner

McAdoo. But as immigrants, as a people of key significance in the Christian scheme, and as a folk with legendary business talents, Jews, like the city itself, occupied an equivocal place in the popular imagination. In an era pledged to the city beautiful, "Jewtown," or the "Oriental district," which "smites the nose and offends the eye," made the city's Jews a target for censure. The Jewish community in "its lowest stages" furnished New York with its most repulsive elements, chided the popular writer Rupert Hughes. If the quarters of others were "more helplessly and hopelessly bad than lowest Jewry," Jews, because of a "higher average of intelligence and energy" seemed the most culpable of the city's slum dwellers. In times of social upset, fear of the future and distrust of the stranger focused on New York, center of change, and the site of a folk who evoked a "vivid sense of a new and overpowering vitality." [1]

The prevailing stereotype of the Jew, foreign, mysterious, associated with trade and a world financial cabal, indiscriminately embraced counting house and sweatshop, Fifth Avenue mansion and Rivington Street slum. Rich and poor were implicated equally with the wickedness immanent in the New York citadel of finance and monopoly. Battening on the vaunted Jewish money prowess, a *Puck* cartoonist even portrayed a disaster like the Moscow expulsions of 1891 as a catapult that advanced refugee business to Broadway. In the apocalyptic presidential election year 1896, the Reverend Isaac M. Haldeman of New York's First Baptist Church echoed the populist cry that fevered the western hustings.

The time is coming when the Jews will rule the world. They are already its financial masters. In a few years they will control every profession and every branch of commerce and industry. The largest commercial interests of New York are already in their hands. The day is fast approaching when an anti-Christ will rise among the Jews who will devastate the nations of Europe and build up in Palestine the most powerful kingdom on earth. [2]

In the first decade of the century, nativist fears of a worldwide Jewish financial conspiracy faded. But publicists and literary men, affecting solemnity and omniscience, appropriated the

populist rhetoric, if not the populist rancor, and the image of
a new Jerusalem replaced the earlier image of a new Rome on
the Hudson. A "Hebrew conquest," mused Henry James,
"swarming Israel," echoed Herbert Casson, "the Great Jewish
Invasion," insisted Burton J. Hendrick, had turned New York
into "a city of Asiatics." Clifton Harby Levy's portrait in the
Independent of the "New York Jew as he is, with his faults and
his virtues," had to compete with the "Jewish specter" that
haunted the imagination of the gentiles. A sensitive Christian,
dismayed by "the hovering vision of Israel that is thrown upon
the screen of our religious consciousness," devoted a book to
exorcizing the metaphorical Jewish ghosts with which English
rhetoric had overstocked the common mind and to cleansing
the landscape of the romantic vision of history to which Jew
and gentile alike had succumbed. Madison Peters and others
called for "justice to the Jew," but the Jewish specter that colored the popular imagination was not to be expelled so easily.[3]

New York, the nation's immigrant terminal, with the highest
proportion of newer immigrants among the nation's major
cities, became the focus for anti-immigration sentiment. The
reorganization of the Immigration Station at Ellis Island, the
tightening of regulations to bar undesirables at embarkation
ports, and increased deportations by the executive discretion of
officials foreshadowed the closing of the gates. The forty-one-
volume Dillingham Commission report explicitly labeled the
latest immigrants inferior to the earlier ones on scientific
grounds and recommended that national policy be based on this
finding. Ethnic and religious considerations were inseparable.
To New York's Protestant minority, the apparently high Catholic birth rate, "families where 'race suicide' is unknown," and
the even higher Jewish birth rate seemed ominous. "The children swarmed above all—here was multiplication with a vengeance," grieved a great American novelist, after a visit to the
Lower East Side. In 1906 the social worker Walter Laidlaw, first
executive secretary of the Federation of Churches and Christian
Organizations in New York City, felt the need to remind Americans of their heritage: "The labor trust that would keep immigrants out in order that wages may rise with the decreased sup-

ply of toilers, and the church trust that would keep out aliens, in order that a homogeneous faith may be preserved on Pilgrim and Puritan soil, are both anachronisms." [4]

In a secular society, religiously rooted prejudices slid into racist forms. If few patricians clothed their fears and discomforts in the later scientific garb of Madison Grant's anthropology, they assumed attitudes that made them vulnerable to racist writings. Despite the city's cosmopolitanism, the thinking of influential New Yorkers, drawn from all parts of the nation, tended to become fixed in racist channels. Jews, the most mobile and the most numerous of the newer immigrants, were to become the most vulnerable to penalty.

A more secure patrician New York had admired the aloof Jewish great merchants of the mid-nineteenth century. "[They are] remarkable for their haughtiness, high sense of honor and their stately manners." Moses Lazarus, father of Emma, had been a founder of the Knickerbocker Club; Joseph Seligman, a founder of the Union League Club; and Benjamin Nathan, a member of the Union Club, the Union League Club, and the St. Nicholas Society. As late as 1872 a leading society journal featured the news of a fashionable "Hebrew Wedding" in the Orthodox Thirty-Fourth Street Synagogue.

But in the socially compulsive years following the Civil War, the German-accented Jews, who aspired to social acceptance, were rejected by the city's foremost clubs. Jews chafed, but disregarded these rebukes as well as the occasional slights at hotels and summer resorts. In the late 1870's, however, social discrimination attained an openness that challenged Jewish self-respect. The New York Bar Association blackballed a Jew in 1877 and in 1878 the Greek letter societies at City College barred Jewish members, a slight that Bernard Baruch never forgave. In the decade's most celebrated incident, the Grand Union Hotel in Saratoga Springs, upon order of Judge Hilton, its executor-proprietor, refused accommodations to Joseph Seligman, a long-time patron. Aroused by the public humiliation to the nation's most prominent Jew, one hundred leading Jewish merchants successfully boycotted Stewart's Department Store, which was administered by Hilton. Alarmed, the judge pledged $1000 to

Jewish charities. In a two-page cartoon, *Puck's* Christmas Day issue mocked Hilton and in an accompanying editorial, New York's leading comic weekly commended Jews for refusing to be bribed.

> Alas! Poor Hilton.
> It is to be regretted that Mr. Hilton is as unsuccessful as a dry-goods man and a hotel-keeper as he notoriously was as a jurist. But the fact remains. He took it upon himself to insult a portion of our people, whose noses had more of the curvilinear form of beauty than his own pug, and he rode his high-hobby horse of purse-proud self-sufficiency until he woke up one day to find that the dry-goods business was waning . . . Then Mr. Hilton arouses himself. He turns his great mind from thoughts of the wandering bones of Stewart; he brings the power of his gigantic brain to bear upon the great question, "How shall I revive trade?" He has remembered that he has insulted the Jews. Aha! we'll conciliate them. So out of the coffers that A. T. Stewart filled he gropes among the millions and orders the trustees of a few Hebrew charities to bend the pregnant hinges of their knees at his door, and receive a few hundred dollars.
> But in this country the Jew is not ostracized. He stands equal before the law and before society with all his fellow-citizens, of whatever creed or nationality. And the Jew has stood up like a Man and refused to condone the gross and uncalled for insults of this haphazard millionaire, merely because he flings the offer of a thousand dollars in their faces. All honor to the Jews for their manly stand in this instance.[5]

Still, the pattern of social exclusion was set. The *Social Register,* as a matter of course, closed its list to Jews. Fashionable clubs, hotels, summer resorts, and private schools followed suit. In 1892 the Union League Club blackballed Theodore Seligman, son of one of the club's founders, and gave conspicuous finality to the exclusion of Jews, regardless of origin, from the city's most socially desirable associations. In the first decade of the twentieth century, the Lotos and Manhattan clubs alone, the one intellectual, the other Democratic, counted a fair number of Jews. By then, fashionable Jews, enjoined by their own needs and the bond of rejection from high society, had coalesced into a "Hebrew Select" society with its own exclusive standards.[6]

Even had they been so inclined, in these years the old Knick-
erbockers no longer could be guided in their social codes by the
earlier distinction between "Sephardic" and "German" Jews,
the "Nathan-type" and the "Seligman-type," "refined Hebrew
ladies and gentlemen" and "vulgar Jews." By the turn of the
century, distinctions between "the better class of Jews" and the
others collapsed beneath the pressure of numbers. To the dismay of German Jews, anxious to dissociate themselves from the
Russians by insisting that they were "Hebrews" not "Jews," few
could distinguish between German and Russian. Jacob Schiff,
Louis Marshall, Oscar Straus, and Abraham Jacobi might be
hailed as outstanding Jews and Americans, but these were the
exceptions who were contrasted with the rest.

Of the older types, the untrimmed hair, long caftans, and unin-
telligible language render their presence here uncouth . . . As we
will not don Polish costumes or learn their jargon, we expect these
Jews in the course of time to adopt our customs. Meanwhile, Yiddish will be spoken on the stage of the Bowery theatre where Mali-
bran sang and Vestris danced.[7]

THE COMMON BOND

Whatever the social snubs, whole areas of the common life
showed little susceptibility to racism. Irish and German New
Yorkers, filling a place midway between older Americans and
the newer immigrants, were often hostile to the new arrivals.
But these sentiments sprang largely from their own status and
economic insecurities. To newer immigrants, the Irish represented American New York, as even recent arrivals from the
Emerald Isle were quick to assume a native air of proprietor-
ship, meting out a proverbially rough welcome to newcomers.
But despite friction and rivalry, social relations were not overly
strained. Youngsters who worshipped John L. Sullivan, the fistic
idol of the day, met Celtic pugnacity on its own terms and many
a Jewish lad competed for the Irish-American Athletic Club.
Burton J. Hendrick noted that it was "a matter of common
notoriety" that "a majority of the prize-fighters in New York are
really Jews who operate under Irish names," and the Yiddish

nationalist press trumpeted the valor of Jewish strong men from
Gideon and Samson to fighting Joe Choynski.[8]

The Fatherland's nurture of modern anti-Semitism did not
noticeably influence the attitudes of New York's German gentiles. Jews joined German clubs, patronized German theaters,
which often featured Jewish themes, and leading rabbis participated prominently in German literary circles. The nation's
foremost German daily, the *New Yorker Staats-Zeitung*, opposed
all forms of anti-Semitism and the *New Yorker Handels Zeitung*
repeatedly defended Jews against misrepresentation and ap-
plauded Jewish leadership in charitable and cultural affairs.
Court-preacher Adolph Stoecker made little impression and
Rector Ahlwardt, another imported professional anti-Semite,
guarded by an escort of forty Jewish policemen assigned to him
by Police Commissioner Roosevelt, drew small and unapprecia-
tive audiences. For a time the largest of all German clubs excluded Jews. But the sudden death of the touring Edward
Lasker in 1883 brought an Arion Society delegation to the
Temple Emanu-El funeral services for this prominent Reich-
stag member. In 1893, when the city of Düsseldorf refused to
accept Ernst Herter's Lorelei Fountain as a memorial to Hein-
rich Heine from his New York German admirers, the Arion
Society presented the sculpture to the City of New York.

A few racist titles by German Americans did appear, but the
new racist categories did not gain acceptance in the German
community. Professor Faust's scientific scruples forbade him to
cite more than a handful of Jews in his prize-winning study of
the Germans in the United States "because of their racial dis-
tinctness." Less scientific German-American compilers, however, showed a greater sensitivity to the life around them and
ignored the categories of the academy. Edward Lauterbach, "a
great supporter of Jewish institutions," was claimed by German
America in a history of New York "Deutschthum" because of
his German parentage. And a German biographical dictionary
included the president of the Jewish Theological Seminary,
the chief of the New York Public Library's Slavonic Division,
a Yiddish newspaper publisher, a star of the Yiddish stage, and
other East European Jews.[9]

EMERGENT ANTI-SEMITISM

Yet, Jews, unable to forget their historic ostracism, were distressed by the growing social "antipathy towards persons of the Jewish faith" and were anxious to dispel the haze that engulfed their people. In 1890 the editors of the *American Hebrew* invited the "foremost Christians" to express their thoughts on the nature, causes, and remedies for social prejudice. But however encouraging, the replies, like the questions, only underlined the ambivalence of many old-stock Americans, unable to square precept with practice. In an individualistic era and in a climate unfavorable to civil rights protection for minorities, resort to legislation proved futile. The New York civil rights code which prohibited discrimination at places of public resort for reasons of "race, color or previous condition of servitude" was amended in 1881 to include creed as well; in 1913 the statute was further amended so as to prohibit discriminatory advertisements. But in these years even Finley Peter Dunne's ridicule failed to dull the social prejudice against Jews.[10]

By the close of the first decade of the twentieth century, as the mobile Yiddish population began to press into areas closed to it earlier, anti-Jewish prejudice threatened to become acute. Abraham Cahan's insistence that Jewish socialists never encountered discrimination only called attention to the seriousness of the problem. Increasingly the great firms rejected or ignored Jewish applicants. Like social exclusion earlier, economic discrimination became overt. "Help wanted" ads specified "Christians" and thus singled out Jews from all other New Yorkers. "It is remarkable that many firms which cater to the trade of Jews display this form of prejudice." Soon apartment house ads ticketed Jews as undesirable. By 1912 matters had become sufficiently serious in New York to warrant the founding of a Jewish-sponsored defense publication, the *American Citizen.* "A National Magazine of Protest Against Prejudice and Injustice." [11]

After 1900 Jewish acts and Yiddish speech patterns attained wide popularity on the stage and in magazines, Pat and Mike giving way before Abe and Sol. Yiddish dialect became dominant when the *Saturday Evening Post* published the "Potash and

Perlmutter" stories that scored the agonies of entrepreneurship in the needle trades. But in an era of racism, gibes often acquired a sting. Previously, Jews, like others, had been hurt by newspaper tagging of lawbreakers that specified their color or origin. But now to be singled out became odious and involved serious economic and social penalties. A whole religious community, no longer a small minority, was ridiculed even by its own sons and patronized as inferior.[12]

In these years Irish Catholics rather than Jews were portrayed as a political menace. The specter of New York as a second Rome ruled by Celtic acolytes still haunted the imagination of upstate nativists and gravely amused metropolitan Yankee critics. Satirically, in *The Last American, a Fragment from the Journal of Khan-Li Prince of Dimph-Yoo-Chur and Admiral in the Persian Navy,* the editor of *Life* predicted that in 2951 the chronicler of a vanished New York would leave "the reader much confused concerning the period between the massacre of the Protestants in 1927 and the overflow of the Murfy dynasty in 1940." [13] Jews were not yet in a position to aspire to top elective offices, but political nativists detected a tendency among Jews to combine with Catholics for political ends. In 1909 the editor of a Jewish periodical saw in the election of a Jewish mayor the antidote to anti-Jewish prejudice. Indeed, in the 1914 gubernatorial campaign, the anti-Catholic cry cocked a double-barrel. "If a Catholic is elected, perhaps a Jew next." Even a Protestant clergyman of advanced religious views regarded Catholic and Jewish candidates for high executive office with equal alarm. "If he is a bad Jew, a renegade, he is not the man for us; if he is a good and loyal Jew, it is a question of what his race would do to us." [14]

The outbreak of World War I halted an immigration wave that showed signs of surpassing the peak years of Jewish immigration in 1906 and 1907. The war, stranding tens of thousands of immigrants at a score of transfer points and embarkation ports, sundered husbands from wives, parents from children. The regions of Central and Eastern Europe most heavily Jewish were at the center of the war inferno. When the Russian Revolution triumphed amid the carnage and the age-long dream of a reconstructed Zion was proclaimed in the Balfour Declaration, the Yiddish world pulsated with the hopes of a new era.

In the years between two great wars, bitterness often frustrated good intentions. But the voice of the immigrant, echoed in his sons, remained the voice of stubborn hope. By the mid–twentieth century, in a world changed beyond recall, the Jews of the great migration had become welded to the great metropolis in their lives and in their descendants. To the most American and the most European of the nation's cities, they have communicated a liberalism of culture and outlook and a zeal for ethnic democracy that might be expected of a folk trained in their history and domiciled in New York. In this they were true to New Amsterdam's most distinctive tradition.

The Jews of New York are the direct heirs of the Jewish enlightenment and the great migration, the Lower East Side and the great strikes in the needle trades, socialism and the settlements. To the extent that this American baptismal still operates in their lives, they retain a vivid sense of the promise of a democratic community in a metropolis where few observers are inclined to be sanguine about such possibilities.

Appendix

Table 1. East European Jewish immigration, 1881–1914 [a]

Year	Total	Russia	Austria-Hungary	Rumania	United Kingdom, France, and British North America	Turkey
1881	5,692	3,125	2,537	30		
1882	13,202	10,489	2,648	65		
1883	8,731	6,144	2,510	77		
1884	11,445	7,867	3,340	238		
1885	15,389	10,648	3,938	803		
1886	19,936	14,092	5,326	518		
1887	32,064	23,103	6,898	2,063		
1888	27,854	21,216	5,985	1,653		
1889	24,394	18,338	4,998	1,058		
1890	27,880	20,981	6,439	462		
1891	50,201	43,457	5,890	854		
1892	73,636	64,253	8,643	740		
1893	32,079	25,161	6,363	555		
1894	27,279	20,747	5,916	616		
1895	23,292	16,727	6,047	518		
1896	30,743	20,168	9,831	744		
1897	19,251	13,063	5,672	516		
1898	23,036	14,949	7,367	720		
1899	37,003	24,275	11,071	1,343	188	81
1900	60,424	37,011	16,920	6,183	150	114
1901	57,818	37,660	13,006	6,827	130	154
1902	57,486	37,846	12,848	6,589	64	138
1903	75,720	47,689	18,759	8,562	431	211
1904	105,548	77,544	20,211	6,446	857	313
1905	128,984	92,388	17,352	3,854	14,637	173
1906	152,491	125,234	14,884	3,872	6,621	461
1907	148,131	114,932	18,885	3,605	8,156	918
1908	102,061	71,978	15,293	4,455	9,078	635
1909	56,604	39,150	8,431	1,390	6,490	690
1910	83,321	59,824	13,142	1,701	6,699	1,388
1911	90,257	65,472	12,785	2,188	7,740	1,177
1912	79,748	58,389	10,757	1,512	6,791	1,381
1913	100,194	74,033	15,202	1,640	6,161	2,053
1914	136,645	102,638	20,454	2,646	6,976	2,252

[a] The statistics for 1881–1898 are based on country of birth; for 1899–1914 on country of last residence. With some exceptions, Jews coming from the United Kingdom, France, and British North America may be assumed to be transmigrants from Eastern Europe. Of the over 10,000 Jewish immigrants from Germany between 1899 and 1914, perhaps half were transmigrants from Eastern Europe. There were also over 2800 Jewish immigrants from Africa between 1899 and 1914, of whom many were transmigrants. As there is no way of separating natives from transmigrants, Jewish immigrants from Germany and Africa have not been included in the table.

Source: Adapted from Samuel Joseph, *Jewish Immigration to the United States* (New York, 1914), p. 93; Imre Ferenczi and Walter F. Willcox, eds., *International Migrations* (New York, 1929), I, 464.

Table 2. The foreign-born of New York City, 1870–1910 [a]

Origin	1870	1880	1890	1900	1910
Total Foreign Born	567,812	656,364	901,643	1,270,080	1,944,357
Europe	557,181	636,542	878,215	1,230,567	1,883,840
United Kingdom	56,020	64,707	82,818	90,358	103,385
Ireland	275,984	277,409	275,156	275,102	252,672
Germany	187,972	218,821	305,521	322,343	274,666
Scandinavia	4,400	9,729	26,176	45,328	65,230
The Low Countries	2,478	3,571	2,820	3,829	6,453
France	10,132	11,846	12,937	14,755	18,293
Switzerland	2,844	5,514	6,355	8,371	10,452
Greece	49	78	301	1,309	8,038
Italy	3,018	23,411	49,514	145,433	340,770
Russia	1,224	4,760	52,187	158,934	445,628
Austria-Hungary	5,227	17,776	49,813	117,998	242,545
Poland (Austrian)	2,602	9,521	8,466	32,873	73,703
Rumania	—	—	—	10,499	33,586
Turkey	54	98	303	1,401	9,855
China [b]	133	870	2,648	6,080	3,936
Spain	682	1,048	1,413	1,491	3,359
Latin America	2,835	4,079	4,343	7,144	18,795
Canada	5,251	8,573	14,295	21,826	26,320

[a] Before 1900, the figures cover only the totals for the cities of Brooklyn and New York as then constituted. Countries with less than one thousand nationals in New York in 1910 have not been included; except for Japan with 957, all of these numbered less than 500.

[b] Includes all those born in China. In 1870 only 19 were Chinese. Thereafter, virtually all were Chinese but the census compilers no longer recorded the China-born by race.

Source: Derived from *Ninth Census, 1870: The Statistics of the Population of the United States* (Washington, 1872), p. 386ff; *Tenth Census, 1880: Population* (Washington, 1883), p. 538f; *Eleventh Census, 1890: Population* (Washington, 1895), pt. I, p. 670f; *Twelfth Census, 1900: Population* (Washington, 1901), pt. I, p. 800f; *Thirteenth Census, 1910: Population, General Report and Analysis* (Washington, 1913), pt. I, p. 854f.

Table 3. Occupations of East Side Jews (1890)

Tailors	9595
Peddlers	2440
Cloakmakers	2084
Clerks	1382
Laundry workers	1043
Cigar workers	976
Hat makers	715
Painters	458
Carpenters	443
Tinsmiths	417
Butchers	413
Food purveyors	370
Goldsmiths	287
Bakers	270
Cigar merchants	270
Melamdim (Hebrew Teachers)	251
Saloon keepers	248
Machinists	149
Glaziers	148
Printers	145
Old clothes dealers	86
Shoemakers	83
Musicians	67
Milk dealers	62

Source: Adapted from Table of Baron de Hirsch study in E. Tcherikower, ed., *Geshikhte fun di idishe arbeter bavegung in di feraynikte shtatn* (New York, 1943–1945), I, 258–259.

Table 4. The Eighth Assembly District vote for president

Year	Republican	Democrat	Prohibition	Socialist Labor	Socialist	Progressive
1884	4824	4040				
1888	5043	4168				
1892	4622	7445		109		
1896	2519	1851	20	628		
1900	2178	2462	20	157	253	
1904	2225	1934	5	54	764	
1908	2100	3146	7	46	835	20 [a]
1912	686	2211	1	13	683	2313

[a] Independence League.

Sources: City Record Official Canvass of the County of New York, 12:6–7 (December 15, 1884); 16.4:8–10 (December 14, 1888); 20:14–15 (December 15, 1892); 25.1:62–63 (January 2, 1897); 28.12:4, 20, 35, 43, 51 (December 13, 1900); 33:4, 20, 36, 52, 68 (January 21, 1905); 36.12:16, 32, 48, 64, 80, 96 (December 31, 1908); 40.12:20, 40, 60, 80, 100, 120 (December 31, 1912).

Table 5. The Eighth Assembly District vote for governor

Year	Republican	Democrat	Prohibition	Socialist Labor	Socialist	Progressive
1898	2285	1760		383		
1906	1623	5387 [a]			452	
1908	1768	3353	6	45	809	265 [c]
1910	1480	2798		172	783	
1912	233	1654			448	3352
1914	1657	2627 [a]	1012 [b]	17	527	93

[a] Includes Independence League vote as well.
[b] Includes American party vote.
[c] Independence League.
Source: *City Record Official Canvass of the County of New York*, 27.2:3 (March 13, 1899); 35:3 (January 13, 1907); 36.12:98 (December 31, 1908); 38.12:2 (December 29, 1910); 40.12:122 (December 31, 1912); 42.12:2 (December 31, 1914).

Table 6. The Eighth Assembly District vote for mayor

Year	Republican	Democrat	Fusion	Socialist Labor	Socialist	Independence League
1886	3436	2241		2671 [b]		
1897	1182	1916	1021 [a]	446		133 [c]
1901		2168	2100		257	
1903		2716	1498		595	
1905	579	1890			182	1980
1909	486	2559		27	243	2173
1913		2370	2835		689	

[a] Citizens Union.
[b] United Labor party.
[c] Single Tax party.
Source: *City Record Official Canvass of the County of New York*, 14.4:10 (December 6, 1886); 25.4:9 (December 31, 1897); 30.1:9 (January 4, 1902); 31.12:2 (December 31, 1903); 34.2:3 (February 27, 1906); 37.12:3 (December 31, 1909); 41.12:13 (December 31, 1913).

Table 7. The Ninth Congressional District vote for congressman [a]

Year	Republican	Democrat	Socialist Labor	Socialist	Progressive
1894			2,358		
1896	8,379 [b]	11,002	4,371		
1898	6,447	11,694	2,396		
1900	7,438	13,570	1,261	1,190	
1902	4,235	7,739	499	1,355	
1904	5,667	5,982	186	3,167	
1906	2,734	7,276		3,586	
1908	2,313	6,194	151	2,483	
1910	1,850	4,606		3,322	
1912	839	4,592		3,646	2,602
1914	1,136	4,947		5,969	

[a] Became the Twelfth Congressional District in 1912.
[b] Includes National Democratic vote as well.
Source: City Record Official Canvass of the County of New York, 22:32–33 (December 15, 1894); 25.1:80 (January 2, 1897); 27.2:27 (March 13, 1899): 30.12:43 (December 31, 1902); 28.12:82 (December 13, 1900); 33:146 (January 21, 1905); 35:59 (January 13, 1907); 36.12:146 (December 31, 1908); 38.12:57–58 (December 29, 1910); 40.12:177 (December 31, 1912); 42.12:58–59 (December 31, 1914).

Bibliographical Note

This bibliographical note is intended to outline the source materials essential to the writing of this book. A more complete guide to material relating to this subject is available in my critical essay and bibliography, *An Inventory of American Jewish History* (Cambridge, 1954).

In transliterating from the Hebrew and the Yiddish, I have adhered to a simple phonetic system. In book titles I have capitalized only the first letter of the first word, as the Hebrew alphabet does not have capitals; the reader is thus able, at a glance, to distinguish Yiddish from German. The already transliterated titles of newspapers and periodicals, however, have been retained intact. Unless otherwise noted, I am responsible for all translations.

BASIC SOURCES

Newspapers and Periodicals

For almost every aspect of this study, the immigrant press, especially the Yiddish press, provided the core. No other source so effectively bared the facts and the texture of Yiddish New York. The newspaper and periodical collections of the YIVO Institute of Jewish Research, the Jewish Division of the New York Public Library, the Library of the Jewish Theological Seminary, and Harvard's Widener Library, taken together, provided a network of files for a full-scale portrait of a complex immigrant community. In part, Chapter 7 may be viewed as a bibliographical essay of the Yiddish and collateral Jewish immigrant press. *Jewish Newspapers and Periodicals on Microfilm* (American Jewish Periodical Center: Cincinnati, 1957), and its supplements, is a handy guide. Had it been available some years ago, it would have eased my way but deprived me of the privilege of working with the originals.

Examined in connection with special events and problems, the *New York Times*, the *New York Tribune,* and the *New York Sun* were useful both for the information they contained and the attitudes they expressed. Especially attentive to the city's immigrant communities were the fastidious and literary *New York Commercial Advertiser* and *Evening Post.* The mass circulation *New York World, New York American and Journal, Daily News,* and *Morning Journal* were but at one remove from the immigrant press in covering what was taking place in the immigrant communities. (Clippings from the English and German editions of the last two dailies have been preserved in the Barondess Scrapbooks, in the keeping of Mrs. Jean Barondess.) The Anglo-Jewish weeklies, like the general newspapers, proved supplementary. I came to them with special questions and therefore my research in them was highly selective. The *Jewish Times* was important for the 1870's; in subsequent years, the *American Hebrew,* the *Hebrew Standard,* and the *Jewish Messenger* were most useful. The *New Yorker Staats-Zeitung,* the *New Yorker Volks-Zeitung,* and *Il Giornale Italiano* were valuable for data on the attitudes toward Jews of the two major non-English-speaking groups in the city. The Robinson Locke Collection (NYPL) of theater clippings is the most convenient of its kind.

The city's considerable labor press proved important for understanding the make-up of New York's labor movement. The *Journal of the Knights of Labor,* the *Official Journal of the Central Labor Union,* the *Bakers' Journal,* and the *Garment Worker,* were helpful. *John Swinton's Paper,* available on microfilm, is almost illegible and could not be used to advantage. I benefited from the reading of a rare complete file of the *Cap-Makers' Journal* (YIVO Institute). Trade publications, generally neglected by labor historians, such as the *Clothiers' and Haberdashers' Weekly,* the *Clothing Gazette,* and the *Fur Trade Review,* were helpful for a view of employer attitudes to labor; unfortunately, Fairchild Publications did not permit me to examine their unique but fragile file of the *Daily Trade Record,* the later *Daily News Record.*

Especially useful for an understanding of the views of reformers were: the *Christian Union,* the later *Outlook; The Hammer and the Pen,* organ of the Church Association for the Advancement of the Interests of Labor; *Charities Review,* under various titles; the *Social Economist,* subsequently *Gunton's Magazine;* and *Federation,* published by the Federation of Churches and Christian Organizations in New York City.

Manuscripts

The letterbooks (New York Public Library) and scrapbooks of Joseph Barondess, the letterbooks (American Federation of Labor Building) and scrapbooks (NYPL) of Samuel Gompers, the William Edlin Papers (YIVO Institute), and the Paul Abelson Collection (New York School of Industrial and Labor Relations) provided insight in those areas where the interests of Jewish immigrants, labor, and the larger community intersected. The Edward King Collection (New York State School of Industrial and Labor Relations) and the Marc Eidlitz Papers (NYPL) contained useful labor materials but the Terence V. Powderly Collection (Catholic University) was only incidentally helpful. The records of the Hebrew-American Typographical Union (YIVO Institute) document the rise of the oldest Jewish union.

The James B. Reynolds Correspondence (University Settlement Society) proved rewarding for understanding the role of the settlements in the 1890's but the Lillian D. Wald Collection (NYPL) proved disappointing. The Louis Marshall Letterbooks (American Jewish Archives), the Edwin R. A. Seligman Papers (Columbia University Library), and the Oscar Straus Papers (Library of Congress) shed light on the relations between

Russian and German Jews. The selected Marshall correspondence, *Louis Marshall*, ed. Charles Reznikoff (Philadelphia, 1957), 2 vols., contains the best of the Marshall materials. The Jacob H. Schiff Papers for the period before 1914 and the Meyer London Papers, unfortunately, have been destroyed.

The People's Institute Collection (NYPL), consisting of over thirty scrapbooks of clippings, memorabilia, correspondence, etc., made vivid the role of this metropolitan crossroads forum. The vast Seth Low Collection and the correspondence of Lemuel E. Quigg and Herbert Parsons (all Columbia University Library) helped shed light on reform politics; Elting E. Morison, ed., *The Letters of Theodore Roosevelt* (Cambridge, 1951–1954), 8 vols., was also important.

Government Documents

Government documents proved to be especially valuable for quantitative data. The printed summaries of the United States Census, particularly the decennial volumes on population and, after 1899, the more frequent census of manufactures, supplied the basic statistical data. The manuscript federal census schedules for 1890 were destroyed by fire and subsequent census schedules are not yet available to scholars. But considering the thoroughness of contemporary sociologists and statisticians, it is unlikely that an analysis of original census data would alter the general outlines of our knowledge. The published summary of the New York State Census of 1892 was incomplete and failed to include New York City. The printed summaries of the New York State censuses of 1905 and 1915 were too scant to be useful; the original schedules may be examined at the New York County Court House but are crude and unwieldy. Walter Laidlaw, *Statistical Sources for Demographic Studies of Greater New York* (New York, 1912), 2 vols., tabulates the data of the United States Census by ethnic origin. Henry Chalmers, "The Number of Jews in New York City," *American Statistical Association*, March 1914, critically examines Jewish population estimates based on ingenious statistical techniques. The statistical tables in the *Reports of the United States Industrial Commission* (1900–1902), 19 vols., and in the *Reports of the United States Immigration Commission* (1911), 41 vols., were not arranged in categories useful to my needs.

Of the state documents, the reports of the New York Bureau of Statistics of Labor and the Board of Mediation and Arbitration provided basic coverage for labor developments. The special reports of the tenement house investigations of 1884 and 1894 and the industrial directories of the state, published in 1913 and 1914, which provided a detailed industry-by-industry breakdown for the city, were important.

Private Reports

Since Jews displayed their traditional sense of social responsibility, the reports of private organizations, rather than the reports of public agencies, proved most rewarding. Basic were the reports of the United Hebrew

Charities and to a lesser extent the reports of the Executive Committee of the Jewish Community (kehillah). As might be expected, the reports of the Charity Organization Society and the Association for the Improvement of the Condition of the Poor had little to tell about Jewish immigrants. The reports of the University Settlement, however, carried detailed social surveys of the Lower East Side and the reports of the Consumers' League, the Legal Aid Society, and the Provident Loan Society contained relevant data.

Miscellaneous

Biographical albums and encyclopedias, guidebooks, travel accounts, dictionaries, language manuals, and business, club, and newspaper directories were indispensable at many points. The slim *Hebrew American Directory and Universal Guide* (New York, 1892), the first comprehensive register of immigrant Jewish life, and the massive *Jewish Communal Register of New York City 1917–1918* (New York, 1918) reflected in their contents and in their physical size the transformation wrought by a quarter of a century of migration.

The Jewish Immigrant Saga

Abraham Cahan, *Bleter fun mayn lebn* (Leaves from My Life) (New York, 1926–1931), 5 vols., the memoirs of Yiddish America's outstanding citizen, is a repository of information. Gregory Weinstein, *The Ardent Eighties* (New York, 1928), portrays the impact of the social reformers of that decade upon an educated immigrant. Marcus E. Ravage, *An American in the Making* (New York, 1917), is a penetrating psychological study. Morris R. Cohen, *A Dreamer's Journey* (Boston, 1949), by the beloved City College philosopher, is tenderly eloquent. Miriam Blaustein, ed., *Memoirs of David Blaustein* (New York, 1913), collects the pertinent observations of a director of the Educational Alliance. Of the manuscript autobiographies on file at the YIVO Institute of Jewish Research, Ephraim Wagner's Memoir was the most sharply drawn. A view of the Lower East Side as seen by scholars of the Hebrew enlightenment is to be found in Alexander Harkavy, *Prokim mehayay* (Chapters from my Life) (New York, 1935), and Max Raisin, *Dapim mepinkoso shel rabbi* (Leaves from a Rabbi's Notebook) (Brooklyn, 1941).

Philip Cowen, *Memories of An American Jew* (New York, 1932), by the editor of the *American Hebrew,* and Julius H. Cohen, *They Builded Better Than They Knew* (New York, 1946), are important accounts written by American Jews close to the immigrant community.

SECONDARY SOURCES

The East European Background

For the East European background, the author relied upon a variety of sources. S. N. Dubnow, *History of the Jews in Russia and Poland*, trans.

by I. Friedlaender (Philadelphia, 1916–1920), 3 vols., is useful for its major outlines; Louis Greenberg, *The Jews of Russia* (New Haven, 1944–1952), 2 vols., contains some fresh material but closely follows Dubnow. Bernard D. Weinryb, *Neueste Wirtschaftsgeschichte der Juden in Russland und Polen* (Breslau, 1934), is an excellent monograph that surveys the economic history of the Jews of Russia and Poland to 1880 and Jacob Shatsky, *Di geshikhte fun idn in varshe* (New York, 1947–1953), 3 vols., is a major study of the Jews in Warsaw. But the story of economic development and cultural change had to be reconstructed from contemporary dissertations, monographs, and journalistic accounts which have been surprisingly neglected. For the final decades of the nineteenth century indispensable is *Receuil de Materiaux sur la Situation Economique des Israelites de Russie* (Paris, 1906–1908), compiled by the Jewish Colonization Association and summarized by I. M. Rubinow in "Economic Conditions of the Jews in Russia," *United States Labor Department* (Washington, D.C., 1907).

Thomas Masaryk, *The Spirit of Russia* (New York, 1919), 2 vols., is masterful and indirectly casts light on the Russian Jewish mind. Abraham J. Heschel, "The Eastern European Era in Jewish History," *YIVO Annual of Jewish Social Science* (1946), is a lyric portrait; also see Heschel's *Man Is Not Alone* (New York, 1951). Maurice Samuel's pastiches, *The World of Sholem Aleichem* (New York, 1942) and *Prince of the Ghetto* (Philadelphia, 1943), based on the writings of J. L. Peretz, are without equal for social insight and literary charm. Except for individual selections, the mordant social satire of Mendele Moicher Sforim, the first of the Yiddish literary triumvirate, must be read in the original. Shalom Spiegel, *Hebrew Reborn* (New York, 1930), and Simon Halkin, *Modern Hebrew Literature Trends and Values* (New York, 1950), are admirable studies.

Hertz Burgin, *Geshikhte fun der idisher arbeter bavegung in amerika* (New York, 1915), although outdated and often inaccurate, is still the most comprehensive study of all phases of the Jewish labor movement in Europe and America. *Historishe shriftn* (Vilna, 1939), 3 vols., is a collection of careful studies of the Jewish labor movement in Eastern Europe. Koppel S. Pinson, "Arkady Kremer, Vladimir Medem and the Ideology of the Jewish Bund," *Jewish Social Studies*, July 1945, is an important article.

Mark Wischnitzer, *To Dwell in Safety: The Story of the Jewish Migration Since 1800* (Philadelphia, 1948), is the best over-all study but the full story of the great Jewish migration still awaits its social historian. M. Silber, *America in Hebrew Literature* (New Orleans, 1928), is sketchy but useful.

New York City and New York State

Both David Ellis, et al., *A Short History of New York State* (Ithaca, 1957), fresh and tightly packed, and A. C. Flick, ed., *History of the State of New York* (New York, 1933–1937), 10 vols., are useful but they focus on the state and tell the story of the city only incidentally.

A full-dress history of New York City is badly needed. Martha J. Lamb and Mrs. Burton Harrison, *History of the City of New York: Its Origin, Rise and Progress* (New York, 1877–1896), 3 vols., and J. G. Wilson, ed., *Memorial History of the City of New York from its first settlement to the year 1892* (New York, 1892–1893), 4 vols., still can be consulted with profit. Isaac N. P. Stokes, *The Iconography of Manhattan Island, 1498–1909* (New York, 1916–1925), 6 vols., a prodigious labor of love, contains in volumes 4 and 5 a detailed chronology of events in the city's history enriched by excerpts from the contemporary press. Allan Nevins and John A. Krout, ed., *The Great City—New York 1898–1948* (New York, 1948), contains five worthwhile essays by Carl Carmer, Margaret Clapp, Thomas C. Cochran, and the editors. If undiscriminating, *New York Panorama* (New York, 1938), and its companion, *New York City Guide* (New York, 1939), prepared by the Federal Writers' Project, provide a mine of information for which the historian can only be grateful. *Regional Survey of New York and Its Environs* (New York, 1927–1931), 8 vols., prepared by Thomas Adams and his associates, contains valuable ecological and economic data, illustrated by tables, charts, and maps, that for the first time depict the city in its regional and metropolitan aspects. It is comprehensive and has historical sweep. Bayrd Still, *Mirror for Gotham* (New York, 1956), is a discriminating, composite portrait of the city as seen by visitors, but is concerned essentially with externals. Bayrd Still, "The Personality of New York City," *New York Folklore Quarterly,* Summer 1958, makes a valiant attempt to get at the essence of New York.

The Jewish Labor Movement and Socialism

William M. Leiserson, "History of the Jewish Labor Movement in New York City" (B.A. thesis, University of Wisconsin, 1908; on deposit, YIVO library) is a pioneer study for the years to 1892 and depends heavily on the Yiddish labor press and *John Swinton's Paper.* E. Tcherikower, ed., *Geshikhte fun der idisher arbeter bavegung in di feraynikte shtatn* (New York, 1943–1945), 2 vols., a collective effort of wide scope, covers the years to 1893 but is uneven in execution. Melech Epstein, *Jewish Labor in USA 1882–1914* (New York, 1950), although journalistic and often inaccurate, captures the flavor of the period. Hyman Berman, "Era of the Protocol: A Chapter in the History of the International Ladies Garment Workers' Union" (unpublished doctoral dissertation, Columbia University, 1955), and Morris Berg, "Contributions of Adolph Strasser to Organized Labor in America" (M.A. thesis, Brooklyn College, 1953), explore special topics. M. D. C. Crawford, *The Ways of Fashion,* rev. ed. (New York, 1948), a learned and felicitous treatise on the aesthetics of garment making, contributes as well to an understanding of the social economy of the needle trades. Of the recent studies of American socialism, David A. Shannon,

The Socialist Party of America (New York, 1955), proved the most judicious and Howard Quint, *The Forging of American Socialism* (Columbia, S.C., 1953), the most original.

Politics, Progressivism, and Reform

Neither Gustavus Myers, *History of Tammany Hall*, 2nd ed. (New York, 1917), nor M. R. Werner, *Tammany Hall* (New York, 1928), examine the ethnic dimensions of New York politics, except in passing. [Interesting contemporary accounts do, e.g.: L. F. Post and F. C. Leubuscher, *An Account of the George-Hewitt Campaign in the Municipal Election of 1886* (New York, 1887) : Frank Moss, *The American Metropolis* (New York, 1897), 3 vols.; Matthew P. Breen, *Thirty Years of New York Politics Up-to-Date* (New York, 1899)]. Mark D. Hirsch, *William C. Whitney, Modern Warwick* (New York, 1948), and Allan Nevins, *Abram S. Hewitt with Some Account of Peter Cooper* (New York, 1935), tell the story of the city's politics through two of its leading political figures. Jacob A. Friedman, *The Impeachment of Governor William Sulzer* (New York, 1939) is a careful monograph. John W. Pratt, "Boss Tweed's Public Welfare Program." *New York Historical Society Quarterly*, October 1961, treats a neglected aspect of machine politics.

Aaron I. Abell, *The Urban Impact on American Protestantism, 1865–1900* (Cambridge, 1943), and Henry F. May, *The Protestant Churches and Industrial America* (New York, 1949), are the most pertinent of a number of good volumes concerned with the rise of the social gospel. Richard Hofstadter, *The Age of Reform* (New York, 1955), portrays the climate of reform with freshness and imagination but deals only peripherally with the immigrant communities; the same is to be said for Eric Goldman, *Rendezvous with Destiny* (New York, 1952). George E. Mowry, *The Era of Theodore Roosevelt 1900–1912* (New York, 1958), ably synthesizes the latest insights and researches into the progressive movement. Robert H. Bremner, *From the Depths: The Discovery of Poverty in the United States* (New York, 1956), is a sweeping survey. Lawrence A. Cremin, *The Transformation of the School* (New York, 1961), which appeared after this book went to press, depicts the educator as reformer with erudition and verve.

Immigration

John Higham, *Strangers in the Land* (New Brunswick, 1955), is the key book on American nativism for the years 1860–1925. Barbara M. Solomon, *Ancestors and Immigrants* (Cambridge, 1956), focuses on the Brahmin nativist with sensitivity. Oscar Handlin, *Race and Nationality in American Life* (Boston, 1957), especially chapter 5, "Old Immigrants and New," punctures the scientific and racist rationale for immigration restriction presented in the 41-volume United States Immigration Commission Report of 1911.

Robert Ernst, *Immigrant Life in New York City 1828–1863* (New York,

1949), is a background account for post–Civil War immigrant New York. Florence P. Gibson, *The Attitudes of the New York Irish toward State and National Affairs 1848–1892* (New York, 1951), does not get below the surface; Thomas N. Brown, "The Origins and Character of Irish-American Nationalism," *Review of Politics,* July 1956, does. John Talbot Smith, *The Catholic Church in New York* (New York, 1905), 2 vols., is an unusally candid history of the church and its conflicting constituencies. Federal Writers' Project, *Gli Italiani Di New York* (New York, 1939), is more comprehensive than its English equivalent, *The Italians of New York* (New York, 1938). Federal Writers' Project, *The Foreign Language Press in New York* (1941, typescript on deposit, Columbia University School of Journalism Library), is a useful but not always reliable compendium.

The Jews

Oscar Handlin, *Adventure in Freedom* (New York, 1954), is a valuable interpretative history of the Jews in the United States. H. B. Grinstein, *The Rise of the Jewish Community of New York 1654–1860* (Philadelphia, 1947), is useful for that period. Rudolf Glanz's studies of the Jews of German America are based on investigations into rare source materials; see, for example, "German Jews in New York City in the 19th century," *YIVO Annual of Jewish Social Science,* 1956–1957.

There are a number of valuable recent studies of anti-Semitism in the larger nativist context: Oscar Handlin, "American Views of the Jew at the Opening of the 20th Century," *Publications of the American Jewish Historical Society,* June 1951; Oscar and Mary F. Handlin, "The Acquisition of Political and Social Rights by Jews of the United States," *American Jewish Yearbook,* 1955; and John Higham, "Anti-Semitism in the Gilded Age: A Reinterpretation," *Mississippi Valley Historical Review,* March 1957, and "Social Discrimination against Jews in America," *Publication of the American Jewish Historical Society* September 1957. Also see, Rose A. Halpern, "The American Reaction to the Dreyfus Case" (M.A. thesis, Columbia University, 1941).

Notes

Chapter 1. City Unlimited

1. Samuel Osgood, *New York in the 19th Century: A Discourse Delivered Before the New York Historical Society November 20, 1866* (New York, 1888), pp. 55, 56.

2. Daniel Van Pelt, *Leslie's History of the Greater New York* (New York, 1898), I, 502f; R. G. Albion, *The Rise of New York Port* (New York, 1939), p. 240f; J. W. Gerard, "Impress of Nationalities on New York City," *Magazine of American History*, 23:59 (January 1890).

3. C. M. Depew, ed., *One Hundred Years of American Commerce, 1795-1895* (New York, 1895), p. 60; T. E. Rush, *The Port of New York* (New York, 1920), pp. 126, 129; *Fifty-first Annual Report, Chamber of Commerce, State of New York, 1908*, p. xxxvi.

4. *Thirteenth Census, 1910: Manufactures 1909, Reports for Principal Industries* (Washington, 1913), p. 815; *Fifty-first Annual Report, Chamber of Commerce, State of New York, 1908*, p. xliii; Thomas Cochran, "The City's Business," *The Greater City*, ed. Allan Nevins and John A. Krout (New York, 1949), pp. 125, 180.

5. *Tenth Annual Report, Bureau of Statistics of Labor, State of New York, 1892* (New York, 1893), 39f; *Thirteenth Census, 1910: Manufactures 1909*, p. 815; *United States Bureau of the Census, Census of Manufactures, 1914* (Washington, 1918), I, 986; George H. Evans, Jr., "Geographical Differences in the Use of the Corporation in American Manufacturing in 1899," *Journal of Economic History* 14:117f (Spring 1954).

6. *Valentine's Manual for the City of New York, 1916-1917*, ed., H. C. Brown (New York, 1916), pp. 132-133; Van Pelt, *Leslie's History*, I, 520; *Sixteenth Annual Report, Bureau of Statistics of Labor, State of New York, 1898*, pp. 986, 1052-1053; United States Industrial Commission, *Reports* (1900-1902), VII, 810; XIV, 42; XV, 312-313, 428-429; W. M. Leiserson, *Unemployment in the State of New York* (New York, 1911), pp. 45-46.

7. *Federation*, 2:39 (June 1902); *Federation*, 2:41 (July 1902); cf. Table 2; *Thirteenth Census, 1910: Population, General Report and Analysis* (Washington, 1913), p. 1023; Van Pelt, *Leslie's History*, I, 545; Edward E. Pratt, *Industrial Causes of Congestion of Population in New York City*

(New York, 1911) , p. 136; *New York Illustrated* (New York, 1891) , pp. 58–59; Rupert Hugher, *The Real New York* (New York, 1904) , pp. 241–242; William P. McLoughlin, "Evictions in New York's Tenement Houses," *Arena,* 7:54 (December 1892) ; *Das deutsche Element der Stadt New York* (New York, 1913) , p. 12; J. L. Bahret, "The Growth of New York and Suburbs since 1790," *Scientific Monthly,* 11:40f (November 1920) .

8. Adna F. Weber, *The Growth of Cities* (New York, 1899) , p. 450.

9. *Historical Statistics of the United States, 1789–1945* (Washington, 1949) , p. 11; Abram C. Dayton, *Last Days of Knickerbocker Life in New York* (New York, 1880) , p. 9.

10. James Creelman, "The New York Subways," in Robert M. La-Follette, ed., *The Making of America* (Chicago, 1906) , III, 455; Henry C. Van Dyke, *The New New York* (New York, 1909) , p. 403.

11. M. P. Breen, *Thirty Years of New York Politics* (New York, 1899) , p. 840; Frank Moss, *The American Metropolis* (New York, 1897), I, ix; II, 347.

12. H. C. Merwin, "Irish in American Life," *Atlantic Monthly,* 73:289 (March, 1896) ; "Power of Irish in Cities," *Littell's Living Age,* 172:383–384 (November 6, 1886) ; John Talbot Smith, *The Catholic Church in New York* (New York, 1905) , II, 447; United States Industrial Commission, *Reports,* VII, 302f, 809.

13. *New York Panorama* (WPA: New York, 1938) , p. 66; Samuel B. Thomas, *The Boss, or the Governor* (New York, 1914) , p. 54.

14. D. G. Thompson, *Politics in a Democracy* (New York, 1893) , p. 97; Harold F. Gosnell, *Boss Platt and His New York Machine* (Chicago, 1924) , 47f, 232f; *Thirty Seventh Annual Report, Chamber of Commerce, State of New York, 1894–1895,* p. 55.

15. *Trow's New York City Directory 1882–1883,* pp. iv–v; Edith Wharton, *A Backward Glance* (New York, 1936) , pp. 21–22, 55–56.

16. Mrs. John King Van Rensselaer, *The Social Ladder* (New York, 1924) , 205f; Ward McAllister, *Society As I Have Found It* (New York, 1890) , p. 378f; Ralph Pulitzer, *New York Society on Parade* (New York, 1910) , p. 2; Dixon Wecter, *The Saga of American Society* (New York, 1937) , p. 368f.

17. Carl Schurz to Mrs. R. W. Gilder, February 15, 1898, *Speeches, Correspondence and Political Papers of Carl Schurz,* ed., Frederick Bancroft (New York, 1913) , V, 451.

18. Mark Sullivan, *Our Times* (New York, 1932), IV, 206; Martha J. R. N. Lamb and Constance B. Harrison, *History of the City of New York* (New York, 1896) , III, 791.

Chapter 2. The East European Captivity

1. M. Silber, *America in Hebrew Literature* (New Orleans, 1928) , p. 51; Leo Wiener, *The History of Yiddish Literature in the 19th Century* (New York, 1899) , p. 134; Abraham G. Duker, "Polish Political Emigration

in the United States and the Jews, 1833–1865," *Publ. Amer. Jew. Hist. Soc.*, 33:149f (December 1949).

2. L. Hersch, "International Migration of the Jews," Imre Ferenczi and Walter F. Willcox, eds., *International Migrations*, National Bureau of Economic Research (New York, 1929–1931), I, 86; II, 471f: M. L. Schlesinger, *Russland in XX Jahrhundert* (Berlin, 1908), p. 134; K. Durland, *The Red Reign* (New York, 1907), p. 468.

3. L. Hersch, *Le Juif Errant d'Aujourd'hui* (Paris, 1913), pp. 105, 283f; B. D. Weinryb, *Neueste Wirtschaftsgeschichte der Juden in Russland und Polen* (Breslau, 1934), p. 19; W. Kaplan-Kogan, *Die Jüdische Wanderbewegungen in der Neuesten Zeit* (Bonn, 1919), pp. 13, 15–16.

4. Weinryb, *Neuste Wirtschaftsgeschichte*, pp. 7–8; I. M. Rubinow, "Economic Conditions of the Jews in Russia," *United States Department of Labor* (Washington, 1907), pp. 488–489.

5. Gregor Alexinsky, *Modern Russia* (New York, 1913), p. 304; E. B. Lanin, *Russian Characteristics* (London, 1892), p. 484f.

6. *Receuil de Materiaux sur la Situation Economique des Israelites de Russie* (D'apres l'enquete de la Jewish Colonization Association) (Paris, 1906–1908), I, 34, 199; I. M. Rubinow, "The Jews in Russia," *Yale Review*, 15:152 (August 1906); Margaret Miller, *The Economic Development of Russia 1905–1914* (London, 1926), pp. 225–226; R. Andree, *Zur Volkskunde der Juden* (Leipzig, 1881), pp. 292–294.

7. Jacob Lestschinsky, "The Jews in the Polish Cities," *Yivo Bleter*, 21:24, 34 (January–February 1943); Francis Henry Skrine, *The Expansion of Russia* (Cambridge, England, 1915), p. 318f.

8. Trans. from original song in Schlesinger, *Russland in XX. Jahrhundert*, pp. 140–141; Hugo Ganz, *The Land of Riddles* (New York, 1904), p. 21.

9. Rubinow, "Economic Conditions," pp. 524, 555; F. H. E. Palmer, *Russian Life in Town and Country* (New York, 1901), 147f; *Receuil*, I, 256f; S. Liss, *Autobiography* (MS, YIVO), p. 15.

10. L. C. A. Knowles, *Economic Development in the 19th Century* (London, 1932), p. 184; Skrine, *The Expansion of Russia*, p. 321; Henry W. Nevinson, *The Dawn in Russia* (New York, 1906), p. 288; R. Luxemburg, *Die industrielle Entwickelung Polens* (Leipzig, 1898), p. 34; B. Baskerville, *The Polish Jew* (New York, 1906), p. 47; United States Consular Reports, *Labor in Europe* (Washington, 1885), p. 1468f; M. Sudarsky, ed., *Lite* (New York, 1951), p. 941f.

11. Leonty Soloveitchik, *Un prolétariat méconnu* (Bruxelles, 1898), p. 98f; J. B. Weber and W. Kempster, *A Report of the Commissioners of Immigration upon the Causes which Incite Immigration to the United States*, (Washington, 1892), p. 74; Victor Bérard, *The Russian Empire and Czarism* (London, 1905), p. 128; Rubinow, "Economic Conditions," p. 526.

12. Rubinow, "Economic Conditions," p. 522; *Receuil*, I, 394f; *Forward* August 3, 9, 26, 1910, February 24, 1912.

13. Phillipp Friedmann, "Wirtschaftliche Umschichtungsprozesse und

Industrialisierung in der Polnischen Judenschaft, 1800–1870," *Jewish Studies in Memory of G. A. Kohut,* S. W. Baron and Alexander Marx, eds., (New York, 1935), p. 178f.

14. Rubinow, "Economic Conditions," pp. 502–503, 543f; Weinryb, *Neueste Wirtschaftsgeschichte,* pp. 99, 116–117; Bérard, *The Russian Empire,* p. 129; Maurice Fishberg, *The Jews* (London, 1911), pp. 538–539; A. Menes, "Di idishe arbeterbavegung in russland fun onhaib 70er bizn soyf 90er yorn, "*Historishe shriftn* (Vilna, 1939), III, 4f; Soloveitschik, *Un prolétariat,* p. 101; S. R. Landau, *Unter Judischen Proletariern* (Vienna, 1898), p. 46; F. Bielschewsky, *Die Textilindustrie des Lodzer Rayons* (Leipzig, 1912), pp. 41, 110.

15. Rubinow, "Economic Conditions," pp. 533–535; *Receuil,* I, 423, 429, 435–436; Miriam Blaustein, ed., *Memoirs of David Blaustein* (New York, 1913), p. 185; quoted from Bérard, *The Russian Empire,* p. 129; Fishberg, *The Jews,* p. 364.

16. Rubinow, "Economic Conditions," pp. 506–515; *Receuil,* I, 47–57; Sudarsky, ed., *Lite,* 997f; Liss, *Autobiography,* p. 28; Lanin, *Russian Characteristics,* p. 528.

17. Lanin, *Russian Characteristics,* p. 528; Soloveitschik, *Un prolétariat,* p. 102; L. Errera, *The Russian Jews* (London, 1894), p. 116; Bérard, *The Russian Empire,* p. 134.

18. Palmer, *Russian Life,* p. 142; Fishberg, *The Jews,* pp. 363–365; *Receuil,* II, 216, 221f; Rubinow, "Economic Conditions," pp. 570–572.

19. Traub, *Judische Wanderungen* (Berlin, 1922), pp. 26, 29; Weber and Kempster, *A Report of the Commissioners of Immigration,* p. 101; Phillipp Friedmann, *Die Galizischen Juden in Kampfe am ihr Gleichberechtigung 1848–1868* (Frankfurt am Main, 1929), pp. 1, 27; Andree, *Zur Volkskunde,* p. 291; Landau, *Unter Judischen Proletariern,* pp. 13–14.

20. Jacob Thon, *Die Juden in Oesterreich,* Bureau für Statistik der Juden, Heft 4 (Berlin, 1908), p. 118f; J. Bross, "Der onhoyb fun der idishe arbeter bavegung in galitsia," *Historishe shriftn* (Vilna, 1939), III, pp. 485–487; Benzion Rubstein, "Der ekonomisher kamf in galitsien," *Di Yudishe Velt* (Vilna), March 1913, 120f.

21. J. Kissman, "A kapitl geshikhte fun der idisher arbeter bavegung in rumania," *Historishe shriftn* (Vilna, 1939), III, 448; A. Ruppin, *Die Juden in Rumanien* (Berlin, 1908), p. 29f; Soloveitschik, *Un prolétariat,* p. 82f; Joseph Jacobs, *Studies in Jewish Statistics* (London, 1891), p. 26; (U. S.) Industrial Commission, *Report* (Washington, 1902), XIV, 122.

22. Traub, *Judische Wanderungen,* pp. 49–50; G. M. Price, *Di yuden in amerika* (Odessa, 1891), 14f.

Chapter 3. Torah, Haskala, and Protest

1. S. A. Birnbaum, "The Cultural Structure of East Ashkenazic Jewry," *The Slavonic and East European Review,* 25:76f (1946–1947); Abraham J. Heschel, "The Eastern European Era in Jewish History," *YIVO Annual of*

Jewish Social Science (1946), I, 86f; J. H. Greenstone, *The Messiah Idea in Jewish History* (Philadelphia, 1906), *passim*.

2. Birnbaum, "East Ashkenazic Jewry," p. 80f: *Hebrew Standard*, September 29, October 6, 1893; J. H. Adeney, *The Jews of Eastern Europe* (London, 1921), 48f; E. B. Lanin, *Russian Characteristics* (London, 1892), p. 482; L. Deitch, *Di yuden in russisher revolutsiya* (Berlin, 1924), p. 19; N. Slouschz, *The Renascence of Hebrew Literature, 1743–1885* (Philadelphia, 1909), 95f, 107; I. M. Rubinow, "Economic Conditions of the Jews in Russia," *United States Department of Labor* (Washington, 1907), p. 576f.

3. N. Goldmann, "Zur Psychologie der Ostjuden," *Ostjuden* (February, 1916), p. 821f; *Idishe familien un familien kraysen fun new york* (New York, 1939), p. 9f; Trans. from S. I. Abramovitch, *Shloymele reb chayim's gezamelte shriftn fun mendel moicher sforim* (Warsaw, n.d.), XVIII, 105–106.

4. M. Sudarsky, ed., *Lite* (New York, 1951), pp. 417, 1045; E. Deinard, *Zikhronos bath ami* (St. Louis, 1920), p. 79; I. Levitats, *The Jewish Community in Russia, 1772–1844* (New York, 1943), pp. 105f, 246f.

5. Z. H. Masliansky, *Sermons* (New York, 1926), p. 193; G. Weinstein, *The Ardent Eighties* (New York, 1928), p. 25; Sudarsky, *Lite*, p. 979; Levitats, *The Jewish Community*, p. 237f: Deinard, *Zikhronos*, p. 40f; F. H. E. Palmer, *Russian Life in Town and Country* (New York, 1901), p. 144; Lanin, *Russian Characteristics*, p. 477.

6. S. Levin, *The Arena* (New York, 1932), pp. 164–165; J. S. Raisen, *The Haskallah Movement in Russia* (Philadelphia, 1913), p. 137.

7. Wolf von Schierbrand, *Russia, Her Strength and Her Weakness* (New York, 1904), p. 200f; Albert F. Heard, *The Russian Church and Russian Dissent* (London, 1887), p. 137f; G. Drage, *Austria-Hungary* (London, 1909), p. 34.

8. Leo Wiener, *The History of Yiddish Literature in the 19th Century* (New York, 1899), pp. 132–133; quoted in L. Greenberg, *The Jews in Russia* (New Haven, 1944–52) I, 32, 35–36.

9. Simon Halkin, "Socio-Historical Implications of Modern Hebrew Literature," *Historia Judaica*, 10:1f (April 1948); Trans. from S. I. Abramovitch, *Di taxe, gezamelte shriftn*, IV, 119.

10. Sudarsky, *Lite*, pp. 353–354, 511f; R. Mahler, *The Struggle Between Haskallah and Hassidism in Galicia in the First Half of the 19th Century* (New York, 1942), pp. 38, 82; Anon., "Die litauischen Juden," *Ostjuden* (February 1916), p. 829f; S. Schechter, *Studies in Judaism* (Philadelphia, 1896), I, 117–118.

11. Deitch, *Di yuden*, pp. 30–32; Trans. from Abramovitch, *Schloimele reb chayim's gezamelte shriftn*, XVIII, 38–40; M. Baring, *The Mainsprings of Russia* (London, 1914), p. 194f; cf. T. Masaryk, *The Spirit of Russia* (New York, 1919), II, 556.

12. Trans. from A. Liesin, "Ahin, Ahin," *Lider un poemen* (New York, 1938), III, 271.

13. Greenberg, *The Jews in Russia*, I, 117.

14. H. Burgin, *Geshikhte fun der idisher arbeter bavegung in amerika* (New York, 1915), p. 189; C. Zhitlowsky, *Zikhroines fun mayn lebn* (New York, 1935–1940), III, 158f; Baron E. Von der Brüggen, *Russia of Today* (London, 1904), p. 193.

15. A. Menes, "Di idishe arbeter bavegung in russland fun onhaib 70er bizn soif 90er yorn," *Historishe shriftn* (Vilna, 1932), III, 2f; Trans. from N. A. Buchbinder, *Geshikhte fun der idisher arbeter bavegung in russland* (Vilna, 1931), pp. 61, 114–115; Trans. from M. Winchevsky, *Gezamelte verk* (New York, 1927), II, 76.

16. A. Menes, "Di idishe arbeter bavegung in russland;" Koppel S. Pinson, "Arkady Kremer, Vladimir Medem, and the Ideology of the Jewish 'Bund,'" *Jewish Social Studies*, 7:235, 239 (July 1945); *Bialostocki Komitet Robotniczy* (May 1898; broadside in S. Solomon Archives, YIVO Institute of Jewish Research); A. L. Patkin, *The Origins of the Russian Labor Movement* (Melbourne and London, 1947), pp. 192–193.

17. I. M. Rubinow, "The Jews in Russia," *Yale Review* 15:156 (August 1906); H. W. Nevinson, *The Dawn in Russia* (New York, 1906), pp. 298–299.

18. *Ah tsusterte simkha* (Bialystok, August 1900; broadside in S. Solomon collection); Burgin, *Geshikhte*, pp. 193, 223; Menes, "Di idishe arbeter bavegung," p. 49; S. Rabinowitsch, *Die Organisationen des Judischen Proletariats in Russland* (Karlsruhe, 1903), pp. 161–162; Rubinow, "Economic Conditions of the Jews in Russia," *United States Department of Labor* (Washington, 1907), p. 53f; Buchbinder, *Geshikhte*, pp. 63–64, 170f; T. K. A. Pashitnow, *Die Lage der Arbeitenden Klasse in Russland* (Stuttgart, 1907), pp. 271–272.

19. M. S. Miller, *The Economic Development of Russia, 1905–1914* (London, 1926), p 234f; M. Davitt, *Within the Pale* (New York, 1903), pp. 74–75; *Unzer protest gegn tsarishen mishpot* (Grodno, September 1904; broadside in S. Solomon collection); *Ah tsusterte simkha* (Bialystok, August 1900; broadside in S. Solomon collection).

20. Rubinow, "The Jews," p. 157; J. Melnik, ed., *Russen über Russland* (Frankfurt am Main, 1906), pp. 585f; J. A. Nillesen, *De Sociale Toestand der Joden in Rusland onder de Tsaren En De Sowets* (Nijmegen-Utrecht, 1939), pp. 101–102.

21. *Ah tsusterte simkha; Der onfall fun politsay in shklov* (Mogilev, June 1904; broadside in S. Solomon collection); *Blut vieder blut* (August 1905; broadside in S. Solomon collection); *Tsu alemen* (Minsk, October 1905; broadside in S. Solomon collection); *Memoirs of Count Witte*, ed. A. Yarmolinsky (New York, 1921), p. 378.

22. J. Meisl, *Haskallah* (Berlin, 1919), p. 201; I, Friedlaender, *The Jews of Russia and Poland* (New York, 1915), p. 207; Burgin, *Geshikhte*, pp. 208, 217.

23. Pinson, "Arkady Kremer," p. 239; A. Menes, "J. L. Peretz un di idishe arbeter bavegung," *Zukunft*, 57:127 (March 1952).

24. J. Kissman, *Shtudies tsu der geshikhte fun rumanishe idn in 19sten*

un onhaib 2osten yorhundert (New York, 1944), 53f; J. Bross, "Der onhaib fun der idishe arbeter bavegung in galitsia," *Historishe shriftn* (Vilna, 1939), III, 488f; S. R. Landau, *Unter Judischen Proletariern* (Vienna, 1898), p. 12.

Chapter 4. Urban Economic Frontiers

1. Cf. Walter Barrett, *The Old Merchants of New York City* (New York, 1885), I, 116f; II, 121–122, 128; M. J. Kohler, "The Board of Delegates of American Israelites, 1859–1878," *Publ. Amer. Jew. Hist. Soc.* 29:119–120 (1925); I. Markens, *Hebrews in America* (New York, 1888), p. 159; Paul H. Nystrom, *The Economics of Retailing* (3rd ed., New York, 1930), p. 137; R. Edwards, *New York's Great Industries* (New York, 1885), pp. 111, 144, 158, 185, 240, 245, 276; *American Hebrew*, November 24, 1905.

2. Max Cohen, "The Jews in Business," *The American Hebrew*, May 22, 1891; Markens, *Hebrews*, p. 140; cf. M. H. Smith, Henry L. Williams, and Ralph Bayard, *Wonders of a Great City; or the Sights, Secrets, and Sins of New York* (Chicago, 1887), p. 414; M. D. C. Crawford, *The Ways of Fashion* (New York, 1948), p. 101; *New York Sun*, May 31, 1891; Edwards, *New York's Great Industries*, pp. 89, 101, 247, 313.

3. Cf. *Twenty-Eighth Annual Report, Corporation of the Chamber of Commerce, State of New York, 1885–6* (New York, 1886), p. 121f and subsequent reports; *Souvenir Book of Fair Educational Alliance* (New York, 1895), p. 97f; John S. Billings, "Vital Statistics of the Jews," *United States Census Bulletin No. 19* (December 30, 1890), p. 7f; "Will the Jews Own New York?" *New York Journal*, June 14, 1896; S. Ratner, ed., *New Light on the History of Great American Fortunes* (New York, 1953), pp. 57f, 185.

4. Cohen, "The Jews in Business."

5. *Arbeiter Zeitung*, November 4, 1892; *New York Times*, November 18, 1957, p. 31; *Zukunft*, December 1905, p. 703; *The Hebrew Album of Prominent Israelites in America* (New York, 1904), p. 15; A. L. Belden, *The Fur Trade in America and Some of the Men Who Made and Maintain It* (New York, 1917), *passim*.

6. *Fourteenth Annual Report, Board of Relief of the United Hebrew Charities, City of New York, 1888*, pp. 19–20; M. Wischnitzer, *To Dwell in Safety* (Philadelphia, 1948), pp. 61f, 125f; Boris Bogen, *Jewish Philanthropy* (New York, 1917), p. 121; Samuel Joseph, *History of the Baron de Hirsch Fund* (Philadelphia, 1935), p. 205f; Zigismund Pestkof to Paul Abelson, May 20, 1907 (Abelson Collection).

7. *New Yorker Idishe Volks-Zeitung*, November 5, 1886; H. Idell Zeisloft, *The New Metropolis* (New York, 1899), p. 531; *Fourteenth Annual Report, Board of Relief of the United Hebrew Charities, City of New York, 1888*, p. 40.

8. Jacob Riis, *How the Other Half Lives* (New York, 1890), p. 90;

W. McAdoo, *Guarding A Great City* (New York, 1906) , p. 143; *Eighteenth Annual Report, Bureau of Labor Statistics, State of New York, 1900*, pp. 292–293; Bertha H. Poole, "The Way of the Pushcart," *The Craftsman*, 9:218f (November 1905) ; *Report of the Mayor's Push-Cart Commission The City of New York* (New York, 1906) , pp. 37, 89, 199f; *Social Reform Club Circular* (1898); Hutchins Hapgood, "The Earnestness That Wins Wealth," *World's Work*, 6:3459 (May 1903) ; *Yearbook, University Settlement Society of New York, 1899–1900*, pp. 89–90.

9. Markens, *Hebrews*, pp. 156–157; R. A. Clemen, *The American Livestock Industry* (New York, 1923) , pp. 156f, 169, 453, 460; I. Kopeloff, *Amol in amerika* (Warsaw, 1928) , p. 402f; cf. Faith M. Williams, *The Food Manufacturing Industries in New York and Its Environs* (New York, 1924) , p. 20.

10. *Yearbook, University Settlement Society*, (1900) , p. 35f; *Forward*, September 28, 1909; *Fourth Annual Report, Bureau of Statistics of Labor, State of New York, 1886*, p. 485f; *State of New York, Preliminary Report of the Factory Investigation Commission, 1912*, I, 209, 217–218; Williams, *Food Manufacturing Industries*, p. 24; *Forward*, April 23, 1910; *Second Annual Industrial Directory, New York, 1913*, pp. 574–575.

11. *Forward*, April 27, 1906, April 23, 1910; *Wilson's Business Directory 1880–1881*, pp. 705–706; *The Trow Business Directory of Greater New York, 1907*, pp. 1039–1040; M. E. Ravage, *An American in the Making* (New York, 1917) , p. 124f.

12. G. M. Price, *Di yuden in amerika* (Odessa, 1891) , p. 12; *Eighteenth Annual Report, United Hebrew Charities*, pp. 25–26; United States Industrial Commission, *Reports* (Washington, 1900–1902) , XIV, 1200; Crawford, *Ways of Fashion*, p. 148; C. S. Bernheimer, "The Jewish Immigrant as an Industrial Worker," *Annals of the American Academy of Political and Social Science*, 33:399f (March 1909) ; cf. Ann Reed, "The Jewish Immigrants of Two Pittsburgh Blocks," *Charities and Commons*, January 2, 1909, 609f; *Forward*, April 8, 1913.

13. L. Hersch, "International Migrations of the Jews," *International Migrations*, ed. Imre Ferenczi and W. F. Willcox (New York, 1930) , II, 497–498, 504–505.

14. H. S. Goldstein, *Forty Years of Struggle for a Principle* (New York, 1928) , pp. 32–33; *The Hebrew American Directory and Universal Guide* (New York, 1892) , p. 137; *Arbeiter Zeitung*, June 6, 1890; *Sixteenth Annual Report, Bureau of Statistics of Labor, State of New York*, p. 1046; *Thirteenth Annual Report, Bureau of Statistics of Labor, State of New York*, II, 388–389; *Forward*, February 20, June 12, 1914; Sol Blum, "Trade Union Rules in the Building Trades," J. H. Hollander and G. E. Barnett, ed., *Studies in American Trade Unionism* (New York, 1912) , p. 300.

15. *Fifth Annual Report, Bureau of Statistics of Labor, State of New York*, p. 220; *Sixth Annual Report, Bureau of Statistics of Labor, State of New York*, p. 829; E. S. Martin, "East Side Considerations," *Harper's Magazine*, 40:861 (May 1898); A. Cahan, *Bleter fun mayn lebn* (New York,

1926), II, 95; *Arbeiter Zeitung*, February 10, 1893; Markens, *Hebrews*, p. 162; *Forward*, July 20, August 24, 1906, June 21, 1907, April 4, 1910, October 16, 1911, February 8, 1914; *University Settlement Studies* (October 1906), pp. 24–25.

16. G. Weinstein, *The Ardent Eighties* (New York, 1928), p. 11f; S. Sheinfeld, *Zikhroines fun a shriftzetzer* (New York, 1946), p. 61; S. Sheinfeld, *Fuftsig yor geshikhte* (New York, 1938), pp. 48–49; *Thirteenth Census, 1910: Manufactures Reports for Principal Industries* (Washington, 1913), pp. 910–912; cf. A. F. Hinrichs, *The Printing Industry in New York and Its Environs* (New York, 1924), p. 16; H. S. Linfield, "Jews in Trade Unions in the City of New York," *The Communal Organization of the Jews in the United States, 1927* (New York, 1930), p. 129; *Forward*, December 22, 1915.

17. Riis, *The Other Half*, p. 108; *Report of the Committee on Manufactures on the Sweating System*, 52nd Congress, 2nd Session, H. R. Report no. 2309, 1893, pp. 219–220; *Annual Report, Chamber of Commerce, State of New York, 1858*, pp. 38–39; Martin E. Popkin, *Organization, Management and Technology in the Manufacture of Men's Clothing* (London, 1929), p. 8.

18. Crawford, *Ways of Fashion*, pp. 95, 145–146; I. N. P. Stokes, *The Iconography of Manhattan Island, 1498–1909* (New York, 1918), III, 819–820; Popkin, *Organization, Management and Technology*, p. 19; Charles E. Zaretz, *The Amalgamated Clothing Workers of America* (New York, 1934), p. 20f; *Tenth Annal Report, Bureau of Statistic of Labor, State of New York, 1892*, pp. 47–51; Jesse Pope, *The Clothing Industry in New York* (Columbia, Mo., 1905), p. 292.

19. *New York Labor Bulletin*, 10:309 (September 1908); Pope, *The Clothing Industry*, pp. 289–290; E. E. Pratt, *Industrial Causes of Congestion* (New York, 1911), p. 79f; *New York State Department of Labor, 16th Annual Report of Factory Inspection*, p. 17.

20. United States Industrial Commission, *Reports*, XV, 320; Crawford, *Ways of Fashion*, p. 95; quoted by Louis Levine, *The Women's Garment Workers* (New York, 1924), p. 11f.

21. H. Koht, *The American Spirit in Europe* (Philadelphia, 1949), p. 98; Paul H. Nystrom, *Economics of Fashion* (New York, 1928), p. 289f; *Forward*, August 19, 1909; Florence S. Richards, *The Ready-to-Wear Industry 1900–1950* (New York, 1950), p. 11.

22. Belden, *The Fur Trade*, pp. 179–180; *Twelfth Census, 1900: Manufactures VIII* (Washington, 1902), p. 624; *Forward*, May 16, 1910; B. Weinstein, *Di idishe unions in amerika* (New York, 1929), p. 442f.

23. C. M. Depew, *One Hundred Years of American Commerce, 1795–1895* (New York, 1895), II, 563; Riis, *The Other Half*, pp. 121, 123; Pope, *The Clothing Industry*, pp. 291–292; Crawford, *Ways of Fashion*, p. 91; "In Defense of the Immigrant," *American Jewish Yearbook*, 12:29 (1910–1911).

24. *Second Annual Industrial Directory of New York*, pp. 105, 436–438,

477f, 491f; *Tenth Annual Report, Bureau of Statistics Labor, State of New York*, pp. 47–51.

25. U. S. Industrial Commission, *Reports*, XIV, 92; Price, *Di yuden*, pp. 4–5; *Report, Committee of the Senate, Relation between Capital and Labor, 1885*, I, 259–260; *Autobiography 4*, p. 14f, *Autobiography 52*, p. 36, *Autobiography 70*, pp. 50–51, *Autobiography 115*, p. 16f (manuscripts at the YIVO Institute of Jewish Research); *Jewish Communal Register, 1917–1918*, 708f; *New York Times*, December 26, 1957, p. 19.

26. Willis N. Baer, *The Economic Development of the Cigar Industry in the United States* (Lancaster, Pa., 1933), pp. 41, 92; Jacob Wolf, *Der Tabak und Die Tabak-Fabrikate* (Leipzig, 1912), p. 243f; Samuel Gompers, *Seventy Years of Life and Labor* (New York, 1925), I, 34; United States Industrial Commission, *Reports*, XV, 385–386; *University Settlement Society Quarterly* (October 1906), pp. 23–24; Lucy W. Killough, *The Tobacco Products Industry in New York and Its Environs* (New York, 1924), p. 33.

27. William W. Young, *The Story of the Cigarette* (New York, 1916), pp. 7–9, 69, 114–115; R. B. Tennant, *The American Cigarette Industry* (New Haven, 1950), p. 35f; *Eighth Annual Report, Bureau of Statistics of Labor, State of New York, 1890*, p. 1023; *Forward*, March 23, 1906, February 15, 1907; *Zukunft*, January, 1913, p. 37; Killough, *Tobacco Products Industry*, pp. 44, 47, 50; cf. *Trow Business Directory of Greater New York, 1907*, pp. 254–255, contrast with the *Trow Business Directory of New York City, 1897*, pp. 251–252 and *Wilson's Business Directory, 1880*, p. 173; *Abendblatt der Arbeiter Zeitung*, January 11, 1896; *Zukunft*, December 1905, p. 702; *Idisher Zhurnal*, November 11, 1904.

28. *Report, Select Committee, H. R., Importation of Contract Laborers, Paupers, Convicts, and Other Classes* (Washington, 1889), p. 507; B. Weinstein, *Di idishe unions in amerika* (New York, 1929), p. 44; Sheinfeld, *Fuftzig yor geshikhte*, pp. 83–84; *Forward*, December 10, 1904; Jacob Panken, "The Jew as Proletarian, *"United Hebrew Trades Souvenir Journal* (New York, 1933), p. 28; Rubinow, "Economic Conditions of the Jews in Russia," *United States Department of Labor* (Washington, 1907), pp. 502, 532; Frank J. Sheridan, "Italian, Slavic and Hungarian Unskilled Immigrant Laborers in the United States," *United States Department of Labor* (Washington, 1907), pp. 403–404; Maurice Fishberg, *The Jews* (London, 1911), p. 398.

29. *Ninth Census: Population, New York City 1870*, XXX, 9th elect. dist., 6th ward, pp. 7, 30, 35 (National Archives, Washington); Kopeloff, *Amol*, p. 294; *Hebrew Standard*, August 11, 1893; *Report of the Committee of Manufactures on the Sweating System, 1893*, p. 194; *Report to the Council of the University Settlement Society* (March 1900), p. 2; Rubinow, "Economic Conditions," p. 506; *Second Annual Report, Board of Relief of the United Hebrew Charities, City of New York, 1876*, p. 17; cf. United States Immigration Commission, *Report* (Washington, 1907–1910), XXVI, 219.

30. Abraham Cahan, *The Rise of David Levinsky* (New York, 1917),
p. 216; Price, *Di yuden,* pp. 19–20; A. J. Rongy, "Half A Century of Jewish Medical Activities in New York City", *Medical Leaves,* 1:151 (1937);
Laws of the State of New York (1893), pp. 1540f; A. Flexner, *History of
Medical Education in the United States* (New York, 1910), p. 207f;
James J. Walsh, *History of Medicine in New York* (New York, 1919), I,
107; II, 591; M. A. Lipkind, "Some East Side Physicians," *Medical Leaves,*
4:103f (1942); C. E. A. Winslow, *Hermann M. Biggs* (Philadelphia, 1929),
p. 171; Solomon R. Kagan, *Jewish Contributions to Medicine in America*
(Boston, 1939), pp. 61, 323–326, 332–333; *New York City Guide* (WPA:
New York, 1939), p. 245.

31. *Autobiography 178* (MS, YIVO Archives), p. 89; Hutchins Hapgood, *The Spirit of the Ghetto* (New York, 1902), pp. 79, 85; Nina N.
Selivanova, *Russian Women* (New York, 1923), p. 154; *First Bulletin of
the Educational Alliance, 1898,* p. 3; *Arbeiter Zeitung,* October 13, 1893;
Forward, January 2, 1904, November 11, 1908; Kopeloff, *Amol,* 412f; Cahan, *Bleter,* II, 335f; Miriam Blaustein, ed., *Memoirs of David Blaustein*
(New York, 1913), pp. 139–140; James Creelman, "Israel Unbound," *Pearson's Magazine,* 17:252 (February 1907). My estimates are based on a study
of the *Trow Business Directory of New York City* for 1897 and 1907 and
Jewish Encyclopedia (New York, 1905), XII, 370; J. L. Cardozo, ed. *Hebrew-American Manuel for New York for 1887* (New York, 1887), estimated there were 900 Jewish physicians in the city, which is wide of the
mark, and 300 Jewish lawyers, which is also too high.

32. Cf. Table 3; Blaustein, *Memoirs,* pp. 139–140; *Arbeiter Zeitung,*
October 13, 1893; *Abendblatt der Arbeiter Zeitung,* January 11, 1896; B. J.
Hendrick, *The Story of Life Insurance* (New York, 1907), p. 263f; *Forward,* January 23, 29, 1900, January 4, April 20, October 5, 14, 1906;
Zeitgeist March 1, 1907; B. Weinstein, *Fertzig yor in di idishe arbeter
bavegung in amerika* (New York, 1924), pp. 73–74; *American Jewish Yearbook, 1907–1908,* p. 329.

33. A. E. Costello, *Our Police Protectors* (New York, 1885), p. 527f;
E. Morison, ed., *The Letters of Theodore Roosevelt* (Cambridge, 1952),
III, 79; Arnold Bennett, *Your United States* (New York, 1912), p. 184;
The City Record Supplement (July 31, 1901), XXIX, 15f; B. J. Hend-
rick, "The Jewish Invasion of America," *McClure's Magazine,* 40:140f
(March 1913); Winslow, *Biggs,* p. 190.

34. *New York Herald,* November 26, 1905.

35. Jacob Riis, *The Children of the Poor* (New York, 1892), p. 35f;
Price, *Di yuden,* p. 6.

Chapter 5. The Lower East Side

1. Abraham Cahan, *Yekl, A Tale of the Ghetto* (New York, 1896), p.
28; United States Immigration Commission, *Reports* (Washington, 1907–
1910), XXVI, 167; *Seventeenth Annual Report, University Settlement So-*

ciety, (1903), p. 8; *Arbeiter Zeitung*, June 20, 1890; *Forward*, March 23, 24, 1904; February 20, 1906, February 8, 1911; *Volksblatt*, February 18, May 27, 1910; I. L. Nascher, *The Wretches of Povertyville* (Chicago, 1909), p. 10f; Miriam Blaustein, ed., *Memoirs of David Blaustein* (New York, 1913), pp. 123–124.

2. Gregory Weinstein, *The Ardent Eighties* (New York, 1928), p. 79; *Yiddishes Tageblatt*, March 20, 1910; *Forward*, February 14, 1912; *Report, Committee on Manufactures on the Sweating System*, 52nd Congress, 2nd Session, H. R. Report no. 2309, 1893, p. 182; *Wegweiser in der Amerikaner bizness velt*, February 8, 1892; Nascher, *The Wretches*, p. 12.

3. H. B. Grinstein, *The Rise of the Jewish Community of New York, 1654–1860* (New York, 1945), p. 31f; United States Industrial Commission, *Reports* (Washington, 1900–1902), XV, 476, 478; P. Cowen, *Memories of An American Jew* (New York, 1932), p. 103; B. Weinstein, *Fertsig yor in di idishe arbeter bavegung in amerika* (New York, 1924), pp. 21–22.

4. *New York Labor Bulletin*, 10:314–315, 322 (September 1908); E. E. Pratt, *The Industrial Causes of Congestion in New York City* (New York: 1911), pp. 19–20; *Report of the University Settlement Society* (1897), p. 3; Arnold Bennett, *Your United States* (New York, 1912), p. 187; Harold M. Finley, "New York's Populous and Densest Blocks," *Federation*, 4:8 (November 1906); H. C. Brearley, *The Problem of Greater New York and Its Solution* (New York, 1914), p. 28; *Report of the University Settlement Society* (1896), p. 10.

5. G. M. Price, *Di yuden in amerika* (Odessa, 1891), p. 13; *New York Herald*, November 25, 1892; Louis Waldman, *Labor Lawyer* (New York, 1944), pp. 23, 28; *Autobiography 45* (MS, YIVO Institute of Jewish Research), p. 153.

6. Z. Szjaikowski, "The Attitude of American Jews to East European Jewish Immigrants, 1881–1893," *Publ. Amer. Jew. Hist. Soc.*, 40:272–273 (March 1951); *Report, Select Committee, H. R. Importation of Contract Laborers, Paupers, Convicts and Other Classes* (Washington, 1889), p. 289f; W. T. Elsing, *The Poor in Great Cities* (New York, 1898), p. 103. The following are the 1910 population figures for East Europeans in New York City:

	Total	Male	Female
Rumania	33,584	16,461	17,123
Hungary	76,625	35,224	41,401
Austria	190,237	95,941	94,296
Russia	484,189	257,418	226,771

Walter Laidlaw, *Statistical Sources for Demographic Studies of New York, 1910* (New York, 1912), I, i.

7. W. M. R., "A Sabbath Among Orthodox Jews," *Galaxy*, 14:379f (September 1872); *Report, Committee of the Senate, Relations between Capital and Labor* (Washington, 1885), I, 94.

8. C. D. Wright, *The Housing of the Working People* (Washington, 1895), p. 196; *Forty-third Annual Report, New York Association for the Improvement of the Condition of the Poor, 1886*, p. 43f; Allen Forman, "Some Adopted Americans," *The American Magazine*, 9:51–52 (November 1888) : *Report of the Tenement House Committee of 1894, New York* (1895), pp. 8, 12, 104.

9. Daniel Van Pelt, *Leslie's History of Greater New York* (New York, 1898), I, 544; *21st Annual Report, University Settlement Society, 1907*, pp. 27–28; *Abendblatt der Arbeiter Zeitung*, January 11, 1896; *Idisher Zhurnal*, July 14, 1899; *Fifth Report, Tenement House Department, City of New York, 1909*, pp. 106–107, 112–113.

10. *Report of the Year's Work, University Settlement Society, 1900*, p. 34; William P. McLoughlin, "Evictions in New York's Tenement Houses," *Arena*, 7:50–52 (December 1892) ; *Hebrew Standard*, August 25, 1893; Samuel Gompers to Henry Goldfogle, September 14, 1893 (Gompers Papers) ; *Yiddishes Tageblatt*, January 1, 1901.

11. United States Industrial Commission, *Reports*, XIV, 87; Frank Moss, *The American Metropolis* (New York, 1897), III, 205; Joseph Barondess to Charles D. Spivak, June 11, 1908 (Barondess Papers) ; *Report, Tenement House Department, 1902–1903*, I, 141; *Fifth Report, Tenement House Department*, New York, 1909, pp. 19, 103; Ralph D. Paine, "Are Riches Demoralizing American Life?" *World's Work*, 6:3917f (September 1903) .

12. Stephen Jenkins, *The Greatest Street in the World* (New York, 1911), p. 191; B. J. Hendrick, "The Jewish Invasion of America," *McClure's Magazine*, 40:134 (March 1913) ; M. Feinstone and H. Lang, eds., *Geverkshaftn* (New York, 1938), pp. 100–102; Donald H. Davenport, et al., *The Retail Shopping and Financial Districts in New York* (New York, 1927), p. 23; George Filipetti, *The Wholesale Markets in New York* (New York, 1925), p. 46.

13. M. Fishberg, "Health and Sanitation of the Immigrant Jewish Population of New York," *Menorah*, August-September 1902, pp. 4, 14; M. Fishberg, "Materials for the Physical Anthropology of the Eastern European Jews," *Memoirs of the American Anthropological and Ethnological Societies* (June, 1905), vol. I, pt. I, pp. 36–37, 41–42; Szjaikowski, "The Attitude of American Jews," p. 243; *Report of the Tenement House Committee of 1894*, pp. 21–22, 47–48; United States Immigration Commission, *Reports*, XXVI, 165; Joseph Barondess to Mrs. M. A. Davis, March 22, 1902 (Barondess Papers) ; cf. *Wilson's Business Directory of New York City, 1880–1881*, p. 45; *The Trow Business Directory of New York City, 1897*, pp. 86–87; *Trow Business Directory of Greater New York, 1907*, pp. 102–103.

14. C. E. A. Winslow, *The Life of Hermann M. Biggs* (Philadelphia, 1929), pp. 80, 95–96; *Eighteenth Annual Report, United Hebrew Charities, 1892–1893*, p. 21; United States Industrial Commission, *Reports*, XIV, 87; *Twenty-fifth Annual Report, United Hebrew Charities, 1899*, p. 35;

Ernest Poole, *The Plague In Its Stronghold* (New York, 1903), p. 3f; Joseph Barondess to Dr. J. S. Billings, September 9, 1908 (Barondess Papers); M. Fishberg, "Tuberculosis Among Jews," *American Israelite*, October 18, 1908; A. J. Rongy, "Half a Century of Jewish Medical Activities in New York City," *Medical Leaves*, 1:159 (1937). Cf. advertisements by specialists in "men's diseases" like "Old Dr. Grey," *Yiddishes Tageblatt*, January 16, 1899; *Forward*, March 2, 1901.

15. *Abendblatt der Arbeiter Zeitung*, January 13, 1896; *Forward*, February 14, 1912; Ida Van Etten, "Russian Jews as Desirable Immigrants," *Forum*, 15:178 (April 1893); S. Foster, "The Workingman and the Synagogue," *Yearbook, Central Conference of American Rabbis*, 20:482 (1909); Hutchins Hapgood, *The Spirit of the Ghetto* (New York, 1902), p. 14; *Forward*, March 23, 1904; *Report of the Tenement House Committee of 1894*, p. 431.

16. M. Fishberg, *The Jews* (London, 1911), pp. 367, 530–531; *Arbeiter Zeitung*, June 20, 1890; *Forward*, July 26, August 13, 1897, March 25, 1908; M. Osherowitch, "Di geshikhte fun forverts, 1897–1947" (MS, New York Public Library); 17; *Nayer Gayst* (December 1897), p. 133; L. K. Frankel, "Jewish Charities," *The Making of America*, ed. R. M. LaFollette (Chicago, 1906), X, 64; United States Industrial Commission, *Reports*, XIV, 119, 121; K. H. Claghorn, "Jewish Immigration and Pauperism," *Jewish Charity*, 3:31–32 (November 1903); L. K. Frankel to Herbert Parsons, January 12, 1905 (Parsons Papers).

17. Grinstein, *The Rise of the Jewish Community*, p. 16; *Trial of Pesach Rubinstein for the Murder of Sarah Alexander in the Town of New Lots* (New York, 1876), *passim*; Frank Weitenkampf, *Manhattan Kaleidoscope* (New York, 1947), p. 82; prison statistics are cited in Allen Tarshish, "The Rise of American Judaism; A History of American Jewish Life from 1848–1881" (doctoral dissertation, Hebrew Union College, 1938), p. 433; George Walling, *Recollections of a New York Chief of Police* (New York, 1887), pp. 19, 280f; A. E. Costello, *Our Police Protectors* (New York, 1885), p. 324; I. Markens, *Hebrews in America* (New York, 1888), p. 24; Nascher, *The Wretches*, pp. 12, 40, 63, 129–130; Jacob Riis, *How The Other Half Lives*, p. 109; Moss, *The American Metropolis*, II, 366, III, 55, 154; Rupert Hughes, *The Real New York* (New York, 1904), pp. 333–334; *Report, University Settlement Society, 1896*, p. 10; C. C. Regier, *The Era of the Muckrackers* (Chapel Hill, 1932), p. 80.

18. *Arbeiter Zeitung*, January 26, October 12, 1894; *Yearbook, University Settlement Society, 1899*, p. 89; Nascher, *The Wretches*, pp. 10–12, 40; *Forward*, May 15, 1908; United States Industrial Commission, *Reports*, XIV, 124; David Blaustein to Paul Abelson, January 29, 1907 (Abelson Papers); *American Hebrew*, December 17, 1909.

19. *Twenty-Sixth Annual Report, President, Treasurer, and Attorneys, Legal Aid Society, 1901*, p. 18; Joseph Barondess to Desertion Bureau, United Hebrew Charities, May 27, 1908 (Barondess Papers); S. Lowenstein, "Jewish Desertions," *Jewish Charity*, 5:143 (February, 1905); *Year-*

book, University Settlement Society, 1900, pp. 28–29; J. B. Reynolds to Henry C. Potter, October 1, 1900 (Reynolds Papers) ; *Hebrew Standard,* August 25, 1893; *Twenty-Third Annual Report, United Hebrew Charities, 1896,* p. 45; *Twenty-Eighth Annual Report, Legal Aid Society, 1903,* p. 31.

20. *American Hebrew,* December 17, 1909; *Report of the Tenement House Committee of 1894,* p. 81f; *Importing Women for Immoral Purposes* (New York Senate, Doc. 196, 1909), p. 14; *Jewish International Conference on the Suppression of Traffic in Girls and Women* (London, 1910), *passim; Forward,* January 10, 1901, January 1, 1902.

21. Morris D. Waldman, *Nor By Power* (New York, 1953), p. 298; J. D. Eisenstein, *Otser Zikhronotsay* (New York, 1929), pp. 79, 98, 112; S. Sheinfeld, *Zikhroines fun a shriftzetser* (New York, 1946), p. 33; Rose A. Halpern, "The American Reaction to the Dreyfus Case" (M.A. thesis, Columbia University, 1941), pp. 85–86.

22. Anatole Leroy-Beaulieu, *Les Immigrants Juifs et le Judaisme aux Etats-Unis* (Paris, 1905), pp. 11–12; Felix Klein, *In the Land of the Strenuous Life* (Chicago, 1905), p. 3; Peter Wiernik, *History of the Jews in America* (New York, 1912), pp. 270–272; Fishberg, *The Jews,* p. 368; C. S. Bernheimer, *The Russian Jew in the United States* (Philadelphia, 1905), p. 112. Cf. ads for Schleicher and Weser pianos; *Abendblatt der Arbeiter Zeitung,* January 11, 1896; *Yiddishes Tageblatt,* January 16, 1899.

23. *New York City Guide* (WPA: New York, 1939), p. 498; *The Menorah,* 27:298 (November 1904) ; *Weekly Bulletin of the Clothing Trades* 3:11 (April 29, 1904) ; H. C. Syrett, *The City of Brooklyn, 1865–1898* (New York, 1944), p. 237.

24. Eisenstein, *Otser,* pp. 70, 124; United States Industrial Commission, *Reports,* XIV, 477; United States Immigration Commission, *Reports,* XLI, 198; *Weekly Bulletin of the Clothing Trades* 3:14 (April 29, 1904) ; Joseph Barondess to Thompson, November 12, 1907 (Barondess Papers).

25. W. Laidlaw, *Population of the City of New York, 1890–1930* (New York, 1932), pp. 52, 53; Regional Survey, *Population, Land Values, and Government* (New York, 1929), p. 63.

26. W. M. Rosenblatt, "The Jews, What They Are Coming To," *Galaxy,* 13:47 (January, 1872), estimated their number at from 60,000 to 100,000; *The New York Times,* December 18, 1870, estimated 70,000; Z. H. Bernstein, "Dvorim achadim al dvar hayehudim lifnay shloshim v'arba shonim b'New York," *Yalkut Maarabi,* 1:4 (1904), estimated 80,000; Wiernik, *History,* p. 256. The religious census conducted by the Board of Delegates of American Israelites in 1878, by the nature of its method, appeared to err on the side of conservatism. 60,000 Jews for New York City, where the religiously unaffiliated were numerous indeed, seems low. *Statistics of the Jews of the United States* (Philadelphia, 1880), p. 9. In 1885, Carl Schurz estimated that New York's German Jews alone numbered 85,000. Rudolf Glanz, *Jews in Relation to the Cultural Milieu of the Germans* (New York, 1947), p. 27; the figure 1,400,000 for 1914 is based on estimates for the years 1913 to 1917, *Jewish Communal Register of New*

York City, 1917–1918 (New York, 1918), p. 89. For a discussion of the problems of Jewish demography see *Jewish Communal Directory* (New York, 1912), p. 1f, and Henry Chalmers, "The Number of Jews in New York City," *Publications of American Statistical Association,* 14:68f (March 1914).

Chapter 6. Germans versus Russians

1. Alice Hyneman Rhine, "Race Prejudice at Summer Resorts," *Forum,* 3:527f (July 1887); *The Annual Club Book of New York and Vicinity, The Elite Catalogue of Clubs for 1890–1891* (New York, 1890), pp. 43, 74; *The New York Hebrew Select Directory and Visiting List* (New York, 1896), *passim;* Francis Gerry Fairfield, *Clubs of New York* (New York, 1873), pp. 107, 112, 145, 155, 210, 271, 288, 331, 341–342; George J. Manson, "The Foreign Element in New York City, The Germans," *Harper's Weekly,* 32:581f (August 4, 1888); cf. *Deutsch-Amerikanisches Conversations-Lexicons* (New York, 1873), VIII, 79; *Das deutsche Element der Stadt New York* (New York, 1913), pp. 19–20, 305–306; Theodore Lemke, *Geschichte des Deutschtums von New York* (New York, 1891), p. 77f.

2. Henry Whittemore, *Progressive Patriotic and Philanthropic Hebrews of the New World* (New York, 1907), p. 141f; *Der Stadt Anzeiger,* October 15, 1893; cf. J. Chaiken, *Idishe bleter in amerika* (New York, 1946), p. 78.

3. *New York Times,* December 18, 1870; R. J. H. Gottheil, *The Life of Gustav Gottheil* (Williamsport, Pa., 1936), p. 33f; H. B. Grinstein, "Reforms at Temple Emanuel of New York, 1860–1890," *Historia Judaica,* 6:163f (October 1944).

4. Henry A. Pochmann and A. R. Schultz, eds., *Bibliography of German Culture in America to 1940* (Madison, Wisconsin, 1953), p. 71f; Lemke, *Geschichte des Deutschtums,* p. 104; *Jewish Times,* April 14, 1871; K. Kohler in *Menorah,* November 1888, quoted by Max J. Kohler, "The German-Jewish Migration to America," *Publ. Amer. Jew. Hist. Soc.,* 9:104 (1901); cf. *American Hebrew,* November 24, 1905.

5. Felix Adler, *The Anti-Jewish Agitation in Germany* (New York, 1881), *passim; American Hebrew,* December 6, 1889; *Hebrew Standard,* June 15, 1894; Emma Lazarus, "The New Colossus," *Poems* (Boston, 1889), I, 202–203.

6. *New York Times,* August 19, 1877; J. A. Mandel, "The Attitude of the American Jewish Community to East European Immigration," *American Jewish Archives,* 3:31–32 (June 1950); *Eighteenth Annual Report, United Hebrew Charities, City of New York,* pp. 11–12; Lincoln Steffens, *Autobiography* (New York, 1931), p. 243; B. G. Richards, "The Attitude of Jews Towards Jewish Fiction," *The Reader,* 1:45f (November 1902); *Sixteenth Annual Report, United Hebrew Charities,* p. 26; *The Jewish Messenger,* May 30, October 3, 1890; H. L. Mencken, *The American Language, Supplement I* (New York, 1945), p. 614.

7. *New York Times,* August 5, 1883; *American Hebrew,* November 18,

1887; *Official Correspondence Relating to the Immigration of Russian Exiles* (Washington, 1889), p. 1f; P. Cowen, *Memories of an American Jew* (New York, 1932), pp. 94–95; C. S. Bernheimer, ed., *The Russian Jew in the United States* (Philadelphia, 1905), p. 64; *Fifth Biennial Session, The National Conference of Jewish Charities in the United States, 1908* (Baltimore, 1909), p. 54.

8. G. Pollak, *Michael Heilprin and His Sons* (New York, 1912), p. 205f; *Official Correspondence of Russian Exiles*, p. 10f; Mark Wischnitzer, *To Dwell in Safety* (Philadelphia, 1948), pp. 74–75; *The Hebrew-American Directory and Universal Guide* (New York, 1892), pp. 80–81; *Fifteenth Annual Report, United Hebrew Charities*, p. 32.

9. *Souvenir Book of the Fair, Educational Alliance* (1895), p. 142; *The Hebrew American Directory*, p. 84f; *First Bulletin of the Educational Alliance, 1898*, p. 3; Samuel Joseph, *History of the Baron de Hirsch Fund* (Philadelphia, 1935), pp. 254, 258; B. Liberson, "Slum Clearance and Low Rent Housing on the Lower East Side of New York City, 1901–1931" (M.A. thesis, Graduate School of Jewish Social Work, 1938), p. 77.

10. Jeremiah J. Berman, "Jewish Education in New York City, 1860–1900," *YIVO Annual of Jewish Social Science* (New York, 1954), IX, 262f; Cowen, *Memories*, p. 52; A. Cahan, *Bleter fun mayn lebn* (New York, 1926), II, 152f; Rebecca Kohut, *My Portion* (New York, 1925), pp. 249, 255; Gottheil, *Gustav Grottheil*, p. 179; Gertrude Friedlander, "Need of Jewish Day Nurseries on Lower East Side," *Jewish Charity*, 4:210 (April 1905); *American Jewish Yearbook, 1900–1901*, p. 357.

11. *Order of Exercises at the Dedication of the Hebrew Institute* November 8, 1891; *Souvenir Book, Educational Alliance* (1895), p. 23; *The Hebrew-American Directory*, p. 82; Boris Bogen, *Jewish Philanthropy* (New York, 1917), pp. 57, 234f; *First Bulletin of the Educational Alliance* (1898), p. 3; *Prospectus of Concerts, Entertainments and Special Celebrations* (1900–1901); *First Annual Report, Educational Alliance*, p. 20; Paul Abelson, "The Education of the Immigrant," *Journal of Social Science*, 24:167 (1906); M. J. McKenna, *Our Brethren of the Tenements and Ghetto* (New York, 1899), p. 87; Sam Franko, *Chords and Discords* (New York, 1938), p. 87; *Yearbook, University Settlement Society 1895*, p. 14; *Forward*, January 5, 1904; Lillian D. Wald, *The House on Henry Street* (New York, 1915), p. 198.

12. Miriam Blaustein, ed., *Memoirs of David Blaustein* (New York, 1913), pp. 47, 217f; William McAdoo, *Guarding A Great City* (New York, 1906), p. 162; I. B. Berkson, *Theories of Americanization* (New York, 1920), pp. 56–57; B. Z. Eisenstadt, *Hachmai yisroel b'amerika* (New York, 1903), p. 76; *First Annual Report, Russian-American Hebrew Association; The Hebrew-American Directory*, p. 94; *American Jewish Yearbook, 1907–1908*, p. 299; *American Jewish Yearbook, 1900–1901*, pp. 380–381; *Fourth Report, Russian-American Hebrew Association*, pp. 43–44; *Sixth Report, Russian-American Hebrew Association*, pp. 12, 21.

13. *Independent*, 45:1 (September 7, 1893); Kohler, "The German-

Jewish Migration," p. 105; *New York Times*, August 5, 1883; *The Hebrew American Directory*, pp. 89–90, 94; Cyrus Adler, *Jacob H. Schiff His Life and Letters* (New York, 1928), I, 395; *The Jewish Communal Register of New York City, 1917–1918* (New York, 1918), pp. 656, 1095f, 1136f, 1318.

14. Quoted from *Yiddishe Gazetten*, April, 1894, in Harold Silver, "Some Attitudes of the East European Jewish Immigrants Toward Organized Jewish Charity, 1890–1910" (M.A. thesis, Graduate School of Jewish Social Work, 1934), p. 219.

15. McKenna, *Our Brethren*, p. 60; Bernheimer, *The Russian Jew*, pp. 14–15; *Hatsofe Ba-Arets Hahadasha*, June 28, 1872; H. B. Grinstein, *The Rise of the Jewish Community of New York, 1654–1860* (New York, 1945), pp. 473–474; J. D. Eisenstein, "The History of the First Russian-American Jewish Congregation, The Beth Hamedrash Hagadol," *Publ. Amer. Jew. Hist. Soc.* 9:64f (1901); *The Hebrew American Directory*, pp. 116, 118, 120, 126f.

16. *Di idishe lansmanshaftn fun New York* (WPA: New York, 1938), pp. 69–70; A. S. Sachs, *Di geshikhte fun arbeter ring, 1892–1925* (New York, 1925), I. 74f; *Jewish Communal Register, 1917–1918*, pp. 732f, 888, 935, 958, 871, 961; *Yearbook, University Settlement Society, 1899*, p. 27f; *Idishe Zhurnal*, September 14, 1900.

17. *Jewish Communal Register, 1917–1918*, pp. 334–335, 689, 1014–1015, 1241; Eisenstein, "Beth Hamedrash"; *Report of the Passover Relief Committee, Beth Hamedrash Hagadol, 1896*, p. 2; *Report of the Passover Relief Committee, 1897*, p. 9; *Hebrew American Directory*, p. 138f.

18. *New York Times*, May 29, 1952; A. J. Rongy, "Half A Century of Jewish Medical Activities in New York City," *Medical Leaves*, 1:154f (1937); James J. Walsh, *History of Medicine in New York* (New York, 1919), III, 763; Whittemore, *Hebrews of the New World*, 137f; Peter Wiernik, *History of the Jews in America* (New York, 1912), p. 379.

19. David De Sola Pool, *An Old Faith in the New World* (New York, 1955), pp. 197, 443; *Hebrew American Directory*, p. 111; *Forward*, February 18, 1911; David De Sola Pool, "The Levantine Jews in the United States," *American Jewish Yearbook, 1913–1914*, p. 209f; *Jewish Communal Register, 1917–1918*, p. 1005.

20. Berman, "Jewish Education," *ibid.*, 271; Miriam Blaustein, ed., *Memoirs of David Blaustein* (New York, 1913), p. 141; Z. Scharfstein, *Toldos hahinuch b'yisroel b'doros ha-akhronim* (New York, 1947), II, 175f; I. Friedlaender, *Past and Present* (Cincinnati, 1919), p. 368.

21. A. Dushkin, *Jewish Education in New York City* (New York, 1918), pp. 81f, 104; *Jewish Communal Register* (New York, 1912), p. x; Wiernik, *History*, p. 376; Chaiken, *Yidishe bleter*, p. 356; S. Niger, *In kamf far a nayer dertsieung* (New York, 1940), p. 31f; Ira Kipnis, *The American Socialist Movement, 1897–1912* (New York, 1952), pp. 256, 260–261; Joseph Cohen, *Di idishe anarkhistishe bavegung in amerika* (New York, 1945), p. 299f.

22. James B. Reynolds to Dr. Jane E. Robbins, February 19, 1897 (Rey-

nolds Papers) ; W. R. Stewart, *The Philanthropic Work of Josephine Shaw Lowell* (New York, 1911), pp. 363–364; *American Hebrew*, March 24, 1905; Theodore Bingham, "Foreign Criminals in New York," *North American Review*, 188:384 (September 1908) ; *Charities and the Commons*, 21:270 (November 14, 1908): *Nineteenth Report, Educational Alliance*, p. 67f.

23. A. G. Warner and M. R. Coolidge, *American Charities* (New York, 1908), pp. 404–405; *Hebrew American Directory*, pp. 80–81; Silver, "Attitudes of East European Jewish Immigrants," pp. 77, 91; *Twenty-fifth Annual Report, United Hebrew Charities*, pp. 13, 15.

24. John M. Maguire, *The Lance of Justice, A Semi-Centennial History of the Legal Aid Society, 1876–1926* (Cambridge, 1928), pp. 3, 160–161; *Twenty-fifth Annual Report, Legal Aid Society*, p. 12; James Speyer to James B. Reynolds, December 17, 1894, April 13, 1895 (Reynolds Papers) ; *First Annual Report, Provident Loan Society of New York, 1894–1895*, p. 6; *Seventeenth Report, Provident Society*, pp. 1, 9.

25. Bernheimer, *The Russian Jew*, p. 1f; *Hebrew American Directory*, p. 123; *Volksblatt*, February 18, May 27, 1910; *New Yorker Yiddishe Volks-Zeitung*, September 3, 1886; I. Kopeloff, *Amol in Amerika* (Warsaw, 1928), pp. 165–166.

26. J. Drachsler, *Democracy and Assimilation* (New York, 1920), p. 121; *Forward*, March 11, 1902, June 29, 1909.

27. Silver, "Attitudes of East European Jewish Immigrants," pp. 259–261; *Twenty-Seventh Annual Report, United Hebrew Charities*, p. 18; Maurice B. Hexter, "The Business Cycle, Relief Work and Desertion," *The Jewish Social Service Quarterly*, 1:14, 18 (February 1924) ; *American Jewish Yearbook 1907–1908*, p. 330.

Chapter 7. Voices of Enlightenment

1. Peter Wiernik, *History of the Jews in America* (New York, 1912), p. 303; Leon Kobrin, *Fun deitchmerish tsu idish in amerika* (New York, 1944), p. 3f; *Yiddishe Gazetten*, January 20, 1892; Abraham Cahan, *Bleter fun mayn lebn* (New York, 1926), II, 240f; S. Niger, "Kapitlach amerikaner idishe literatur geshikhte," *Zukunft*, February 1940, pp. 98, 101; Joseph Schlossberg, "A halber yorhundert idishe arbeter bavegung," *Zukunft*, July 1942, p. 415; *Yiddishes Tageblatt*, March 20, 1910.

2. Z. Reisin, *Lexicon fun der idisher literatur presse un filologie* (Vilna, 1928–1929), I, 799; A. Harkavy, *Complete English-Jewish Dictionary* (New York, 1891), pp. iii–iv; A. Harkavy, *A Dictionary of the Yiddish Language* (New York, 1898), p. iii; P. Wiernik, "Vie lang vet unzer literatur bleehen?" *Nayer Gayst* (March 1898), pp. 356–357; *Menschenfreind*, December 27, 1899; M. Kostoff, "Etliche verter funem *Zukunft* zetster vegn der idisher ortografia," *Zukunft*, January 1912, p. 117.

3. Niger, "Kapitlakh," *Zukunft*, April 1940, pp. 214–215; Hutchins Hapgood, *The Spirit of the Ghetto*, (New York, 1902), p. 10; *Der Amer-*

ikaner Folks Calendar, 1894–1895, p. 38; *Yiddishes Tageblatt,* March 20, 1910; Harkavy, *Complete Dictionary,* pp. 245, 296, 466.

4. *Report, Special Committee of the National Jewish Immigration Council,* (Washington, 1914), p. 5f; M. Osherowitch, "Di geshikhte fun forverts 1897–1947," pp. 105–106 (typescript, New York Public Library).

5. *Yiddishes Tageblatt,* March 20, 1910; E. Schulman, *Geshikhte fun der idisher literatur in amerika, 1870–1900* (New York, 1943), pp. 34–35, 38; K. Marmor, *Der onhaib fun der idisher literatur in amerika, 1870–1890* (New York, 1944), pp. 6, 10; Niger, "Kapitlakh," *Zukunft,* April 1940, p. 213; J. D. Eisenstein, *Otser zikhronotsai* (New York, 1929), p. 57; S. N. D. North, *The Newspaper and the Periodical Press* (Washington, 1884), p. 301; George P. Rowell, *American Newspaper Annual* (Philadelphia, 1884), p. 403; N. W. Ayer, *American Newspaper Annual* (Phildelphia, 1885), p. 66; *Yiddishe Gazetten,* January 20, 1893, October 11, 1901; quoted and translated from *Yiddishe Gazetten* (1890) in Harold Silver, "Some Attitudes of the East European Jewish Immigrants toward Organized Jewish Charity in the Years 1890–1900" (M.A. thesis, Graduate School of Jewish Social Work, 1934), pp. 1–2.

6. Cahan, *Bleter,* II, 226; III, 9f, 426f; *Freie Arbeiter Shtimme,* October 6, 1899, November 2, 9, 1928; *New Yorker Yiddishe Volks-Zeitung,* September 13, 1886; *Volksadvocat,* November 2, 1888; *Arbeiter Zeitung,* August 1, 1890; *Zukunft,* September 1892; *Zeitgeist,* June 28, 1907; *Naye Lebn,* June 1908; *Arbeiter,* April 20, 1907.

7. Reisin, *Lexicon,* I, 226–227; H. Burgin, *Geshikhte fun der idisher arbeter bavegung in amerika* (New York, 1915), pp. 640–641; *Judisches Lexicon* (Berlin, 1930), IV, 1103f; *Capmakers' Journal,* September 1903; *Garment Worker,* May 1896; *Arbeiter Welt,* May 14, 1904; *Ladies Garment Worker,* December 1911; *Painter,* October 21, 1911; *Hoffnung,* July 1913; *Yiddishe Presse,* January 21, 1913.

8. Reisin, *Lexicon,* I, 532–534; J. Chaikin, *Idishe bleter in amerika* (New York, 1946), p. 135; *Stadt Anzeiger,* October 15, 1893; *Yiddisher Gayst,* January 1910; *Volksblatt,* February 18, 1910; *Theatre and Moving Pictures Review,* October 17, 1913; *Unzer Shrift,* January 1912.

9. Reisin, *Lexicon,* I, 42, 152; *Yudisher Puck,* March 22, 1896; Rose S. Batchelis, *Unzer fawter shomer* (New York, 1950), pp. 150–151; *Die Groise Beitch* (The Big Whip) (1888), *Der Litvakel* (1889), *Fledermoiz* (?), *Der Nayer Telephun* (1890), *Der Floidersack* (The Chatterer) (1893), *Der Land Chochem* (1893–1894), a series of Jewish festival journals, *Der Ashmedai* (The Devil) (1894), *Der Laitz* (1908), *Der Kuker* (1908), *Der Taivel* (1908) and *Der Idisher Gazlon* (1910); H. Rogoff, *Der gayst fun forverts* (New York, 1954), p. 258; *Der Groiser Kibitzer,* February 19, March 5, 1909; *Groiser Kundes,* March 19, 1909.

10. Morris Rosenfeld's *Di Zun* (1892), Jaffe's *Der Kritiker* (1892), *Der Wechter* (1893), Minikes' *Yom Tob Bleter* (1895–1897), Jacob Terr's *Natur un Lebn* (1897–1898) and Sharkansky's *Di Naye Welt* (1897), Rosenfeld and Sharkansky's *Pinkos* (1900), *Di Yiddishe Natsion* (1902–

1903), and *Di Fraye Shtunde* (1904); *Hoizfreind,* September 19, 1889; *Menschenfreind,* December 6, 1889; *Nayer Gayst,* December 1897; *Yiddishe Natsion,* August 1902; *Yiddishe Wochenshrift,* January 19, 1912; H. B. Grinstein, "The Memoirs and Scrapbooks of the late Joseph I. Bluestone of New York City," *Publ. Amer. Jew. Hist. Soc.* 35:54f (1939); cf. *Yiddishe Natsion,* August 1902; *Yiddisher Kempfer,* April 5, 1907; *Yiddishe Folk,* April 23, 1909.

11. *Yiddishes Tageblatt,* March 20, 1910; J. Schlossberg, "A halber yorhundert idishe arbeter bavegung," *Zukunft* (July 1942), p. 414. Schlossberg's recollections were verified by an examination of the *Tageblatt,* March 15, 16, 18, 20, 1892, January 3, 1894 and *Yiddisher Herold,* April 13, 1894; Alfred M. Lee, *The Daily Newspaper in America* (New York, 1937), p. 743; Burgin, *Geshikhte,* p. 891; Reisin, *Lexicon,* I, 135; II, 423; III, 861; Cahan, *Bleter,* IV, 512; *Arbeiter Zeitung,* August 1, 8, 1896; *Yiddisher Recorder,* April 17, 1893, February 23, 1895; *Abendzeitung,* March 18, 30, 1906.

12. Moses Rischin, "Abraham Cahan and the *New York Commercial Advertiser,* 1897–1901: A Study in Acculturation," *Publ. Amer. Jew. Hist. Soc.* 43:10f (September 1953); Reisin, *Lexicon,* III, 861; *Forward,* March 6, 1907, August 27, 1909; French Strother, "Abraham Cahan, A Leader of the Jews," *World's Work,* 26:472 (August 1913); James Creelman, "Israel Unbound," *Pearson's Magazine,* 17:236 (March 1907); *American Hebrew,* March 18, 1910. N. W. Ayer, *American Newspaper Annual* (Philadelphia, 1915), p. 639 gives the circulation of the four Yiddish dailies as:

Forward	174,699
Warheit	108,000
Morgen Journal	106,258
Yiddishes Tageblatt	66,665

13. "The Foreign Language Press in New York" (WPA: typescript on deposit at the Columbia School of Journalism Library, 1941), p. 564; *La America,* November 11, 1910, May 12, 26, June 2, 1911.

14. *Hatsofe Ba-Arets Hahadasha,* June 11, 1871, February 2, 16, July 5, August 23, September 20, November 22, 1872; Z. H. Bernstein, "Dvarim akhadim al dvar hayehudim lifnai shloshim v'arba shona b'new york," *Yalkut Maarabi* (1904), I, 128f; Niger, "Kapitlakh," *Zukunft,* May 1940, p. 270; Bernard Drachman, "Neo-Hebraic Literature in America," *Proceedings, Seventh Biennial Convention, Jewish Theological Seminary Association* (New York, 1900), p. 87; Hapgood, *The Spirit of the Ghetto,* p. 99f.

15. Jacob Riis, *The Children of the Poor* (New York, 1892), p. 45; Solomon Ornstein, *Shmay Toker Comes to America* (Yid.) (New York, 1951), p. 76; Herman Rosenthal, "Die neueste Literatur," *Vorträge und Discussionen, Deutschen Geselig-Wissenschaftlichen Verein von New York,* no. 17 (1889), *passim; Sonntagsblatt der New Yorker Staats-Zeitung,.* December 3, 10, 1905; *Federation,* 2:92 (December 1902); Rupert Hughes, *The Real New York* (New York, 1904), p. 238; W. T. Elsing, *The Poor*

in Great Cities (New York, 1895), pp. 101–102; "The Foreign Language Press" (WPA), pp. 22, 32, 35, 40, 49, 57–58; Jerome Davis, *The Russian Immigrant* (New York, 1922), p. 126; Burgin, *Geshikhte,* pp. 152, 671, 724f; Reisin, *Lexicon,* I, 188, 519; K. Marmor, *Jacob Gordin* (New York, 1953), pp. 51–52; Nicholas Rosenauer to Jacob Gordin, November 13, 1907); Ernest J. Bohm to Nicholas Rosenauer, October 26, 1908 (Hebrew Printers' Union Papers, YIVO); *Der Arbeiter,* October 17, 1908; *Warheit,* October 21, 1908.

16. M. Shtarkman, "Fun popular vissenshaft biz vissenshaft, 1882–1942," *Jewish Book Annual* (1942), I, 83f; Chaiken, *Idishe bleter,* p. 75f; E. Schulman, "Jewish Popular Romances in America," *YIVO Amoptayl* (New York: 1938), I, 238–239, 244f; A. Litwin, "Di zhargonishe literatur in bilder," *Zukunft,* June 1905, p. 311f; Reisin, *Lexicon,* IV, 758; *Yiddishes Tageblatt,* January 8, 1897, October 11, 1901.

17. M. Osherowitch, "Di geshikhte fun forverts, 1897–1947," pp. 109, 221, 245 (typescript, New York Public Library); Cahan, *Bleter,* V, 35; Ernest Poole, "Abraham Cahan Socialist—Journalist Friend of the Ghetto," *Outlook,* 99:478 (October 28, 1911); J. Gollomb, "Editor of *Forward,*" *American Magazine,* 74:674 (October 1912); *Abendblatt der Arbeiter Zeitung,* January 13, 1896; *Forward,* February 24, 1901, September 6, October 23, 1902; *Yiddishe Gazetten,* January 8, 1897, January 2, 1901; *Yiddishes Tageblatt,* April 27, 1909.

18. Drachman, "Neo-Hebraic Literature"; William James to E. R. A. Seligman, November 12, 1896 (Seligman Papers); *American Jewish Yearbook, 1907–1908,* p. 332.

19. *Yiddisher Zhurnal,* June 17, 1902; Niger, "Kapitlakh," *Zukunft,* January 1940, p. 9; Niger, "Kapitlakh," *Zukunft,* August 1940, p. 469; Chaiken, *Idishe bleter,* p. 342f; Osherowitch, "Geshikhte," p. 203; cf., for example, L. W. Zwisohn, *Tuberkulosa* (New York, 1902), William Edlin, *Velt berimte operetten* (New York, 1907); *Zukunft,* December 1906, p. 767f; A. Cahan, *Historia fun di feraynikte shtatn* (New York, 1912), II, 716; Joseph Cohen, *Di idish anarkhistishe bavegung in amerika* (New York, 1945), p. 283.

20. *Fifteenth Annual Report, University Settlement Society,* (1901), p. 26f; Hapgood, *The Spirit of the Ghetto,* pp. 117–118; *Freie Arbeiter Shtimme,* August 22, 1890; *Arbeiter Zeitung,* July 7, 1893; J. Shatzky, *Arkhiv far der geshikhte fun idishen teater un drama* (New York, 1930), I, 250–251.

21. G. C. D. Odell, *Annals of the New York Stage* (New York, 1927–1949), XII, 108, 513, 543; XIII, 313, 529–530; XV, 371, 399f; *New Yorker Yiddishe Volkszeitung,* March 4, 1887; *Hoizfreind,* October 4, 1889; L. Kobrin, *Erinerungen fun a idishen dramaturg* (New York, 1925), p. 27; A. Mukdoni, "Jewish Drama of the Immigrants," *YIVO Amoptayl* (New York, 1938), I, 258f; Reisin, *Lexicon,* I, 283; *New York Journal,* November 25, 1913; cf. advertisements appended to Joseph Lateiner, *David's Violin* (New York, 1900).

22. Cahan, *Bleter*, II, 327; *Hoizfreind*, September 19, 1889; *Der Stadt Anzeiger*, October 15, 1893; Judith Herz, "East Side Jewish Plays and Playwrights," *The New Era* 4:32 (December 1903) ; *American Hebrew*, January 18, 1909; Reisin, *Lexicon*, I, 523; *Arbeiter Zeitung*, February 13, 1891; *Forward*, January 1, 1904; Joseph Barondess to Louis Marshall, June 6, 1910 (Marshall Papers) ; Karl Lamprecht, *Americana Reiseeindrucke* (Freiburg, 1906), pp. 61–62; Marianne Weber, *Max Weber: Ein Lebenbild* (Tubingen, 1926), p. 316–317; Arnold Bennett, *Your United States* (New York, 1912), p. 184; Lillian D. Wald, *The House on Henry Street* (New York, 1915), p. 272.

23. Alvin Harlow, *Old Bowery Days* (New York, 1931), pp. 454, 463; I. L. Nascher, *The Wretches of Povertyville* (Chicago, 1909), pp. 14–16; Odell. *Annals*, XIII, 317–318; J. D. Eisenstein. *Otser zikhronotsai* (New York, 1929), p. 124; H. S. Goldstein, *Forty Years of Struggle for a Principle* (New York, 1928), pp. 56–57; *Forward*, February 6, 1904; B. Gorin, *Di Geshikhte fun idishen teater* (New York, 1918), II, 171f.

24. *Forward*, October 4, 1913; Odell, *Annals*, XV, 659; Kobrin, *Erinerungen*, p. 13–14; *Fifth Annual Report, Educational Alliance*, p. 37; Reisin, *Lexicon*, II, 781f; Gorin, *Geshikhte*, II, 222–223; *American Hebrew*, May 12, 1905, April 15, 1910; A. Cahan, "Der itstigen tsushtand fun idishen teater," *Zukunft*, March 1913, p. 278f.

25. *Forward*, March 17, April 12, 1902; Marmor, *Gordin*, p. 215; *New York Commercial*, February 5, 1905 and *New York Telegraph*, June 4, 1903 (Robinson Locke Collection).

26. *American Hebrew*, March 24, 31, 1905; L. Kobrin, "Di idn," *Zukunft*, May 1905, p. 1; *The Theatre*, 5:315 (Christmas 1905) ; Emma Goldman, *Living My Life* (New York, 1931), I, 366, 370f; *New York Globe*, January 10, 17, 1906; *New York Herald*, November 14, 1906 (Robinson Locke Collection) ; Anatole Chujoy, *The Dance Encyclopedia* (New York, 1949), p. 90; Chalif Russian Normal School of Dancing, *Announcement*, 1907; George Amberg, *Ballet in America* (New York, 1949), pp. 10, 19.

27. L. Wiener, *The History of Yiddish Literature in the 19th Century* (New York, 1899), pp. 119–120; Meyer Beer, "The Composer of Eili Eili," *Metronome* 35:70 (September 1919) ; Hapgood, *The Spirit of the Ghetto*, p. 118; cf. advertisements in Lateiner, *David's Violin;* Eisenstein, "Beth Hamedrash," p. 74; Wiernik, *History*, pp. 284–285.

28. Ethel Peyser, *The House Music Built* (New York, 1936), pp. 57–58, 66; Russian Symphony Society of New York, *Programs, 1904–1906; Forward*, January 1, 1904; *Russian Artists in America* (New York, 1932), I, 240–241.

29. Jack Burton, ed., *The Blue Book of Tin Pan Alley* (New York, 1950), p. 148; *Arbeiter Zeitung*, September 22, 1893; *Forward*, January 5, 1904; *Fifth Report, Educational Alliance*, p. 37; *Second Report, Educational Alliance*, p. 26; *Fourth Report, Educational Alliance*, p. 47; *American Jewish Yearbook, 1907–1908*, p. 331.

30. I. Weichsel, "Der maler fun der idisher gass," *Zukunft*, February

1913, p. 143f; *Fourth Report, Educational Alliance*, p. 18; *University Settlement Society's Report* (1895), pp. 12–13; Saul Raskin, "Der proletariat un der kunst," *Zeitgeist*, March 1, 1907, p. 6; Cahan, *Bleter*, V, 296.

31. *Fifteenth Report, University Settlement Society*, p. 21; *Abendblatt der Arbeiter Zeitung*, January 11, 1896; Letter of Educational League, 1900 (Abelson Collection); Burgin, *Geshikhte*, p. 326; M. E. Ravage, *An American in the Making* (New York, 1917), pp. 174–175; *Der arbeter ring zammelbukh* (New York, 1910), pp. 167, 172; *Forward*, January 1, 9, 1904, March 3, 1906.

32. D. M. Hermalin, "Jews of Rumania," *American Jewish Yearbook, 1901*, pp. 101–102; Ravage, *An American*, pp. 88f, 124f; *Die Freie Gesellschaft* (December 1899), pp. 98, 100; Ida Van Etten, "Russian Jews as Desirable Immigrants," *Forum*, 15:178–179 (April 1893); *Seventeenth Report, University Settlement Society*, p. 8; *Hebrew Standard*, November 16, 1900; Hapgood, *The Spirit of the Ghetto*, p. 255.

33. *Report, University Settlement Society, 1897*, pp. 38–39; *Abendblatt der Arbeiter Zeitung*, January 11, May 20, 1896; *Forward*, January 1, 1904, January 2, 1906; M. J. McKenna, *Our Brethren of the Tenements and the Ghetto* (New York, 1899), p. 57; A. Cahan, *Yekl* (New York, 1896), p. 32; Osherowitch, "Di geshikhte," pp. 54–55; I. Rivkind, *Der kamf kegn azarshpiler bay idn* (New York, 1946), pp. 82, 93; *Abendblatt der Arbeiter Zeitung*, January 11, 1896; *Forward*, February 14, 28, 1912; *Groiser Kundes*, December 10, 1909.

Chapter 8. The Great Awakening

1. G. M. Price, *Di yuden in amerika* (Odessa, 1891), p. 9; Israel Davidson, *Parody in Jewish Literature* (New York, 1907), pp. 99; Hutchins Hapgood, *The Spirit of the Ghetto* (New York, 1902), p. 239; E. Schulman, *Di geshikhte fun der idisher literatur in amerika, 1870–1900* (New York, 1943), p. 130f; *Laws of the State of New York* (Albany, 1893), p. 1883f; *Arbeiter Zeitung*, August 4, 1893; *Freie Arbeiter Shtimme*, December 25, 1891; *Forward*, April 13, 1911; Jacob Riis, *The Children of the Poor* (New York, 1892), p. 43.

2. M. Fishberg, *The Jews* (London, 1911), p. 530; M. J. McKenna, *Our Brethren of the Tenements and the Ghetto* (New York, 1899), p. 63.

3. I. Kopeloff, *Amol in amerika* (Warsaw, 1928), pp. 90–91; A. Cahan, *The Imported Bridegroom* (Boston, 1898), p. 12; M. E. Ravage, *An American in the Making* (New York, 1917), pp. 79, 118f, 169; R. S. Baker, *The Spiritual Unrest* (New York, 1909), pp. 117–118; S. Solomon, *Autobiography* (MS, YIVO Institute), p. 209f; Hapgood, *The Spirit of the Ghetto*, p. 10f; A. Cahan, *Yekl* (New York, 1896), p. 27.

4. *Annual Report University Settlement Society, 1898*, p. 25; S. Foster, *The Workingman and the Synagogue* (Newark, 1909), p. 57f; Joseph S. Bloch, *Ein Besuch beim Judentum in New York und Umgebung* (Wien, 1912), p. 34; *Report, Executive Committee, Fifth Annual Conference, Jewish Community (Kehillah) New York* (April 25 and 26, 1914), pp. 16–17;

Fishberg, *The Jews*, p. 539; *Forward*, February 4, 1906; *Volksblatt*, February 25, 1910; J. D. Eisenstein, *Otser zikhronotsai* (New York, 1929), pp. 77–78, 113; *Shabos Zhurnal*, April 1905.

5. *Arbeiter Zeitung*, September 30, 1892, September 11, October 4, 1896; *Forward*, October 5, 7, 1897; *Yiddishe Gazetten*, October 11, 1901; S. Solomon, *Autobiography* (MS, YIVO Institute), p. 23; Miriam Blaustein, ed., *Memoirs of David Blaustein* (New York, 1913), p. 140; Baker, *The Spiritual Unrest*, p. 112; cf. Hapgood, *The Spirit of the Ghetto*, p. 3.

6. M. Weinberger, *Yehudim veyahadus benew york* (New York, 1887), pp. 55–56; *New York Times*, August 19, 1877; E. A. Steiner, *On the Trail of the Immigrant* (New York, 1906), pp. 162–163; M. Raisin, *Dapim mepinkoso shel rabbi* (Brooklyn, 1941), pp. 175–176; Hapgood, *The Spirit of the Ghetto*, pp. 54, 62, 64; H. Hapgood, "The Earnestness That Wins Wealth," *The World's Work*, 6:3460–3461 (May 1903); E. Deinard, *Zikhronos bas ami* (St. Louis, 1920), p. 39; A. Cahan, *Bleter fun mayn lebn* (New York, 1926), II, 401; J. J. Berman, *Shehitah* (New York, 1941), p. 295f; *Jewish Messenger*, August 15, 1902; Abraham J. Karp, "New York Chooses A Chief Rabbi," *Publ. Amer. Jew. Hist. Soc.*, 44:162f (March 1955); *Jewish Communal Register of New York City, 1917–1918* (New York, 1918), p. 287.

7. *Zukunft*, January 1896; A. Cahan, *Rafael nertsich vert a sotsialist* (New York, 1896), p. 165.

8. M. Ivensky, *Aaron Lieberman* (New York, 1934), p. 23; David Hecht, *Russian Radicals Look to America, 1825–1894* (Cambridge, 1947), pp. 142f, 219f; A. Menes, "The Am Olam Movement," in E. Tcherikower, *Di geshikhte fun der idisher arbeter bavegung in di fareynikte shtatn* (New York, 1945), II, 293f.

9. Cahan, *Bleter*, II, 87, 102, 123, 142, 166, 178, III, 457; Helena Von Racowitz, *Autobiography* (New York, 1910), p. 341; Emma Goldman, *Living My Life* (New York, 1931), I, 119; Samuel Gompers, *Seventy Years of Life and Labor* (New York, 1925), I, 26, 50, 53; G. Weinstein, *The Ardent Eighties* (New York, 1928), pp. 47–48; Kopeloff, *Amol*, pp. 232–233, 261, 323; H. Burgin, *Geshikhte fun di idishe arbeter bavegung in amerika* (New York, 1915), p. 126; J. Schlossberg, "A halber yorhundert idisher arbeter bavegung," *Zukunft*, July 1942, pp. 413–414; *Forward*, August 14, 15, 1913.

10. I. Mirovitch and B. Goldgar, *Der Amerikaner, A Practical Book of Self-Instruction To Speak, Read, and Write the English Language*, 2nd ed. (New York, 1891), *passim*; *Arbeiter Zeitung*, January 2, 1891, October 7, 1892, September 22, 1893; *Freie Arbeiter Shtimme*, May 22, 1891; *Daily News*, March 24, 1892; M. Hillquit, *Loose Leaves from A Busy Life* (New York, 1934), p. 38f; Cahan, *Bleter*, II, 106, 154; Cahan, *The Imported Bridegroom*, p. 79.

11. *New Yorker Yiddishe Volks-Zeitung*, March 4, 1887; *Der Nayer Gayst* (May 1898), p. 433; *Volksadvocat*, November 2, 1888; *Zukunft*, January 1892 and January 1896.

12. B. Feigenbaum, *The Passover Haggadah According to a New Version* (Geneva, 1900), quoted in Davidson, *Parody in Jewish Literature,* pp. 82–83; cf. *Arbeiter Zeitung,* November 25, 1892; J. A. Riis, *Out of Mulberry Street* (New York, 1898), pp. 33–34.

13. *Zukunft,* 1892–1897, *passim; Hoizfreind,* 1:2–3 (September 19, 1889); A. Cahan, "Kritishe shtudien iber zhargonishe meisterverk," *Zukunft,* October 1895, p. 53f; also see *Zukunft,* May 1896, p. 229; October 1896, p. 485f; November 1896, 523f; cf. S. Niger, "Kapitlakh fun der idisher literatur in amerika," *Zukunft,* December 1940, p. 722.

14. B. Weinstein, *Fertsig yor in di idishe arbeter bavegung in amerika* (New York, 1924), 149f; *Arbeiter Zeitung,* April 11, July 4, 1890, January 9, 1891, October 21, 1892, June 1, 1894; Cahan, *Bleter, III,* 200–201.

15. Kopeloff, *Amol,* p. 234; P. Kranz, "God, Religion, and Morality," *Zukunft,* January 1892, p. 14; M. Hilkowitz, "The Flood," *Zukunft,* December 1892, p. 14; A. Ginsberg, "Der idisher gott, amol un haynt," *Die Freie Gesellschaft,* December 1899, p. 56; *Arbeiter Zeitung,* May 26, June 2, 1893, January 17, 1896; A. Cahan, "The Apostate of Chego-Chegg," *Century,* 59:96 (November 1899).

16. S. Yanovsky, *Ershte yorn fun idishen frayhaytlikhen sotsialism* (New York, 1948), p. 117f; Kopeloff, *Amol,* pp. 232–233; Burgin, *Geshikhte,* p. 126f, 140; Cahan, "The Apostate of Chego-Chegg," p. 94; A. Cahan, *Rafael nertsikh vert a sotsialist* (New York, 1896), pp. 157, 165; Eisenstein, *Otser,* p. 72; Schulman, *Di geshikhte,* p. 48, 69; ticket translated in *New York Sun,* September 24, 1890 and quoted in *Tcherikower, Di geshikhte,* II, 444.

17. *Freie Arbeiter Shtimme,* September 19, 1890; cf. *Arbeiter Zeitung,* May 26, June 2, 1893; M. Katz, *Geklibene shriftn* (New York, 1939), p. 38.

18. B. Feigenbaum, "Der gedank vegn an ayntsiken gott," *Nayer Gayst* (October 1897), p. 18; B. Feigenbaum, "Der sotsialismus fun toras moshe," *Zukunft,* September 1896, p. 10; B. Feigenbaum, *Kosher un trayf* (New York, 1909), pp. 1, 9, 10; Schulman, *Di geshikhte,* pp. 71–72; B. Feigenbaum, *Liebe un familien lebn loit idishkayt* (New York, 1904), p. 66f; Kopeloff, *Amol,* p. 327; L. Kobrin, *Mayn fuftsig yor in amerika* (Buenos Aires, 1955), p. 81; Cahan, *Bleter, II,* 300; Hapgood, *The Spirit of the Ghetto,* pp. 77f.

19. *Zukunft,* January 1892, 1–2; *Autobiography 45* (MS, YIVO Institute), p. 61.

20. Cahan, *Bleter, II,* 243–244; III, 205–206; B. Feigenbaum, *Di geula* (New York, 1893), pp. 42–43; *New Yorker Yiddishe Volks-Zeitung,* April 8, August 12, 1887.

21. *Arbeiter Zeitung,* August 29, 1890, March 3, 1893, May 4, 11, 1894.

22. M. Hilkowitz, "Politik," *Zukunft,* January 1895, p. 41; *The People,* July 26, 1896; Kobrin, *Mayn fuftsig yor,* pp. 317–318; Cahan, *Rafael nertsikh,* p. 157; *Forward,* July 22, 1897; Cahan, *Bleter, III,* 452f.

23. *Di tegliche volkszeitung ershaynt* (1899); *Arbeiter Zeitung,* Janu-

ary 31, 1896; *Forward,* December 31, 1899, February 17, 1901, April 11, 1902; J. Milch, *Di anstehung fun forverts* (New York, 1936), p. 117f; J. Barondess to L. Landes, November 9, 1901, J. Barondess to Friedman, October 20, 1902 (Barondess Papers); *The Inquisition in the Socialist Labor Party* (brochure); *Abendblatt der Arbeiter Zeitung,* August 10, 20, November 28, 1898; *Freie Arbeiter Shtimme,* March 16, 1900; Paul Abelson, "The Education of the Immigrant," *Journal of Social Science,* 44:165 (1906); M. Osherowitch, *Di geshikhte fun forverts, 1897–1947,* 35f.

24. *Forward,* November 27, 1897; J. Barondess to editor, *Social Democratic Herald* (Chicago), May 9, 1900, J. Barondess to Emma Goldman, December 28, 1903, J. Barondess to Solove, October 11, 1906 (Barondess Papers); Cameron H. King to William Edlin, January 3, 1901 (Edlin Papers).

25. Cahan, *Bleter,* IV, 512f; *Forward,* April 7, October 12, 1901, March 27, November 7, 1902, March 31, 1903, March 20, 1904, July 9, 16, 1906; *Jewish Gazette,* October 11, 1901.

26. *Forward,* August 1, 1902, March 25, 1904, September 5, 1905, April 24, 1907.

27. Hapgood, *The Spirit of the Ghetto,* p. 190; *Freie Arbeiter Shtimme,* October 6, 1899, September 20, 27, October 8, November 22, December 6, 1901, January 24, 1902; Joseph Cohen, *Di idish-anarkhistishe bavegung in amerika* (Philadelphia, 1945), p. 119; E. Goldman, *Living My Life,* I, 312, 316; cf. Sidney Fine, "Anarchism and the Assassination of McKinley," *American Historical Review,* 60:794–795 (July 1955); P. Kropotkin, *Tsum yungen dor* (New York, 1901), p. iii.

28. Max M. Laserson, *The American Impact on Russia, 1784–1917* (New York, 1950), pp. 196–199; Cahan, *Bleter,* II, 115–117, 135–137, 164–165, 178, 278; *Despotism vs. Liberty or, The Czar of Russia and the Blue-Blooded Aristocracy of America versus the People 1887; Russian-American National League 1893* (circular); *Free Russia* (February 1891), p. 8; W. A. Williams, *American-Russian Relations, 1781–1947* (New York, 1952), p. 380; Burgin, *Geshikhte,* pp. 36–37, 96–97, 123, 227, 320–321.

29. *Abendblatt der Arbeiter Zeitung,* January 11, 1896; *Forward,* December 14, 1903; *The Little Grandmother of the Russian Revolution, Reminiscences and Letters of Catherine Breshkovsky,* ed. Alice Stone Blackwell (Boston, 1917), p. 124; *Evening Call,* November 4, 1908. In 1887, all immigrants from Armenia, reported to be Jews expelled by an edict of 1885, were doubtless Russian-speaking, but it seems unlikely that any of these immigrants were members of the Armenian Revolutionary Federation, Dashnaktzostune-Dashnags, a Democratic-Socialist club organized in 1890 in New York by Russian Armenians. *Report, Select Committee, H.R., Importation of Contract Laborers* (Washington, 1889), pp. 291, 296; F. J. Brown and J. S. Roucek, *Our Racial and National Minorities* (New York, 1937), p. 304; M. Baranov, "Di drei revolutsionere parteien in rusland un new york." *Zukunft,* September 1905, p. 510f.

30. *Forward,* January 6, October 2, 4, 15, 1903, January 9, July 29, Sep-

tember 1, 1904, January 1, April 20, November 24, 29, December 5, 11, 1906; Anna Rappaport, "Resurrection," *Zukunft*, July 1905, p. 189; cf. *Yiddisher Zhurnal*, November 3, 1905; Burgin, *Geshikhte*, p. 668f.

31. Cahan, *Bleter*, IV, 398, 407; Burgin, *Geshikhte*, p. 668f; Cowen, *Memories*, pp. 155–156, 311; L. Wald, *The House on Henry Street* (New York, 1915), p. 230; T. A. Bailey, *America Faces Russia* (Ithaca, 1950), pp. 209–210; *Forward*, June 10, 1903, January 1, 6, 21, 1904, January 23, 1906, January 5, 1907; *New York Times*, quoted in Morris Werner, "L'Affaire Gorky," *New Yorker*, September 28, 1946, p. 64; *Arbeiter*, December 31, 1906.

32. S. Yanovsky, "Di ershte tsvantsig yor *Freie Arbeiter Shtimme*," *Freie Arbeiter Shtimme*, January 11, 1929; Osherowitch, "Di geshikhte," pp. 54, 60, 62; *Forward*, January 2, February 26, 1906, October 2, 1908; M. Winchevsky, "Di *Zukunft* . . . ihr oifgabe," *Zukunft*, January 1912, p. 10; P. Kranz, "Idishe mythologie," *Zukunft*, April 1905, p. 240; B. Feigenbaum, *Kosher un treif* (New York, 1909), pp. vii, x.

33. *Forward*, August 14, 1909, April 13, 1911; Kopeloff, *Amol.* pp. 333–334; M. Zametkin, "Idishe abgesundertkayt," *Zeitgeist* (January 25, 1907), pp. 8–9; "Kritik, M. Zametkin's 'a rusisher shylock,' " *Zukunft*, August 1906, p. 108; B. Feigenbaum, "Alts heisst assimilation," *Zukunft*, July 1912, p. 444f.

34. J. Milch, "Marx un zayn kritiker," *Zukunft*, April 1905, p. 197f; Cahan, *Bleter*, IV, 508; *Zeitgeist*, November 17, 1906; *Naye Welt*, October 1909, p. 5.

35. P. Wiernik, "Vie lang vet unzer literatur bleehen?" *Nayer Gayst*, March 1898, p. 355; J. Milch, "New Movements Among the Jewish Proletariat," *International Socialist Review*, 7:354–355 (December 1906); O. Janowsky, *The Jews and Minority Rights, 1898–1919* (New York, 1933), p. 145; K. Fornberg, "Di lehre fun tsvantsig yor," *Zukunft*, January 1912, p. 41f; Cahan, *Bleter*, IV, 423; M. Zametkin, "A greenhorn remains a greenhorn," *Zeitgeist*, June 21, 1907, p. 25f; Chaiken, *Idishe bleter*, p. 154; *Dos Naye Lebn*, 1:3 (June 1908); L. Kobrin, *Fun deitshmerish tsu idish in amerika* (New York, 1944), pp. 11, 14, 15, 26; Z. Reisin, *Lexicon fun der literatur presse un filologie* (Vilna, 1928–1929), I, 1118f, 1246; *Zukunft*, April 1906, p. 214; C. Zhitlowsky, *Der sotsialism un di natsionale frage* (New York, 1908), *passim;* Charles Spivack, "Loshen kodesh iz der vinkelshtayn fun idish," *Zukunft*, January 1912, p. 33f.

36. *Forward*, September 26, October 3, 1910, March 11, 1911, April 29, 1912; *Daily Call*, May 30, 1908; *Arbeiter Zeitung*, March 27, 1891.

37. *Arbeiter Zeitung*, July 18, 1890, March 6, 13, 1891, April 21, May 5, 1893, September 7, 1894; *Volksadvocat*, November 9, 1888; *Forward*, November 12, 1897, January 2, 1901, May 24, 1902, June 17, 23, November 4, 1904, May 4, 5, 1907, July 19, August 18, 1908; *Warheit*, August 18, 1908; Cahan, *Bleter*, II, 280; K. Fornberg, "Fuftsen yor proletarisher yom tov," *Zukunft*, May 1905, p. 255f; *Headquarters Allied Conference for Cheap Kosher Meat*, May 24, 1902 (brochure); *Tageblatt*, June 17, 1912;

J. Schlossberg, "A halber yorhunder idisher arbeter bavegung," *Zukunft,* July 1943, p. 415.

38. *Forward,* July 4, 1911.

Chapter 9. Labor's Dilemma

1. *Tenth Annual Report, Bureau of Statistics of Labor, State of New York, 1892,* pp. 11ff; *United States Industrial Commission, Reports* (Washington, 1900–1902), VII, 823.

2. Herbert Harris, *American Labor* (New Haven, 1939), p. 75; L. F. Post and F. C. Leubuscher, *An Account of the George-Hewitt Campaign* (New York, 1886), p. 3; *New York Tribune,* October 26, 1890; G. Weinstein, *The Ardent Eighties* (New York, 1928), pp. 170–171; *Report, Committee of the Senate upon the Relations between Capital and Labor,* 1885, I, 559; P. A. Speek, *The Single Tax and the Labor Movement* (Madison, Wis., 1917), p. 6of.

3. *Minutes of Central Labor Union,* February 1, 1885 (Edward King Papers); Speek, *The Single Tax,* pp. 9, 16, 37–38, 136; Weinstein, *The Ardent Eighties,* pp. 93–94, 147–148; Edward F. Roberts, *Ireland in America* (New York, 1931), p. 176; F. A. Sorge, "Die Arbeiter-bewegung in den Vereinigten Statten, 1886–1892," *Die Neue Zeit,* 1894–1895, pp. 132, 337; *Report, Committee of the Senate, Relations between Capital and Labor,* II, pp. 82–83; Robert A. Christie, *Empire in Wood, A History of the Carpenter's Union* (Ithaca, 1956), pp. 31–32, 68.

4. *New York Times,* March 31, 1888; *Constitution und Neben-Gesetze der Central Labor Union von New York* (New York, 1890), *passim;* A. N. Young, *The Single Tax Movement in the United States* (Princeton, 1916), p. 115; N. J. Ware, *The Labor Movement in the United States, 1860–1895* (New York, 1929), pp. 277–278, 297–298; *The Bakers' Journal,* December 9, 1893; B. Weinstein, *Fertsig yor in di idishe arbeter bavegung in amerika* (New York, 1924), p. 173.

5. *Documents of the Senate of the State of New York,* 1887, I, 23f; *Tenth Annual Report, Bureau of Statistics of Labor, State of New York,* pp. 36–37.

6. F. R. Fairchild, *Factory Legislation of the State of New York* (New York, 1906), p. 106; *Minutes of the Central Labor Union,* January 10, 11, March 28, 1885 (Edward King Papers); H. Laidler, *Boycotts and the Labor Struggle* (New York, 1913), p. 82f; H. Hurwitz, *Theodore Roosevelt and Labor in New York State, 1880–1900* (New York, 1943), p. 60; Sorge, "Die Arbeiter-bewegung," pp. 132, 332–333; *Tenth Annual Report, Bureau of Statistics of Labor, State of New York,* pp. 37–38.

7. J. M. Budish, *A History of the Cloth Hat and Cap and Millinery Workers International Union* (New York, 1925), p. 27; United States Industrial Commission, *Report,* XV, 328; S. Gompers, *Seventy Years of Life and Labor* (New York, 1925), I, 78, 115, 187, 189; Meyer Jacobstein, *The Tobacco Industry in the United States* (New York, 1907), p. 161; Morris

Berg, "Contributions of Adolph Strasser to Organized Labor in America" (M. A. thesis, Brooklyn College, 1953), pp. 40, 47, 52, 57, 142; *President Perkins Report, Twenty-second Convention, International Cigarmakers Union, 1912, passim.*

8. M. Hillquit, *Loose Leaves from a Busy Life* (New York, 1934), p. 16; J. Pope, *The Clothing Industry of New York* (Columbia, Mo., 1905), p. 47; *Report, Select Committee of the House on Contract Laborers* (Washington, 1889), pp. 222, 365, 385, 393; Samuel Joseph, *History of the Baron de Hirsch Fund* (Philadelphia, 1935), p. 27; Samuel Gompers to Miss J. E. Bloom, May 22, 1893 (Gompers Papers); S. Gompers, *Seventy Years of Life and Labor*, II, 153; J. M. Price to E. R. A. Seligman, March 4, 1887 (Seligman Papers); *Volksadvocat*, November 2, 16, 1888; trans. from I. Kopeloff, *Amol in amerika* (Warsaw, 1928), p. 135; trans. from *Freie Arbeiter Shtimme*, July 4, 1890.

9. *Third Annual Report, Bureau of Statistics of Labor, State of New York, 1885*, p. 289; *Minutes of the Central Labor Union*, February 15, 1885 (Edward King Papers); *Report, Committee of the United States Senate upon Relations between Capital and Labor, 1885*, I, 144; *New Yorker Yiddishe Volks-Zeitung*, July 2, 30, October 17, November 5, 1886; *Official Journal of the Central Labor Union*, September 3, 1888.

10. B. Weinstein, *Fertsig yor in di idisher arbeter bavegung in amerika* (New York, 1924), pp. 75f, 127; H. Lang and M. Feinstone, *Geverkshaftn* (New York, 1938), pp. 16, 29f; Hillquit, *Loose Leaves*, pp. 19–20, 29; *Arbeiter Zeitung*, March 4, September 19, October 10, 1890; A. Cahan, *Bleter fun mayn lebn* (New York, 1926), III, 25–26; *Hebrew American Directory and Universal Guide* (New York, 1892), p. 157f; *New Yorker Volks-Zeitung*, February 21, 1903; *Official Book of the AFL* (1892); H. Burgin, *Geshikhte fun der idisher arbeter bavegung in amerika* (New York, 1915), p. 165, 198; *Forward*, July 28, 1899.

11. S. Yanovsky, *Ershte yorn fun idishen freiheitlikhen sotsialism* (New York, 1948), p. 117f; *New Yorker Yiddishe Volks-Zeitung*, October 17, 1886; A. Rosenberg, *Di clokemacher un zayre unions* (New York, 1920), pp. 10, 12, 19f.

12. *New York Yiddishe Volks-Zeitung*, July 30, 1886; *Forward*, May 7, 1913; Robert Waters, *Career and Conversations of John Swinton* (Chicago, 1902), p. 69; John Swinton, *A Momentous Question—The Respective Attitudes of Labor and Capital* (Philadelphia, 1895), p. 39f; W. M. Leiserson, "History of the Jewish Labor Movement in New York City" (B.A. thesis, University of Wisconsin, 1908), p. 27; Rosenberg, *Di clokemacher*, p. 23.

13. *New Yorker Volks-Zeitung*, February 21, 1903; Post and Leubuscher, *The George-Hewitt Campaign*, p. 6; *Who's Who in New York City and State* (1904), pp. 475, 628; *Official Journal of the Central Labor Union*, September 3, 1888, September 7, 1891; *Official Book of the AFL*, 1892; R. H. Harvey, *Samuel Gompers* (Stanford University, 1935), pp. 66, 75; Gompers, *Seventy Years of Life and Labor*, II, 153; Samuel Gompers to

Meyer Jonasson, December 30, 1891 (Gompers Papers); *Evening World,*
July 22, 24, 1896; *The Outlook* 49:354 (February 24, 1894); *New York
Journal,* August 2, 1896.

14. *Arbeiter Zeitung,* August 25, September 1, 1893, February 9, 1894;
New York Sun, August 18, 23, 1893, February 14, 1894; *Social Economist,*
5:171–172 (September 1893); *World,* August 22, 1893; W. R. Stewart, *The
Philanthropic Work of Josephine Shaw Lowell* (New York, 1911), p. 362;
A Call to All Organized Elements of the Labor Movement, December 22,
1893; *Outlook,* 49:354 (February 24, 1894).

15. United States Industrial Commission, *Report,* VII, 190; M. J.
McKenna, *Our Brethren of the Tenements and the Ghetto* (New York,
1899), p. 45; *Arbeiter Zeitung,* July 11, 25, 1890; Joseph Barondess to Albert Maroschek, May 1, 1900 (Barondess Papers); *Daily News,* February 27, 1892; *Morning Journal,* February 29, March 20, 1892; *Morgen
Journal,* March 17, 1892; *World,* February 23, 1892.

16. *Outlook,* 50:414–415 (September 15, 1894); *American Hebrew,* Sep-
tember 21, 1894; *New York Times,* November 30, 1894; *New York Tribune,*
August 4, 1896; *Yiddishe Gazetten,* February 22, 1892; *Yiddishes Tageblatt,*
October 25, 1894.

17. *Arbeiter Zeitung,* July 11, 1890, August 25, October 13, 1893; *New
York Yiddishe Abend Post,* January 2, 1901; *Forward,* May 22, 1901, August 8, 1910; cf. *Di idishe lansmanshaftn fun new york* (WPA: New York,
1938) p. 80; *Zeitgeist,* November 22, 1907.

18. *New York Tribune,* July 20, 1890, October 2, 1891; *Evening World,*
March 10, 1891; *American Hebrew,* March 13, 1891; *Arbeiter Zeitung,*
March 14, May 21, 1891; Samuel Gompers to Joseph Barondess, October 10,
1891 (Gompers Papers); *Ninth Annual Report, Bureau of Statistics, New
York,* pp. 905, 921; Howe and Hummel to Joseph Barondess, March 26,
1892 (Barondess Scrapbooks); Rosenberg, *Di clokemacher,* p. 55; *Journal
of the Knights of Labor,* May 28, 1891; *Morning Journal,* June 5, 1892.

19. *Thirteenth Annual Convention, New York Protective Association
Affiliated with District Assembly 49, 1895; Fourteenth Annual Convention,
New York Protective Association Affiliated with District Assembly 49, 1896;*
Speek, *The Single Tax,* pp. 40–42; T. V. Powderly to Edward E. Kunze,
May 31, 1888 (Powderly Papers); *Fifteenth Annual Official Handbook,
District Assembly 49, Knights of Labor and Affiliated Trades, 1897;* J. R.
Commons, *History of Labor in the United States* (New York, 1918–1935),
II, 422, 428–429.

20. Weinstein, *Fertsig,* p. 175f; *Arbeiter Zeitung,* January 31, 1896; J. B.
Reynolds to J. S. Lowell, March 17, 1896 (Reynolds Papers); *People,*
May 24, 1896; *Forward,* March 16, 1900; *An alle genossen un publikum in
algemayn* (1897); *Clothing Gazette* (August, 1901), p. 3; *Zeitgeist,* Sep-
tember 1, 1905; A. Cahan, "The Russian Jew in America," *Atlantic
Monthly,* 82:139 (July 1898).

21. *Di idishe lansmanshaftn* (WPA), p. 80; Lang and Feinstone, *Geverkshaftn,* p. 17; A. Cahan, *The Rise of David Levinsky* (New York, 1917),

p. 380; *Forward*, May 16, 1907, August 31, 1909, December 4, 1912, May 15, 1952; B. Weinstein, *Di idishe unions in amerika* (New York, 1929), pp. 273, 276; *Autobiography 4* (MS, YIVO Institute), pp. 15–16.

22. *Fifteenth Convention, American Federation of Labor, 1895, Report of Proceedings*, p. 9; *Gunton's Magazine*, 13:292 (October 1897); United States Industrial Commission, *Report*, XVII, 100; *Bakers' Journal*, I:4 (July 14, 1888); G. A. Tracy, *History of the Typographical Union* (Indianapolis, 1913), p. 108of; *Fourth Annual Report, Bureau of Statistics of Labor, State of New York*, p. 496; H. Schluter, *The Brewing Industry and the Brewery Workers' Movement in America* (Cincinnati, 1910), p. 188f; *New Yorker Volks-Zeitung*, February 21, 1903; C. Wright, *Regulation and Restriction of Output* (Washington, 1904), p. 324.

23. *Industrial Conference National Civic Federation* (December 1902), p. 197; Samuel B. Donnelly to E. R. A. Seligman, August 10, 1905 (Seligman Papers); Marc Eidlitz to Beatrice Wellington, March 10, 1910 (Eidlitz Papers); United States Industrial Commission, *Report*, XV, 426; R. C. Chapin, *The Standard of Living Among Workingmen's Families in New York City* (New York, 1909), p. 247; Theodore Roosevelt to Herbert Parsons, December 28, 1907 (Parsons Papers); William S. Bennett, *Reminiscences* (Oral History Project, Columbia), pp. 29–30; C. O. Gregory, *Labor and the Law* (New York, 1946), pp. 76, 77, 80; C. G. Groat, *Trade Unions and the Law in New York* (New York, 1905), pp. 132–134; United States Industrial Commission, *Report*, VII, 95.

24. *Forward*, October 22, 1898, November 21, 1900, February 23, 1901, May 9, 1902, September 13, 1904; cf. Joseph Barondess, "Trade vs. Industrial Unionism," *Zukunft*, April 1906, p. 24f; cf. J. W. Sullivan, *Socialism as an Incubus on the American Labor Movement* (New York, 1909), p. 84.

25. Rosenberg, *Di clokemacher*, p. 138f; *The Cloakmakers' Strike* (New York, 1910), pp. 28, 38, 53, 61; Franklin Matthews, "Vacations for the Workers," *World's Work*, 6:357f (June 1903); *Zeitgeist*, September 1, 1905; *Capmakers' Journal*, February 1909, p. 12; *Garment Worker* (December 1911), pp. 27–28; *Forward*, July 28, 1909.

26. *New Yorker Yiddishe Volks-Zeitung*, August 20, 1886; *Eighth Annual Report, Bureau of Statistics of Labor, State of New York*, p. 231; *Arbeiter Zeitung*, April 18, 1890; S. Sheinfeld, *Zikhroines fun ah shriftzetser* (New York, 1946), p. 99; S. Sheinfeld, *Geshikhte fun der idisher shriftzetser union* (New York, 1938), pp. 21, 45, 48–50, 56, 60, 89f; Wright, *Regulation*, p. 79f; *Scale of Prices, Hebrew American Typographical Union, June 6, 1898, April 19, 1907* (YIVO Institute); *The Typographical Journal*, (?), 1909 (YIVO Institute); *Forward*, December 19, 1913.

27. Budish, *History*, p. 11f; *Arbeiter Zeitung*, May 8, 1891; *Ninth Annual Report, Bureau of Statistics of Labor, State of New York*, p. 885f; *The Cap Makers' Journal*, July, 1904, p. 20.

28. *Cap Makers' Journal*, June 1903, p. 18, June 1905, p. 30f; Donald B. Robinson, *Spotlight On A Union* (New York, 1949), p. 115; *Forward*, May 5, 29, 1903, December 21, 23, 1904; *Di Arbeiter Welt*, May 14, 1904.

29. *Arbeiter Zeitung*, October 10, 1890; *Proceedings, First Convention of the American Federation of Musicians in the United States* (Indianapolis, October 19–22, 1896), pp. 43–44; A. F. Harlow, *Old Bowery Days* (New York, 1931), pp. 449–450; *Forward*, November 10, 1897, February 13, 1901, May 4, August 4, 1906, March 22, April 27, 1907, March 13, 1908, May 24, November 28, 1910, June 30, 1911, July 21, 1913.

30. *Thirteenth Annual Report, Bureau of Labor, State of New York*, II, 388–389; *Sixteenth Annual Report, Bureau of Labor, State of New York*, pp. 1046, 1050–1051; Wright, *Regulation*, pp. 324–325; *Zeitgeist*, March 8, 1907; *Forward*, April 20, 1906, March 11, 1909, June 12, 1914; *The Painter*, October 21, 1911.

31. *Forward*, May 8, 1898, June 29, July 28, 1904, April 3, 1908, August 7, September 18, 1913; J. Barondess to John Moffett, May 1, 1900 (Barondess Papers); *Cap Makers' Journal*, October 1904, p. 31; J. Barondess to Local Union No. 308, United Brotherhood of Carpenters and Joiners of America, April 6, 1903 (Barondess Papers); *Weekly Bulletin of the Clothing Trades*, July 15, 1904; *The Garment Worker*, September 1896; Pope, *The Clothing Industry*, p. 211.

32. *The Clothiers' and Haberdashers' Weekly*, January 22, 1897; Marcus M. Marks to Oscar S. Straus, January 9, 1908 (Straus Papers); *Weekly Bulletin of the Clothing Trades*, 3:1 (April 15, 1904); *National Labor Bureau Clothing Manufacturers, Proceedings of the Annual Meeting, 1906*, pp. 10, 16; *Daily Trade Record*, July 1, 1904 quoted in R. S. Baker, "The Rise of the Tailors," *McClure's* 24:137 (December 1904); Joseph Barondess to Joseph S. Marcus, May 17, 1900 (Barondess Papers); L. Levine, *The Women's Garment Workers* (New York, 1924), p. 141; Rosenberg, *Di clokemacher*, p. 110f; J. Oneal, *A History of the Amalgamated Ladies Garment Cutters' Union Local 10* (New York, 1927), pp. 25, 31, 85–86.

33. *Forward*, August 22, 1902, January 1, 13, 24, 1904, January 6, June 4, 1911; Burgin, *Geshikhte*, pp. 655f, 613f; Rosenberg, *Di clokemacher*, p. 116; *Der Cooperativer Magazin* (August, September 1908), *passim*.

34. *Forward*, November 22, 1905, March 23, June 30, July 20, 1907; *Der Arbeiter*, March 3, 17, June 23, September 1, 1906, June 15, 1907; *Rule or Ruin Policy of the Industrial Workers* (pamphlet); P. Brissenden, *The IWW, A Study of American Syndicalism* (New York, 1919), pp. 118–119, 134–135, 362, 364; *Zukunft*, January 1914, p. 15.

35. Charles L. Brace, *The Dangerous Classes of New York* (New York, 1872), pp. 25, 29; William O. Stoddard, *The Volcano Under The City* (New York, 1886), pp. 4, 316f; Oscar Handlin, "American Views of the Jew at the Opening of the 20th Century," *Publ. Amer. Jew. Hist. Soc.*, 40:340 (June 1951); *Sun*, August 23, 1893; Ida Van Etten, "Russian Jews as Desirable Immigrants," *Forum*, 15:172f (April 1893); interview with Dr. Paul Abelson, October 20, 1951; *Guardian of Liberty* (February 1913), p. 11.

36. Lincoln Steffens, *Autobiography* (New York, 1931), p. 211; *New York Tribune*, January 3, 13, 1901; Harold Seidman, *Labor Czars, A His-*

tory of Labor Racketeering (New York, 1938), pp. 45–46; Hurwitz, *Theodore Roosevelt*, p. 154f; Pope, *The Clothing Industry*, p. 205.

37. *Arbeiter Zeitung*, February 17, 1893; *Abendblatt der arbeiter zeitung*, January 11, 1896; *Forward*, July 13, October 5, 1906, March 29, September 4, 1908, January 9, 11, 1909; *Letters to the Commissioners of Police of New York City, the Mayor, and Governor Hughes from Robert Hunter, May 15, 1908; Evening Mail*, April 2, 1908.

38. *Jewish Tribune*, July 4, 1924, p. 6; Speek, *The Single Tax*, p. 136; *New York Journal*, July 27, 1898; J. Barondess to John Swinton, July 15, 1901 (Barondess Papers); Benjamin Barondess to author, February 16, 1952; J. Barondess to City Editor, *New York World*, August 11, 1900; W. T. Jerome to J. Barondess, February 28, 1912; Morris Waldman to A. S. Elkus, June 25, 1913 (Barondess Papers).

39. G. E. Bevans, *How Working Men Spend Their Spare Time* (New York, 1913), pp. 37, 39; *Autobiography 117* (YIVO Institute), p. 36; *Forward*, February 4, 1904, June 24, 1907; *Cap Makers' Journal*, October 1903, p. 16.

Chapter 10. Reform in Full Stride

1. R. W. Gilder to Seth Low, May 12, 1897, Stewart L. Woodford to Seth Low, May 11, 1903 (Low Papers); Helen Campbell, *et al.*, *Darkness and Daylight; or Lights and Shadows of New York* (Hartford, 1892), pp. 39–40; Matthew H. Smith, *Sunshine and Shadow in New York* (Hartford 1868), p. 712; *John Swinton's Paper*, February 10, 1884; *Addresses in Memory of Ernest Howard Crosby, 1856–1907* (New York, 1907), pp. 9–10, 20; quoted by J. H. Girdner, *New Yorkitis* (New York, 1901), p. 162f.

2. Campbell, *Darkness*, p. ix; Grace Mayer, *Once Upon a City* (New York, 1958), *passim*; The Federation of Churches and Christian Workers in New York City, *First Sociological Canvass* (New York, 1896), p. 3; *Yearbook, University Settlement Society 1899–1900*, p. 12.

3. *Nation*, February 5, 1891; Frank Presbrey, *The History and Development of Advertising* (New York, 1920), p. 352; J. B. Reynolds to Dr. Jane E. Robbins, February 19, 1897 (Reynolds Papers); O. Carlson, *Brisbane, A. Candid Biography* (New York, 1937), pp. 98–99, 106–107, 114f; O. Carlson and E. S. Bates, *Hearst, Lord of San Simeon* (New York, 1936), p. 137.

4. Charles A. Barker, *Henry George* (New York, 1955), pp. 465, 486f, 571f; *The Hammer and the Pen*, 1:6–7 (June 1897); *Who's Who in New York City and State, 1909*, pp. 421–422; Thomas N. Brown, "The Origins and Character of Irish-American Nationalism," *Review of Politics*, 28:351 (July 1956); Aaron Abell, "Origins of Catholic Social Reform in the United States, Ideological Aspects," *Review of Politics*, 11:307f (July 1949); Aaron Abell, "The Reception of Leo XIII's Encyclical in America, 1891–1919," *Review of Politics*, 7:478f (October 1945); William L. Riordon, *Plunkett of Tammany Hall* (New York, 1948), p. xxxi; Daniel T. McColgan, *A Century of Charity* (Milwaukee, 1951), p. 370.

5. *American Hebrew*, December 5, 12, 1879; *Twenty-eighth Annual Report, New York Association for the Improvement of the Condition of the Poor*, p. 943; *First Annual Report, Central Council of the Charity Organization Society of the City of New York, 1883*, p. 3; *Twenty-fifth National Conference, Charities and Corrections, Local Committee of One Hundred* (1898), *passim*.

6. *Report, Tenement House Committee of 1894*, p. 430; *Publ. Amer. Jew. Hist. Soc.*, 14:213–214, 384–385 (1906); H. Hapgood, *A Victorian in the Modern World* (New York, 1939), pp. 335–336.

7. M. Fishberg, "Health and Sanitation of the Immigrant Jewish Population in New York," *Menorah*, August–September 1902; *Addresses, in Memory of Ernest Howard Crosby*, p. 20; A. E. Thompson, *A Century of Jewish Missions* (New York, 1902), pp. 236f, 272; George Hodges, *Henry Codman Potter* (New York, 1915), pp. 280, 282; A. Abell, *The Urban Impact on American Industrial Society, 1865–1900* (Cambridge, 1943), pp. 140, 141; J. Riis, *How the Other Half Lives* (New York, 1890), p. 112.

8. J. Riis, *Out of Mulberry Street* (New York, 1898), pp. 33–34; M. J. McKenna, *Our Brethren of the Tenements and the Ghetto* (New York, 1899), p. 56; Harold M. Finley, "New York's Populous and Densest Blocks," *Federation*, 4:11 (November 1906); William McAdoo, *Guarding A Great City* (Chicago, 1906), p. 165; Myra Kelly, *Little Citizens* (New York, 1904), p. 3f; Myra Kelly, *Wards of Liberty* (New York, 1907), p. viii f; United States Industrial Commission, *Report*, VII, 191; United States Immigration Commission, *Report* (Washington, 1900–1902), XXIX, 721–722, 743–744, 780–781, 791–793; Jacob Riis, *The Children of the Poor* (New York, 1892), p. 47; S. W. Rudy, *The College of the City of New York: A History 1847–1947* (New York, 1949), pp. 173–174, 293–294; B. J. Hendrick, "The Jewish Invasion of America," *McClure's Magazine*, 50:140 (March 1913).

9. *New York Herald*, August 31, 1892; Louis Filler, *Crusaders of American Liberalism* (New York, 1939), p. 118; R. Glanz, "Jewish Social Conditions as Seen by the Muckrackers," *YIVO* (New York, 1954), IX, 308: Royal A. Gettman, *Turgenev in England and America* (Urbana, 1941), p. 9; Ernest Poole, *The Bridge* (New York, 1940), p. 113f; M. Laserson, *The American Impact on Russia, 1784–1917* (New York, 1950), 416–417; Morris Werner, "L'Affaire Gorky," *New Yorker*, September 28, 1946, p. 61f; Herbert Parsons to J. M. Price, April 12, 1910 (Parsons Papers).

10. Stow Persons, *Free Religion An American Faith* (New Haven, 1947), pp. 70–71; *Twenty Years of the Ethical Movement in New York and Other Cities* (Philadelphia, 1896), 35f; *The Ethical Record* (April 1888), I, 25; C. Wright, *The Housing of the Working People* (Washington, 1895), p. 251; *New York Evening Post*, November 16, 1923; W. H. Tolman, *Handbook of Sociological Information with Special Reference to New York City* (New York, 1894), p. 251; Horace J. Bridges, ed., *Aspects of Ethical Religion, Essays in Honor of Felix Adler* (New York, 1926), pp. 332–333; Barker, *Henry George*, p. 418; Felix Adler, *An Ethical*

Philosophy of Life (New York, 1918), p. 44; *Jewish Messenger*, December 2, 1887; *Garment Worker*, December 1898, p. 3; *Weekly Bulletin of the Clothing Trades*, January 20, 1904, p. 5; S. Gompers, *Seventy Years of Life and Labor* (New York, 1925), I, 433.

11. *The Christian Union*, 32:3–4 (July 16, 1885), 31:6 (March 26, 1885), 32:9 (December 3, 1885); Lyman Abbott, *Reminiscences* (New York, 1915), pp. 392, 396.

12. Charles H. Hopkins, *The Rise of the Social Gospel in American Protestantism, 1865–1900* (New Haven, 1940), pp. 32–34, 72–73, 91.

13. *The Hammer and the Pen*, 1:4–5 (November 1895), I (n.s.):5–6 (March 1898); Spencer Miller and J. F. Fletcher, *The Church and Industry* (New York, 1930), p. 52f; *Gunton's Magazine*, 10:399–400 (June 1896); United States Industrial Commission, *Reports*, XIV, 1–3, 10; H. A. Keyser, *Bishop Potter* (New York, 1910), pp. 54–55, 61f; *Report, University Settlement Society, 1897*, p. 68.

14. Abell, *Urban Impact*, p. 147f; Rebecca Kohut, *My Portion* (New York, 1925), pp. 249, 255; *American Citizen* (November 1912), pp. 237–238; *Souvenir Program, Twenty-Fifth Anniversary Neighborhood Guild* (January 20, 1912), p. 3; Hopkins, *The Rise of the Social Gospel*, pp. 154–155.

15. C. S. Bernheimer, ed., *The Russian Jew in the United States* (Philadelphia, 1905), p. 193; *Eighteenth Annual Report, Bureau of Statistics of Labor, State of New York*, pp. 247, 271; C. R. Henderson, *Social Settlements* (New York, 1899), p. 43f; *Report, University Settlement 1898*, p. 30; *Report, University Settlement, 1895*, p. 32.

16. *Report, Henry Street Settlement, 1893–1913* (New York, 1913?), pp. 13, 14, 17, 25; C. E. A. Winslow, *The Life of Hermann M. Biggs* (Philadelphia, 1929), p. 186; *The Settlement Journal*, 1:1–2 (April 1904).

17. *Report, Henry Street Settlement*, p. 47; J. K. Paulding, *Charles B. Stover* (New York, 1938), p. 75f; *Report, University Settlement, 1899*, p. 32f; Charles Zueblin, *American Municipal Progress* (New York, 1916), pp. 268–269; A. Nevins, ed., *Selected Writings of Abram S. Hewitt* (New York, 1937), p. 372; J. B. Reynolds to William L. Strong, December 7, 1895 (Reynolds Papers). In 1895 Jacob H. Schiff erected a fountain at Rutgers Square. C. Adler, *Jacob H. Schiff His Life and Letters* (New York, 1928), I, 351.

18. *Charities Review*, 2:151, pp. 180–183 (January 1893); R. W. De Forest and L. Veiller, *The Tenement House Problem* (New York, 1903), II, 35, *Eighteenth Annual Report, Bureau of Statistics of Labor State of New York*, p. 339; United States Industrial Commission, *Report*, XIV, 80; *Fifteenth Annual Report, University Settlement*, pp. 46–51; J. B. Reynolds to Seth Low (Reynolds Papers); *Forward*, March 3, 1906; L. Wald, *The House on Henry Street* (New York, 1915), pp. 282–283.

19. *Report, University Settlement, 1896*, p. 12; *Alliance Review*, 1:11 (April 1901).

20. Daniel Van Pelt, *Leslie's History of Greater New York* (New York,

1898), I, 503–504; *Report, Tenement House Committee, 1894*, p. 512f; Sidney Ditzion, *Arsenals of A Democratic Culture* (Chicago, 1947), p. 146f; *Order of Exercises, Dedication of the Hebrew Institute*, November 8, 1891, p. 16; Cleveland Rodgers and Rebecca B. Rankin, *New York, The World's Capital City* (New York, 1948), p. 322; H. U. Faulkner, *The Quest for Social Justice, 1898–1914* (New York, 1931), pp. 279–280.

21. Gompers, *Seventy Years of Life and Labor*, I, 486; *Official Journal, Central Labor Union*, September 3, 1888; *Annual Report, Working Women's Society, 1892*, p. 3; *Report, Tenement House Committee of the Working Women's Society, 1892*, pp. 3–8; Abbie Graham, *Grace H. Dodge* (New York, 1926), p. 66f; Wald, *The House on Henry Street*, p. 207; G. Boone, *The Women's Trade Union League* (New York, 1942), p. 43; *Annual Report, Consumer's League, New York, 1894*, p. 2f; J. B. Reynolds to Edward King, January 28, 1896 (Reynolds Papers); *Edward King Memoir* (King Papers); Maud Nathan, *The Story of an Epoch-Making Movement* (New York, 1926), p. 21f.

22. E. L. Godkin, "Rich Men and Democracy," *Nation*, 71:362 (November 8, 1900; "True Americanism," *The Forum* (April, 1894) and "The College Graduate," *Atlantic Monthly* (August, 1890), reprinted in *The Works of Theodore Roosevelt* (New York, 1926), XIII, p. 20f.

23. W. H. Tolman, *Municipal Reform Movements in the United States* (New York, 1895), pp. 70, 71, 75, 85f; *Report, University Settlement, 1895*, p. 15; *The Social Economist*, 58:38 (July 1892); R. Gilder, ed., *Letters of R. W. Gilder* (New York, 1916), pp. 223, 263, 319; W. J. Schieffelin, *Reminiscences* (Oral History Project, Columbia), pp. 10, 18, 23; C. Rodgers, *Robert Moses* (New York, 1952), p. 15f.

24. James G. Wilson, ed., *The Memorial History of the City of New York* (New York, 1893), IV, 253; R. J. H. Gottheil, *The Life of Gustav Gottheil* (Williamsport, Pa., 1936), p. 89f; *How to Make New York A Beautiful City* (pamphlet pub. by Nineteenth Century Club, 1894–1895); *New York Times*, December 9, 1887; E. R. L. Gould to E. R. A. Seligman, June 9, 1897 (Seligman Papers); J. Dombrowski, *The Early Days of Christian Socialism in America* (New York, 1936), p. 101; Tolman, *Municipal Reform Movements*, pp. 128, 140.

25. Ruth L. Frankel, *Henry M. Leipziger, Educator and Idealist* (New York, 1933), pp. 83, 106–109; quoted from *Report, Committee of the Senate Upon the Relations between Capital and Labor, 1885*, III, 462–463; *The Free Lecture Course in New York City* (May 4, 1899), p. 3; Mrs. John M. Gitterman to Herbert Parsons, December 17, 1906 (Parsons Papers); Nevins, ed., *Selected Writings of Hewitt*, p. 402; *Sixth Annual Report, Educational Alliance, 1897–1898*.

26. John Collier, "The People's Institute," *Independent*, 72:1144 (May 30, 1912); Charles S. Smith, *Working with the People* (New York, 1904), p. 50; *The Civic Journal, Memorial Number, C. S. Smith*, 1:3 (April 30, 1910); *First Annual Report, Managing Director to the Corporation, People's Institute, 1898, passim*; J. Riis to C. S. Smith, May 25, 1897, R. Ful-

ton Cutting to C. S. Smith, May 24, 1897, C. S. Smith to E. R. A. Seligman, June 15, 1897 (People's Institute Papers) ; *The People's Institute 20th Anniversary Yearbook* (New York, 1918) , p. 7.

27. *Minutes, Meetings of the Board of Trustees, People's Institute* (July 7, 1897) , p. 1; quoted from *Third Annual Report, People's Institute,* 17f; *Second Annual Report, People's Institute,* 14f; quoted from J. A. Riis, "The People's Institute of New York," *Century,* 79:851 (April 1910); cf. Smith, *Working With the People.* pp. 19, 151–152, 159.

28. *Third Annual Report, People's Institute,* p. 5; *Fifth Annual Report, People's Institute,* pp. 2, 19, 20–21; C. Stelzle, *A Son of the Bowery* (New York, 1926) , pp. 118, 121, 123; Riis, "The People's Institute," p. 861.

29. *Ninth Annual Report, People's Institute,* p. 12; *The People's Institute Bulletin,* November 12, 1905; *The Civic Journal,* November 13, 20, December 4, 28, 1909; Samuel M. Jones to C. S. Smith, May 7, 1903; Henry George, Jr., to C. S. Smith, May 10, 1903 (People's Institute Papers) ; *Sixth Annual Report, People's Institute,* p. 14; *Memorial to Henry Codman by the People's Institute,* (New York, 1909) , pp. 14–17; *Civic Journal, Memorial Number, C. S. Smith,* April 30, 1910.

30. C. S. Smith, "Saloon Substitutes in New York and Elsewhere," *Federation,* 2:54 (March 1903) ; *Lecturer's Report, People's Institute,* January 27, March 26, 1900 (People's Institute Papers) .

31. Thomas Davidson, *The Education of the Wage-Earners* (New York, 1904) , pp. 96–97, 220; *Second Annual Report, People's Institute,* pp. 3–4; *Seventh Annual Report, Educational Alliance,* p. 17; Thomas Davidson to Charles P. Daly, April 15, 1889 (Daly Papers, New York Public Library) ; Thomas Davidson, "American Democracy as a Religion," *International Journal of Ethics,* 1:20 (October 1899) .

32. Thomas Davidson to My Dear Willie, June 21, 1900 (Abelson Collection) ; William Knight, ed., *Memorials of Thomas Davidson* (London, 1907) , p. 206; Morris R. Cohen, *A Dreamer's Journey* (Glencoe, Ill., 1949) , p. 103f; Louis I. Dublin, "Thomas Davidson, Educator for Democracy," *American Scholar,* 17:201f (Spring 1948) .

33. Paulding, *Charles B. Stover,* p. 115; M. Sullivan, *Our Times* (New York, 1930) , III, 388; A. M. Schlesinger, *The Rise of the City* (New York, 1935) , p. 302; Rupert Hughes, *The Real New York* (New York, 1904) , p. 238; quoted in "Frank Damrosch and the New Music School in New York," *Musician,* 10:420 (October 1905) ; L. P. Stebbins, *Frank Damrosch* (Chapel Hill, N.C., 1943) , p. 136f; Bernheimer, *The Russian Jew,* pp. 196–197; J. H. Cohen, *They Builded Better Than They Knew* (New York, 1946) , pp. 51–53, 59–60; Faulkner, *Quest for Social Justice,* p. 269; *Eighteenth Annual Report, Bureau of Statistics of Labor, State of New York,* p. 297; *Annual Report, Music School Settlement, 1906–1907,* pp. 6–7, 13; David Mannes, *Music is My Faith* (New York, 1938) , pp. 125f, 170f, 57.

34. *Report of First Season, People's Symphony Concerts,* p. 2f; *Fourth Annual Report, People's Institute,* p. 5; *The People's Institute 20th An-*

niversary Yearbook (New York, 1918), p. 51; *New York Times,* June 8, 1903, January 6, 1905; Riis, "The People's Institute," pp. 851–852; *The Settlement Journal,* 2:6 (May 1906).

35. Gilder, *Gilder,* pp. 221–222; Paul Abelson, *Purposes for Organizing East Side Civic Club* (December 7, 1901); L. Veiller to P. Abelson, December 22, 1903, C. S. Smith to P. Abelson, February 23, 1903 (Abelson Tenement House Scrapbook); cf. *Yiddishe Welt,* March 26, 1903; *Forward,* February 16, 1903; *Jewish Morning Journal,* February 10, 1903; *New York Times,* March 27, 1903; *World,* March 5, 1903 (Abelson Tenement House Scrapbook); East Side Civic Club to Board of Estimate, October 3, 1904 (Abelson Tenement House Scrapbook); G. Weinstein, *Pressing Problems of the East Side and the Opportunities of Our Civic Club* (January 2, 1904); *Notice of East Side Civic Club* (April 30, 1904); *East Side Club Souvenir Journal* (December 30, 1904); Weinstein, *The Ardent Eighties,* p. 120; B. Liberson, "Slum Clearance and Low Rent Housing on the Lower East Side of New York City, 1901–1931" (M.A. thesis, Graduate School of Jewish Social Work, 1938), p. 77.

36. I. Kipnis, *The American Socialist Movement, 1897–1912* (New York, 1953), p. 258; *Forward,* November 13, 1911; Harriet Stanton Blatch to William Edlin, January 15, February 23, 1906 (Edlin Papers); H. S. Blatch and Alma Lutz, *Challenging Years* (New York 1940), p. 92f; *Evening Post* [?], 1908 (Hillquit Papers); *From the Bottom Up—The Life of Alexander Irvine* (New York, 1910), pp. 144–145.

37. *Forward,* November 14, 1906; A. Cahan, *Bleter fun mayn lebn* (New York, 1928), IV, 551f.

Chapter 11. The Political Wilderness

1. William C. Gover, *Tammany Hall Democracy of the City of New York* (New York, 1875), p. 173; *The Hebrew Album of Prominent Israelites in America* (New York [?], 1904), p. 10; *Diary of John Bigelow,* October 16, 1893 (New York Public Library); D. S. Alexander, *Four Famous New Yorkers* (New York, 1923), pp. 225–226; *Tammany Times,* September 13, 1897, July 4, 1908; *Ha-Tsofe Ba-Aretz Ha-Hadasha,* September 20, November 8, 1872; M. Silber, *America in Hebrew Literature* (New Orleans, 1928), p. 83; interview with Dr. Abraham Wolbarst, September 21, 1951; S. Sheinfeld, *Zikhroines fun ah shriftzetser* (New York, 1946), pp. 53–54; *Yiddisher Recorder,* November 9, 1894; Samuel B. Thomas, *The Boss, or the Governor* (New York, 1914), p. 54.

2. Miriam Blaustein, ed., *Memoirs of David Blaustein* (New York, 1913), p. 166; William McAdoo, *Guarding A Great City* (New York, 1906), p. 155; *World,* August 11, 1902; *Evening Sun,* September 16, 1902; P. Cowen, *Memories of an American Jew* (New York, 1932), pp. 293–294; *Yearbook, University Settlement Society, 1900,* p. 12; *Report, University Settlement Society, 1901,* p. 58; Alden Chester, *Courts and Lawyers of New York* (New York, 1925), II, 908, 910.

3. *Report, University Settlement Society* (December 1898), p. 21–22; Edgar L. Merlin, *The Red Book, an Illustrated Legislative Manual of the State of New York* (Albany, 1894), p. 466; *New York Times,* November 4, 1880; Frank Moss, *The American Metropolis* (New York, 1897), III, 55f; Meyer Berger, *The Eight Million* (New York, 1942), p. 93.

4. A Cahan, *Bleter fun mayn lebn* (New York, 1926), II, 218; Samuel Joseph, *Jewish Immigration to the United States* (New York, 1914), p. 163. Cf. Table 4.

5. Charles A. Barker, *Henry George* (New York, 1955), p. 481; B. Weinstein, *Fertsig yor in di idishe arbeter bavegung* (New York, 1924), p. 195f; H. Burgin, *Di geshikhte fun der idisher arbeter bavegung* (New York, 1915), p. 124; *New Yorker Yiddishe Volks-zeitung,* October 29, 1886; G. Weinstein, *The Ardent Eighties* (New York, 1928), p. 108. Cf. Table 4.

6. *Hebrew-American Directory and Universal Guide* (New York, 1892), pp. 163–164; R. T. Ely, *The Labor Movement in America,* 3rd ed. (New York, 1890), pp. 276, 278; F. A. Sorge, "Die Arbeiter-bewegung in den Vereinigten Staaten, 1886–1892," *Die Neue Zeit* (1894–1895), pp. 133, 337; William F. Kamman, *Socialism in German American Literature* (Philadelphia, 1917), pp. 30, 32; *New York Times,* April 16, 1883; *New York Tribune,* July 20, 1890; Cahan, *Bleter,* II, 306f, 419–420; Burgin, *Geshikhte,* 157f; Anna P. Johnson to E. R. A. Seligman, April 5, 1886 (E. R. A. Seligman Papers).

7. Max Beer, *Fifty Years of International Socialism* (New York, 1935), p. 110; C. S. Gorsira to F. A. Henry, May 31, 1918, J. M. L. Maduro to W. J. Ghent, June 25, 1929 (in possession of Solon DeLeon); interview with Solon DeLeon, April 3, 1954; Arnold Petersen, *Daniel DeLeon; Social Architect* (New York, 1941), pp. 16, 18, 40, 257–258; Cahan, *Bleter,* III, 280–281.

8. *Arbeiter Zeitung,* June 20, 1890, November 4, 1892, October 13, 1893, March 16, September 28, October 12, November 7, 1894; *Zukunft,* August 1896, p. 5; M. Hilkowitz, "Politik," *Zukunft,* January 1895, p. 41.

9. Cf. Table 7; *New York Times,* November 8, 1896; *Der Seder,* extra edition of the *Yiddishe Puck,* March 22, 1896; cf. *Arbeiter Zeitung,* October 18, 1896; *The City Record Official Canvass of the County of New York,* vol. 27, pt. 2, p. 36 (March 13, 1899); Beer, *Fifty Years,* p. 115; Cahan, *Bleter,* III, 398–399; *Yiddishes Tageblatt,* November 4, 1896.

10. Burgin, *Geshikhte,* pp. 372f, 637–638; *Letter of Resignation, Miller to Arbeiter Zeitung Publishing Association,* March 21, 1895 (YIVO Institute); *An alle genossen un publikum in algemayn* (1897); *Forward,* July 6, December 9, 1897.

11. *Zukunft,* December 1896, p. 23f; *Forward,* July 5, 1897.

12. *Zukunft,* January 1897, pp. 13–18, February 1897, p. 41, March 1897, pp. 41–42, May 1897, pp. 22–29, June 1897, pp. 22–30, July 1897, pp. 15, 17.

13. R. Rocker, *Johann Most* (Berlin, 1924), p. 378; *Forward,* December 11, 1908; Burgin, *Geshikhte,* p. 422; *City Record, Official Canvas of the County of New York,* vol. 28, pt. 12, p. 98f (December 13, 1900), 33:16of (January 21, 1905).

14. *Works of Theodore Roosevelt* (New York, 1926), XIV, 226, 234; James B. Reynolds to Isaac H. Klein, October 8, 1896 (Reynolds Papers) ; A. L. Wolbarst to Theodore Roosevelt, October 3, 1898, Theodore Roosevelt to Lemuel Quigg, October 21, 1898 (Quigg Papers) ; Henry White to Seth Low, October 5, 1897, J. S. Lowell to Seth Low, October 17, 1897, L. Wald to Seth Low, October 27, 1897 (Low Papers) ; *The Social Evil with Special Reference to Conditions Existing in the City of New York* (New York, 1912), *passim;* Alfred Hodder, *A Fight for the City* (New York, 1908), pp. 21–22, 35f; Everett P. Wheeler, *Sixty Years of American Life* (New York, 1917), pp. 390–391; *New York Times,* November 6, 1901.

15. E. E. Morison, ed., *Letters of Theodore Roosevelt* (Cambridge, 1952), III, 254–255, 647; J. Magidoff, *The Mirrors of the East Side* (New York, 1923), p. 148f; *Yiddisher Zhurnal,* November 4, 1904; Marcus Braun to Herbert Parsons, February 23, 1909 (Parsons Papers) ; Oliver H. P. Garrett, "Nize Sam, Ett Opp All the GOP," *New Yorker* (March 6, 1926), pp. 15–16; *New York Times,* November 9, 1904, November 8, 1905, March 18, 1955; cf. Tables 4, 5, and 7.

16. F. Lundberg, *Imperial Hearst—A Social Biography* (New York, 1936), pp. 96, 101–102; Carl G. Winter, "The Influence of the Russian-American Treaty of 1832 on the Rights of American Jewish Citizens," *Publ. Amer. Jew. Hist. Soc.,* 41:182 (December 1951) ; Morris Werner, "L'Affaire Gorky," *New Yorker* (September 28, 1946), p. 62; J. Chaiken, *Idishe bleter in amerika* (New York, 1946), pp. 324–325; *New York American and Journal,* May 16, 17, 22, 1903; T. A. Bailey, *America Faces Russia* (Ithaca, 1950), pp. 182–183; Theodore Roosevelt to Oscar Straus, October 9, 1906 (Straus Papers) ; *Warheit,* November 2, 1906; *Forward,* September 11, November 7, 1906, November 9, 1908. Cf. Tables 5 and 6.

17. B. J. Hendrick, "The Great Jewish Invasion," *McClure's Magazine,* 28:321 (January 1907) ; *Yiddishes Tageblatt,* November 1, 1896; *The Hebrew Album,* p. 9; United States Immigration Commission, *Reports* (Washington, 1907–1910), XLI, 236; J. D. Eisenstein, *Oster zikhronotsai* (New York, 1929), p. 191; Magidoff, *Mirrors,* p. 117f.

18. *Forward,* June 16, 1901, April 29, 1903, December 24, 1909.

19. *Yiddisher Zhurnal,* November 9, 1900; *Yiddishes Tageblatt,* October 29, 30, 1908, October 31, 1912; J. Salwyn Schapiro, "Henry Moskowitz: A Social Reformer in Politics," *Outlook,* 102:447, 449 (October 26, 1912) ; *American Hebrew,* November 2, 1912; *Warheit,* October 27, 29, 31, November 4, 1912.

20. *Warheit,* September 7, 11, October 4, 31, November 2, 1912; *Forward,* October 24, 1906. The *Warheit* tabulated straws for president, governor, and congressman.

Party	President		Governor		Congressman	
Rep.	Taft	618	Hedges	345	Wolf	4
Dem.	Wilson	1782	Sulzer	807	Goldfogle	100
Soc.	Debs	1602	Russell	681	London	812
Prog.	Roosevelt	4564	Straus	6709	Moskowitz	269

In Yiddish theater polls Straus received 178 of 225 straws cast for governor. *Warheit*, November 2, 1912.

21. *City Record, Official Canvass of the County of New York*, vol. 40, pt. 12f (December 31, 1912) ; Jacob A. Friedman, *The Impeachment of Governor William Sulzer* (New York, 1939), pp. 247–248, 259f; L. Wald, *The House on Henry Street* (New York, 1915), pp. 255–256. Cf. Tables 4–6.

22. *Forward*, July 23, September 11, October 9, 15, 17, 18, 29, 1906; *Worker*, November 3, 1906; *New York Times*, October 28, 1906; *Evening Post*, October 8, 1908.

23. *Forward*, September 11, November 7, 1906, May 14, 1907, November 9, 1908, November 16, 1909; *Groiser Kundes*, December 10, 1909; M. Hillquit, *Loose Leaves from a Busy Life* (New York, 1934), pp. 107–108; *New York Call*, November 4, 1908; Florence Kelly to E. R. A. Seligman, June 1, 1908 (Seligman Papers) ; *Yiddishes Tageblatt*, November 2, 1908, October 29, 1912; *Warheit*, November 3, 1908, October 28, 1912. Cf. Table 7. *Die Volkstimme*, March 29, 1912; S. Solomon, *Autobiography* (MS, YIVO Institute), p. 183f.

24. "The Representative With A Million Constituents," *Independent*, 80:281 (December 1914) ; *Ladies' Garment Worker* (November, 1912), p. 1f; *Forward*, October 29, 1910, October 29, 1911, November 1, 1912; *Warheit*, October 28, 29, 1912; *Arbeiter*, November 12, 1910; Schapiro, "Henry Moskowitz," p. 449; A. Liesin, "Der kongressional campayn oifn new yorker east side," *Zukunft*, November 1914, p. 1083f; A. Liesin, "Unzer groiser zieg," *Zukunft*, December 1914, p. 1197f. Cf. Table 7.

25. Cahan, *Bleter*, III, 488; *Forward*, October 8, 24, 1897, August 23, 1912.

Chapter 12. Dawn of a New Era

1. F. L. Mott, *Golden Multitudes* (New York, 1947), p. 325.

2. Edwin E. Slosson, *Great American Universities* (New York, 1910), p. 442f; C. Adler, *Jacob H. Schiff* (New York, 1928), II, 10.

3. Moses Rischin, "A History of the American Jewish Committee, 1906–1956" (typescript on deposit, Blaustein Library, AJC Institute of Human Relations), p. 2f; B. J. Hendrick, "The Great Invasion," *McClure's Magazine*, 27:307 (January 1907) ; *Fifth Biennial Session, The National Conference of Jewish Charities in the United States, 1908*, pp. 64–65.

4. *Jewish Gazette*, October 11, 1901; *Forward*, March 24, April 17, 1902, June 11, 1908; C. Reznikoff, ed., *Louis Marshall* (Philadelphia, 1957), II, 1125–1126; Joseph Barondess to Jacobs, May 14, 1908 (Barondess Papers).

5. H. M. Lydenberg, *History of the New York Public Library* (New York, 1923), pp. 376–377; Marshall Sklare, *Conservative Judaism* (Glencoe, III, 1955), p. 161f; Edgar Shimer to Paul Abelson, March 23, 1903 (Abelson Papers); Ernest Poole, *The Bridge* (New York, 1940), p. 73; Cyrus Adler, *Louis Marshall* (New York, 1931), p. 31; Louis Marshall to

E. Sarasohn, July 15, 1904 (Marshall Papers); Z. H. Masliansky, *Zikhroines: fuftsig yor lebn un kemfen* (New York, 1924), p. 244; United States Immigration Commission, *Reports* (Washington, 1907–1910), XLI, 199.

6. *Yiddishe Welt*, July 4, 1903; *The Educational Alliance Department of Civics* (Pamphlet; September 21, 1905); I. B. Berkson, *Theories of Americanization* (New York, 1920), p. 57; *Forward*, February 2, 1906; *Thirteenth Annual Report, Educational Alliance*, pp. 9, 38–39; *Fifteenth and Sixteenth Annual Reports, Educational Alliance*, pp. 18–19; *Educational Alliance Prospectus, 1908–1909* (New York, 1909); A. Cahan, *Bleter fun mayn lebn* (New York, 1926), II, 121; Paul Abelson, "The Education of the Immigrant," *Journal of Social Science*, 44:168 (1906).

7. *American Jewish Yearbook, 1900–1901*, p. 346; *American Jewish Yearbook, 1907–1908*, p. 331; "In Protest of Restrictive Legislation," *Official Program, Cooper Union*, June 4, 1906; A. S. Schomer, *How We Can Help Ourselves, a Logical Solution of the Jewish Question Addressed to all Israel* (New York, 1907), p. 12.

8. Israel Goldstein, *A Century of Judaism in New York* (New York, 1930), p. 228f; cf. *Menorah*, 10:91f (January, 1891), for Rabbi Joseph Silverman's sermon, "Socialism or Individualism"; Stephen S. Wise, *The Challenging Years* (New York, 1949), pp. 95, 98, 102, 109f; J. H. Schiff, "Social Service and the Free Synagogue," *Free Synagogue Pulpit* (December 15, 1907), p. 49; Lillian Wald to Seth Low, October 20, 1897 (Low Papers); *American Hebrew*, June 16, 1905; *The Personal Letters of Stephen Wise*, ed. J. W. Polier and J. W. Wise (Boston, 1956), p. 136.

9. N. Bentwich, *For Zion's Sake* (Philadelphia, 1954), pp. 45f, 55f, 78f; Julius Haber, *The Odyssey of an American Zionist* (New York, 1956), p. 45f; *Report, Executive Committee Presented at the First Annual Conference, Jewish Community (Kehillah)* (February 26 and 27, 1910), p. 17; *Report, Fourth Conference, Kehillah* (April 12 and 13, 1913), pp. 9–10; *Report, Fifth Conference, Kehillah* (April 25 and 26, 1914), p. 17.

10. B. J. Hendrick, "The Jewish Invasion of America," *McClure's Magazine*, 40:314 (March 1913); H. Burgin, *Di geshikhte fun der idisher arbeter bavegung in amerika* (New York, 1915), p. 668f; B. Weinstein, *Fertsig yor in di idishe arbeter bavegung in amerika* (New York, 1924), p. 238; H. Frank, *Abraham S. Sachs* (New York, 1943), p. 160; *Forward*, July 6, 1906.

11. *Morning Journal*, June 4, 1892; James B. Reynolds, *Strike Report*, July 21, 1896, J. B. Reynolds to John Franey, December 18, 1895, J. B. Reynolds to Henry White, February 5, 1896, J. B. Reynolds to A. Shapiro, January 5, 1897, J. B. Reynolds to Lillian Wald, March 18, 1897, J. B. Reynolds to Meyer Jonasson, June 6, 1900 (all in Reynolds Papers); H. A. Keyser, *Bishop Potter* (New York, 1910), p. 77; *Hammer and Pen*, 1 (n.s.):5–6 (July 1898), 3 (n.s.):146 (June 1900), 5 (n.s.):58 (August 1902); Joseph Barondess to Harriet Keyser, December 12, 1903 (Barondess

Papers); L. D. Wald, *The House on Henry Street* (New York, 1915), p. 205f; *Outlook*, 56:927–928 (August 14, 1897); C. Adler, *Jacob H. Schiff* (New York, 1928), I, 292.

12. *Eighth Annual Report, Bureau of Statistics of Labor, State of New York*, p. 1037; *World*, July 16, 1890; W. R. Stewart, *The Philanthropic Work of Josephine Shaw Lowell* (New York, 1911), pp. 366–368; J. H. Schiff to J. B. Reynolds, January 7, 1895, J. B. Reynolds to Henry White, February 15, 1896, Josephine S. Lowell to J. B. Reynolds, May 27, 1897 (Reynolds Papers); Joseph Barondess to J. K. Paulding, May 17, 1900 (Barondess Papers); Keyser, *Bishop Potter*, p. 75; *Forward*, January 3, 7, 1901, January 21, 1902, April 20, 1906; *American Hebrew*, August 2, 1907; *New York Labor Bulletin*, 2:273 (September 1905); *Hammer and Pen*, 9 (n.s.):8 (February 1906)'.

13. *Forward*, November 13, 1900, April 17, 28, 1902, May 16, 1900; M. D. C. Crawford, *The Ways of Fashion* (New York, 1948), p. 106f; interview with Max Meyer, January 7, 1952; J. H. Cohen, *They Builded Better Than They Knew* (New York, 1946), p. 182; *Second Annual Industrial Directory, New York State, 1913* (Albany, 1914), pp. 501, 515; *Yiddishes Tageblatt*, March 20, 1910; Hyman Berman, "Era of the Protocol" (doctoral dissertation, Columbia University, 1956), p. 121.

14. *Forward*, March 23, April 24, 26, May 16, 1907, February 19, June 25, 1908, April 23, 1910; *Yiddisher Kemfer*, April 5, 1907, p. 14, May 17, 1907, p. 15; A Rosenberg, *Di clokemacher un zayre unions* (New York, 1920), pp. 132f, 151f. D. M. Schneider and A. Deutsch, *The History of Public Welfare in New York State* (Chicago, 1941), pp. 200–201; *The Call*, June 18, 22, 1908; Joseph Barondess to A. Michaels, June 25, 1908 (Barondess Papers).

15. *Forward*, September 6, 1909; C. C. Catt and N. R. Shuler, *Woman Suffrage and Politics* (New York, 1923), p. 280; J. K. Paulding, *Charles B. Stover His Life and Personality* (New York, 1938), 76; Solomon Foster, "The Workingman and the Synagogue," *Yearbook, Central Conference of American Rabbis* (1909), XX, 432f; David Philipson, *My Life As an American Jew* (Cincinnati, 1941), p. 213; the Jewish oath is quoted from L. Levine, *Women's Garment Workers* (New York, 1924), 144f; G. Boone, *The Women's Trade Union League* (New York, 1942), p. 64; *American Hebrew*, December 24, 1909.

16. *Forward*, December 7, 10, 14, 16, 21, 1909, February 15, 1910; *Arbeiter*, January 29, 1910; Mark Sullivan, *Our Times* (New York, 1930), III, 366; Boone, *Women's Trade Union League*, pp. 43, 79f; C. S. Bernheimer, *The Shirt Waist Strike* (New York, 1910) p. 6; Levine, *Women's Garment Workers*, pp. 165–166; Berman, "Era of the Protocol," p. 86f.

17. Mary W. Ovington, *Half a Man, The Status of the Negro in New York* (New York, 1911), p. 163; George E. Haynes, *The Negro at Work in New York City* (New York, 1912), pp. 75–76; quoted from Theresa Malkiel, *The Diary of a Shirtwaist Striker* (New York, 1910), p. 5; *Sunday Journal*, May 20, 1892; *Gli Italiani Di New York* (WPA: New York,

1939), p. 147f; *Il Giornale Italiano,* January 1, 2, 1910; *Autobiography 182* (YIVO Institute); p. 41, F. H. LaGuardia, *The Making of an Insurgent* (Philadelphia, 1948), p. 95f.

18. James Oneal, *A History of the Amalgamated Ladies' Garment Cutters' Union Local 10* (New York, 1927), pp. 85–86; B. Weinstein, *Di idishe unions in amerika* (New York, 1929), p. 378, 409; *Forward,* June 12, 30, July 2, 6, 9, August 8, 28, 1910; A Rosenberg, "Metoden un taktik fun der idisher arbeter bavegung," *Zukunft,* November 1910, p. 706; Rosenberg, *Clokemacher,* pp. 177–178, 184; I. Salutsky, "Di lehre fun di clokemacher strike," *Zukunft,* October 1910, p. 613, 617; *Yiddishes Tageblatt,* July 8, 1910; Cohen, *They Builded,* p. 274; *Il Giornale Italiano,* July 8, 1910; *Yearbook, Society for Ethical Culture, New York City, 1904–1905,* pp. 14–15.

19. *The Cloakmakers' Strike* (New York, 1910), pp. 26, 100, 120–121.

20. Samuel Gompers to John B. Lennon, August 26, 1910 (Gompers Papers); Levine, *Women's Garment Workers,* pp. 187, 192–193; *The Cloakmakers' Strike,* p. 141; Cohen, *They Builded,* p. 221; Louis Marshall to Meyer London, September 1, 1910 (Marshall Papers); *Daily Trade Record,* September 3, 1910; *Forward,* September 4, 1910.

21. *Forward,* March 14, 25, 1911; Cohen, *They Builded,* p. 239; *The Madison,* April 12, 1913; *New York Post,* November 16, 1923; George M. Price, "Two Years Work of the Joint Board of Sanitary Control," *The Ladies' Garment Worker* (November 1912), pp. 7–8.

22. *Forward,* March 26, 29, April 3, 6, 1911; L. Waldman, *Labor Lawyer* (New York, 1944), pp. 33–34; Lowell Limpus, *History of the New York Fire Department* (New York, 1940), p. 307f; *Autobiography 52* (YIVO Institute), p. 62; Wise, *Challenging Years,* p. 62f; Boone, *Women's Trade Union League,* pp. 99–100; *Free Synagogue Pulpit,* April 1911, p. 181; F. R. Dulles, *The American Red Cross, A History* (New York, 1950), p. 117; J. D. Eisenstein, *Otser Zikhronotsai* (New York, 1929), p. 121.

23. *First Public Hearing, New York State Factory Investigation Commission,* October 10, 1911; p. 2; David M. Ellis, et al., *A Short History of New York State* (Ithaca, 1957), pp. 389–390; A. C. Flick, *History of the State of New York* (New York, 1935), VII, 262–263.

24. I. Kohn to H. Yoshpe, August 11, 1911 (YIVO Archives); *Forward,* June 19, September 9, 24, 1912; *Yiddishes Tageblatt,* June 21, 1912; P. B. Foner, *The Fur and Leather Workers' Union* (Newark, 1950), p. 43; J. Budish and G. Soule, *The New Unionism in the Clothing Industry* (New York, 1920), p. 96; *Fur Trade Review,* 41:63–64 (October 1912); *Report, Executive Committee, Fourth Annual Conference, Jewish Community Kehillah* (April 12 and 13, 1913), pp. 9–10.

25. *Forward,* January 13, 23, 1913; *New York Times,* January 22, 1913, January 25, 1913, Cohen, *They Builded,* p. 245; Boone, *Women's Trade Union League,* p. 109; Berman, "Era of the Protocol," p. 154f.

26. *Census of Manufactures, 1914* (Washington, 1918), I, 986; II, 178–179, 188; *Forward,* October 16, 1910, February 16, August 14, 1911, Decem-

ber 28, 1912; H. Best, *The Men's Garment Industry of New York and the Strike of 1913* (New York, 1914), pp. 3, 15–16; *Report, Jewish Community, 1914*, p. 17; A. Cahan, *Bleter fun mayn lebn* (New York, 1931), V, 248f; John L. Elliott, "Better Industrial Relations," *The Standard*, August 1914, p. 5.

27. *Addresses, Labor Conventions, and Labor Meetings*, I, 3–5 (Gompers Scrapbooks); cf. A. Liesin, "Tsum finf un tsvantsig yorigen yubilaum fun di feraynikte idishe geverkshaftn," *Zukunft*, February 1914, p. 115; *Forward*, January 24, 1914.

28. M. Josephson, *Sidney Hillman* (New York, 1952), p. 90f; *Documentary History of the ACWA*, pp. xvi–xvii; *Ladies Garment Worker*, September 1912, p. 6, November 1912, p. 4; A. Rosenberg to Joseph Barondess, August 1, 1912 (Barondess Papers); M. Winchevsky, "Der kamf bay der clokemacher," *Zukunft*, January 1914, p. 23f; Levine, *Women's Garment Workers*, pp. 249–250, 273–274; *Zukunft*, February 1914, p. 120.

Epilogue

1. William McAdoo, *Guarding A Great City* (New York, 1906), p. 158; A. E. Costello, *Our Police Protectors* (New York, 1885), p. 324; Rupert Hughes, *The Real New York* (New York, 1904), p. 337; Mary K. Simkhovitch, *Neighborhood* (New York, 1938), p. 60.

2. *Puck*, July 29, 1891; *New York Journal*, June 14, 1896.

3. Herbert N. Casson, "The Jew In America," *Munsey's Magazine*, 34:382 (January 1906); B. J. Hendrick, "The Great Jewish Invasion," *McClure's Magazine*, 28:307f (January 1907); Clifton Harby Levy, "The New York Jew Today," *Independent*, 59:1279 (November 30, 1905); George H. Warner, *The Jewish Spectre* (New York, 1905), pp. 3, 315–316; Madison C. Peters, *Justice to the Jew* (New York, 1899), *passim*.

4. Harold M. Finley, "New York's Populous and Densest Blocks," *Federation*, 4:10 (November 1906); Henry James, *The American Scene* (W. H. Auden, ed., New York, 1946), p. 131; Walter Laidlaw, "Immigration at the Port of New York," *Federation*, 4:17 (April 1906).

5. Walter Barrett, *The Old Merchants of New York City* (New York, 1862), V, 65; *Constitution and Rules, The Knickerbocker Club, 1872*, 25f; *Constitution, Union Club, 1880*, 9f; *Constitution, Union Club, 1910*, 29f; *Charter, St. Nicholas Society, City of New York*, p. 50f; *Harper's Magazine*, 55:300 (July 1877); S. W. Rudy, *The College of the City of New York: A History 1847–1947* (New York, 1949), p. 294; Bernard Baruch, *My Own Story* (New York, 1957), pp. 58–59; Andy Logan, "That Was New York," *New Yorker*, February 2, 1958, p. 110; *Puck*, December 25, 1878.

6. F. L. Allen, *The Lords of Creation* (New York, 1935), p. 96f; *Hebrew Standard*, November 2, 1900; James Creelman, "Israel Unbound," *Pearson's Magazine*, 17:259 (March 1907).

7. Rudolf Glanz, "German Jews in New York City in the 19th Century," *YIVO Annual* (New York, 1956–1957), pp. 10, 36; Philip Cowen,

ed., *Prejudice Against the Jew* (New York, 1928) , *passim* (reprinted from the *American Hebrew*, April 4, 1890) ; Louis Windmuller, "The Commercial Progress of Gotham," *The Progress of the Empire State*, ed., Charles A. Conant (New York, 1913) , pp. 325–326.

8. Paul L. Ford, *The Honorable Peter Stirling* (New York, 1894) , p. 260; Miriam Blaustein, ed., *Memoirs of David Blaustein* (New York, 1913) , p. 160; A. Cahan, *Yekl* (New York, 1896) , pp. 3, 12; Meyer Berger, *The Eight Million* (New York, 1942) , p. 90f; *Gaelic American,* January 14, 1905; S. B. Frank, *The Jew in Sports* (New York, 1936) , pp. 148–155; B. J. Hendrick, "The Jewish Invasion of America," *McClure's Magazine*, 40:140, 144 (March 1913) ; *Warheit*, August 12, 1908.

9. Glanz, "German Jews in New York City," p. 10f; *Arbeiter Zeitung*, July 4, 1890; *New York City Guide* (WPA: New York, 1939) , p. 520; Theodor Lemke, *Geschichte des Deutschtums von New York* (New York, 1891) , pp. 77, 138; *New Yorker Staats-Zeitung*, May 30, 1881; J. R. Marcus, *Index to Americana in Foreign Jewish Periodicals, 1806–1938* (Cincinnati, 1939) , pp. 27–28, 364; A. B. Faust, *The German Element in the United States* (New York, 1909) , I, x; *Das deutsche Element der Stadt New York* (New York, 1913) , *passim*.

10. Cowen, *Memories, passim; Laws of the State of New York, 1873*, p. 303; *Laws of the State of New York, 1881,* I, 541; C. Reznikoff, ed., *Louis Marshall* (Philadelphia, 1957) , I, 249f.

11. E. A. Ross, "The Hebrews of Eastern Europe in America," *Century*, 89:791 (September 1914) ; *Sixth Annual Report, American Jewish Committee* (New York, 1913) , pp. 17–18; *American Citizen*, March 1913, p. 83, September 1913, p. 168.

12. Reznikoff, ed., *Louis Marshall*, I, 395; *American Citizen*, April 1913, pp. 150–151.

13. M. H. Smith, *Sunshine and Shadow in New York* (Hartford, 1880) , pp. 692–693; J. A. Mitchell, *The Last American* (New York, 1889) , p. 4.

14. *Federation Review* (March 1909) , p. 71; *Warheit*, November 2, 1914; *American Citizen*, January 1913, p. 5.

Index